Research Methods for Empirical Legal Studies

An Introduction

Research Methods

for

Empirical Legal Studies:

An Introduction

Catrien Bijleveld

eleven

Published, sold and distributed by Eleven
P.O. Box 85576
2508 CG The Hague
The Netherlands
Tel.: +31 70 33 070 33
Fax: +31 70 33 070 30
e-mail: sales@elevenpub.nl
www.elevenpub.com

Sold and distributed in USA and Canada
Independent Publishers Group
814 N. Franklin Street
Chicago, IL 60610, USA
Order Placement: +1 800 888 4741
Fax: +1 312 337 5985
orders@ipgbook.com
www.ipgbook.com

Eleven is an imprint of Boom uitgevers Den Haag.

ISBN 978-94-6236-938-2

Preface

Empirical Legal Studies or ELS is a field of study where the law is studied using empirical methods. Examples of questions that are studied in ELS are: to what extent do labour laws achieve their intended effect (namely: reduction of short and temporary contracts)? Are potential offenders deterred by heftier penalties? What is the role of apologies in medical malpractice cases? What percentage of divorce proceedings is dealt with timely?

ELS is a somewhat peculiar subdiscipline, wedged in between the normative legal discipline and an array of empirical disciplines. It finds itself on the cusp of widely different paradigms: the empirical sciences are interested only in phenomena in as far as they can be empirically registered, and legal scholarship – loosely said – does not study how things are but how they should be. ELS constitutes a field where methodologies from one set of disciplines are applied to another discipline. Some additional awkwardness may emerge from the fact that very few legal scholars are trained in empirical research methodology – and very few empirical scholars in law. Much still has to be discovered, and a shared methodological language does not exist yet.

At the same time, ELS is a hugely exciting field. New facts are discovered daily, the welding of disciplines and different methodological traditions brings forth novel syntheses and unique approaches, and the field has a strong tail wind with new technological developments and the increasing availability of digitized legal data.

This book was written for a course 'Empirical Legal Studies: An Introduction to Research Methods'. As such, the book can give only a summary introduction to those empirical research methods that are most commonly used in ELS. Introductions will be cursory, at times to the detriment of precision and nuance. Numerous examples are to make the text better digestible, from empirical legal research practice but also from related disciplines. Techniques are described as conceptually as possible, with a minimum of formulas.

The author hopes that the book will contribute to the burgeoning field of empirical legal studies. As a simple research methodologist with a degree in law, she benefited much from discussions with Arno Akkermans, Masha Antokolskaia, Gijs van Dijck, Anja Eleveld, Erik Wesselius, Lidewyde Berckmoes, Lianne Wijntjens, Paul Verbruggen and Bert Marseille. Koosje Heurter and Frits Bijleveld solved technical issues. I especially thank Joris Bekkers for his help and patience.

CB
Amsterdam, July 2023

Contents

Preface v

List of Figures xi

List of Tables xiii

I INTRODUCTION 1

1 Empirical legal studies **3**
1.1 Introduction . . . 3
1.2 Various definitions of empirical legal studies . . . 4
1.3 The trias ELSica or the three pillars of empirical legal research . . . 5
1.3.1 Positioning of ELS vis-à-vis other disciplines . . . 8
1.4 Methods for empirical legal research . . . 11
1.4.1 Qualitative and quantitative methods . . . 12
1.5 Outline of this book . . . 15

2 ELS research methodology: general issues **17**
2.1 Introduction . . . 17
2.2 Empirical cycle . . . 17
2.3 Literature search and source evaluation . . . 21
2.4 Conceptual and operational definitions . . . 22
2.5 Pilot study . . . 24
2.6 Validity and reliability . . . 24
2.6.1 Reliability . . . 24
2.6.2 Validity . . . 26
2.7 Qualitative and quantitative studies . . . 29
2.7.1 Mixed methods and triangulation . . . 30
2.8 Macro-, meso- and micro-level studies . . . 32
2.9 Primary and secondary data . . . 32
2.10 Research ethics: rules and conventions . . . 34
2.10.1 Legal framework: the GDPR . . . 35
2.10.2 Code of conduct: the ALLEA Code . . . 36

2.10.3 Internal review boards 37

II MEASUREMENT **39**

3 Measurement units **41**
3.1 Populations and samples 41
3.2 Representativeness and generalizability 42
3.3 Types of samples 45
3.3.1 Probability samples 46
3.3.2 Non-probability samples 54
3.4 Bias and noise 61
3.5 Sample size 63
3.6 Sample nonresponse and representativeness 65

4 Data collection methods **69**
4.1 Introduction 69
4.2 Interviews and questionnaires 70
4.3 Design of interviews, questionnaires and questions 80
4.3.1 Interview design 80
4.3.2 Questionnaire design 81
4.3.3 Types of questions and question design 83
4.4 Interviewing: skills and approach 89
4.5 Observation 90
4.6 Data collection from documents 93
4.6.1 Coding schemes 93
4.7 Relative strengths and weaknesses 96

5 Measurement design **99**
5.1 Introduction 99
5.2 Dependent and independent variables 103
5.3 Causality 104
5.4 Interventions and change 106
5.4.1 Threats to internal validity 108
5.5 Types of (experimental) designs 114
5.6 Longitudinal and cross-sectional designs 117
5.7 Vignette studies 117
5.8 Pros and cons of various designs 118
5.9 Natural experiments 119
5.10 Further reading 122

III DATA ANALYSIS **125**

6 Quantitative data: univariate and bivariate analysis **127**
6.1 Analysis units versus variables 127

6.2 Measurement levels 129
6.2.1 Nominal to absolute measurement level 129
6.2.2 Implications for analysis 132
6.3 Describing the variables 132
6.3.1 Central tendency: the mean, median and mode 133
6.3.2 Measures of variability 134
6.3.3 Graphs for visualizing the variables 135
6.4 Describing the association between variables 137
6.4.1 Correlation coefficients 138
6.4.2 Other measures of association 143
6.4.3 Graphs for describing the association between variables . . . 149
6.5 Duration variables: survival analysis 150
6.6 Wrapping up 157

7 Qualitative data analysis **159**
7.1 Introduction 159
7.1.1 The iterative nature of qualitative research 160
7.1.2 Modes of qualitative data collection and analysis 162
7.2 Coding qualitative data 164
7.2.1 Description: first-level coding 165
7.2.2 Analysis: second-level coding, patterns and typologies 170
7.3 Content analysis 173
7.3.1 Systematic case law analysis 176
7.4 Analysing other material 177
7.5 Reliability and validity in qualitative analysis 178
7.6 Wrapping up 179
7.7 Further reading 180

8 Inferential statistics **181**
8.1 Statistical testing 182
8.1.1 Day-to-day statistical reasoning 182
8.1.2 More formalized statistical reasoning 184
8.2 Distributions and tests 187
8.2.1 Standard scores and testing 190
8.3 Sampling, significance and power 194
8.3.1 Hypotheses revisited 197
8.4 Theoretical foundations of sampling and testing 199
8.5 Estimation and uncertainty 201
8.5.1 Point estimates versus interval estimates 201
8.5.2 Confidence intervals 202
8.6 Practical limitations in sampling and testing 203
8.7 Wrapping up 204

9 Quantitative data analysis: multivariate analysis **207**
9.1 Models . . . 208
9.1.1 Models with dependent and independent variables . . . 209
9.1.2 Model building . . . 210
9.1.3 Model fit . . . 212
9.2 Regression model . . . 214
9.2.1 When to employ regression analysis . . . 214
9.2.2 Simple regression analysis . . . 215
9.2.3 Multiple regression analysis . . . 219
9.2.4 Model fit . . . 221
9.2.5 Tests . . . 222
9.2.6 The workhorse of multivariate analysis . . . 223
9.3 Analysis of variance model . . . 226
9.3.1 When to employ analysis of variance . . . 226
9.3.2 Analysis of variance proper . . . 227
9.3.3 Factorial analysis of variance . . . 232
9.3.4 Tests . . . 235
9.3.5 Model fit . . . 235
9.4 Wrapping up . . . 238
9.5 Further reading . . . 239

10 Three worked ELS examples **241**
10.1 Introduction . . . 241
10.2 Experiences with mandatory work programmes: qualitative analysis . 242
10.2.1 Data collection . . . 243
10.2.2 Analytic methods: coding and discovering patterns . . . 243
10.2.3 Answering the research questions . . . 250
10.3 Apologies: systematic case law analysis . . . 253
10.3.1 Data collection . . . 254
10.3.2 Analytic methods: coding . . . 255
10.3.3 Analytic methods: classification and finding patterns . . . 256
10.3.4 Answering the research questions . . . 258
10.4 International sentencing: multivariate analysis . . . 259
10.4.1 Data collection . . . 260
10.4.2 Analytic methods: bivariate data analysis . . . 261
10.4.3 Analytic methods: multivariate data analysis . . . 262
10.4.4 Answering the research questions . . . 265

11 Conclusion: some generic methodological issues **267**
11.1 The particular setting of empirical legal research . . . 267
11.2 Correlation is not causation . . . 268
11.3 Replication, triangulation and mixed methods . . . 268

Bibliography **271**

Subject index **279**

List of Figures

1.1 Abstract representation of quantitative and qualitative research 13

3.1 Example of spread of sample members in the Netherlands 44
3.2 Example neighbourhood layout for systematic sample with inadequate periodicity 49
3.3 Example neighbourhood layout for systematic sample 49
3.4 Fictional example of a random sample in a village 54
3.5 Fictional example of a systematic sample in a village 55
3.6 Fictional example of a cluster sample in a village 55
3.7 Visual representations of bias and noise 62

4.1 Example of rating scales 85
4.2 Example of answering categories to prevent socially acceptable answers 86
4.3 Example of rating scales with 'escape' category 87
4.4 Scoring list for court rulings file 94
4.5 Percentage of cases with contribution required for subsidized legal aid 95
4.6 Nominal contribution paid for government-subsidized legal aid . . . 96

5.1 Representation of relation between independent and dependent variable 103
5.2 Representation of more complex relations between independent variables and dependent variable 104
5.3 Spurious association between number of firefighters and damage . . . 105
5.4 Model for the relation between alcohol consumption and risk of breaking legs 105
5.5 True relation between alcohol consumption and fracture risk, including exposure time 106
5.6 Well-being scores before and after therapy 'intervention' 106
5.7 Development of well-being scores from month 1 to 10 107
5.8 Control for threat *history* through use of control group 109

6.1 Pie chart of employment status 136
6.2 Bar chart of employment status 136
6.3 Histogram for distribution of age in 5-year categories 137
6.4 Scatterplots for associations of various direction and strength 139

6.5 Relation between association and prediction 141
6.6 Non-linear association between X and Y 142
6.7 Outlier 143
6.8 Example of stacked bar chart for type of abuse and recidivism 150
6.9 Clustered histogram for distribution of ratings by age group 150
6.10 Kaplan–Meier survival curve 154
6.11 Kaplan–Meier survival analysis of days until treatment entry for all parents 155
6.12 Kaplan–Meier survival analysis of length of time until child's end of involvement in the child welfare system 156

7.1 Schematic representation of three modes of qualitative data collection 164
7.2 Descriptive codes vignette study of international sentencing 168
7.3 Descriptive and axial codes in vignette study of international sentencing 174

8.1 Overview of testing 186
8.2 Normal distribution of wing span of *Ardea cinerea* 188
8.3 Area under the curve 189
8.4 Standard normal distribution 191
8.5 Standard normal distribution with critical standard scores 192
8.6 Normal distribution with critical raw values 193
8.7 Distribution of coping skills under H_0 and H_1 with α=1% 195
8.8 Distribution of coping skills under H_0 and H_1 with α=5% 196
8.9 Test situation for two-sided null hypothesis with critical raw values . . 198
8.10 Test situation for one-sided null hypothesis with critical raw value . . 198

9.1 Visual representation of model with predictors and dependent variable 210
9.2 Visual representation of association between X and Y, and prediction of Y from X 215
9.3 Scatterplot of shoe size against height 217
9.4 ANOVA example: improvement in calculus before and after course . . 229
9.5 ANOVA example: calculus improvement with less variability 229
9.6 ANOVA example: interaction effect 233
9.7 ANOVA example: mean justness for different gender constellations . 238

List of Tables

5.1 Results of experiment on compensatory punishment 118

6.1 Example of notation of variables and respondents 128
6.2 Frequency tabulation of employment status 135
6.3 Observed frequencies of sentence type and gender 144
6.4 Expected frequencies if sentence type and gender were unassociated . 144
6.5 Observed frequencies of sentence type and gender 146
6.6 Positions of the administrative authorities and court judgment 148
6.7 Type of administrative authority and court judgment 149
6.8 Months, recidivism and censoring, number of persons *at risk*, event chance, survival chance and cumulative survival chances 152

9.1 Dataset with shoe size, height and gender 217
9.2 Unstandardized regression weights of gender and hourly wage in euros 224
9.3 Example ANOVA results 231
9.4 ANOVA example with interaction terms 234
9.5 ANOVA example on workplace misbehaviour 236
9.6 Category means for age 237

10.1 First- and second-level codes and quotations 245
10.2 Second-level codes and quotations 246
10.3 Grouping second-order codes related to meaningful work experiences 247
10.4 Grouping second-order codes related to meaningless work experiences 248
10.5 Identifying patterns 251
10.6 Data reduction in apologies study 257
10.7 Apologies versus outcome for apologizing party 258
10.8 Sentence length in years, by offence, offender rank, guilty plea and mode of individual responsibility 261
10.9 Regression analysis of ICTY sentence lengths in years 263

Part I

INTRODUCTION

Chapter 1

Empirical legal studies

1.1 Introduction

Empirical legal studies, or empirical legal research, is a label given to studies that focus on the law by gathering empirical facts. Empirical legal studies is not a traditional academic discipline like psychology, economics, or biology. Empirical legal studies (or ELS) is a subfield in a sense at the fringes, or at the intersection, of law and social sciences. It is regarded differently by different scholars: by some as an ancillary discipline to law, by others as a particular object science within the broader social sciences. It is also encountered under different names, such as 'empirical legal research' or 'legal realism'/'new legal realism'. Similar – but not exactly identical – areas of study are denoted as 'law in action' or 'legal sociology'.

We will therefore start by defining what we understand empirical legal studies or empirical legal research to be. We believe that it will be impossible to exactly outline or demarcate what empirical legal studies is, and what it is not. Rather, we will attempt to describe and define what is at the core of empirical legal research, what distinguishes it from related fields, and in doing so hopefully outline a prototype. As we will see, some (sub)disciplines share properties with empirical legal research: criminology does, and so do legal sociology and legal anthropology. Rather than embark upon or elicit ontological discussions, we will point out similarities and differences, and leave things there. Our aim is to define what is particular or even quintessential for empirical legal research.

We accept that some disciplines share properties with ELS, or partially overlap with our arena of empirical legal research. As this book focuses mainly on the research methods and techniques for empirical legal research, we believe that any remaining ambiguities or fuzzy demarcations need not bother us much. We assume that legal scholars are the main readership of this book, with ELS revolving around questions relevant for law and its application.

1.2 Various definitions of empirical legal studies

Some examples of questions that are studied under the umbrella of empirical legal research are: 'Do judges understand the evidentiary strength of DNA evidence correctly?', 'Has the new labour law resulted in the aimed-for reduction in temporary contracts?', 'What type of compensation do victims of sexual abuse who participate in compensation schemes wish to receive?', 'Is international sentencing haphazard?', 'Are divorce cases settled faster under a 'one judge – one case' regime?', 'Do judges administer more lenient sentences when evidence is weak?'

These questions have two elements in common: (1) they all enquire after empirical facts, and (2) they all focus on the law, its operations or effects. This is still fairly vague, however. A quick scan of a (non-random and non-exhaustive) selection of textbooks and handbooks in fact results in a jumble of definitions. We discuss a few.

Epstein & Martin (2014, pp. viii–ix) define empirical legal research perhaps most broadly. They state that it is: "Research carried out by law students, lawyers, judges and scholars interested in law and legal institutions". In this definition, we see that it is required that the research be carried out by legally trained persons and that the questions asked pertain to law and legal institutions – but the definition does not contain the element 'empirical'.

Henster & Gasperetti (2017) do incorporate 'empirical' as an element when they define empirical legal studies as the "investigation of legally relevant facts using diverse methods and theories derived from the social sciences". It is the mention of 'facts' in this definition that classifies the studies as empirical. In contrast with Epstein and Martin, Henster and Gasperetti do not require the research to be carried out by legal scholars; the facts should simply be 'legally relevant'.

Leeuw & Schmeets (2016, p. 3) state that empirical legal research "addresses developments and actions in the 'real social world' as relating to legal arrangements, either to influence this world, to facilitate it, or to legalize what has been the 'usual' practice". These authors also – without using the term 'empirical' – refer to research being empirical in that research should address phenomena in the 'real social world'.

In the *Oxford Handbook on Empirical Legal Research* (2010, p. 4), the editors Cane and Kritzer describe empirical legal research as "the systematic collection of information and its analysis according to some generally accepted method". They subsequently note that the systematic nature of the research process is of central importance, both in the collection of data and in their analysis. The authors next state that traditional historical research ('legal history') is in their view *not* part of empirical legal research because of its already long-standing traditions with its own discrete norms, methodologies and standards. Second, they explicitly exclude the traditional analysis of formal legal documents, such as court decisions and legislative materials. Thus, case law analysis and the analysis of jurisprudence (often referred to as 'doctrinal analysis') do not belong to empirical legal research according to these authors.

As the authors of the *Oxford Handbook* also write, and as the reader will perhaps have gathered, there are of course examples of research that have both empirical and doctrinal elements. Such studies are in that sense hybrids or syntheses and may be categorized as belonging to both categories. It is namely not the case that doctrinal legal and empirical legal research take place in separate worlds. Davies (2020) states that these two types of research are mutually dependent activities, which can (and should) mutually influence each other.

A prototypical hybrid – regarded by some as a synthesis between classical dogmatic analysis and ELS – is systematic content analysis of judicial opinions, or, briefly, systematic jurisprudence or case law analysis: that branch of empirical legal endeavour where a systematic selection of cases, such as verdicts, is coded systematically and analysed. The aim of systematic legal analysis is to reveal associations, patterns or developments in legal practice, and to do so in a manner that is structured ('systematic') and replicable (Verbruggen, 2021, pp. 8–9; Hall & Wright, 2008).

Systematic legal analysis can be regarded as a hybrid or synthesis because while the sampling strategy is clearly empirical, the analysis of the content of judicial opinions strongly resembles classic dogmatic analysis: reading and analysing legal decisions. However, the focus of systematic legal analysis is different. The focus is not on the analysis of a small number of the most important legal decisions with conclusions that are strongly authority-based, but on the description and evaluation of an entire set of legal decisions, in which all decisions are equally important and conclusions are based on empirical description, such as tallying or associations. The focus is on systematizing the content of these decisions, describing patterns, trends and quantities. The selection of decisions is systematic and preferably representative for a larger universe of decisions, and the analysis of the decisions is also systematic and transparent, so that the entire research process is objective, reliable, reproducible and replicable.

As we announced, we will not attempt to draw watertight boundaries, and therefore not strive to demarcate the domain of empirical legal research exactly. What is important at this stage is to note that from the various definitions, three characteristics of empirical legal research emerge, namely that (1) an empirical legal study poses questions about the law, that (2) it uses empirical data to answer those questions, and that (3) the answers to the questions are legally relevant. A number of authors do not classify certain types of research as empirical legal studies, because of either the particular type of data used, the questions posed, the methods (case law) or differing paradigmatic views (historical research).

1.3 The trias ELSica or the three pillars of empirical legal research

Our exploration of the various definitions and demarcations as given by handbooks and overview articles has brought us a little further, but we cannot say that it has given us an overview of what the field of empirical legal studies covers. If we combine the various definitions, it emerges that we are dealing with research that poses questions about the law or is after legally relevant facts. Also, the idea is that this research is pursued by legal scholars (which can be interpreted as saying that the findings must be of relevance to lawyers or legal practice), that the research collects and analyses empirical facts, and that traditional historical research on the law and doctrinal analysis are excluded. But what then *is* empirical legal research? What types of substantive issues does ELS address?

If one reviews empirical legal scholarship – whether it deals with administrative law, international law, civil or criminal law – three substantive topics or 'pillars' can be recognized into which empirical legal research can be grouped. We will discuss these briefly.

Law is one of the most important instruments to accommodate desirable human behaviour. Indeed, from the manner in which laws are drafted, and rules and regulations designed, it can be seen that politicians, law makers and legal policy makers make numerous assumptions about the subjects of these legal instruments. For instance, drafters of criminal law assume that sanctions deter potential criminals. Moving to civil and tort law, it is assumed that monetary payouts compensate victims for damages they suffered. But are these assumptions always true? The US which is one of very few developed nations to still have the death penalty, also has very high crime rates. Apparently those extremely severe penalties do not deter criminals, or do they? From recent surveys of victims of sexual abuse joining compensation schemes, it appears that many may not just welcome some kind of monetary compensation, but mainly wish their voice to be heard, their suffering recognized, and that the procedures they entered help to prevent future abuse. The proposal for a EU directive on improving working conditions in platform work assumes that platform workers such as food delivery riders want to be employees rather than freelance, in order to be protected by labour law. But is there an empirical basis for these assumptions? This is the first pillar of empirical legal studies: the study of the *empirical* assumptions on which laws and regulations are based.

Then, laws are administered and enforced, and legal decisions proclaimed. Numerous questions can be posed about this process, ranging from contextual issues such as the training of lawyers and practical obstacles in the judicial process, to questions regarding the length of procedures, to substantive questions about the applications of legal rules and interpretation of legal principles. We briefly mention a number of examples. Are new procedures, such as the 'one judge – one case' principle, practically feasible? Is the training of judges sufficient for them to be able to judge novel forms of evidence? How often and in what type of cases is the *actio pauliana* invoked? What factors influence the length of court proceedings? And lastly, what legal rules are employed in legal decision making? How do judges interpret legal principles, such as proportionality, in international criminal procedures? This we distinguish as a second pillar of empirical legal research: the study of how the law is interpreted and applied *in practice*.

Last, the law aims to influence people's behaviour, and the operation of institutions. Veerman (2021, pp. 221–222) distinguishes two approaches when we talk about that function: the legal and the sociological. The legal approach regards the question of how the standards laid down in the law are applied when conflict needs to be resolved, and what their meaning is. Many laws have been enacted with lofty ideals, such as promoting justice, correcting mistakes, equality before the law. According to Veerman, this legal effect is about the validity of standards and their significance in the application by the court. Research into this traditionally takes place within the legal discipline, by lawyers.

In the sociological approach, on the other hand, the emphasis is on the effects of legislation in or on society. According to Veerman (2021, p. 222), this sociological approach is about "the social changes that take place after the entry into force of laws, through an adjustment of the behaviour of actors where the changes or adjustments are wholly or partly the result of legislation that has made this behaviour possible or imposed".

That the two should not be studied in isolation is shown by the fact that effectiveness in a sociological sense is perceived by some as essential to legitimacy. Davies (2020) also argues that the doctrinal and empirical study of law should in some way enrich each other. Van Boom, Desmet, & (2018, pp. 5–6) write that the empirical study of law enriches doctrinal legal research, more than through empirical fact checking, because it allows a deeper understanding of not only the plain facts but also the underlying mechanisms of legal interaction, such as insight into both explicit reasoning as well as unconscious processes in legally relevant decision making.

It is predominantly within this more sociological approach that empirical questions have been asked. Many laws have been enacted with lofty ideals, such as promoting justice, repairing wrong, equality before the law. But more mundane goals have also been formulated. For instance, laws came into force in the Netherlands recently that forbid employers to hire staff in consecutive temporary contracts ('revolving-door contracts'), adopted with the explicit purpose that more (young) employees would acquire tenured positions. Did this work out in the foreseen way? Did the law indeed induce or force employers to hire people on permanent contracts? Whether laws and regulations have their intended effects is an important, empirical, question. Such intended effects are also referred to as 'effectiveness'. And studies that then investigate whether laws have been effective are generally referred to as 'evaluation studies' or 'impact assessments'.

However, laws can also have unintended side-effects. The Dutch Rent Act that was enacted in 1950 provided tenants with virtually unlimited protection against eviction. One of the aims of the Act had been to strengthen the legal position of tenants, who were generally in a more vulnerable position than landlords. After the new law, once a landlord had rented out a place, whether by contract or not, and whether payment was official or monetary or in kind, the tenant had indeed a very strong legal position, and – unless a tenant left voluntarily – it was now practically speaking impossible for landlords to vacate rented-out living quarters. The side-effect of this law was, however, that it had now become very 'risky' for home owners to let their premises. And the consequence of this was that shortages of rented spaces quickly became a major problem that those looking for a place to live were faced with. All in all, both the intended *effects* and unintended or side-effects of laws are the object of study in the third pillar of empirical legal research.

It is good practice to study the impact of laws and regulations not only after laws have been enacted, but to try to gauge their likely impact already before the laws are implemented. If such a – more hypothetical – investigation of a law's likely effects already shows that it would have flaws or undesirable side-effects, this can hopefully be remedied before the law comes into effect. Such an evaluation that takes place before a law comes into force, and in fact mostly when a law is still in its design stage, is referred to as an 'ex-ante evaluation'. We will return to the topic of ex-ante evaluations in chapter 5.

In summary, empirical legal studies can be defined as comprising three pillars or areas of study:

(1) *the assumptions about the real world on which laws are built*

(2) *the operations in the real world of the legal system*

(3) *the effects of the law in the real world*

The pillars should not be regarded as disconnected, as we said, and in fact they are also empirically intrinsically related. If the assumptions on which laws are built are incorrect, or if tradition or lack of intrinsic support for new rules stand in the way, then it is very unlikely that the laws would have their desired effect. If the assumptions are correct, but if the law would not be applied as planned (for instance, cases take extraordinarily longer to process, judges do not understand new rules), it is also unlikely that the foreseen effect would materialize. The three pillars form in that sense a trias ELSica.

1.3.1 Positioning of ELS vis-à-vis other disciplines

As we stated in section 1.1, empirical legal studies is not a traditional field of study, although it is more and more recognized as a subdiscipline or even an integral part of the legal discipline. As we also said, there are similar areas of research denoted as '(new) legal realism', 'law in action' or 'legal sociology' for which it is perhaps not immediately obvious how these would differ from empirical legal studies as we defined it. In fact, the attentive reader may have noted us also using the terms 'empirical legal studies' and 'empirical legal research' interchangeably. We do so because we do not believe that there are differences between these two that are significant for the purpose of this book.

Areas of study denoted by 'legal realism' or 'new legal realism' resemble empirical legal studies or empirical legal research. Legal realism was a movement that started in the 1930s in the US, and that aimed to test hypotheses about the (workings of the) law using large-scale quantitative datasets. With a slightly different focus, the new legal realism movement attempts the same. It appears that the focus in both is mainly on quantitative research, a choice which severely limits the scope of methods that can be employed, and a choice that we do not consider fruitful.

The Law and Society Association (`lawandsociety.org/history.html`) publishes a journal that aims to publish original work on the relationship between society and the legal process. Its focus is quite broad, as it aims to further theoretical and empirical understandings of law, legal decision making by individuals and groups, and the impact of specific reforms and behaviour of people and institutions with regard to the law, but also "the operations of law as a perspective for understanding ideology, culture, identity, and social life". Its disciplinary outlook is predominantly socio-legal.

We have so far regularly mentioned legal sociology, a fairly broad field that does use social science methods and focuses on the empirical workings of the law. In that sense, one could ask, is legal sociology perhaps empirical legal studies under a different name? Opinion is divided here. While some regard legal sociology as a part of empirical legal studies, others regard it as a subspecialization of sociology, and others again regard it as a separate discipline wedged in between law and sociology.

Either way, we believe that legal sociology differs from ELS in that the focus of legal sociology studies is essentially mono-disciplinary: the theoretical framework of sociology is applied to study the law. This means that legal sociology can at the least not fully overlap with empirical legal studies, as empirical legal studies is not particular to one social science paradigm: there is no inherent reason why empirical legal studies would not also employ theories from psychology, economics, anthropology or even neurosciences. In fact, much of the rich and extensive literature on perceived (procedural) justice employs theories and methods from social psychology.

A similar reasoning can to a certain extent be applied when asking about (sub)disciplines such as criminology or legal psychology. Criminology focuses on one particular kind of behaviour: criminal behaviour. It studies the prevalence of crime, the causes of crime, the manner in which society responds to crime, and victims. Surely the last two could be said to fall under the scope of empirical legal studies too? Or consider legal psychology, which focuses on all the ways in which psychology plays a role in the operations of the law: examples are psychological factors in sentencing decisions or the reliability of witness testimony. Those surely could be regarded as fitting in our second pillar? Several such subdisciplines do indeed fit to some extent in our definition of empirical legal studies. All have however a narrower scope than empirical legal studies as we defined it. The scope is narrower either because the types of data and analyses are limited to quantitative (e.g. legal realism), or because one disciplinary vantage point is employed (e.g. sociology). For instance, 'law and economics' seeks to explain phenomena such as the manner in which humans respond to legal rules employing an economic theoretical vantage point, that of rational choice. One could argue that these subdisciplines in a sense partially overlap with empirical legal studies: some empirical legal studies may be labelled as 'criminology' or 'legal sociology', but empirical legal research is broader. Also, not all criminology or all 'law and economics' is empirical legal research.

Regardless of such partial overlap, we believe that there is one important element that distinguishes empirical legal studies from subdisciplines such as criminology, law and economics, or legal sociology. In empirical legal studies the goal is to describe and explain the workings of the law and the legal system in a broad sense. So, where legal sociology or law and economics are essentially about testing sociological theories or economic theories – for which the law is ancillary – in empirical legal research this is the opposite. Here, the central focus is the law and the various disciplines are the tools. Empirical legal research is therefore essentially multi-disciplinary: any disciplinary focus or theory may be used and the field is not particular to any paradigmatic viewpoint.

A second aspect is important to position empirical legal studies. For example, jurimetrics is defined as the application of science to the law, in the sense of measuring by mathematical and statistical methods the outputs of the legal system or the system itself, or as computer-assisted legal research, or even, very broadly, as the study of science and the law (for an overview see `legal-dictionary.thefreedictionary.com/jurimetrics`). An important subarea of study within jurimetrics is for instance how statistics can be used to support judicial decision making. Examples are studies into statistical aspects of the use of DNA evidence, or into the manner in which Oslo confrontations should be set up to deliver as much evidentiary value as possible. Such jurimetric studies, which generate findings to be used in the actual processing of cases or the legal decision making process, however, differ from our description of empirical legal studies in an important respect. Empirical legal research is namely involved with studying the legal system, in a sense, *from the outside*: empirical legal research observes the workings of and in the system, its impact, empirical facts underlying rules and regulations. While its findings may be useful for lawyers as background information, empirical legal scholars will hardly be called to assist in individual legal cases or judicial decision making. The information that empirical legal studies generates about the law is, one could also say, *indirectly* of use.

To clarify our point, take again as an example jurimetrics, which we just introduced. Jurimetrics generates knowledge and gives clear rules that are useful for actual legal practice: jurimetric knowledge will tell practitioners how to use DNA or fingerprint evidence in court. Similarly, legal psychology will provide judges with information on the reliability of a certain witness's statement. It is indeed not uncommon that a legal psychologist is called to testify about the scientific merit of a certain piece of evidence, just like a forensic psychologist may be called in to testify about the psychological state of a defendant. Findings from the examples we gave about empirical legal studies, on the other hand, would generally not advise individual cases.

Empirical legal studies provides information on legally relevant topics in a *generic* sense. As such, ELS may very well influence judicial outcomes, but not in the sense that it aids by giving guidance in a specific case. Rather, ELS findings may advise judges about the general properties of cases such as the current case, trends in the interpretation of legal norms, or on the effectiveness in general of measures such as may be chosen from. Phrased differently, empirical legal research focuses more on the *context* of the law and its general application, but will hardly ever be used to determine evidentiary value in a particular instance, or a recommended intervention in an individual case.

Finally, there is a third important difference. This has to do with the fact that not all criminology or all 'law and economics' and not all sociology of law is empirical legal research. In empirical legal studies, the aim is to describe and explain the functioning of law and the legal system in a broad sense. So, referring back to the first point we made, where the goal in sociology of law or legal economics is essentially to test sociological theory or, respectively, economic theory – where the legal examples function as indeed no more than illustration or a specific area within which disciplinary questions are addressed – in empirical legal research the opposite is the case. In ELS the *law* is the focus of attention. An ELS researcher is fundamentally and exclusively interested in law. The ELS researcher conducts research to advance the legal discipline. To illustrate our position in this we should perhaps write 'empirical-legal': the dash between 'empirical' and 'legal' would then indicate that ELS is a particular type of *legal* research. The questions asked are about the law, and the answers generated by this research are relevant for law.

Before we proceed to a summary, we must admit that in order to make our case, we have sometimes (considerably) simplified and even exaggerated. For example, legal psychological research may in some cases also be seen as ELS, for example when it comes to psychological processes that play a role in judicial decision making, or the willingness of consumers to take collective action under the influence of the coverage of legal expenses insurance. And the same goes for some types of jurimetrics or studies labelled as 'law and economics'.

In summary, empirical legal studies is that field of study in which the assumptions about the real world on which laws are built, the operations of the legal system and the effects of laws and legal procedures are studied, using a variety of disciplinary viewpoints and a variety of methodological approaches. The primary and ultimate focus of interest is the law. As such, empirical legal studies describe and explain the context within which the law is applied, the application itself of the law, and the impact the application of laws and regulations has on the empirical world. Having said this, many (sub)disciplines have partial overlaps with empirical legal studies and it is impossible to demarcate the field exactly.

1.4 Methods for empirical legal research

Thus far, we have discussed various definitions of empirical legal research, and attempted to outline, sketchily, the domain of empirical legal studies. This book does not deal with empirical legal research as such, however, but rather with the *research methods* employed for such studies. In this section, we will briefly sketch an overview of these research methods as they can be used in empirical legal research.

Our previous definitions told us that certain research types and their methods do not belong in empirical legal research. A first prominent one is doctrinal analysis, a method that in a sense does not use empirical data. We might be tempted to conclude that all methods that make use of empirical data therefore belong in the toolkit of empirical legal scholars. This is also not the case, as historical methods, given history's idiosyncratic paradigm, are excluded as well. Given these exemptions, we again move to inspect what textbooks tell us about empirical legal methods.

Lawless, Robbennolt, & Ulen (2009, p. xxi), in their seminal volume, define empirical *methods* in law as "the entire process of posing an empirical research question, deciding on the method or methods by which to pursue that research question, gathering and coding the data, analyzing the data, and then communicating one's results – with an emphasis on legal research". A little further on in their book they state that the research in which these methods are used is "empirical research based on observation (...), oriented towards testing hypotheses (...), concerned with aggregate effects (...), an incremental and ongoing process" (2009, pp. 10–15). All in all, Lawless et al. define the methods of empirical legal research as comprising the posing of the research question itself, the choice of method, the data collection procedure and coding of the data, analysis and reporting. In the second quote that we just gave, they limit the scope of empirical legal research to those questions that are quantitative and that can be answered by testing ("testing hypotheses"). This would seem a reductionist view of empirical legal studies that not all scholars, including this author, ascribe to. In fact, the *Oxford Handbook on Empirical Legal Research* explicitly includes many examples of studies that are of a more exploratory nature, where no hypotheses were tested. It even features an entire chapter on qualitative methods for empirical legal research (Cane &

Kritzer, 2010, chapter 38). Kritzer (2021, chapter 1) defines empirical legal research as research that employs methods of collecting information to examine, in some way, legal phenomena.[1] Van Dijck & Hagenaars (2017, chapter 1) explicitly mention that the methodology of empirical legal research is "much and much more" than statistics. They state that many types of empirical legal studies exist in which statistics do not play a role at all, for instance because they focus on a small sample or when questions are more of an exploratory or qualitative nature.

In empirical legal research, we therefore find the entire gamut of methods that are employed in those disciplines that study empirical facts. These are the social science methods – albeit not always originally so. As we will see in some chapters below, the social sciences have also at times borrowed methods designed in other disciplines when social science data resembled the formal structure of such 'foreign' data. A good example is the use of survival analysis techniques from epidemiology to analyse how long court cases 'survive' until they can be considered dealt with (either because they were withdrawn, a settlement was reached or a judge decided what the outcome was). Even though the formal structure is not exactly the same as the data structure we have when studying actual physical survival of people (people only die once and cannot 'resurrect' as court cases in a sense may do on appeal; all people die eventually while some cases are simply never dispositioned), the technique of survival analysis is very well usable for ELS. It can be used to investigate the shelf life of court cases (and to investigate what particulars of the cases or the courts predict a long shelf life) or to assess whether prison sentences are associated with more recidivism than community service orders. Criminologists have often used techniques from anthropology, such as participant observation, when they wanted to learn more about segments of society that they were unfamiliar with, such as drug or street gangs. Similar to a 'classical' anthropologist, they would first attempt to become acquainted with their research subjects, live like them, participate in their lives, witness their daily hassles, chores and moments of joy, to be able to understand why gang members make the choices they make, or feel forced to live in a certain way.

All in all, methods for empirical legal studies comprise the starting point of empirical research, such as phrasing the research question, defining what exactly needs to be measured, what data need to be collected, how the data will be processed and analysed, and how findings are reported. The methods used for empirical legal research comprise therefore those methods used in the empirical, social sciences. In line with what we discussed above in section 1.3, it is pivotal that, given the fact that the focus of empirical legal studies is on the law and the legal system, articles and research reports reflect not only on the findings as such, but also, importantly, on their implications for laws, legal norms and the legal system.

1.4.1 Qualitative and quantitative methods

An often-used categorization of research that we already briefly touched upon, is that into qualitative and quantitative studies. Formulated a bit simplistically, we can characterize the two as follows: while quantitative studies aim to measure the volume or

[1] The book by Kritzer contains a nice, somewhat US-centred history of ELS.

Figure 1.1: Abstract representation of quantitative and qualitative research

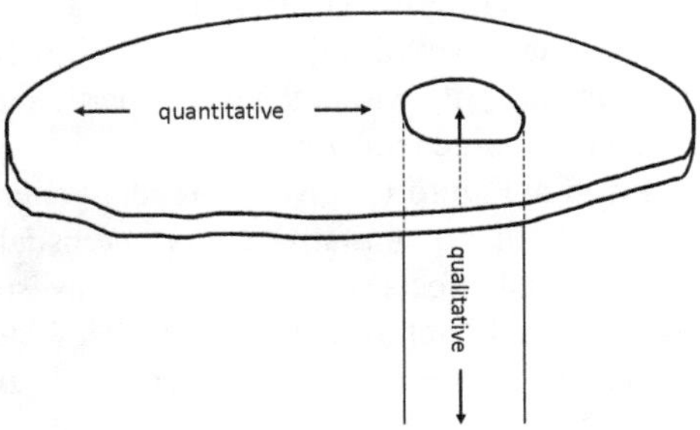

quantity of some variable of interest, qualitative studies are geared towards finding out the *quality*, 'nature', 'why' or 'how' of phenomena.

In a study that uses quantitative methods, we would want to find out *how often* something occurred, such as: 'How often are cases of domestic violence acquitted?', or 'What percentage of citizens have trust in the criminal justice system?', or 'How many citizens with a certain type of legal problem take their case to court?' Quantitative studies typically follow a fairly strict format (the empirical cycle), in which hypotheses are formulated and where statistical testing is employed to investigate these. Also, in quantitative research, samples are generally large, and standardized instruments (such as questionnaires or web surveys) are often used. An explicit aim is to generalize findings from the sample that was studied to a larger universe or a population.

Qualitative methods are used, on the other hand, if we want to understand *why* things happened or *how*, or explore new phenomena. Examples of questions we would pose then are: 'What are the reasons for taking or not taking a business conflict to court?', or 'Under what circumstances are domestic violence filings settled through mediation?', or 'What deliberations do judges make in divorce procedures when one parent has accused the other of sexual abuse?' Qualitative studies are generally much less strictly formatted beforehand than quantitative studies. Hypothesis testing is rare, and statistics is therefore used much less often. Qualitative designs differ from quantitative methods: in general smaller, not necessarily representative samples are used. Open interviews and observation are common, and analytic methods less prescribed and more exploratory, often spread over several iterations.

Quantitative research generally produces a broad, generalizable, quantitative summary of a phenomenon. Qualitative research gives a rich understanding of a particular problem within a particular context. As the two are different methods for answering seemingly different kinds of questions, neither is superior to the other. We do not use the adverb 'seemingly' without purpose, however, as many questions can be addressed using either quantitative or qualitative methods. The approach may then be different, depending on what type of methods one uses, and the type of answers generally are as well.

In qualitative research, the aim is much less to produce generalizable quantitative statements, but to unravel a number of mechanisms, to *understand* what happened, or to understand the meaning that the research subjects give to phenomena that are being studied. This is why the inherent juxtaposition of qualitative and qualitative research is often (slightly simplistically) portrayed as in Figure 1.1. As qualitative scholars work from the assumption that "everything is contextual", they tend to study phenomena, and understand phenomena, only within the given, particular context. This makes qualitative research inherently non-generalizable.

A quantitative study as portrayed in Figure 1.1 gives a broadly generalizable result, but it is like a pancake: it is shallow. In a quantitative study one usually investigates but a few factors or variables. Contextual effects are generally not investigated but seen as a nuisance: quantitative researchers attempt to separate out such factors, control for any contextual factors that might distort the picture. Examples of such studies are experimental studies into the effectiveness of medicines. One then has a group of patients and administers among the group – at random – the medicine-to-be-tested and a placebo. Any differences between the group that received the medicine and the group that received the placebo are then attributable to the medicine and to the medicine only. In such a design, the medicine is 'isolated', and the impact of any contextual effects (such as the expectations patients had, any other medical conditions patients have, gender, personality) evened out by the randomization.

In summary (and admittedly leaving out nuances), a qualitative study picks a small part of the population of interest, but it delves deep, it goes to the bottom of things and generates a rich and contextual understanding – but we cannot be sure whether the same result would have been found elsewhere as the findings apply only within that particular context. A quantitative study studies but a few aspects of the problem at hand but does so broadly, and tries to find the impact of factors regardless of any particular context. That makes the findings of a quantitative study more easily generalizable across contexts, but as it largely disregards context it investigates only a limited number of aspects of the problem at hand.

Why is it important to already touch upon this distinction in our first chapter? Because the two 'traditions' or paradigms use partially different methods. Qualitative studies rely more on open interviews, legal texts, observations, immersing oneself in the context to be studied. Samples are generally small. Studies can be planned only to a certain extent as one is unsure what one will encounter. Analysis is generally lengthier and iterative. Quantitative studies on the other hand rely more heavily on pre-designed measurement instruments such as programmed questionnaires or web surveys. Extensive piloting is necessary. Samples are generally larger, and testing, model building and statistics are common.

Many students prefer qualitative methods to quantitative, assuming that qualitative research – without maths and formulas – is easier. The latter is however generally not the case. Qualitative research requires strong theoretical skills, hard and good analysis, perseverance, and constitutes more often than not a substantive investment (and may entail much more – tedious – work than quantitative research). Whether the outcomes are useful is also often more uncertain beforehand. A solid qualitative study is a feat that requires extensive training, and is much harder to learn through textbook recipes, such as can be used for teaching quantitative skills. We will return to the difference between quantitative and qualitative methods in chapter 2, where we will also detail why a combination of the two types of methods is – when possible – the preferred approach. We will in chapter 7 illustrate how the two can also be regarded as situated on a spectrum, where they regularly encounter each other.

1.5 Outline of this book

In chapter 2 of this introductory part of the book, we will first introduce and discuss some concepts and issues that are important for empirical research, such as reliability and validity, macro-, meso- and micro-level studies and primary and secondary data.

Next, part II of this book deals with data collection. In three chapters, which discuss sampling (chapter 3), measurement (chapter 4) and design (chapter 5), we will discuss data collection methods for both qualitative and quantitative research.

In part III, we discuss analysis methods, separately for quantitative and qualitative data. In chapter 6 we discuss analysis methods to describe the properties of quantitative data, using statistics such as the mean and correlation coefficients and other association measures. In chapter 7, we discuss methods for the analysis of qualitative data, focusing on the coding of texts and textified material, and on content analysis. The next two chapters are more technical. In chapter 8 we introduce statistical testing, and in chapter 9 we move on to more complex quantitative multivariate data analysis.

Towards the end of the book, we set out a number of worked examples to show how all the dry, abstract methodological notions are applied in practice. The first of these, in section 10.2, regards a study on recipients of social assistance benefits and the impact of employment status on both the experienced meaningfulness of their often-tedious tasks as well as protection against arbitrary power exercised by case managers and work supervisors. With data from 42 qualitative interviews, it showcases the various stages and intricacies of qualitative coding strategies, and illustrates how open coding can reveal unexpected viewpoints. The second example (section 10.3) details systematic legal analysis. In this study, a large number of judicial decisions in civil and disciplinary cases were systematically sampled and coded, and the legal arguments by parties analysed to investigate to what extent apologies implied admitting legal accountability in practice. In the third example, in section 10.4, multivariate analysis was used to investigate to what extent international sentencing at the International Criminal Tribunal of the former Yugoslavia could be considered consistent, combining both perpetrator and crime characteristics in one model to predict sentence length. In our final chapter (chapter 11) we summarize some general issues that those who wish to use empirical methods to study the law should be particularly aware of.

Chapter questions

1. What three elements characterize empirical legal research? (section 1.2)
2. What types of research focused on the law are generally not regarded as part of empirical legal studies? (section 1.2)

3. What are the three pillars that constitute the trias ELSica? (section 1.3)
4. What is an ex-ante evaluation? (section 1.3)
5. Give an example of how the three pillars are interconnected (section 1.3)
6. What two features distinguish empirical legal studies from subdisciplines such as criminology, legal sociology or legal psychology? (section 1.4)
7. In what respects does qualitative research differ from qualitative research? (section 1.4.1)

Chapter 2

ELS research methodology: general issues

2.1 Introduction

This chapter discusses a number of issues that are at the basis of empirical legal research methodology. They deal with preparatory issues such as research question formulation, research ideas and specifics such as hypothesis formulation. Extensive attention will be given in this chapter to quality aspects of measurement, such as validity and reliability of the measurement of constructs. We will do so for quantitative as well as qualitative research, and discuss reasons why combining the two – in a so-called mixed methods design – generally strengthens our conclusions. Next we discuss a number of commonly used categorizations of research questions and designs, at the micro- meso- and macro-level, and briefly touch on the distinction between primary and secondary data. We end the chapter with research ethics, the rules that researchers should stick to by law and disciplinary convention.

2.2 Empirical cycle

Researchers can come across a research idea at any time, in any place. No rules describe how researchers should identify a research idea. Some researchers come upon ideas when they are peeling potatoes, others while sitting in their study bent over thick books, others while jogging along a canal in the rain. No rules prescribe how you as a researcher should arrive at a new research idea.

Some refer to this phase as the 'observational phase': you as a researcher observe phenomena, you walk around and take notice of things – out of which an idea bubbles up. Obviously, quite often researchers are approached by governmental bodies who ask them to answer a certain policy- or practice-relevant research question.

This research idea is what starts the so-called *empirical cycle*. As said, this idea can be a very rough notion of what you as a researcher want to zoom in upon. However, once you have identified a research idea (say: the relation between tort victimization and well-being, or the recruitment process of law firms) there are a number of steps to follow for that idea to be turned into a researchable question and for us as researchers to find an answer to our question. That sequence of steps is often referred to as the 'empirical cycle'. Qualitative and quantitative research may differ in how they progress through that cycle, and we start by describing the steps in the research cycle for quantitative studies.

So: let us suppose that the research idea has been identified. After a research idea has been decided upon, it should next be translated into a question. This phase is what is called the *inductive phase*. Here the rough notion is transformed to a question to which you want to find the answer. That question could be, for our example: are criminal law judges less intelligent than civil law judges? (It could also be: is there a difference in intelligence between criminal law judges and civil law judges?) These two varieties may seem only superficially different but, as we will see in chapter 9, the exact formulation of the research question does have implications for statistical testing. This inductive phase is also referred to as the phase where hypotheses are formulated, or the 'hypothesis phase'.

Suppose that the research question we choose is: 'are criminal law judges less intelligent than civil law judges?' Then, before we can start carrying out our research to provide an answer to this question, we must become much more concrete. It is for instance unclear in this question what we mean by intelligence. Intelligence is what is often referred to as a 'construct' or 'hypothetical construct': something people have a common understanding of, but something we cannot observe directly like we could someone's height or weight or eye colour. We assume that it exists, but it is not observable, it is only hypothesized to exist. As the construct is not an observable property, we have to define how we measure the construct, in this case: intelligence. Do we intuitively infer it from someone's appearance? Do we infer it from someone's educational level? Or do we use someone's score on a validated IQ test?

Next we have to decide what we mean by a criminal and civil law judge. Is that someone who has worked as a judge only in criminal or civil courts respectively? Or someone who has done so over the past five years, regardless of what other type of cases s/he tried? Or who is doing so currently? And how do we measure this? Do we ask judges in what type of court they worked? And whether they did so exclusively? What do we do with those who have experience in administrative cases as well? Suppose we do our study in the Netherlands, do we include judges at the International Criminal Court?

Subsequently, we also need to decide when we will answer our question in the affirmative. Suppose that criminal judges' average IQ is 120.0000, and that that of civil law judges 120.0001, do we then answer our question in the affirmative? Or do we only identify a difference as 'telling' from a certain magnitude onwards (for instance a 10-point difference, or a 5-point difference)?

In this phase the research question or hypothesis becomes testable. It is specified to such an extent that we will actually be able to find the answer to the questions through measurement. From the general question that was formulated in the inductive phase in which we wrapped the question in vague words, we have now come 'down to earth' in this next phase, the *deductive phase*, and defined exactly how we are going to *measure* the concepts or constructs. It is sometimes jokingly said that after the deductive phase, after the questions have been turned into testable hypotheses, if the researcher were to suddenly be run over by a tram in front of the university building, the research could go ahead as planned. After his or her untimely demise another researcher could take over and would conduct the research in exactly the same way as the deceased researcher would have done. All decisions have been made, all steps have been outlined. The path or 'recipe' for the study has been outlined. This process, of defining exactly what is meant by a construct and how it can be measured, is called *operationalization*. Operationalization is the process through which general ideas are turned into concrete to-do lists. With operationalization, you lay down exactly through what operations you are going to answer the research question. After operationalization, the research has become *reproducible*, by which we mean that if asked to re-do the study, the authors would be able to do so.

Reproducibility – the extent to which the original researchers can reproduce their findings – is different from replicability, the desirable situation where findings conducted in one study by a set of researchers are replicated in a different study by different researchers (it should be noted that replicability and reproducibility are at times defined differently in different disciplines). Replicability can also be regarded as a form of external validity, namely the situation where the conclusions from one study generalize to other contexts (see section 2.6.2).

After the deductive phase, the research proper can go ahead. According to the precise prescriptions, measurements can be made and we will be able to determine whether civil law judges are indeed more (or less) intelligent than criminal law judges. This phase is often referred to as the 'testing phase', that is, the phase where data are collected in the empirical world, to test the hypothesis.

Lastly, after the hypothesis has been accepted or rejected, the last phase encompasses the consideration of this result and its meaning for theory. Suppose – for our silly example – that criminal law judges are found to be on average indeed less intelligent than civil law judges, what are the implications for our empirical legal theories? Can this finding be due to an effect in the sense that the cleverer law students are more often assigned to the 'superior' civil bench? Or is it that after working for many years as a criminal court judge, your mind becomes numb and your IQ decreases? Or is there perhaps a *confounder* at play, in the sense that the criminal law judges are older (it is known that IQ decreases with age)? Here, in this so-called *evaluation phase*, we are assessing what the findings mean: is it really true that the type of chamber in which a judge works is associated with intelligence. And suppose that were the case, of course we would immediately ask ourselves why that would be? Clearly, an answer to the first question immediately raises a follow-up question to be studied.

In that sense, we generally have not come full circle after these five steps. And indeed, the empirical cycle is generally not regarded as a cycle, but as a spiral, with each answer to a question generating new research ideas. Viewing the empirical cycle as a spiral rather than a cycle concurs with the idea that research is accumulative and leads to knowledge in small steps, with each step and each subsequent study constituting progress and taking us further along the path to understanding the world around us.

The research cycle as we have described it just now is characteristic of positivist, quantitative research. It is much less typical for qualitative research. In qualitative research, testing is generally not done, nor are 'instruments' (in the sense of an instrument such as a questionnaire to measure intelligence) commonly used. This is mainly due to the fact that the types of questions posed in qualitative research are generally different. In qualitative studies, we are generally not so much interested in the magnitude, frequency or scale of phenomena. Rather, we ask questions referring to the 'why' or the 'how' of phenomena. For instance, we may be interested to know why people like to work as a barrister. Obviously, we could also answer that question using quantitative research. We could present members of the bar with a set of answers to this question (for instance: a. 'Because I want fast money'; b. 'Because I want to change the world'; c. 'Because I know nothing better to choose'), but that is not the manner in which qualitative studies aim to answer questions. Rather, qualitative studies aim to always study phenomena within their context. Thus, here, a researcher would not simply sit down with a number of barristers or e-mail them questionnaires, but would – if s/he chose a more ethnographic approach – immerse him- or herself in the bar, in staff meetings, sit in on cases being tried, talk to the lawyers also after work, drink beer with them, bike with them to the day care centre where they pick up their children after work. As such, the researcher would try to *understand* through frequent interaction, observation, getting to know barristers, why decisions such as applying for the bar are made, and what gratifications its member receive for their work. The understanding of the subject matter would be deeper, contextual and in all likelihood more variegated. Researchers might also stumble upon motivations they could not have foreseen. Qualitative research might be able to uncover how for different people, a different set of motives operated, depending on the particular phase in their life and choices they were facing, or depending on child care support they could enlist, or not. For that matter, qualitative research is also referred to as *interpretative* empirical, with quantitative research conversely labelled as *analytical* empirical.

The way qualitative research operates is therefore generally much less prescribed and much more open than quantitative research. At the most qualitative end of the spectrum, researchers often start by interacting with the people they aim to study, and draw up hypotheses as they go along. In such studies, each interaction or interview may be seen as a separate mini-research cycle, after which each time new research questions or explanations (not often referred to as such, though) are distilled, which are then tested again with every new research activity. A qualitative study is in that sense by itself a spiral of small research cycles. By the time the explanation or interpretation of the phenomenon under study converges, the research ends. The researcher then has an overview of the phenomenon.

In qualitative research, the research cycle can even be inverted, with researchers starting with data collection, and formulating questions on the basis of what they observe. This type of research is referred to as *grounded theory* and the data gathered in this fashion as *grounded data*; the 'grounded' refers to the fact that the questions thus formulated are based on empirical observation, and not decided upon before observation starts. As Strauss & Corbin have said (1990, p. 23), a theory is:

> "*inductively derived from the study of the phenomenon it represents. That is, it is discovered, developed and provisionally verified through systematic data collection and analysis of data pertaining to that phenomenon.*

> *Therefore, data collection, analysis and theory stand in reciprocal relationship with each other."*

Grounded theory (see Glaser & Strauss, 1967 and Strauss & Corbin, 1998 for the classic references, and Charmaz, 2014 for a more recent update) is an approach that is useful or even necessary if one wants to study phenomena that are largely uncharted terrain. As Stern (1995) has said:

> *"the strongest case for the use of grounded theory is in investigations of relatively uncharted water, or to gain a fresh perspective in a familiar situation."*

We have so far described qualitative and quantitative research in a fairly caricatural manner: qualitative research as open and grounded, with researchers immersing themselves in uncharted communities, and not working from any existing theoretical notions or categorizations, and quantitative research on the other hand as inflexible and deterministic and without any options for open answers or contextual understanding. In practice, the twain regularly meet. Quantitative questionnaires however often also contain some open-ended questions, and qualitative researchers may also quantify their data to be able to tally or compute correlations. They had perhaps, for that reason, best not be seen as entirely different unmarriageable approaches but as complementary, with mixtures and blends being quite feasible.

2.3 Literature search and source evaluation

Often the research idea, the first phase of the empirical cycle, is not a sudden revelation or a lightning bolt. In fact the idea phase often coincides with the period where reading is done. One may for instance be reading up on the scientific literature on employment careers, and find a number of studies that postulate that many lawyers end up at the bar because of the networks they built when they were students. Such 'pointers' from previous research often generate new research ideas.

In general, it is in fact highly inadvisable to start out on research without a thorough literature search. Once a vague idea or direction for the research has been formed (such as 'I want to know more about barristers'), a first exploration should be done of the scientific literature. Reading recent work on the topic tells you what has already been found, what is still an enigma, what new directions are considered fruitful by the cognoscenti in the discipline. Reading up will also warn you against embarking upon topics that are very hard to study in practice, and reading about other researchers' struggles will save you time and money, and prevent you from making the same mistakes.

Literature searches can be done through the internet, or in literature databases. Not all academic literature is 'open access' yet (meaning it can be read without charge) and for many articles in scientific journals you still need to search their content through a university e-mail account that grants you access. It is important to be (extremely) critical when using information from the internet. For scientific purposes, it is in fact best to use only sources that have been published in academic, peer-reviewed journals. Even though that does not guarantee high-quality research, it does give a layer of checking that was done by journal editors and reviewers. Academic work published in academic peer-reviewed journals is ranked as more noteworthy and telling than studies published in non-academic or non-peer-reviewed journals, or work published on researchers' own websites. Top-ranking journals are *The Lancet* (for medical research), and *Nature* and *Science* for various disciplines, mostly from the harder sciences – the latter two so highly ranked that they are in a sense in a separate universe.

For empirical legal studies, a few journals stand out. The first of these is the *Journal of Empirical Legal Studies* (`onlinelibrary.wiley.com/journal/17401461`), with a relatively select and small readership. A second journal that publishes empirical work (with a socio-legal focus) is the *Journal for Law and Society* (`onlinelibrary.wiley.com/journal/14676478`). The European Society for Empirical Legal Studies (`esels.eu`) aims to publish its own *European Journal for Empirical Legal Studies* as of 2024.

Searches are generally done using keywords such as *lawyer*, *barrister* or *legal professional*. In describing the findings, it is common to list, apart from the keywords, the databases searched, the date the search was conducted and the number of hits. Your output is then reproducible. Many researchers next 'snowball' in the sense that they scan the reference list of each of the publications found, retrieve those publications, in turn scan the latter's reference lists, and so forth.

Some academic conferences publish abstracts on their websites that can also be searched. Often, these do not contain sufficient material to refer substantively to these conference presentations, but it is not uncommon to e-mail the presenters and ask them for their PowerPoint slides or any unpublished papers they may have.

2.4 Conceptual and operational definitions

If we want to make statements about the explanatory power of theories, we need data. Empirical data are necessary to test for instance whether the extent to which suspects' experience of procedural justice accurately predicts to what extent they were content with the sentence handed down. We could sit in and witness a large number of randomly selected criminal law cases, note to what extent the defendant was allowed to speak, whether s/he was addressed by the judge in a respectful manner, and in general tick off all the other variables that are assumed to be relevant in the theory of procedural justice (Tyler, 1990). Next, after the sentence has been handed down, we interview the defendant and note his or her 'contentedness' on some scale with the outcome. If we find correlations between the various aspects of procedural justice and the extent to which defendants were content with the outcome, this supports the theory of procedural justice. If we find no such correlation, we have little empirical support for the theory.

If the theory says that – regardless of the severity of the sanction – defendants who are addressed in a condescending manner will be less content with the outcome than those who were treated with respect, and if the theory holds, we should have found the patterns as predicted by the theory. But if that is not the case, something is wrong. Did we investigate the type of cases that the theory supposedly holds for? Should the theory be adapted? If measurements fail to support theories, this can also be because the operationalization of the variables was different from what the theory purports they should be.

Many theories employ so-called hypothetical constructs, abstract notions that in quantitative research need to be defined precisely before they can be measured. Earlier, we used 'intelligence' as an example of such a construct.

Tyler (1990) is regarded as having minted the construct of *procedural justice* (also encountered as 'procedural fairness'), by which it is meant that legal procedures are seen to be conducted in line with principles of fairness. Procedural justice is assumed to be an important pillar of legitimacy. The theory of procedural justice posits that if citizens regard the justice process as having been conducted in line with fairness principles, they are more likely to comply with the outcome, even when the outcome of the process is unfavourable for them. Formulated differently: the theory posits that how citizens regard the justice system is tied more to the perceived fairness of the justice process (including the manner in which citizens are approached) than to the perceived fairness of the outcome.

The construct of procedural justice is generally regarded as being multidimensional, although these dimensions are encountered in the literature in slightly different constellations. Notable dimensions are (1) voice (citizens are given the opportunity to express their side of the story); (2) respect (officials treat parties with dignity and respect); (3) neutrality (the decision making process is unbiased); and (4) transparency (parties are able to see the above being done). Other dimensions that may be postulated are (5) understanding (citizens understand the process and how decisions are made); and (6) helpfulness (perception that system players are interested in your personal situation to the extent that the law allows).

This shows that, while scholars may employ one and the same wording for a construct, their exact definition of that construct may regularly vary. Also, definitions of the same term may evolve over time. A good example again is the hypothetical construct 'intelligence'. While the word intelligence is common usage in many languages, numerous definitions and measurement strategies have emerged over the years it has been employed in psychological research. In the early years, the Stanford–Binet test was used to measure people's intelligence level. As the science of psychology evolved, more dimensions were added to the construct, particularly capturing nonverbal abilities. Currently, many tests are available, such as the WISC or the Raven, which each operationalize intelligence (slightly) differently.

After a construct has been defined, after we have described what exactly we understand the construct to be, through a *conceptual definition*, we next need to decide how the construct should be measured. This is done though a so-called *operational definition*. If for instance our conceptual definition of intelligence states that intelligence is the ability that individuals have for language, maths, and logical reasoning, our operational definition would likely state that our test must contain items to capture language skills, mathematical skills, and logical reasoning. If our conceptual definition also includes visual-spatial processing skills, then the operational definition would state that the test also contains items for these.

All this applies strongly to quantitative research. As said above, the definition of constructs in qualitative research is generally done much more inductively, working from empirical reality with constructs emerging from it.

2.5 Pilot study

In general, once the literature has been read, and the variables have been operationalized, studies do not go full steam ahead yet. It is in fact recommended to test all the study's elements before the study goes 'live'. The study's manner of contacting the respondents should be tested, any instruments should be tested, questionnaires should be administered to a number of trial respondents to see whether filling out the forms really does not take too long, whether all the questions are understandable to respondents, non-offensive, and the like. Even interviewers should be 'tested', as well as research protocols, apps that are used, ICT settings. Such a general rehearsal for the study is referred to as a 'pilot study'.

Studies should be piloted before they start. In spite of all the good intentions and years of experience of research staff, it turns out that – as the saying goes – in research too the proof of the pudding is in the eating. Only once the research is actually carried out in the field, can we find out whether it works. And often that research pudding turns out to need a few more tweaks before it is really up to standard. Thus, almost all researchers pre-test the crucial elements of their studies, and almost all find they need to adjust the study at least a bit. Not piloting one's study is considered extremely risky.

Piloting is especially important for quantitative research. Once a questionnaire has been printed 2,500 times, or distributed to an e-mail list of 5,000 respondents, changes cannot be made without great damage to the study, and concomitant costs. That is why it is so extremely important to have a good test-run before the research goes live. In qualitative research, the need for testing is much less crucial. Of course, some kind of testing is inherently necessary, especially with regard to obtaining access to the people one wants to study. Much of qualitative research is however flexible and adaptable, so that as the research proceeds, changes to questions can be made, questions added, the protocol adapted, etc.

2.6 Validity and reliability

We discussed above the need to operationalize constructs such as intelligence. But how can we be sure that our operational definition does give us good measurements of the construct we intend to measure? Perhaps the items with which we aim to measure intelligence have been chosen such that it is easy to guess the right answers. Or perhaps maths skills items have been formulated so 'wordily' that they actually tap language skills, so that only those with sufficient language skills are able to understand what is asked – in that case the test does not capture maths skills.

This issue – whether our operational definition enables us to measure the construct as we defined it – is generally captured in two methodological properties: validity and reliability. Let us first turn to reliability.

2.6.1 Reliability

Reliability refers to the exactness with which we measure our construct. Suppose I would want to measure someone's height. I could do so using a measuring tape. If my measure of height is reliable, this means it is exact: each time I measure that person's height, I get exactly the same result. In the reverse case, namely if I get different results each time I take my measurement, I call my measure unreliable. Using an elastic measuring tape would for instance make for an unreliable measure: one time the result is 170 cm, next it is 172, then it is 167, then 173 etc. If I were to do my measurements 100 times I might on average get the right result, but because of the variability in the measurements, we say that the measure is unreliable.

How can we assess a measure's reliability? The example already gives an indication of that: one way to do this is to test and then re-test: if we obtain the same results upon re-testing we call the measures reliable. If we do not, we call them unreliable. Testing and re-testing is not always an option, however: if we for instance interview respondents, it is not feasible to return to respondents and re-interview them. Even if the objects we are investigating would lend themselves to re-testing (for instance when we are conducting a dossier analysis), it still often does not make sense to re-test: the coder would probably remember the value s/he entered previously.

In such cases, we tend to have two coders investigate the material, independently, and compare their measurements. If the results from these two raters concur, we say that we have *interrater reliability*. Reliability is often expressed as percentage agreement: it is then reported, for instance, that for the variable that measures the number of children over whom custody issues arise in divorce proceedings, interrater agreement is 90, meaning that in 90% of cases the coders arrived at the same value for the variable. Percentage agreement varies from 0 to 100.

Percentage agreement is often regarded as a fairly simplistic measure of interrater agreement. It namely disregards the fact that some agreement may occur by chance. A better measure, which is often preferred, is Cohen's kappa (also written with the Greek letter κ), a statistic that takes the observed level of agreement between coders and corrects for agreement that would have occurred by chance. Kappa ranges from -1 to +1, with 1 indicating perfect agreement, 0 indicating as much agreement as expected by chance, and -1 indicating perfect disagreement. There are no hard rules to judge whether interrater agreement (which will seldom be perfect) is good enough. Most authors rate agreement in a stepwise fashion, with for instance absolute values of 0.41 to 0.60 indicating moderate agreement, 0.61 to 0.80 indicating sufficient agreement, and 0.81 to 1.0 indicating almost perfect or perfect agreement (Landis & Koch, 1977). Others are more strict and believe that only kappa-values indicating that two-thirds or more of the rankings are identical are acceptable.

But both percentage agreement and Cohen's kappa may be less than optimal measures of reliability if we have a numerical variable (such as number of children). Percentage agreement and Cohen's kappa simply look at whether two coders fill out the same value, but they disregard whether the difference between scorers is small ('4' versus '5') or large ('1 child' versus '5 children'). One solution that may be employed is to use a measure of association, such as the correlation coefficient (see section 6.4.1). Versions of kappa are also available that weight the differences between coders. In case the scorings of more than two raters are to be compared, a special statistic should be computed to arrive at an overall measure of consistency across raters (an example is the so-called intraclass correlation coefficient or ICC). For a fairly technical but instructive and comprehensive overview see Hallgren (2012).

Reliability may be less easy to assess in qualitative research. As the qualitative method does not often rely on instruments, and as much of the data may be gathered in interaction with the research subjects, it may be the case that – as is often said – it is the researcher him- or herself who 'is' the instrument. As interactions can only occur when at least two people are present, interactions could not even be replicated through a second researcher or coder.

However, when text has been coded or video material, we have data that is 'patient' and that can be re-coded by another researcher. Then, it is possible to assess reliability. The two (or more) coders then code fragments of text, and one can check whether they attach the same labels to the same chunks of text. Krippendorff's α is a coefficient of agreement between coders that is regularly used when textual units have been coded. It was developed for content analysis, which we will discuss in section 7.3. When Krippendorff's α is 1 there is perfect agreement; when it is 0, agreement is no higher than would have been achieved by chance. It can be used with any number of coders. For more, see Krippendorff (2004, 2011). We return to the topic of reliability in qualitative research in section 7.5.

2.6.2 Validity

Next, validity refers to the extent to which our instruments really measure what we are after. Where reliability has to do with the extent to which we measure our construct precisely, meaning that it would be replicable, validity is much more fundamental in that it reflects to what extent an instrument to measure, say, criminogenic beliefs, actually captures those beliefs and not something else. Designing instruments such that they truly reflect the construct you are after is a skill, and requires extensive testing and probing before you can be confident that the instrument is up to standard.

Focusing again on quantitative research, let us illustrate with an example some of the issues that complicate achieving valid measures. Suppose I would indeed want to measure criminogenic beliefs. Some of the questions I could pose respondents are, for instance: 'It is okay to steal', or 'If someone does not pay me respect, I am willing to use force'. Now some of your respondents who harbour criminogenic beliefs may answer 'yes' to the first question, and 'yes' to the second one. Most respondents with criminogenic beliefs will, however, realize that their beliefs are considered 'not done'. Anticipating disapproval, they may therefore choose to answer 'no' to your questions and present themselves as respectable citizens, just like they believe the interviewer to be. If that happens, we say that the instrument is sensitive to 'social desirability bias'. The instrument then does not capture criminogenic beliefs, but to a large extent what the interviewee believes the interviewer finds a 'correct' answer. Your instrument is then not valid. More tendencies exist that influence respondents' answers and thus affect validity, and we will discuss some additional ones in chapter 4.3.3.

In quantitative social science research methodology, several kinds of validity are distinguished. The first one is the one that we just referred to: does the instrument measure what it is intended to measure? This is denoted more specifically as *construct validity*. For an instrument to have construct validity, it has to meet three criteria. First, the instrument must capture the construct across its entire 'spectrum'. For instance, an intelligence test that has maths items only does not capture intelligence as we understand it: it does not measure language skills or logical reasoning or nonverbal abilities. It therefore assesses the construct only partially. It is then said that the instrument lacks *content validity*. Only an instrument that assesses the construct across its entire breadth or spectrum, is said to have content validity. Second, the instrument must generate measures that correlate in the expected direction with other outcomes. This likely sounds fairly obscure, so we will try to clarify it with an example: the scores on an instrument to measure driving skills should be associated negatively with the likelihood that people cause traffic accidents. If the instrument tells us that someone has good driving skills, we would expect that person to drive safely. This is referred to as *criterion validity*: the scores obtained with the instrument should correlate with an external criterion that you would expect it to be associated with. Third, we want our instrument to really capture the underlying construct, and not something else. It is for instance possible that we might design an instrument that has good content validity (say we are again measuring intelligence, and our instrument encompasses intelligence across all its dimensions), and also has good criterion validity in the sense that people with high scores on the instrument do well in school. However, if our instrument is built using items written in advanced Dutch, it does not capture intelligence but mainly language skills. It would for instance be unable to measure intelligence for recently arrived migrants who have not yet mastered Dutch. Then this instrument still does not measure intelligence. This last criterion is referred to as *construct validity-in-the-narrow-sense*.

All in all, an instrument can only be said to have validity if it meets all of the three criteria: content validity, criterion validity and construct validity-in-the-narrow-sense. If all these three criteria are met, can we then say that the instrument has construct validity? Not yet, as for an instrument to have construct validity, we also require it to be reliable. Formulated in ordinary terms: we cannot say that our instrument measures what we are after if it produces imprecise measurements. So, in summary, we regard an instrument to have construct validity only when the instrument gives us precise measurements of the construct we are after *and* meets all of the three above-described validity criteria. The instrument then has full construct validity.

How then does one assess whether one's instrument has construct validity? This is a lot more complicated than assessing reliability. Researchers generally first assess *face validity*, which may sound sophisticated but is not much more than judging whether, on the face of it, the instrument is likely to be content, criterion and construct (in the narrow sense) valid. More intricate methods investigate whether the scores generated by the construct correlate with other variables in the way they should if they were a valid measure of the underlying construct.

Other kinds of validity exist. We discuss them briefly. *Statistical conclusion validity* or *statistical validity* refers to whether a result is likely to be attributable to anything other than chance. Suppose that we have investigated 100 volunteers, young men aged 15–25 years old. We have administered our intelligence test and asked them whether they have ever been a victim of an accident. Now suppose that we find that our measurements of intelligence correlate with our respondents' accident victimization: the lower the respondents' intelligence scores, the more accidents they suffered. Statistical tests can tell us how likely it is that the observed association is a chance one. If our statistical test tells us that the observed correlation is in fact a highly unlikely outcome if intelligence and accident proneness were unrelated, we say that the correlation is significant. We then conclude that intelligence and accident proneness are related. The finding then has 'statistical conclusion validity'. We discuss statistical testing in detail in chapter 8.

Next, *internal validity* is distinguished. Continuing our example on intelligence and victimization, we might be tempted to believe that, given the statistically significant association between the two, intelligence and accident proneness are in fact causally related, with people with lower intelligence more often suffering accidents: because they do not pay attention, do not learn from past mistakes, etc. We cannot be sure about this, however. It may for instance be that intelligence has nothing to do with accident proneness, but that those with higher intelligence do not like to own up to the fact that they were involved in accidents (in which case our instrument could be said to suffer from social desirability bias.) Or could the lower intelligence score be due to the accident suffered? Or could it be the case that people with lower intelligence work in different jobs that expose them to more risk of accidents?

As there are several alternative explanations – other than that low intelligence causes accidents – for our finding, we do not have internal validity. Even though we captured intelligence with a construct valid measure and even if we have valid measures of the number of accidents that people suffered, and even if the association is significant, we still cannot rule out other explanations than the causal one. This happens very often in observational research: researchers find associations between an intervention and an outcome, but they cannot prove that the outcome has been caused by the intervention. If vegetarians live longer than meat eaters, this may also be due to the fact that vegetarians do more exercise, or smoke less, or are generally more health-conscious. If marathon runners live longer than non-runners, this may also be due to the fact that they are healthier in the first place (which enables them to do those gruelling runs and makes them live longer, so that it is actually a reverse causal relation). These other variables, such as exercise, smoking or health (consciousness), are called *confounders*.

Ensuring internal validity is extremely difficult in observational studies like the examples given here, and in fact in much empirical legal research. The only way to be absolutely certain that a causal relation exists between for instance participation in an anti-discrimination training for municipal workers and the outcome of citizen satisfaction is if we could be certain that those who participate in the training do not differ from non-participants. The only way to be entirely sure about this is to administer the intervention at random: just like in pharmaceutical research, we should then create two groups who randomly do and do not get the anti-discrimination training. If we have such a design, we will have ruled out any alternative explanation. As the two groups (those with and those without the intervention) have been formed by chance, there are no systematic differences between the two groups anymore and they therefore also cannot differ anymore on the confounders. Then, no confounders can be at play, and no alternative explanations are left – only the causal one. We will return to this topic at length in chapter 5.

Lastly, suppose that we have a study conducted with a measure that has construct validity, and suppose our findings have statistical validity, and suppose as well that we have internal validity: can we be certain that trust in the municipal institutions as measured in our sample would also be found in the entire population once all municipal workers had been trained?

External validity can also be conceived of in a broader sense. Suppose that we have studied a pilot neighbourhood court in Rotterdam, and that we found that the court is able to effectively and speedily deal with the underlying problems of defendants (addiction, homelessness, debts, etc.), so that processual costs are massively reduced. We can ask ourselves the question whether we may be confident that we would find similarly successful outcomes if neighbourhood courts were to be rolled out in other cities? More generally: can we be sure that interventions tested in certain 'experimental' settings such as research labs or pilot projects would also be found in the outside world, outside of the artificial research setting induced by academia or the enthusiastic innovative pilot? If that is the case, we have *external validity*: our findings are then also generalizable to other situations than our artificial research environment. We will return to the issue of generalizability from samples in section 3.2.

Note that the four kinds of validity we just discussed constitute in a sense levels or steps: each validity level has to be satisfied before it makes sense to check whether the next type of validity is present. If we do not measure what we are interested in, it does not make sense to test whether a result is statistically significant. If an association is not statistically significant (and is therefore likely to be chance result), it does not make sense to investigate whether an association is causal. Therefore, with each successive validity level reached, we become more confident that our findings are meaningful.

All that has been discussed so far on validity pertains particularly strongly to quantitative research. Assessing validity in qualitative research – especially construct validity and internal and external validity – is often done slightly differently. We return to the topic of validity in qualitative research in section 7.5.

2.7 Qualitative and quantitative studies

An often-used categorization of research, which we have already briefly touched upon, is that into qualitative and quantitative studies. While quantitative studies aim to measure the volume or *quantity* of some variable of interest, qualitative studies are geared to find out the 'why' or the 'how' of phenomena. Quantitative studies typically follow the empirical cycle, are studies where hypotheses are formulated and where statistical testing is employed. For understanding, for instance, why corporate fines do not reduce environmental crime, or what role family lawyers play in the deflection of divorce conflict, qualitative studies may be much better suited.

When we conduct qualitative studies, much is different from what has been discussed up to now. Qualitative studies are generally much less strictly formatted, use lots of unstructured interviews and observation, have more room for adaptation as the research goes along, and leave more room for respondents to put forward unexpected viewpoints. They may be ethnographic, in which case the researcher spends time on a structural basis with his or her research subjects, to understand their world and reality, and to be able to explain 'from within'. Instruments are hardly ever used, statistical testing is hardly ever encountered.

While quantitative research gives a broad, generalizable, quantitative summary of a phenomenon (which are plus points), its downside is that it is reductionist and can deal with only a small number of factors in relatively simple models (which are negative points). Qualitative research is richer in the sense that it can describe complex situations, uncover mechanisms, understand behaviour in context and deal with multiple layers of interrelated causal factors (these are all plus points), but often has limited generalizability and limited reliability (negative points).

In qualitative research, the aim is much less to produce generalizable quantitative statements, but rather to unravel a number of mechanisms, to *understand* what happened, within a certain context. Some qualitative researchers even may find lack of generalizability unproblematic as they regard all behaviour as contextual. This is why the inherent juxtaposition of qualitative and qualitative research is often portrayed as we did in Figure 1.1 in chapter 1.

A quantitative study gives in general a broadly generalizable result. It has nice properties and strengths, amongst which its generalizability, and the fact that all the data that are collected and analyses that are carried out are easily replicable. Other researchers can use the same instruments, draw a sample in the same manner from the same population and would find (approximately, as there will be some chance variation) the same result. In that sense, quantitative studies are strong on reliability, reproducibility and replicability. However, quantitative research is generally limited in the kind of models it can analyse: only so many variables can practically be analysed simultaneously. In addition, quantitative studies can only give you what you were searching for: the questionnaires will generate answers only to the questions that were posed, not to other useful things respondents knew but had no space in the questionnaire to tell you about.

A qualitative study, on the other hand, focuses generally on one or a few particular settings, and investigates behaviour in the complex environment in which behaviour emerges: in interaction with others, understanding and misunderstanding cues, expecting things and asking for one thing but wanting another, analysing symbolic meanings that people give to behaviour, dress code and the like. Qualitative studies can be serendipitous. This makes qualitative studies attractive for getting to the heart of things, for gathering new insights. Phrased differently, qualitative studies can be stronger on validity. The downside is that it will be very hard, if not impossible, to replicate and sometimes even reproduce qualitative studies; the researcher him- or herself may in some cases even be regarded as the 'instrument' in a qualitative study. It is through the interaction with the researcher, through the impact that the researcher had on the respondents, through his or her observations and interpretations that the analysis takes shape.

This may all sound pretty abstract as we have not given many illustrations of what qualitative and quantitative studies are about. We will do so in a stepwise fashion in the next chapters. For now, it is important to remember that a quantitative study is generally relatively strong on reliability, a qualitative study relatively strong on 'validity' in the broad sense of unravelling mechanisms, capturing the intricacies of processes – all, obviously, given a high quality of the study design, measures and staff.

2.7.1 Mixed methods and triangulation

While the two types of research traditions are at times juxtaposed, and researchers from the two traditions often move in their own separate circles, this writer believes that qualitative and quantitative methods can very well be combined. Contrasting the two is an unnecessary 'antagonistic' schematization as, first, no type of tradition has a priori preference over the other. Suppose we are interested to study the 'how much', or 'change' in a variable, for an entire population. Then a quantitative study is clearly best used. If the question on the other hand is one about the why or the how, or a question on a topic that we know very little about, then a qualitative study is likely best chosen.

Second, instead of seeing the two traditions as different, they are perhaps better regarded as complementary. In many instances we are namely not only interested in the – putting it in a very black-and-white way – 'how much', but for sure also in the 'how' or 'why'. And even if we are interested in barristers' motivations for working at the bar, we might still want to have some idea of how often certain motivations prevail, or whether motivations differ for younger and older respondents, or men and women. It is in practice in fact often the case that researchers combine the two types of methods to answer one and the same question. Quantitative methods then give the broad, generalizable, replicable overview, with qualitative methods shedding light on why the data have been observed as they are, what the processes were that generated the observed patterns. The advantage of such a 'mixed methods' approach is not only that we can answer questions about quantities as well as about how those quantities came about, but that each type of method in a sense 'buffers' the weakness of the other type. Such a combination of qualitative and quantitative methods in one study is encountered as 'triangulation', as 'mixed methods', or even as a multi-method study. Various types of mixed methods designs exist. An excellent and concise introduction to such types of research, which compares their strengths and weaknesses and unique suitabilities for specific questions, is Dixon, Singleton, & Straits (2016), chapter 4. Apart from combining qualitative and quantitative approaches in research, other examples of mixed methods exist, combining various quantitative data sources or different methodological approaches to answering the same questions. The terms 'mixed methods' and 'triangulation' are in practice often used interchangeably, although triangulation was originally coined to indicate the combination of qualitative and quantitative lenses on one and the same phenomenon or, more precisely, research question.

Zeng and Eleveld (2022) investigated, focusing on food riders in Amsterdam, the assumptions underlying the proposal for an EU Directive on improving working conditions in platform work (`ec.europa.eu/eures/public/eu-proposes-directive-protect-rights-platform-workers-2022-03-17_en`). Underlying the proposed directive is the assumption that riders wish to be employees rather than freelance, in order to be protected by labour law. For this study, the authors analysed the EU proposal, EU and Dutch labour law, and reviewed relevant literature. In addition, they conducted semi-structured interviews with 20 riders in Amsterdam. The researchers stratified their sample (see section 3.3.1: 'Stratified sample') in the sense that they conducted 10 interviews with riders who were employees and 10 with riders who were self-employed. They also observed popular rider areas, and conducted interviews with professionals such as experts, NGOs and the riders' union.

The authors found that most riders actually did not have much specific knowledge about labour law. Especially those riders who were employed already preferred employee status because it gave them stability and financial security. However, most riders preferred the flexibility and anonymity of being a self-employed rider. Particular reasons for self-employment that had not been identified yet in the EU proposal were, amongst others, the possibility (especially for women) to refuse rides to neighbourhoods deemed unsafe, and the possibility to also cater for undocumented migrants.

2.8 Macro-, meso- and micro-level studies

The macro-meso-micro categorization is often encountered in sociological research where processes and explanations are regularly divided along these lines. The categorization reflects the aggregation level at which studies attempt to draw conclusions.

The *micro*-level is the lowest or smallest possible analysis unit. Often this is the level of the individual, and micro-level studies generally focus on respondents: people (whether they are defendants, lawyers, litigants, citizens) or cases. These are interviewed or observed, or data are collected about them from other sources. Explanations for the phenomena that are observed are then also situated at this level, for example an explanation where it is postulated that greed (an individual trait) causes people to embezzle.

The *macro*-level is found at the other end of the aggregation spectrum. As this is therefore the highest level of aggregation, explanations focus on high levels of aggregation, such as the level of the nation or government. An example of such an explanation is one where it is said that strict tenancy laws lead to a shortage of rental units.

In between the micro- and macro-level is situated the *meso*-level. Here, there is some aggregation over individuals. Examples of this level are neighbourhoods, companies, or trade unions. Explanations for the phenomena that are observed at the meso-level are then also situated at this level, for example the explanation where it is postulated that an open and non-hierarchical corporate culture prevents norm-transgressive behaviour.

2.9 Primary and secondary data

Many researchers collect their own data. They go out into the field, and ring doorbells with bailiffs, interview lawyers, survey citizens, code court cases, and the like. Such data, collected by researchers themselves, according to their own codes and formats and quality standards, are referred to as 'primary' data.

However, when doing empirical legal research, it is very often possible to use data that have already been collected by others. Governmental statistics agencies collect data on the number and nature of cases dealt with in court, the prison service surveys prisoners, law firms have administrations, the records of asylum seekers' applications are held in governmental offices.

Such data, already collected by others, are often attractive to use. Firstly because of cost: if we can use governmental data or data collected by other bodies, we generally spend (if we have to pay at all) but a fraction of what it would cost to collect all that data ourselves. Second, such data are attractive because we then do not need to design and carry out sampling procedures: we may have access to all cases that exist.

In many countries, a wealth of data is available from registries held by national statistics agencies. For instance, for England and Wales the Individual Insolvency Register holds records on all bankruptcy and insolvency cases for a period of three months (`gov.uk/search-bankruptcy-insolvency-register`); Ireland and Scotland have separate registers). The extent of data and coverage over historical periods can be amazing. Statistics of bankruptcy and all civil cases have been collected annually for England and Wales since 1856, and are published and accessible online at Parliamentary Papers: for instance for all cases decided by the House of Lords, cases from late 1996 up to 2009 are available online from `publications.parliament.uk/`; from late 2009 onwards, all decided cases are accessible from the Supreme Court website (`supremecourt.uk/decided-cases/index.html`). Court data in England and Wales are well preserved, extensive and complete, and go back a very long time. Files of bankruptcy cases are held at the National Archives, with notices of bankruptcies from 1665 (!) to 1986; after 1945 the reports are generally held to become more summary. As these case files contain the original data, they can be considered primary data.

For the Netherlands, a selection of court rulings is published since 2016 at `rechtspraak.nl`; as only the rulings are published, these data on rulings can be considered primary data as they are simply the original rulings. However, information on lots of aspects of the case that is present in the original case file is mostly summarized, such as information on victims, or the pleas made by lawyers, or the different arguments used by plaintiffs. Information on the latter as it appears in the rulings should therefore be regarded as secondary data: registrars have summarized the data as far as is relevant for the ruling.

The sample of Dutch court cases at `rechtspraak.nl` unfortunately does not constitute a population (yet) in the statistical sense (see chapter 3). For instance, for criminal law, verdicts in all (completed and attempted) homicide cases are published, but an unclear selection of sexual violence cases is published. All cases decided upon by the Supreme Court are published, as are all cases decided upon by a number of higher appeal boards that are particularly relevant for business and commerce (inter alia the Administrative Law Division of the Council of State, the Administrative Court for Trade and Industry, the Business Chamber of the Amsterdam Court of Appeal, the Intellectual Property Division of the Civil Sector of the District Court of The Hague, and the Agricultural Tenancies Appeal Chamber of the Arnhem Court), that is to say, in as far as the case has not been declared unfounded or non-admissible or has been dealt with through a standard wording model. The Netherlands Council for the Judiciary has announced that it aims to publish *all* rulings within a few years, after which an entire population of rulings will be accessible online.

In all European countries, all decisions are given a unique European identifier (European Case Law Identifier or ECLI). ECLI is a uniform code that has the same recognizable format for all EU member states, composed of five mandatory elements, namely a country code, the code of the court that rendered the judgment, the year the judgment was rendered, and a number that is a unique identifier for the specific country. The Dutch decisions are searchable by this ECLI code, but also through other pointers, such as the specific court, the substantive area of law, or through more open terms such as ‘tort’, which produces numerous hits. The massive amount of hits is then refinable (for instance by adding 'sports' as a more specific second term), which will reduce the set to be much smaller and more workable amount.

In many countries, the prosecution service holds statistics and court files. Until the end of the last century, most documents were paper only. Since the turn of the century, more and more of these case files are held only in digital format. It should be noted that not all data that are of interest to the ELS researcher are held by governmental bodies: for instance insurers hold interesting records (although they might not always be willing to share them), such as on all cases filed claiming legal expenses insurance. The latter would if available (obviously) not entail a complete list of all claimants or even conflicts, but again only a particular selection, namely those who submit a claim with their insurer.

Secondary data can be used only for some research questions. For other questions, we do need to go and collect data ourselves, because the government or other bodies simply do not collect the data we need, or do not collect them in the format or following the quality standards we require. It is therefore important to keep in mind that – while their easy availability may be seductive – there are drawbacks to their use.

2.10 Research ethics: rules and conventions

Whenever we conduct research in which we study humans, we have to observe ethical rules. Every discipline has its own – at times international – ethical rules, which in general share a common core. A first rule is that research subjects or respondents have the right to be treated decently and respectfully. Appointments should be met, on time, and researchers should dress and behave according to the standards of the respondents. The same goes when we approach organizations whose data we might want to use. Attentive e-mails and swift responses generally get you further than informal or cursory responses. And, apart from this being common decency, experience teaches that treating respondents with respect, friendliness and flexibility is also much better for the research: respondents who feel they are not being treated correctly will maybe sooner refuse to participate, or may give only cursory or half-true answers, just to be rid of the researchers or to quickly cash the remuneration.

Second, and more formally, respondents have the right before they agree to participate to be informed what the research is about, who finances it, what will happen with the information they give – in short, they are entitled to be fully informed about all aspects of the research that may be relevant for them in deciding whether they want to participate or not. This is referred to as *informed consent*. We return to this topic in section 4.2. Obviously, researchers should also heed the safety of respondents. Especially in charged environments, such when studying conflict settings, the participation in a study may by itself endanger respondents.

In the following paragraphs, we discuss the legal framework for data protection and research on human research subjects. We describe how internal and independent review boards commonly review research proposals before any research goes ahead, and we delve a little into the implications for data protection and ethical rules when research is conducted online.

2.10.1 Legal framework: the GDPR

The European Union General Data Protection Regulation (`eugdpr.org`) constitutes the legal framework that governs the manner in which the privacy of citizens and therefore also respondents (in general: non-deceased human study objects) should be safeguarded. Because of its relative novelty (it came into force in 2018), it is not yet clear what the exact scope is of what the GDPR prescribes and forbids when it comes to data protection. All research institutions are required to have a data protection officer (DPO) in place, an independent data protection expert responsible for monitoring compliance, informing and advising on data protection obligations, and who is able to help with practical and technical questions. It does appear, from recent experience across the social sciences board, as if procedures have become much more complicated and lengthy, and as if those who need to give permission for the use of data have become much more strict and reticent in granting access to data.

While much is still unclear about the exact implications of the GDPR for scientific research, it is clear that every researcher is obliged to carry out a so-called Data Privacy Impact Assessment (DPIA) before an investigation can go ahead. A DPIA describes the handling of (special) personal data (`gdpr-info.eu/issues/privacy-impact-assessment/`) collected during the research. A DPIA should specify the risk of the investigation for the rights and freedoms of the persons being examined when processing their personal data, and the measures taken for concrete protection.

In doing so, it is helpful to distinguish three types of data: 'red' data (containing personal details or data that can be directly traced back to persons, such as their name, address, date and place of birth), 'orange' data (that do not contain directly personally identifiable data, but data that in combination with other data can reveal the identity of the persons being investigated; this data is also referred to as 'pseudonymized'), and 'green' data (that contain absolutely no personal or personally identifiable data).

Red data is the most sensitive from a privacy point of view, green data is completely insensitive, and orange data is in between. The regimes that apply to the storage and transport of this data are correspondingly strict. Green data files may be transported freely (physically on paper or on a USB stick, or via e-mail), because they cannot violate the privacy of persons. Red files should preferably only be stored on a data carrier that cannot be accessed or is extremely difficult to access by anyone other than the researcher. In more and more institutions, this type of data is stored on a standalone workstation that is not linked to the internet ('air-gapped') so that it is technically 'unhackable' from outside. If red data need to be transported, this is done on a special USB stick that is encrypted. Orange data can be stored on an ordinary workstation such as a laptop or PC (which is therefore connected to the internet) but may not be transported freely.

An often-used practical solution for transporting data collected from individuals in the field is to divide the data into two sets: one set that contains the personal data with a unique code per respondent, and another set that contains the unique code and the research data. The unique code is the key with which the sets can be linked and research data linked to individuals. Transported separately, the two datasets are fairly harmless if they were lost: the first set contains only names and meaningless numbers, and the second meaningless numbers and research data that cannot however be linked to individual respondents.

In general, we recommend that one be too careful rather than easy-going. It is also advised to be extra-careful when conducting research abroad or in collaboration with researchers from other countries. Special agreements must sometimes be laid down for cooperation with certain countries, and in some countries special privacy legislation also applies.

The French Centre National de la Recherche Scientifique (CNRS) has drafted an overview of the GDPR and its implications for research in the humanities and social sciences (downloadable from `inshs.cnrs.fr/sites/institut_inshs/files/pdf/Guide_rgpd_2021_en_0.pdf`; CNRS, 2021) that explains key concepts in the GDPR and describes what they mean in practice. Although geared towards the French situation and the CNRS, and with particular focus on health data, it gives useful examples of consent forms and information notices, and ends with a useful checklist of key issues to achieve compliance with the GDPR on the protection of personal data.

2.10.2 Code of conduct: the ALLEA Code

Since 2017, a European Code of Conduct for Research Integrity has been adopted, a revised version of an earlier code. The Code is quite readable and lists principles, good research practice, as well as violations of research integrity. The principles are briefly summarized as: *reliability* in ensuring the quality of research, reflected in the design, the methodology, the analysis and the use of resources (very much relevant for the topics discussed in this book), *honesty* in developing, undertaking, reviewing, reporting and communicating research in a transparent, fair, full and unbiased way, *respect* for colleagues, research participants, society, ecosystems, cultural heritage and the environment, and *accountability* for the research from idea to publication, for its management and organization, for training, supervision and mentoring, and for its wider impacts.

The Code categorizes fabrication, falsification and plagiarism as research misconduct, and lists a number of unacceptable practices (such as citing selectively to enhance one's own findings or to please editors, reviewers or colleagues, withholding research results and expanding unnecessarily the bibliography of a study), and subsequently lists a number of principles that national institutions and research institutes should adhere to in dealing with violations and allegations of misconduct.

The Code addresses emerging challenges emanating from technological developments, open science, citizen science and social media, among other areas. The European Commission has recognized the Code as the reference document for research integrity for all EU-funded research projects and as a model for organizations and researchers across Europe. The Code was published originally in English on 24 March 2017 and was translated to all official EU languages by the European Commission's Translational Services and with the support of ALLEA Member Academies. See `allea.org/code-of-conduct/`.

2.10.3 Internal review boards

Many research institutes and universities call in the aid of independent or internal review or research and ethical boards for all research in which human subjects are involved. Such committees are hugely important, and are more and more a standard precondition from management to give studies the green light. Not only do they give independent 'clearance' for studies to go ahead, they also constitute more and more often a general requirement for research funding to be released. In addition, they can also be extremely helpful in thinking about the mitigation of risks and the protection of respondents and staff.

Internal Review Boards (IRBs) are thus necessary and invaluable steps in the design and preparation for studies. IRBs will screen study designs and protocols to see whether informed consent is guaranteed, whether respondents' safety is ensured, whether staff safety is secured, and whether any breaches of principles are proportional.

It should be noted that while research ethics generally refer to respondents, they are equally important to consider for researchers. When research takes place in charged or volatile settings, the safety of the researchers is an issue that needs consideration too. Insurance constraints may decide whether research can go ahead, for instance in interviewing forensic staff in conflict areas. But even if insurance covers the researchers, it is important to consider whether one needs or wants to expose interviewers to the risk of getting hurt. IRBs therefore generally also take into account the safety of research staff when assessing research proposals.

Van den Berg, Blommaert, Bijleveld, & Ruiter (2020) investigated the effect of a criminal record on job market opportunities by sending motivation letters with CVs in response to existing vacancies, with one half of the applicants randomly 'confessing' that they had a criminal record for a certain offence, and the other half not. In this study, the employers did not know that the applications had been fabricated and sent by researchers. They participated unknowingly, and without informed consent, in a field experiment. Nevertheless, the exception to informed consent could be defended here, because informed consent in advance would have made it impossible to answer the research question: the employers would then no longer behave 'naturally' because they knew they were being studied and what the focus of the researchers was.

The researchers found, to their surprise, that a criminal record had but a marginal effect on applicants' chances of getting back a favourable reply. The effect of the indicated migrant background of the applicants (the researchers had also randomly varied the names of the applicants, one name indicating a Dutch applicant, and the other name indicating a migrant background) was much stronger, however, with a Dutch applicant who had confessed to having previously committed a sex offence significantly more likely to receive a positive reply than an applicant with a migrant background with a clean rap sheet.

Flood (2005) conducted an ethnographic study in a law firm in Chicago but did not go 'undercover'. He did introduce himself to all staff as a researcher, which takes away any objections regarding informed consent: all firm employees knew who he was, what he was studying and were therefore able to choose – to a certain degree – to what extent they wanted to interact with him. Revealing that you are a researcher and what and for whom you are studying, generally takes away any objections an IRB might have. Obviously, the downside for the Flood study might have been that staff members may have been less eager to talk with him or show him their true feelings or thoughts, let him in on all that was happening at the firm; the research was therefore less *unobtrusive* (a term we will return to in section 4.5), so that validity may have been at stake.

Chapter questions

1. How do the empirical cycles of quantitative and qualitative research differ? (section 2.2)
2. What is the difference between a conceptual and an operational definition? (section 2.4)
3. Look up the definition of legitimacy in political science and the definition in legal scholarship and describe their respective conceptual scopes. What are the implications of any different conceptual definitions for the respective operationalizations? (section 2.4)
4. How are reliability and validity connected? (section 2.6)
5. How is reliability generally assessed? (section 2.6)
6. What types of validity are distinguished? (section 2.6)
7. Give examples of micro-, meso- and macro-data (section 2.9)
8. What is meant by informed consent? (section 2.10)
9. Discuss whether it is unethical when participants in a study have not given full informed consent (section 2.10)
10. Outline the main areas of overlap and difference between the GDPR and the ALLEA Code (section 2.10.1 and section 2.10.2)

Part II

MEASUREMENT

Chapter 3

Measurement units

This chapter deals with important methodological decisions to be taken when conducting a study: the choice of units that will be observed or measured. This chapter is firstly a building block for subsequent chapters that will deal with descriptive and inferential statistics. Descriptive statistics (see chapter 6) are used to describe the general properties of our measurement units, such as their mean, or variability. Inferential statistics (see chapter 8) are used whenever we want to *infer* something from a sample, and declare the findings from that sample applicable to a larger set of research or measurement units, a so-called *population*. This chapter is also a building block for the analysis of data gathered through qualitative methods (discussed in chapter 7).

As in social science research, so also in empirical legal research we very often work with samples, as we generally do not have the time or resources to study an entire population. It is then important to ensure, as far as possible, that a sample resembles the population we are interested in.

In the following, we will first discuss the concepts of sampling and populations. We will discuss what constitutes a useful sample and what constitutes a less useful sample, in terms of representativeness. We list probability and non-probability samples, and discuss their pros and cons. We will also discuss the practical constraints in drawing samples. Next, we detail concepts such as representativeness, bias and noise, sample size and issues of nonresponse.

3.1 Populations and samples

The Netherlands has almost 18 million inhabitants. If I wanted to know how tall Dutch people are, I could set out with a measuring tape to measure all Dutch people, each and every one. This would take a very long time. By the time I am finished, quite a few will have died, new Dutch citizens will have been born, and perhaps I will be ready for my pension by that time too.

The entire population of the Netherlands is what we also call in a statistical sense a *population*: a universe of units that we are interested to know something about. We could also be interested to know the height of all female Dutch citizens, in which case the population would consist of all female Dutch citizens. Or we might want to know the height of all adult Dutch citizens, in which case the population of interest would be the Dutch population aged 18 and over.

In this example, 'population' is taken very literally, in the sense that the statistical population is also literally a population: all inhabitants or citizens within a certain geographically defined unit or with a certain legally defined status. A population could however also be all defendants, or all tort claims in a defined jurisdiction, or all rulings. A population can even be tissue samples, or movies or burglaries or desserts. What matters is that there is a certain total reservoir of units of interest that we want to know something about. The people who together constitute the population, or the females or adults who do, or units, whether they be tort cases or light bulbs or desserts, are the *population members*.

Now in the example that we started with, it is clear that it would be an impossible task to measure all population members. It is clearly undoable. But even if a population were to have 'only' 1,000 members, assessing each and every member of that population would be a hefty task. There is more.

Because what statistics teaches us is that scrutinizing each and every population member is actually not necessary. If we operate wisely and according to certain rules, we can with reasonable precision say something about the entire population even if we investigate only a part of that population, a *sample*. Often, already a small part will do, like a 1% sample, or even less, depending on various issues that we will talk about later. So, basically, what statistical science teaches is that it is not necessary to scrutinize each and every population member to infer something about that population. In fact, within reasonable limits, we can get to know the population reasonably well through the study of only a selection of its members.

Sampling only a part of the population saves a lot of expenses. The other side of the coin is that – obviously – we are not absolutely certain any more of what we say. We have with our savings introduced *uncertainty*.

Statistics is the science that teaches us how to deal with that uncertainty. It gives us the rules and procedures, and in a sense the language in which we communicate how we managed the uncertainty in a sensible way, how uncertain we exactly are – and thereby how confident we are about the conclusions we draw from the sample about the population. Much more about this in chapter 8.

3.2 Representativeness and generalizability

Let us start again with an example. We want to know how Dutch citizens of voting age will vote in the upcoming general election in the Netherlands. In numerous countries, such questions are asked in polls right before elections, when politicians are bashed in TV shows and wise men and women air their views on why such and such party is losing and some other party has gained ground suddenly.

Now if we wanted to conduct such a poll, we could not possibly interview all Dutch citizens of voting age, there simply is no time. We therefore draw a sample. But how do we draw a sample? If I were to do door-to-door interviews in my neighbourhood I would definitely not get a good prediction of the average Dutch person's voting behaviour. My neighbourhood contains quite a few nice houses, no flats: it is a pretty, green, slightly upper-class area, with lots of academicians, some medical specialists and artists. I would predict perhaps, sampling only my fellow neighbourhood inhabitants, that the Dutch liberal party D66 would win, or the Green Party, or the Party for Animals. That would not reflect the voting behaviour of the average Dutch citizen. My sample does not reflect the Dutch population, but a specific segment – and while my conclusions about the types of citizens inhabiting my neighbourhood might be right, I would draw the wrong conclusion about the entire population. Similarly, if I were to interview only inhabitants of the Schilderswijk in The Hague, a neighbourhood where many citizens with a migrant background reside, or of the Bijlmer in Amsterdam, I would probably also not get an accurate picture of Dutch voting behaviour, nor if I were to carry out my investigations in Wassenaar, the Beverly Hills of the Netherlands.

Clearly, what we would want, and what all the options above are lacking, is that my sample would resemble the population, would reflect the population. We would want the sample's properties to be like the properties of the population. In statistics-speak we want a *representative sample.*

So, in this case we want the sample members to exhibit about the same voting behaviour as the population. We cannot check that, as we do not know the population's voting behaviour (that's namely what we're after!). Instead, we could check whether we have sample members with approximately the same age as the population, the same sex ratio, urban/rural composition, the same geographical spread, income, etc. as the Dutch population. See Figure 3.1. The idea behind this is that, if sample members resemble population members in various pertinent characteristics, we expect the sample's voting behaviour to then also resemble the voting behaviour in the larger population.

But how to achieve this? What are the pertinent characteristics for which we must ensure that the sample is similar to the population? How many such characteristics do we need? And how in practice could we achieve that? Luckily, these questions do not need to be answered nor do difficult procedures need to be followed. The best and easiest way namely to ensure that a sample's properties reflect those of the population is to draw that sample by chance, or: *at random.*

Suppose that we want to draw a random sample from the Dutch population. All Dutch inhabitants are registered at their municipality, and all these registrations form a list of the population members. This list is what we call the *sampling frame.* We can imagine random sampling now as follows: we could give every Dutch citizen of voting age a slip of paper with his or her name on it, we'd crumple up all those slips, throw them in a big pan, stir them really well with a very big wooden spoon, and then we'd take out – blindly – as many as we need for our sample. Such a sample is called a *random sample*: it is formed only by chance. Only chance determines whether someone ends up in the sample or not. For a random sample we may always assume that it is representative.

Once a sample is representative, it follows that we can *generalize* the sample properties to the population. So if we find that 36% of our sample members vote Labour, 14% Green, 35% Liberal, we conclude that 36% of Dutch voters would vote Labour, 14% Green and 35% Liberal.

Note that a sample is not just representative for any population, but is representative *for a certain population.* So a random sample of females of voting age is representa-

Figure 3.1: Example of spread of sample members in the Netherlands

tive for female Dutch voters, but not representative for all Dutch voters. And a random sample of all victims of sexual abuse in a compensation scheme is representative for all victims in the compensation scheme, but not representative for all victims of sexual abuse. A random sample of tort cases brought before a judge is not necessarily representative for all tort claims.

Dijksterhuis & Vels (2011) wanted to assess the opinion of Dutch citizens on the methods by which child maintenance is calculated according to Dutch law. They surveyed a random sample of clients of the National Bureau for Maintenance Contributions (LBOI); these are citizens who have to pay child or partner maintenance but who defaulted at some point. Of these the authors only sampled from those who had defaulted on child maintenance obligations. Their response rate was 22%. The authors found that 72% of respondents disagreed with the prevailing methods of calculation of maintenance. The report led to some political commotion and even to an initiative for a bill in which a new method of calculating child maintenance was proposed. However, the sampling frame was not made up of Dutch citizens, nor was it composed of citizens who had to pay some kind of maintenance, nor was it composed of all defaulters. It is therefore unclear how Dutch citizens regard maintenance calculation methods, as well as how the more narrowly chosen but perhaps more immediately relevant group of those who pay (or receive) such maintenance would regard these methods. Given that the sample was composed only of citizens who had defaulted on child maintenance, it is very much doubtful whether the 72% that the study found is generalizable to all citizens who pay or receive maintenance, let alone the entire Dutch population.

Note that if we want to obtain generalizable statements from our research, it follows that the sample is by itself wholly uninteresting. No one is interested in some particular sample. The sample only starts to be of interest once it is representative for a larger entity, once it tells us something about the population we are interested in. If I have interviewed some sample of victims of sexual abuse by the clergy, then the properties of that sample are essentially unnoteworthy. If however that sample was drawn such that it is representative for a larger population, then suddenly my sample findings become relevant. So, if my sample of victims of sexual abuse by the clergy is representative for all victims of such abuse in compensation schemes, then it is interesting to note (and declare applicable to all such victims) that well over one in three had suffered repeated invasive sexual abuse or that only 40% report that the compensation scheme is adequate.

This applies most forcefully in quantitative research. In quantitative research we are interested in making generalizable statements. For that reason, sampling – and ensuring that one has obtained a good sample – is more important in quantitative than in qualitative research. As we said, in section 1.4.1 and later in chapter 2, a qualitative study generally focuses on a particular context, and generalization to other contexts is less aimed for and may in fact be regarded as unattainable given that contexts can be so different and context is inherently so important.

Note, secondly, that within the sample we have no uncertainty. I can with certainty measure (and no one can refute my finding) that the average age of victims of sexual abuse by the clergy whom I was able to interview because they had registered for a compensation scheme, is 53.5. This is a fact. If I attempt to generalize that finding to the population, I would state that the average age of all victims of sexual abuse by the clergy is also 53.5. However, now I am not so dead-sure. I have drawn a sample, so it might be that by chance I have a few too many younger victims because these are more likely to submit claims, or by chance a few too many older victims because these would be more willing to be interviewed. This means that while the sample mean age of 53.5 is a measurement, an irrefutable finding, the population mean of 53.5 is an *estimate*.[1] We will return later to the issue of whether and why the sample mean is a good estimator for the population mean.

3.3 Types of samples

So what kinds of samples are representative for the population, and what kinds of samples are not? In the literature two kinds of samples are distinguished: *probability samples* and *non-probability samples*. Drawing a probability sample, representativeness is

[1] We denote this by writing M_X for the sample mean, and $\hat{\mu}_X$ for the estimate (indicated by the 'hat') of the population mean. By convention we write sample characteristics such as the mean with Latin literals (M, s, r_{XY}); whenever we refer to properties of the population it is the convention to use Greek literals (such as μ for the mean, σ for the standard deviation, ρ for the population correlation coefficient, etc.).

guaranteed; drawing a non-probability sample, representativeness is not ensured. This does not mean that a non-probability sample is always a useless sample, or by definition non-representative. Non-probability samples may very well be representative, but there is no guarantee.

3.3.1 Probability samples

As we argued above, samples are useful only insofar as they tell us something about the population we are interested in. In technical terms: a sample is useful only if it is representative for the population of interest. We already said that random samples may always be considered representative. But how do we assess whether a sample is representative?

The answer to this is fairly straightforward. A sample is representative if every population member had an equal chance of ending up in the sample. This is the litmus test of representativeness.

So, if I draw a sample from the province of Zuid-Holland in the Netherlands to investigate voting behaviour, the sample cannot be taken as representative for the Netherlands – those living outside of Zuid-Holland had a zero chance of ending up in the sample. All law students present at the ELS methods class of Monday morning are not a random sample of all law students at the university: those who have already passed will not sit in, nor will those who on a rainy Monday morning preferred their warm beds over a trip by bike through the rain to the university campus. That the latter is self-chosen and these students could have ended up being sampled does not matter. What matters is that the students who dragged themselves from their warm beds likely differ systematically from those who napped on: the ones in class are probably more motivated, or more in need of the ELS methods class than those who did not show up. The unmotivated or those unfearful of methodology therefore had a smaller chance of ending up in the sample. The sample members in that sense differ in a structural, systematic way from those who did not become sample members.

To know whether each population member really has an equal chance of ending up in the sample sometimes requires a bit of brain cell jogging. As an example, imagine that we carry out a survey in a certain country: we sample household addresses randomly, and at each address we interview that person older than 15 years of age who is the first to celebrate his or her birthday. Is this a random sample of all inhabitants? Obviously not, as those under 15 years of age cannot participate. Is it then a random sample of all inhabitants over 15 years of age? One might be tempted to say yes, as households have been sampled randomly, and as within each household again in a sense randomly a household member is chosen. The sample is not random however, as members of larger households have a smaller chance of ending up in the sample: someone living in a 6-person family has an a priori chance of $\frac{1}{6}$ to be selected, whereas someone in a 2-person household has a chance of $\frac{1}{2}$ to end up in the sample. By constructing the sample this way, we will end up with too many singles, and too few people from large families: persons living in large families are *underrepresented* in the sample, and persons living in smaller families are *overrepresented*.

Four kinds of probability samples are distinguished, and four kinds of non-probability samples. We briefly discuss them, starting with probabilistic samples and ending with the non-probabilistic ones. It should be said ahead that in many studies, mixtures of probability samples are employed.

(1) *Random sample*

The first kind of probability sample is the random sample, also known as the *simple random sample*. A random sample is a sample where sample members are drawn as if we had a huge cooking pot, into which we toss a lot for each population member, stir very well, and draw lots blindly, irrespective of any properties of the sample member. Such a sample one also encounters as a 'simple random sample', as an 'a-select sample' or as a 'flat' random sample.

The simple random sample is not used very often though. The reason for this is firstly that drawing such samples requires quite a bit of administrative infrastructure: if there is no such thing as a pre-existing sampling frame, it is an immense task to draw up a list of population members and then select a few of them randomly. Secondly, if we draw a random sample, we are left in fate's hands as regards the representation of certain segments of the population.

We will clarify this with two examples. Suppose that I draw a sample of 100 registered cases from the police databases; police databases in most European countries contain thousands of cases so it would be logical to draw a sample. I would expect to end up in my sample with 85 male suspects and 15 female suspects as that is the distribution of male and female offenders in the population of suspects. However, it might very well be (as chance decides who ends up in the sample) that I end up with 25 females and 75 males. This is what we call *sampling error*. And even though these sampling errors are due to chance, these deviations can be problematic: suppose for instance that I end up in the above example with 5 females and 95 males. In that case, I have really too little to go on if I wanted to say something about female offenders – 5 is a very small number to draw any conclusions from. So, in this case it might be wise not to let chance have its way entirely: it might be better to try to exert some control over the representation of the group of female offenders in the sample.

Similarly, suppose that I want to assess fear of burglary in a neighbourhood. If I were by chance to select 25 houses in that neighbourhood, I could end up with all houses close to the shopping centre, or relatively many on the edge of the neighbourhood (areas with typically a relatively high risk of burglaries and therefore also a higher fear of being burglarized). Or I might end up with disproportionately many apartments. Also here, it might be desirable to enforce a certain spread over the various areas and types of houses in the neighbourhood.

Lastly, and most importantly, strictly random samples may be expensive. If I were to draw a simple random sample to interview 170 Dutch citizens out of all 17 million inhabitants, it would probably mean that I'd do seven interviews in Rotterdam, ten in Amsterdam, four in Utrecht or The Hague, and that I'd need to travel to another 100 or so municipalities to interview the remaining approximately 135 respondents. That is very time-consuming and costly. It is also unnecessary, as we will see below. For all these reasons, researchers often choose to use more efficient random samples than the simple random sample.

(2) *Systematic sample*

The first alternative to the simple random sample is the systematic sample. Suppose that we are interested in fear of being burglarized and we are investigating a newish neighbourhood in a big city. The neighbourhood has 250 standard family houses (in which we assume that each time 2 adults live). If we want to draw a 10% random sample of these adults, this means that we could visit 50 houses and in each house interview one adult. This would give us a sample of 50, which is 10% of all 500 adults living in this neighbourhood.

The systematic sample gives an efficient framework for achieving this, and it works as follows. All houses are first numbered, from 1 to 250. We next draw at random a starting number, say 137, meaning we start from house 137 on our map. Starting from house 137, we draw a track through the neighbourhood, following the layout of houses, and we take every 5th house (as we want to survey 50 out of 250 houses), ring the doorbell and ask to interview someone, for instance the first adult to celebrate his or her birthday. We move up, stepwise at regular intervals, to house 250 and next finish sampling from house 1 up to house 137. As the first number has been drawn at random, and as after this number all other selected houses depend on this starting number, each house has the same chance of ending up in the sample and so does (given that we assume two adults live in each house) every adult. This is a systematic sample, and it is a random – as well as an efficient – sample.

Two conditions must be met for a systematic sample to be random and representative. First, the starting number must be chosen randomly. Second, the physical layout of the neighbourhood, or in more general terms, the ordering of sampling units on the list, must not have the same *periodicity* as the sampling interval. To understand this, inspect Figure 3.2, which gives a hypothetical example of a neighbourhood plan. In this neighbourhood, houses have been built in blocks of 5. Suppose that our random starting number is 15. There are 30 houses in this example, and suppose we want a sample of 6 houses, this means that we would have to sample each 5th house. However, if we start at number 15, and if we interview someone in every 5th house, this would mean that in our sample we would end up with houses at the corner end of a block only. And, obviously, the risk of a burglary is larger in a corner house than in a house in the middle of a block. This means that we end up with a sample in which people who live in corner houses (which may be assumed to be special) are overrepresented and people who live in ordinary in-between houses are underrepresented. Thus, the sample is not representative for the neighbourhood.

So, in this case it might be better to change the periodicity of the sample and for instance sample every 4th house (in which case you end up with a larger sample), or every 6th house (in which case you end up with a smaller sample), or three times sample every 4th house and the next three times sample every 6th house (in which case you end up with a sample of 6 as planned). See Figure 3.3 which gives the last solution.

Figure 3.2: Example neighbourhood layout for systematic sample with inadequate periodicity

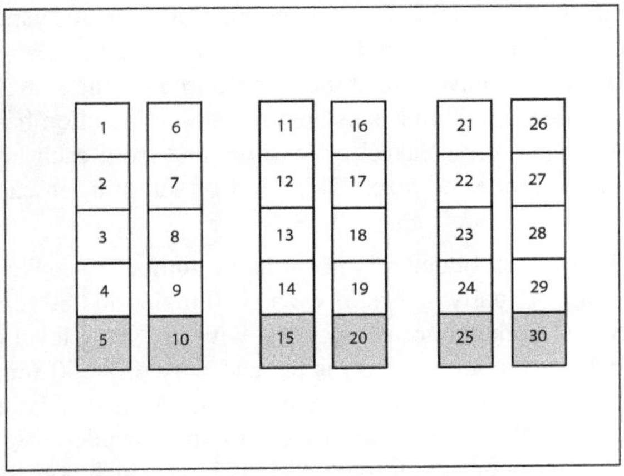

Figure 3.3: Example neighbourhood layout for systematic sample

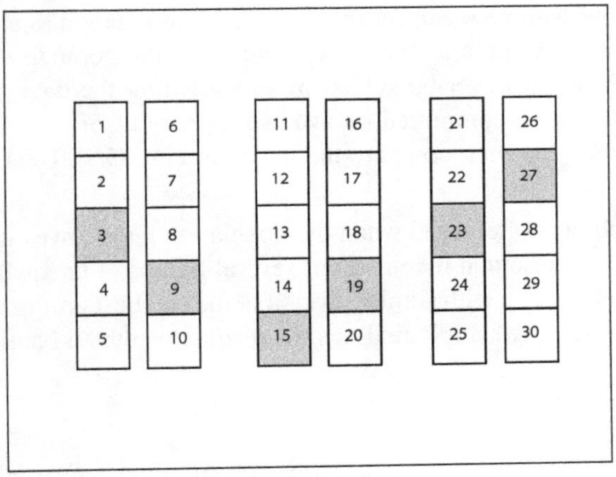

(3) *Stratified sample*

Let us return to the example that we gave above, of male and female police suspects. We said that if we drew a flat random sample of 100 respondents it might occur by chance that we ended up with only 5 female suspects. Five respondents is too small a number to draw meaningful inferences from: statements such as 40% of female suspects had committed a violent offence are based on just two respondents – had it been not 2 but 3 females who had committed a violent offence the percentage would have been 60%! So, if we want to make meaningful inferences about this smaller segment in the population, we have to ensure that we have a sufficient number of females.

There are two ways to go about this. Sticking with the example, we could randomly draw 85 male respondents from the population of male suspects and similarly draw – at random – 15 female suspects from the population of female suspects. In this way, we have forced the sample to have the same proportional representation of males and females as we know the population has. The males and females are considered a 'layer' or *stratum*, and from each layer a sample is then drawn of the requested size. This kind of sampling is called stratified sampling.

Obviously, 15 female respondents is not a large number to make stable inferences about. It might actually be best if we had 50 males and 50 females, so that we could investigate both groups of suspects with the same level of detail and precision. So, what we could also do is to randomly draw 50 female suspects from the population of female suspects, and another 50 males from the population of male suspects. This kind of stratified sampling is called *disproportionate stratified sampling* – as opposed to the previous kind which constituted proportionate stratified sampling. Obviously, now the ratio of males to females has been changed, which means that – while we can carry out computations within each layer – we cannot compute averages over the strata just like that. If we wanted for instance to know how many offences suspects have committed on average, we cannot use the sample mean for that. There are too many female suspects in the sample, and the sample is not representative for the population of suspects anymore. This can however be solved by *re-weighting* the data. Suppose for instance that men have committed on average 2 previous offences, and women on average 1. We can then compute the mean as $2 \times 85/100 + 1 \times 15/100 = 1.85$.

Stratified sampling is often used when the population under investigation is heterogeneous in the sense that it consists of several groups of unequal sizes. If we want to study each group with similar precision, the smallest groups are oversampled, and for presenting sample findings the results 'weighted back' afterwards.

(4) *Cluster sample*

Cluster samples (also referred to as two-stage sampling) are used very often. The reason for that is that they save a lot in terms of time and money, and they can also be carried out very well when precise information about the population distribution is lacking, when we have no sampling frame.

To illustrate how a cluster sample works, suppose that we want to interview prisoners – we are for instance interested to know how they judge the prison climate. In the Netherlands, on any given day, about 10,000 persons are detained. There are 24 penitentiary institutions. Some are larger, some are smaller. There is a centralized database of detainees that keeps track of admissions, transferrals to other institutions, and discharge, so there is a sampling frame. This means that in principle it would be very easy to draw a simple random sample. If we wanted a sample of 200 detainees, we could simply number the detainees in the database and draw them using random numbers. However, if we were to do that, it would mean that we probably would have to visit almost each and every penitentiary institution in the Netherlands.

A much more efficient way is to first randomly sample penitentiary institutions, and next draw random samples of detainees from those selected institutions. Supposing that each institution is of about equal size, this procedure would result in a random sample: each institution has an equal chance of being selected for the sample, and within each institution again each detainee has an equal chance. Obviously, this is very efficient: if we want to interview 200 detainees, we could simply randomly select 5 detention facilities, and from each interview 40 detainees. That would save a lot in travelling cost and time. One could of course argue that in reality detention facilities are not likely to be of exactly equal size (so that detainees in smaller facilities would have a bigger chance to end up in the sample), but even that can be accommodated: we can simply give each detention facility a sampling chance proportional to its size.

Cluster samples have huge advantages, in terms of feasibility and cost. But they come at a price too: in research methodology – as in many areas of life – for every gain usually a price is paid. This has to do with the fact that every time we sample, we introduce sampling error: we might in a flat random sample – by chance – find relatively tall Dutch people, or tort cases with relatively high claim amounts. Such sampling error is all in the game: we know that the price we pay for not investigating each and every population member is uncertainty. We know that when we generalize the findings in the sample to the population, there is always a margin of uncertainty: sampling error.

However, if we now sample twice (as we do in our example cluster sample: once over penitentiary institutions and again over detainees within those centres), we essentially accumulate sampling error. It might for instance be that by chance we have selected those institutions in which detainees have very few distractions and there is a relatively harsh climate, and in second instance that we have selected – by chance again – within those institutions those individuals who have a bleak outlook on life by nature. The fact that we sample in two steps exposes us twice to sampling error. And sampling error in the first instance is in a sense 'multiplied' by sampling error in the second instance. For that reason, results from cluster samples are more susceptible to sampling error, and one could say more 'volatile'.

Such added volatility, or as it is called *noise*, is especially likely to occur if members of clusters resemble each other. To understand what happens, imagine that we have a cluster sample of m clusters, with b respondents per cluster (so that we have b × m sample members, generally written as N). Now, if we add one extra sample member, from one of our clusters, this gives us in principle more information on the population (we now observe more population members). However, suppose now that cluster members are very much alike. Then, adding a sample member from a cluster that is already present in the sample doesn't give that much extra information. Loosely speaking, adding one extra person from the same cluster gives us a bit more of what we already knew.

Practice has revealed that cluster members indeed often share characteristics. Population members from the same cluster are more alike than population members from different clusters. This implies that if we draw a cluster sample of, say, 100 respondents from 5 clusters (so 20 from each), we will have less information about the population than if we had drawn 100 respondents in a flat random sample from the population.

This unfortunate consequence of cluster sampling is referred to as the *design effect*. This design effect, usually abbreviated as DEFF, is expressed in a number that gives the increase in variability of our estimates (and therefore our imprecision) due to the fact that a cluster sample has been chosen – relative to the variability that we would have had, had we chosen a simple random sample. So, if DEFF equals 3, this means that the variability is thrice that of a simple random sample of the same size. If DEFF is 1.40, this means that the variance is increased by 40% – as DEFF is a ratio, a DEFF of 1 would indicate no difference.[2] As a rule of thumb, we find DEFF values higher than 3 problematic.

Now why exactly does this design effect lead to imprecision of our estimates as we said, or differently said, to variability of our estimates? Let us assume that we are interested to measure prisoners' moods. We want to know whether they are depressed or not. If we were to draw a simple random sample of, say, 200 prisoners, we might find that their average depression score is 5. If we were to draw a new random sample of 200 prisoners, that outcome might differ a bit: it might be 4.9, or 5.1, or even 5.3 or 4.7. Chance will give us a different sample each time, with slightly different results. That is the uncertainty we have to accept.

We now draw instead of a flat random sample (where we would need to travel to many different penitentiary institutions, all over the country), a cluster sample. We draw by chance (proportional to their size) two penitentiary institutions, and we interview prisoners from those two institutions. It might be (chance is at work) that we drew two institutions with harsh regimes, bad food, located far away from public transport. This affects prisoners' moods. So we find a mean of 8.3: the prisoners are on average quite depressed. If we were to re-do the cluster sampling, and we again selected just two institutions from which we then interview prisoners, we might, however, by chance end up with two glitzy new facilities: good food, closer to a metro station (so more family visits), open regimes. Prisoners feel much better now, and we end up with a sample mean of 2.2. Depending on what clusters we accidentally sample, we may get widely different sample averages.

---

[2] DEFF is computed as DEFF $=1 + \rho \times$ (b-1) with ρ the so-called intra-class correlation, a measure that reflects the extent to which members from the same cluster resemble each other, and b the cluster size. Note that if ρ is 0, in which case cluster membership does not mean sample members have similar scores, then – as it should – DEFF becomes 1, i.e. there is no difference in variability between the cluster sample and an ordinary random sample. Note also that if b = 1, in which case the clusters have size 1 so that effectively we have a random sample, DEFF also – as should be the case – becomes 1.

What these examples show is that in a cluster sample, the selection of just a few clusters is in fact a tricky business: we are much more vulnerable to ending up with one or two particularly nice or particularly nasty facilities. As a flat random sample generally makes us travel to many facilities, that risk is very much mitigated then.

Hypothetically, if we were to re-do our study 100 times, and draw a flat random sample of prisoners 100 times, the mean depression scores from those samples would not vary much. If however, we were to re-do our study 100 times with cluster sampling, the means of these 100 samples would likely vary – considerably – more. This is expressed by saying that cluster sampling gives more 'noisy' results. This noisiness of cluster samples relative to regular simple random samples is expressed using DEFF.[3]

Many surveys use cluster samples. This is mainly for pragmatic reasons. Unfortunately, key variables of interest are often clustered. Prisons differ in their regime, law firms differ in corporate culture, courts differ in the likelihood to award damages, municipalities differ in the strictness with which they check on recipients of benefits.

DEFF measures are computed *per variable*. So, separate DEFFs can be computed for claims, for sentence length, for socio-economic status. This implies that the DEFF may be high for one variable but need not be so for another.

It is generally advised to aim to employ at least 30 clusters, to keep the design effect within acceptable limits. If then 7 units per cluster are assessed, this results in a sample size of a little over 200. In empirical legal studies this is often not possible: we may for instance have only 20 prisons or only 17 courts from which to sample. Researchers then often impose some kind of stratification over the clusters to ensure spread over pertinent properties, such as by choosing courts from rural as well as urban areas, from the north and south of the county, etc.

The figures below illustrate simple random sampling, systematic sampling and cluster sampling for a hypothetical study into trust in the judiciary, within a village. As can be seen, both the random sample (Figure 3.4) and the systematic sample (Figure 3.5) have an N of 19; the cluster sample (Figure 3.6) in this example simply selects two clusters and thus leads in this example to a much larger sample size (obviously we could have chosen to select 10 sample members from each). Note that for both the simple and the systematic sample the spread over the village is pretty nice: for the systematic sample the area in the bottom left is less well represented but such things are bound to happen by chance. The cluster sample has a nice geographical spread as well. Of course what could easily have happened is that we could have ended up with two adjacent clusters, which may be less desirable as they may be alike in terms

[3]Some researchers use instead of DEFF a measure called DEFT, which is nothing other than the square root of DEFF: DEFT $= \sqrt{\text{DEFF}}$. Given that DEFF relates to the variance in the sample, DEFT relates to the standard deviation (viz. section 6.3.2). DEFT can be interpreted as the increase in the standard deviation relative to the standard deviation had a simple random sample been drawn. All in all, whether DEFF or DEFT is used, both are indicative of the precision-price you pay for the money you save in drawing a cluster sample.

Figure 3.4: Fictional example of a random sample in a village

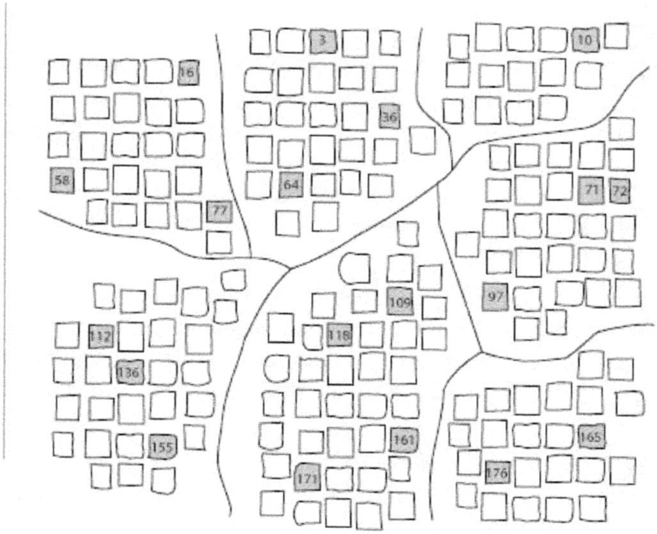

of being less or more affluent neighbourhoods (a property associated with trust in the judiciary). However, as we need to sample randomly to ensure that our sample passes the litmus test, we cannot force this to be so.

3.3.2 Non-probability samples

If we cannot draw a representative sample, we can always draw a non-representative one. Reasons to draw a non-representative sample may be that there is no sampling frame. For instance, we may want to interview illegal residents, a category of persons that typically is not registered. A second reason is that we are not interested in generalization per se: we may be aiming to understand the rationales that judges employ when they have to take decisions in divorce procedures where one parent has accused the other parent of sexual abuse of a child. If we aim to answer such a research question, generalization is a less prominent goal: rather, we would want to have in-depth discussions with judges and lawyers, possibly witness a number of court hearings, interview psychologists and child protection services staff. Our aim is rather to find a reasonable representation of types of cases and be able to find sufficient well-informed actors in these cases so that we can uncover the manner in which judges process information, reason and subsequently take decisions. Other reasons for not drawing a representative sample may be that we do not have the time or resources to do so. Or the study may be just a first pilot study, or researchers may simply be lazy, sometimes combined with there being no need to generalize to a population: we may for instance be studying phenomena deemed universal in people, such as physiological reactions.

Figure 3.5: Fictional example of a systematic sample in a village

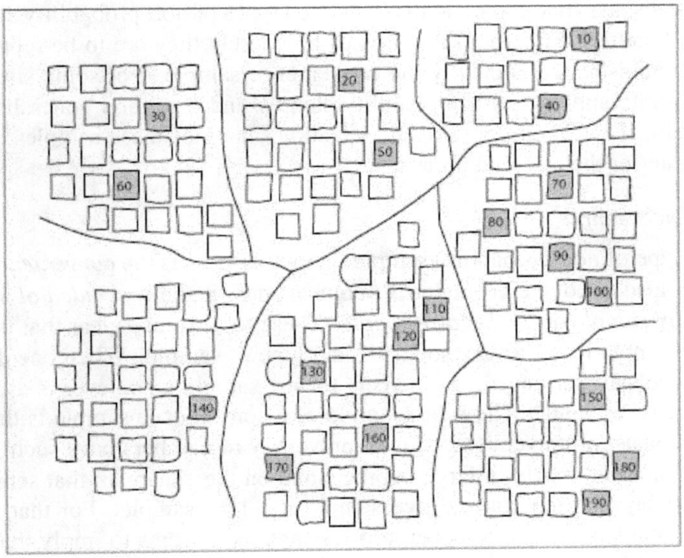

Figure 3.6: Fictional example of a cluster sample in a village

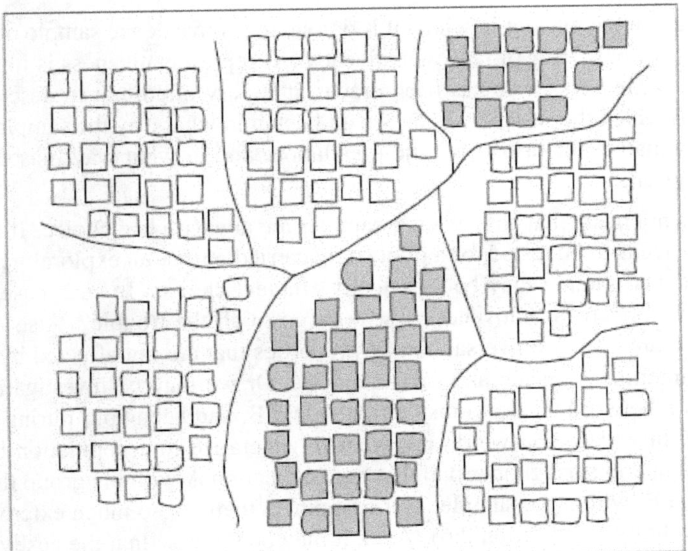

It is not the case that non-probability samples are never representative. Some non-probability samples may in fact very well be adequate or even representative. We however do not have the *guarantee* of representativeness that we have when we draw a probability sample, so we cannot rely on statistical sampling theory (see chapter 8).

We will now discuss four generally distinguished types of non-probability samples. There are clear 'quality' differences in terms of how likely they are to be representative. The least sophisticated is clearly the convenience sample. For some situations, the snowball sample approaches a probability sample and has good generalizability properties. Again, if one's aim is not generalization, many of these samples may be perfectly adequate for the research purposes.

(5) *Convenience sample*

The first type of non-probability sample that we discuss is the *convenience sample*. It is also encountered under different names, namely *accidental sample*, *availability sample* or *haphazard sample*. These terms make clear that the convenience sample is not a very sophisticated type of sample. When one draws a convenience sample, one simply selects for the sample whomever is available, whomever is 'at hand'. The best example of a convenience sample is the samples that consist of university students: university researchers have such sample members in arms' reach, in large numbers and on the cheap. In that sense, one could also say that the convenience sample is a lazy sample. For that matter, the term 'accidental sample' is perhaps less apt, as it seems to imply that some chance or random phenomenon is in operation to form the sample.

Convenience samples can be drawn in many contexts. We already mentioned students, who are very often used in smaller-scale experiments. Other examples are interviews with visitors to a shopping mall, or sending questionnaires to the readership of a journal.

Clearly, given the manner in which it is drawn, the convenience sample offers no perspective whatsoever of representativeness. If representativeness is important and a convenience sample has been drawn, it is very important to describe the manner in which the sample was drawn and detail in what way the sample might be representative for (a part of) the population, and in what way biases might have occurred.

This does not mean that convenience samples are always a bad choice. If a questionnaire needs to be tested, or a pilot study carried out, or an exploratory study, a convenience sample may be a perfectly efficient choice. In such cases there is no need for representativeness – so why go to all the trouble? Also, it may be that we are testing universal human properties that are not affected by social class or intelligence, such as visual memory. Or we may be investigating the association between a certain instruction A and B, and behaviour during an experiment, in which case we do not want to generalize to a population but are interested in comparing the group that had instruction A with the group that had instruction B, within the sample. Our first aim is then not so much external, but internal validity (see section 2.6). Also, it may be the case that the easily available respondents, such as students or shoppers at a supermarket, are precisely the ones a researcher in interested in, for instance for studying student jobs or sexual harassment in fraternities and sororities, or for studying shoppers' awareness of consumer information on products.

(6) *Quota sample*

The second type of non-probability sample we discuss is the quota sample. A quota sample is a non-probability sample that attempts to mitigate some of the drawbacks of the convenience sample by assuring that the distribution of relevant properties in the sample is similar to their distribution in the population. So, as an example, assume again that we want to study 100 police suspects. We do not have a lot of time and/or money so we interview all suspects who have been held by the police and then released: when they leave the police station we ask them whether we may interview them. Obviously, this is not a representative sample: some suspects are transferred to jail after arrest, or to psychiatric wards and we miss out on those. However, given that we know that 15% of police suspects are female and 85% male, we can ensure that our 100 interviewed suspects have the same gender distribution, by interviewing 15 females and 85 males. Once we have interviewed 85 males, we then interview only females to arrive at a quota sample that has the same gender distribution as the population.

The quota sample is like a stratified sample in the sense that per stratum a desired number of sample members is drawn: the researcher attempts to guarantee that the relative representation of certain properties of sample members is as in the population. The manner in which that is achieved is however much less rigorous than in a regular probabilistic sampling procedure: there is no random sampling within strata. For that matter, the quota sample is also often referred to as the non-probabilistic penchant of the stratified sample.

(7) *Purposive sample*

In a purposive sample, sample members are selected because they have certain desirable properties. For instance, they may be mediators employing a specific negotiating strategy in divorce conflicts, or members of a particular international corporate law firm. These categories of people have especially relevant, valid, in-depth, unique information that is of use to the researcher interested in the novel strategies employed by these mediators or in corporate culture in big international business law practices. In a sense, they are selected as 'unrandomly' as possible – they are targeted to provide certain information. Such respondents are also sometimes referred to as *key informants*, as they literally hold the key to the inaccessible topic or sphere. In that sense, this sample is also sometimes referred to as a *targeted* sample.

Purposive samples are used very often in qualitative research. Flood used ethnographic methods to study the workings at a large Chicago law firm. In order to overcome issues with client–attorney privileges, the firm hired him on a temporary basis. Flood thus sat in on meetings, had access to files. Earlier, he had similarly done ethnographic fieldwork with clerks, working with them and participating, and observing their work. Unaccustomed to heavy drinking, he also felt he had to join in as the clerks went to drink (heavily) in pubs, as he felt he had to participate in order to be one of the bunch, to hear gossip and stories "despite the consequences of my own physical collapse. (...) I had to learn to drink and behave in ways that were unfamiliar to me" (2005, p. 44).

At times, the purposive sample is one (N = 1), such as one trade union, or one law firm. In other instances, qualitative researchers speak repeatedly with several persons. Who should be selected for inclusion in the purposive sample then, and when is a purposive sample 'sufficient' or of sufficient size? In general one seeks for a purposive sample persons who are willing to talk, accessible, who have a good overview of what one wants to study either themselves or who give that overview in complementarity with the other sample members. That raises the issue of how one can be sure that the persons interviewed provide that overview. To decide on that, only qualitative criteria are available.

Rubin and Rubin (1995) state that generally in qualitative research two criteria should be used. The first criterion is whether the set of interviews or observations give a complete overview of the phenomenon under study. As a researcher, obviously one cannot be sure about that, so one has to use common sense, reasoning, and the face validity of the data to decide on this. The second criterion is 'saturation', or 'theoretical saturation'. What is meant by that is probably best illustrated with the following. When conducting qualitative research using a purposive (or any) sample, there will usually come a point where new respondents do not add new information. Each new informant tells you as researcher things you already learned from others, reiterates what earlier interviewees said, and as such at most confirms what you already knew. This is what is meant by saturation: the picture becomes clear at a certain point, and adding new respondents does not add to your knowledge. This is also sometimes referred to as *theoretical validity*. This type of sampling up to saturation is also referred to as *theoretical sampling*.

To enhance the significance of the findings, and to prevent 'cherry-picking', some researchers advise even purposely selecting cases that may deviate from the preliminary conclusions of the research, a practice that is called 'negative case analysis' or 'deviant case analysis'. This shows that sampling in qualitative designs is of a different nature than in quantitative designs: adding such a 'cherry-picked' negative case to the sample might even be considered as violating all rules of randomness! We return to this topic in chapter 7.

This shows that while in probabilistic samples a researcher can from the outset in a sense 'compute' the required sample size (for instance 30 clusters × 7 respondents, totalling 210 respondents), such advance planning is less feasible or perhaps even simply impossible when carrying out qualitative research with a purposive sample. It is harder to assess ahead of time how many interviews one needs: one simply does not know beforehand at what point respondents will not give new information. As such, planning is also harder in qualitative research. This shows also how qualitative research is steered by the empirical reality one encounters: it may be that the picture is clear after 20 interviews, but it may equally take 30 or 40 interviews. It should be noted that sampling in qualitative studies is often constrained by practical matters, such as the amount of time that is available for the study or the amount of money. Given that qualitative data are generally quite an investment in terms of ordering the data for analysis, large samples may also become too big for a researcher to have oversight.

A purposive sample is in some cases the only solution for some types of research questions. If respondents are suspicious or anxious, or difficult to access, a solution may be to interview knowledgeable informants: *key-informant sampling*. Key informant sampling can be very efficient: interviewing just a few gives an overview over many. However, the view of these few key informants may be biased, and second, one cannot be sure that the key informants actually do know a lot about the phenomenon or about the inaccessible others – the researcher can never check anyway...

Augusteijn, Bijleveld, & Pemberton (2022) interviewed professionals to investigate whether and if so in what situations compliance with victims' rights is lacking in Dutch criminal proceedings. The authors analysed interviews conducted with a total of 26 professionals. All were either employed in the criminal justice chain, with the police, the prosecution office, at the courts, with Victim Support Netherlands, the Violent Offences Compensation Fund, or Restorative Justice Netherlands, or outside of the criminal justice chain working for either the Victim Support Fund, as a victim support lawyer or personal injury lawyer, or as a scientific researcher. The interviewed professionals were selected in a stratified manner, so that for each relevant part of the justice chain, one or more professionals could be consulted, as well as for each relevant and knowledgeable party outside of that chain. The interviewed professionals were also sampled through 'snowballing' (see next section), that is, through referral by earlier interviewees.

The authors state that their findings – even though they attempted to arrive at a representative sample – should be interpreted with caution. Although they tried to paint as balanced a picture as possible through stratified sampling, it cannot be ruled out that some selectivity occurred in the selection of respondents, and that, for example, more 'critical' persons responded to their request for an interview, or especially more critical persons were referred to them. As a result, it may be that their results are biased towards revealing situations where compliance is lacking.

Findings from a purposive sample are – by definition – not generalizable. In many cases of qualitative research, that does not constitute a limitation. Firstly, one may be interested in one particular group of persons. Another way of formulating this is by saying that if one uses a purposive sample, one has actually studied the entire population of interest, i.e. the one particular youth group, the one particular set of professionals. Secondly, in qualitative research the aim is mostly not to generalize simple facts, such as prevalences or correlations, to additional population members, but to interpret the phenomena that have been studied. That interpretation gives the framework to understand the world around us.

(8) *Snowball sample*

The snowball sample is an important type of non-probabilistic sample. It is often used for investigating inaccessible populations, or groups who are extremely shy or mistrusting. Examples are drug addicts, people who work in the illegal labour market, prostitutes or – indeed – criminals. It is also sometimes referred to as *respondent-driven sampling* (RDS), although respondent-driven sampling is actually a special kind of snowball sampling.

When drawing a snowball sample, one starts with a certain number of accessible respondents (also sometimes called 'starting-respondents' or 'zero-stage respondents'). After interviewing each respondent, one asks the respondent whether s/he knows one or more other respondents who meet eligibility criteria and who might also be interested in being interviewed. The starting respondents are then asked to encourage these respondents to get into contact with the interviewer; sometimes a small fee is offered. When these 'stage-two' respondents have been interviewed the same procedure is repeated, and so forth. When the respondents are extremely shy, the zero-stage respondents themselves may also be asked to conduct the interviews with the stage-two respondents. The snowball sample indeed functions as a snowball, onto which more and more clings with each turn.

Snowball sampling is a workable and relatively cheap way to study groups of persons who would be unsurveyable otherwise, that is, members of a so-called *hidden population*. It is a powerful method in the sense that with a small number of steps – in general – good coverage over the entire population is reached. Heckatorn (1997) has shown that in the USA – under certain conditions – six steps or waves are sufficient.

A disadvantage of snowball sampling is that it may be lengthy: it usually takes a while before respondents have traced new respondents, after which it takes a while before these contact the researcher, etc. In addition, members of hidden populations may not lead the most mundane organized lives and for that reason not be the most punctual.

A second disadvantage of snowball sampling is that its success is dependent on the choice of 'zero-stage respondent'. If this person has only a small circle of acquaintances, or does not instil a lot of trust, the trail will quickly run cold. For that reason Wright et al. (2001) chose for their study of burglars as a zero-stage respondent someone who was a burglar himself, that is, someone absolutely unassociated with the criminal justice system and who was most likely to generate trust in the next wave of respondents.

In snowball sampling it is assumed that all members of the population are sufficiently connected to be able to reach each population member eventually. If that is not case, for instance if there are isolated subgroups (in a sense on social 'islands'), then those on other 'islands' will not be reached by snowball sampling. The method does not succeed in getting the zero- and subsequent stage respondents to leave their islands. To minimize that risk, it is generally advised to use various zero-stage respondents, preferably from different segments of the population. As said, a precondition for any kind of snowball sampling is that respondents know each other. For that matter, drug addicts are a good candidate for snowball sampling as they are likely to know each other from drug dealers, methadone buses, etc. Persons committing social security fraud on the other hand are less or not likely to know each other.

A variation of snowball sampling is so-called *respondent-driven sampling*, in which a respondent receives coupons that s/he can distribute among prospective new respondents. As soon as a successful interview with a new respondent has been completed, both the old and the new respondent receive some kind of bonus. The advantage is that both the old and the new respondent have an incentive for interviews actually to be completed: only then is the remuneration awarded. The second advantage is that the identity of the new respondent remains hidden until the moment the actual interviewing takes place.

Snowball sampling is an accepted method of sampling. It produces – with sufficient numbers of waves – good coverage of the population. However, persons with a large social network have a larger chance of ending up in the sample, and lonely or isolated persons a smaller chance. This means that snowball samples have a certain bias towards 'more sociable' respondents. Secondly, respondents after the zero-stage are likely to resemble those who entered them into the sample, as friends and acquaintances tend to be like each other too. This means that we will also have cluster effects in a snowball sample. In a statistical sense this implies that the estimates of the pertinent properties we are interested in will also be in a sense noisy.

3.4 Bias and noise

In the previous paragraphs we have at several places encountered the terms 'bias' and 'noise'. What is meant by these terms?

Roughly speaking, noise reflects variability. If we are trying to assess citizens' trust in the judiciary, and if there is a lot of variation around the population mean in the samples that we can draw (for instance because we worked with cluster samples), then we have a *noisy* sample. The sample members' averages vary a lot around the true population score that we are interested in. On average, though, they may provide a good estimate of the population mean.

Suppose however that sample means do not reflect the population mean: sample means are consistently lower than the population means, or consistently higher. Then our sample means are *biased*. The sample averages then differ systematically from the population mean: they are most of the time lower, or most of the time higher. Even if we are not bothered by noise, the sample mean is not very useful: it does not give us a valid estimate of the population mean. This means that a biased sample is not a representative sample: it does not reflect the properties of the population.

Does that mean that a noisy sample is therefore always better than a biased sample? Yes and no. A biased sample is not very useful as it does not tell us the properties of the population. A sample that is only noisy gives at least (if we were to draw a large number of samples) on average an unbiased estimate of the population mean. A noisy

Figure 3.7: Visual representations of bias and noise

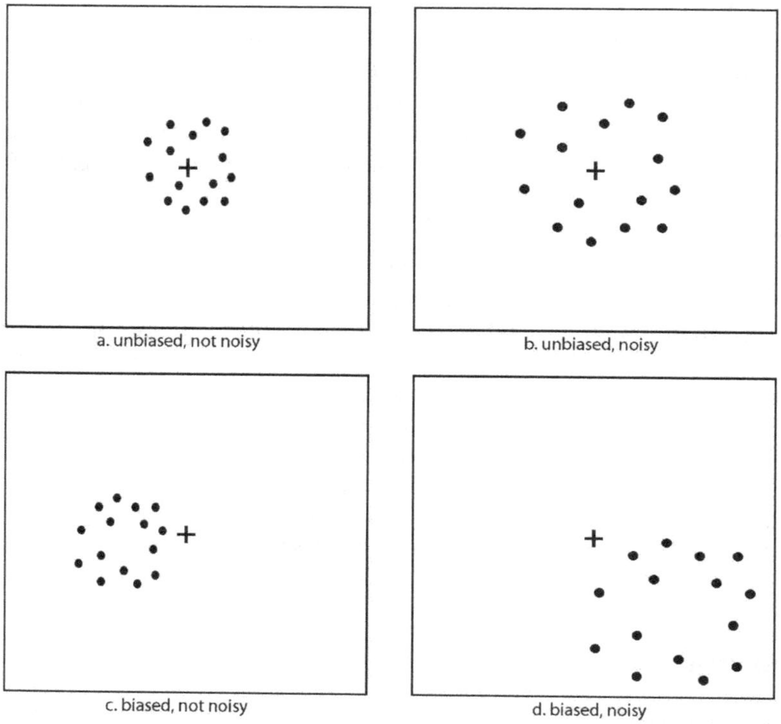

sample however generates problems of its own: in practice we do not draw a large number of samples and repeat our analysis many times. We draw one sample and report our findings. So if we have a noisy sample, our estimate may still be very far 'off'. We will discuss these and related issues much more formally in chapter 8 below.

For now, it is important to remember that both noise and bias are a nuisance. Samples can be noisy, samples can be biased and obviously samples can be noisy as well as biased. Ideally we would want samples to be both unbiased and not noisy. See Figure 3.7.

Figure 3.7 is a visual aid to understand the concepts of bias and noise; each picture should be viewed as a bull's eye that we try to hit with a pistol or with darts. The bull's eye represents the true population mean that we want to estimate, and the holes made by the bullets or darts represent the sample measurements that should aid in arriving at an estimate of that population mean. In this figure, the upper left situation (a) is one where there is little bias and little noise: the cross '+' indicates where the bull's eye/population mean is, and we can see that the hits/sample measurements, indicated as dots, cluster closely around the population mean and would on average equal the population mean. In the upper right situation (b) there is more noise: the measurements spread much more around the population mean but, on average, the measurements tell us what the population mean is. In the lower left situation (c), there is bias: the average of the sample measurements is clearly 'off'. The measurements deviate systematically from the population value. In the lower right situation (d), finally, there is bias as well as noise: the measurements are systematically to the right of where they should be, and they also vary a lot.

3.5 Sample size

So far, we have talked of samples and populations. As we said, in many cases the population is simply too large to investigate member by member, and we therefore have to make do with samples. We therefore 'draw' a sample, a group of members of the population, ideally at random, and what we find in the sample we declare to be generalizable to the population. Obviously, samples are smaller than the population. But how small may a sample be, or how large exactly should a sample be?

Having said that, it is not the case that sample size is always determined by strict iron-fist rules. In practice, a lot also depends on the amount of money and time available, and on the type of question asked. If we conduct qualitative research (see chapter 2, earlier in this chapter and chapter 7), sample sizes depend more on 'saturation' and 'coverage'. Qualitative researchers can decide while their research is ongoing whether they do or do not need additional sample members to study. Qualitative samples vary in size between 1 and a few hundred (and seldom more). Also because qualitative research is generally much more time-intensive, large sample sizes are extremely rare. Sample sizes of 20 to 30 are quite common. Quantitative researchers often work with samples of between 100 to 300, to in some cases 500, or even more respondents. There are various statistical issues that may aid in determining the desired sample size for investigating a certain research question with a certain precision (we will return to such issues in chapter 8). A few basic guidelines may help in understanding issues of sample size.

Firstly, very generally speaking, the larger the sample – assuming it was drawn randomly – the more the sample can tell us about the population. This is logical. Suppose that a sample constitutes about 1% of the population. Anything we measure about that sample, say its mean, may fluctuate quite a bit depending on the sample we accidentally happen to draw, and – although this is not very likely – any statistic, such as the mean, can theoretically even be quite far off the mark. Suppose now however that the sample size increases, to for instance 10% of the population. Again, theoretically speaking, it is still possible that the mean we find for the sample is quite different from the mean in the population, but as we are measuring so many more people, it can only be closer to the population mean. Next, suppose that our sample contains 50% (or even 60%, 70% – or even 90% of the population): the sample mean now approaches the population mean more and more as we are examining larger and larger chunks of the population! It is at 50% highly improbable that the sample mean would be very far off the real population mean, and it becomes almost impossible when we have observed 80% or 90% of respondents. Thus: the larger the sample, the better that sample helps us to conclude something about the population. The larger the sample, the more precisely will our inferences about the population be. In terms of noise: larger samples are in principle less noisy.

This is of course intuitively true: if we investigate more members of the population, we know more about the population, and then we are able to make more precise statements about that population. Adding more sample members adds more information and can thus only improve upon what we do. This however does not help us much in practical situations. Because – while larger is better – exactly how large is then large enough? As mentioned above, time and money often dictate sample size. This is so for qualitative and for quantitative research.

Even though we thus cannot be very precise as to sample size yet, a second general rule is that the number of so-called 'disaggregations' one would like to make also determines the required size. What is meant by that?

Suppose that one is interested to know the contacts that people have had with the courts, as a litigant, plaintiff, defendant, accused or victim or any other mode. One could survey 1,000 persons, and find that 40 persons have had at least one contact the past year. But now suppose that one would want to disaggregate this by men and women, and not only by men and women, but also by age – investigating young men and young women and older men and older women. Now, assuming age and gender are distributed evenly, this would mean that there would be 10 young men, 10 older men, 10 young women, etc. Suppose now that I would also be interested to know the differences between persons with low and high levels of education. Then, the groups would be divided up once more, into groups of 5 persons – generally referred to as 'cells'. And suppose now that I also have reasons to believe that urbanity plays a role: then my groups would dwindle even more. Clearly any differences between the groups now become shaky: what if I find that 2 out of 5 young highly educated women have had a court contact the past year, against 4 out of 5 young highly educated men? How confidently can I report that this chance is twice as high from one group to the other? Suppose I have encountered only 1 young highly educated woman with a court contact the past year: the chance would then have increased fourfold. Within such small groups, one man or one woman extra or less can greatly affect the percentages, so that we may arrive at sweepingly different conclusions, depending on just one or two sample members. The findings are *unstable*.

Clearly, here the fact that one wants to compare so many groups makes it necessary to start out with a larger sample: one would not want to make too strong statements based on just one or two sample members having had a contact with the courts or not. In general, as a rough rule of thumb it is assumed that the number of respondents per cell, i.e. per group one wishes to compare, should not be less than 30. This means that if one wants to investigate just two cells, 60 respondents would be an absolute minimum; for comparing four groups, 120 respondents would be needed, and if one wants to make as many subdivisions that one would be comparing 16 different cells, 480 sample members would be needed.

Thus, summarizing this section, we note that for qualitative studies, sample size is more often guided by 'information gain' or saturation, meaning that sample size will be determined as the research proceeds. Also for practical reasons, sample sizes tend to be smaller in qualitative than in quantitative research. For various viewpoints on desirable sample sizes in qualitative research, see Baker & Edwards (2012). For quantitative studies, bigger samples give a more precise estimate of the properties of the population. For statistical reasons we prefer to work with sample sizes from 100 and up, but this is a rule of thumb. We will return to this issue in chapter 8. Last, we note that if we want to investigate in more depth and want to compare several subdivisions of the sample, for reasons of stability we need a larger sample. This applies to both qualitative and quantitative studies.

3.6 Sample nonresponse and representativeness

Above we said that samples are a part of a population. Instead of investigating all population members, we investigate only part of the population. In choosing that part, our sample, wisely, we hope to have the sample resemble the population. Drawing random samples guarantees representativeness. Obviously, there is uncertainty as we have not investigated each and every sample member, but as we stated, statistics will help us deal with that uncertainty in a sensible and accepted way. Thus, the path to quantitative research seems not too hard: we simply draw a random sample from a population, interview or otherwise assess the sample members, do some statistical wizardry, and we can tell our captivated readers what's likely going on in the population!

Life is unfortunately not that uncomplicated. Suppose that in some quantitative study, we have been able to compile a list of sample members, drawn at random from the population. Therefore we have a random sample and we assume we can generalize the sample results to the population. We start approaching sample members, ringing their doorbells or telephoning them, asking them to participate. Two complications will quickly arise. First, we will be unable to contact all respondents: some will simply never be at home or never answer their phone. Secondly, not all those we establish contact with will consent to participate. Some will say that they are too busy, are not interested, do not like the funding agency for the research. Some may simply be too ill to collaborate. These two mechanisms generate what is called sample *nonresponse* or sample *attrition*.

In most practical situations, sample nonresponse occurs. Depending on the topic of the study, the infrastructural possibilities, the persuasive skills of interviewers and the like, response rates in surveys these days generally hover between 20% and 40%; higher response rates are rare. This means that if we start out aiming for a sample of 100 respondents, we may end up with just 40 completed interviews: a so-called *retention rate* of 40%, and a so-called *attrition rate* of 60%. One might be tempted to think that this is not a real problem, as we could simply draw a larger initial sample of say 250, and then end up with 100 interviewed respondents, reaching our target.

Unfortunately, this does not solve the problem that nonresponse generates. The problem is namely not simply that we are left with fewer respondents, the problem is that nonresponse is generally not accidental. It is not a coincidence that certain respondents do not end up in our realized, interviewed sample. It is the vulnerable and the elderly who are too ill to be interviewed, it is the mistrustful, those who are afraid to talk to strangers or the busy bees with 80-hour work weeks who refuse to talk to us. The final realized sample thus generally contains an overrepresentation of younger and elderly persons, of persons from less urbanized areas, and an underrepresentation of the elderly, of townspeople, of people employed in very busy management positions. In addition, those who refuse to be interviewed generally have more extreme perceptions of the topic under study. Thus it is likely the fervent religious opponents of abortion as well as those who believe that abortion is simply anyone's right and nobody else's business, who will be underrepresented in our survey of citizens' views on abortion.

All in all, even if we start out with a randomly drawn list of sample members, the non-random attrition process will make us end up with a non-random selection of the original random sample. Formulated more loosely: nonresponse messes up the representativeness of a sample. One might be tempted to think that this is a particularly problematic phenomenon when doing surveys with 'live' people to be interviewed, who can be ill and who may say 'no'. Attrition however also plays a role when studying for instance court files or treatment dossiers. Court files of defendants who have their case up for review are typically 'travelling' and not to be found in the archive, the treatment files of recidivists may have been requested for inspection by the investigating psychiatrist or psychologist. Dossiers of withdrawn claims are cleaned earlier than those of cases that were taken to court. Thus, also here, it is the particular, atypical files that will be missed and a non-representative part of the original sample that will be left for inspection by us.

Nonresponse is essentially irreparable. One can inspect the resulting sample, in a so-called nonresponse analysis, and hope that it resembles the population on background characteristics (if one knows them) such as age, gender, type of claim, geographical origin and the like. If there are no serious differences, that is, if the realized sample resembles the population on such background characteristics, then that is more comforting than if we found there were differences. This 'background variables check' however does not tell you whether the nonresponders differ from the responders on the key variables of interest, central to the main research question.

If there are differences between the realized sample and the population, an option would be to 're-weight' the data. What is meant by that is best illustrated by an example. Suppose that it turns out that our realized sample has fewer females than there are in the population. We could then (assuming that the females who did respond are representative for all females – something which is unlikely) give the females' answers more weight than the males' answers, by counting their answers double or something else proportional to their underrepresentation. This solves the problem only if we have too few respondents of one kind. If we miss one kind of respondent altogether (for instance, we were unable to reach any pensioners), there is no way we could correct for this by re-weighting, as we do not have pensioners at all... There is then no way we can know what kind of answers to multiply and add to the existing ones.

Re-weighting has disadvantages as well, however. The easiest one to imagine is that findings become unstable, as they become heavily dependent on the few respondents of the underrepresented category who have been assessed. Suppose that females are underrepresented and that we have only one female respondent, and 50 males. In that case, we would in a sense have to 'multiply' this lone female's answers by 50 and add them to the dataset. The single female who is in our dataset now determines what all cloned females in our dataset report. Had we by chance interviewed another female, the 'female response' could have been wildly different.

Nonresponse rates vary per topic that is studied and per type of study objects (paper or electronic sample members such as case files generally do not generate high nonresponse rates). Nonresponse rates can be so high that generalization to the population becomes increasingly unrealistic. We already mentioned the study by Dijksterhuis & Vels (2011) where the response rate among clients who had defaulted on child maintenance payments was 22%, and the nonresponse rate therefore 78%. Especially when the topic is sensitive, response rates as low as 2% have been encountered. Response rates of 40% to 50% are generally perceived as acceptable, even though then one should always check to what extent the nonresponders differ from the responders.

It should be noted that in so-called longitudinal studies where respondents are followed over time, any so-called *drop-out* that occurs accumulates over waves. So, if we miss, say, 20% of our intended sample at the first measurement wave, meaning we retain a really good 80%, experiencing the same drop-out at wave 2 implies that we will then be left with 64% of our original respondents. Should such *attrition* occur similarly at wave 3, we would then be left with just under 50% of our original sample, and so forth.

By far the best is to prevent nonresponse. This is achieved by careful introduction of the study, good training of interviewers, revisiting of respondents, offering respondents a monetary incentive, and more, which we will detail in chapter 4 below.

Chapter questions

1. Argue whether all cases registered with the prosecution constitute a population, whether all witnesses testifying in international criminal proceedings constitute a population, and whether all medical malpractice cases brought before a disciplinary council do so (section 3.1)

2. What is a sampling frame? Argue whether all tort cases decided upon by the supreme court in a certain country are a representative sample for all tort cases in that country (section 3.2)

3. Order the four types of non-probability samples according to the extent to which you might regard them as being representative for the population from which they were sampled (section 3.3)

4. What is meant by saturation in the context of qualitative sampling? (section 3.3.2)

5. What is negative or deviant case analysis? (section 3.3.2)

6. Order the four types of probability samples according to the extent to which they would generate biased or noisy estimates of properties of the population (section 3.3 and section 3.4)

7. Give two reasons why nonresponse constitutes a problem in empirical research (section 3.6)

Chapter 4

Data collection methods

4.1 Introduction

After it has been decided what the 'units of measurement' are to be – whether they are inhabitants of a certain jurisdiction, court files, newspaper clippings, transcripts from radio shows, verdicts or victim statements – the researcher needs to determine how the required information is going to be 'tapped' from these units.

Humans can be interviewed, we can ask them to fill out questionnaires, or we could observe their behaviour. We can live with them for weeks or months, visit the pubs they frequent, join them in litigation, gossip or fun. We can also get information from paper or electronic files, or CCTV footage (from which analysable units need to be extracted). Court files can be studied: in that case the data in those files need to be accessed in the sense that the generally written information is transferred into the format of variables, or that occurrences of for instance relevant statements are tallied, or coded into categories for later analysis. Data rarely come in a format that is immediately ready for processing and analysis, even though governments increasingly store electronic records, and statistics offices hold registers that are immediately usable for analysis.

This chapter outlines a number of strategies for obtaining such information from different sources, persons or otherwise. Particularly when studying respondents, there is a wide array of choices that can be made. Computer software and the internet offer ever-growing efficient possibilities for this. In the following, we will first discuss the various options for eliciting information from people. The later parts of the chapter deal with data collection from other sources, such as files and registers, and with observation and ethnographic methods as a means of data collection.

Throughout this chapter, we discuss both quantitative and qualitative methods for data collection. While data collection methods used in the two methodological traditions may differ fundamentally, there are also methods used in both, such as the topical interview, or observation, underscoring the overlap between methods employed in the respective approaches. We therefore do not treat the qualitative and quantitative methods separately, but have chosen to integrate them wherever possible.

4.2 Interviews and questionnaires

When we study respondents, we generally want to obtain answers to a number of questions. The information we are after may be fairly factual, such as age, sex, marital status. For other questions we may need some kind of operationalization (see section 2.6), such as for questions after victimization or attitudes. The information we are seeking may however also be such that it is hard to design beforehand as a researcher the exact questions you would want to pose. If we for instance wanted to know why victims of violent crimes would want to speak in court, a pre-designed pencil-and-paper questionnaire will likely not extricate the information needed to understand victims' motivations. In all likelihood, a lengthy interview, where the researcher him- or herself can ask for clarifications, and where repeat sessions may be scheduled to clarify issues, may be needed. Thus, the type of question the researcher wants answers to strongly steers the method of data collection. If one is after fairly factual, objectively determinable issues, a simple questionnaire may do. If one wants to study reasonings, motivations, attitudes, a more nuanced and less pre-set, more flexible approach may be warranted, more like a conversation than an interview, with possibly a lengthy phase for the interviewer and interviewee to get acquainted beforehand.

Tracy (2013) distinguishes several types of interviews, depending amongst others on the goal of the research and the type of participant. The first type she distinguishes is the *ethnographic interview*, with all the appearances of a spontaneous conversation, instigated by the researcher. Questions may be factual, informative, and off the cuff. Questions may be posed when there is respite from work or other business, or expressly during people's daily chores, to illustrate what keeps them busy. The interview feels like a casual chat. Both researcher and interviewee are in their natural roles. By contrast, a *respondent interview* is a more formal setting, where the interviewer assumes an official role, and the interviewee does so as well. Here the interest is not so much factual information but rather the respondent him- or herself, his or her beliefs or motivations. *Informant interviews* on the other hand focus not on the interviewee him- or herself but on a group of people, a set of situations that the informant has special knowledge of or can explain well. Tracy essentially ranks interviews first along a 'natural-ness' scale, with the ethnographic interview actually not feeling like an interview, and other interviews entailing more formalized procedures. Next, she distinguishes whether the interviewer is interested in the interviewee him- or herself, or is after information that the interviewee has on others or certain issues, that is, whether the interviewee is an informant or the object of interest.

The method or stance of interviewing can be ranked along a different scale as well, related to the extent to which the interview is naturalistic or not. This scale reflects the extent to which the questions and answers are pre-determined, and the degree to which the researcher and respondent are constrained by formats and instructions. This scale is best regarded as a 'structuredness' scale. The freest format is exemplified by the unstructured and ethnographic interview; the most strictly regulated and pre-determined is the CAWI questionnaire, where respondents fill out a questionnaire online and are guided through a set of questions to which only a pre-outlined set of answers is possible. This scale along which interviews can be ranked also corresponds with the intensity of contact between respondent and interviewer. The CAWI interview is basically a set of programmed operations that the interviewee follows with no personal interaction or even voice contact necessary between respondent and researcher – and as such a cold and distant mode of data collection. The unstructured interview on the other hand is a vivid, sometimes intense interaction between two people. We will discuss each, and intermediate interview formats below.

It should be noted that all data collection techniques in which one interviews or speaks with respondents depart from three assumptions. A first is that interviewees understand your questions. This may seem like a trivial issue as in daily life if someone asks you a question you do not understand you will ask him or her to clarify that question. In interview situations things may not work that way: respondents may not admit that they do not understand the question, afraid of being considered stupid. Some respondents are too polite or too eager to please the interviewer to let on that they did not get the question entirely – and may simply give that answer they believe pleases the interviewer most or is what the interviewer is after. A second assumption is that respondents still remember the facts you are asking after. Aids to remember events or to place them correctly in time may help, such as a life history calendar (LHC, see Roberts & Horney, 2010). Lastly, an implicit assumption for interviews is that respondents speak the 'truth'. Arguably, if respondents do not speak the truth it does not mean that they lie, or that they lie on purpose. Respondents may tell you what they perceive to be the truth, or may prefer to keep some facts or perceptions to themselves.

Van Dijck (2016), in his review of studies on physicians' fear of malpractice claims and the extent to which this fear impacts their clinical practice (referred to as 'defensive medicine'), relates a fairly wide discrepancy between what physicians *say* they do, and what they *actually* do. Van Dijck goes so far as to say that physician surveys are unreliable for accurately measuring defensive medicine. In a study by Lawthers et al. (1994) it was found that physicians' perception of their risk of being sued was indeed three times higher than their actual risk. This does not mean that physicians' perception of the threat of malpractice suits is irrelevant: as Mello et al. (2004) reported, such fears are clearly associated with their performance, impacting patient contact. It does mean that in some cases it may be advisable to obtain objective data from archival records or court files as well, as triangulation.

Second, it should be noted that an interview, even if it appears to be unstructured, open, free-flowing and natural, is not in all regards a conversation like people have with their friends or relatives. For one, interviewers are non-judgemental. An interviewer is always respectful of the interviewee, and acknowledges the interviewee as someone insightful, who has information or knowledge that is valuable. Interviewers are sensitive in that they pay attention to non-verbal cues that respondents give. In that sense they place the interviewee on a pedestal; the interviewee is one who grants the interview to the researcher, and for that the interviewer should be kind and attentive. Interviews are therefore not two-way, as conversations would be, but focus on the interviewee. And besides being more lenient, more accommodating than ordinary conversations, interviews are at the same time also more forceful. There is usually probing, as interviewers have been trained not to take everything an interviewee says at face value, to point out (in a friendly way) any inconsistencies and to interpret what the interviewee is saying ('Do you mean to say that you actually believe such-and-such to be untrue?'). See Tracy (2013, chapter 8) for more.

Before we continue to discuss the various interview options, it is important to stress once more that ethics requires that all those who participate in research do so willingly, and are fully informed about the research. This is referred to as *informed consent*, by which is meant that research participants should be fully informed about the aims of the study, what the procedures are, who funds the study and how reporting will be done (in most cases researchers guarantee potential research subjects confidentiality, anonymity and unrecognizability). In more formal interview settings, participants are asked to sign a form on which they indicate that they have been fully informed about the study and that they consent to participate. Ethics also prescribes that participants can withdraw their permission at any time, after the interview has started, after data analysis has started. Most ethics boards would agree that once the findings from a study have been published, the data are in a sense 'sealed' and informed consent cannot be withdrawn anymore. See also section 2.10.

We will now discuss the range of interview options, from open, free-format unstructured interviews to highly pre-structured programmed e-questionnaires.

(1) *Open-ended, unstructured interviews*

In an open-ended, unstructured interview, there is basically no format. The researcher wants to get the answers to a number of questions, or understand a number of issues, to understand why for instance a respondent has made certain choices; the respondent has agreed to be interviewed, and the researcher asks accordingly – as long as s/he deems necessary and as long as the respondent manages to sit in, until the interviewer is convinces that s/he 'has the picture'. This type of interview is therefore also referred to as an *in-depth interview*.

An in-depth interview feels more like a conversation than a stylized, pre-determined questioning mode: it is free and naturally flowing, it may deviate here and there, and apparently meander along. This does not mean that there are no rules. The researcher has to introduce him- or herself, explain what the study aims are and what exactly is required, and stress that participation is voluntary and that permission can at all times be withdrawn (the 'informed consent'). It generally helps to establish trust and it increases openness on the part of the interviewee if the interviewer explains well why s/he is interested in the topic, what will be done with the results, when findings will published, etc. A good introduction is highly important for open-ended interviews (and in fact for all types of interviews). After all, the researcher wants the interviewee to share at times private thoughts and feelings. A distant and reclusive, non-committal interviewer is not conducive to people venturing such information.

As said, unstructured interviews generally proceed without a pre-set path. The interviewer can ask whatever questions s/he deems fit or important, as long as questions pertain to the central research question, or indirectly help in getting that question answered. Researchers may ask different questions from one interview to the next, in response to answers that also vary by interviewee. If one respondent voices concern over the outcome of her court case, the interviewer may try to get more information on this and on how she deals with these concerns, or why they concern her. If however another respondent stresses that she has completely different concerns, a different set of follow-up questions will likely be posed.

For unstructured interviews it is hard to predict what questions will be asked and in what order, not only because there is no format, but also because these interviews are supposed to respond to what the respondent says – which cannot be predicted. This means that it is also hard to predict how long unstructured interviews will take. Most take at least one and a half to two hours. Much longer stretches are unlikely as fatigue may set in. It is generally known that if interviews take too long (whether they be unstructured interviews or interviews with the aid of a questionnaire), the quality of the answers decreases, as respondents tire, and may even become fed up with the interview itself – and in the worst case withdraw permission. For that reason, unstructured interviews may extend over several sessions.

Unstructured interviews where respondents are encouraged to relate their experiences or tell stories rather than respond to questions are referred to as *narrative interviews*. Tracy (2013) also distinguishes the *biographical interview* or *life-story interview*. In such interviews the focus is on recounting events of the past, the interviewee's own life or career.

While unstructured interviews are the least tied to rules and format, interviewers should of course at all times behave professionally and decently. This entails not only explaining the purpose of the research well so that the respondent can give informed consent, but also listening attentively, responding in a friendly manner, paraphrasing at times, reacting to verbal and non-verbal signs, creating a pleasant atmosphere. At times, behaving in a professional manner also implies, however, keeping a personal and emotional distance. Interviewees have been reported to ask the interviewer for help, or assistance in practical matters, sometimes extending well beyond what would be possible. A good explanation beforehand of the study's aims and objectives and of the role of interviewer and interviewee may help to prevent such 'incidents' – incidents because obviously the interviewer has to say 'no', which may create tension or an unpleasant atmosphere so that subsequently the respondent may be less willing to divulge his or her feelings and thoughts. Sometimes interviewees ask for little things, such as helping them writing a letter to their children's school. In many such cases and especially when doing ethnographic research, fieldworkers do extend a helping hand.

It may also occur – especially if interviews focus on high-impact or traumatizing events – that an interviewee becomes emotional. Also here the interviewer should remain professional, although it may also be important to show empathy or offer some consolation. Being human, you may simply not be able to hold back your tears, and it would generate a distance if you did not allow your respondent to see that or to pretend that his or her story does not affect you. All in all, there is at times a fine line to tread between human compassion and professional distance. That being said, most interviews generally proceed smoothly, and researchers proceed easily through the questions they want to ask, or issues they want to have covered before the interview ends.

Unstructured interviews are generally lengthy interviews, which ideally should take place in a natural setting, and feel comfortable and conversation-like. For that reason, unstructured interviews may not be taped. Audio- or video-taping may disturb the 'private' feeling of the interview setting, and some respondents dislike having every word recorded. Instead, interviewers may after conclusion of the interviews quickly make a summary of topics touched upon, of pertinent statements made. These are immensely important in later analysis of the findings over several interviews. Such short field notes are called *memos* or *field jottings*: they are quick summaries of what was said, quotes, specific words or marked expressions that respondents used, or other salient observations, which one may forget, or where the specific sound or salience may be lost if one does not capture them exactly. Researchers generally write more extensive summaries of what was said during interviews once they are away from the respondents or the setting where observations took place; these *field notes* are much more elaborate summaries of what was said, and the field jottings serve as memory aides to do so. Both memos or field jottings and the more elaborate field notes together with the researcher's memory constitute (if interviews are not audio- or video-taped) the rough data on which analysis must take place. Such analysis generally starts immediately after interviews or observation has taken place; researchers then write so-called *analytic memos*, in which they describe – diary-like – everything that occurred, what patterns emerge in the data, what hypotheses are formed and rejected, what concepts best synthesize the findings. These analytic memos are an important resource for qualitative data analysis proper, to which we will return in chapter 7.

One important reason, however, to have interviews taped and transcribed is that in unstructured, in-depth interviews, much more than in any other data collection method described below, it may be the *manner* in which respondents formulate matters, the order in which, or the context against which, they bring up issues that is relevant. It may also be the issues that respondents leave out that turn out to be significant for the interpretation of the data and conclusion of the research. These aspects may very well emerge only after careful analysis, after prising apart and piecing together again the bits and pieces that were said. Such significance usually is not clear at the data collection stage, but emerges after (repeated) scrutiny of the material. If an interview is not transcribed (and also not literally – with all the 'erms' and 'ahhs' and 'weeeeelll...'s – as well as indications of whether a respondent laughs, sniffs, or puts particular emphasis on certain words), it is harder to uncover such issues (which would be argument in favour of taping and transcribing). Tracy (2013, pp. 179–180) gives an overview of special characters and conventions to demarcate and transcribe such non-verbal meanings.

It is important to stress that transcription of interviews is an extremely time-consuming process. One hour of interviewing may easily require three to four hours of transcribing. While software is available for automated transcribing, which considerably speeds up the process, all transcriptions need to be checked for consistency and correctness. A disadvantage of such automated transcription is, in addition, that it often is carried out through a web application, where one cannot be sure that the developer does not store the audio material on its own servers as well – a practice that might conflict with confidentiality promises.

Clearly, for transcription, the interview would have to be taped, to which respondents have to consent and which some respondents may not like. In the latter case the only resort is to make notes quickly afterwards or during breaks, and compile extensive field notes and after completion of the interview analytic memos.

A classic about qualitative interviewing is Rubin & Rubin (1995, reprinted in 2004). A number of general books on qualitative research have good chapters on interviewing as well; recommended are Tracy (2013, chapter 7) and Dixon, Singleton, & Straits (2016, chapter 9).

(2) *Topical or semi-structured interview*

A so-called *topical interview*, or an interview with a *topic list* has more structure. The researcher has a list of items that explicitly need to be covered, the 'topics', within one interview session. Thus, contrary to the unstructured interview, the researcher generally has only one session with the respondent, during which the relevant topics need to be covered. The order in which this occurs, or the particular questions that are asked to bring up the topics, are relatively free. Topical interviews are in that sense a mixture of the freest format (the unstructured interview) and the heavily structured varieties that will be discussed below. For that reason, topical interviews are categorized as *semi-structured*.

The free format of the topical interview also makes for a fairly natural and therefore pleasant atmosphere, in which the interview can proceed informally, almost like a conversation, with maximum opportunity for the interviewer to respond flexibly and touch upon topics as they emerge. The list of topics that should be addressed assures on the other hand that no gaps are left, and the breadth of issues discussed is generally narrower and more contained than in the unstructured interview.

Topical interviews, like in fact most interviews, should follow a certain 'intimacy curve'. It would be rude (and unwise) to start the interview with very personal or intimate questions, and it would also be insensitive to end an interview right after sensitive or intimate issues have been brought up. Thus, it is recommended to start interviews with fairly simple 'getting-to-know-you' questions, asking for instance after educational level, or marriage, or number of children. As the interview proceeds, and rapport is built between interviewer and interviewee, and after the interviewee has sketched some previous experiences, more personal or sensitive topics may be delved into. Towards the end of the interview, it is wise to round off the interview by again moving back to a less personal level.

In many interviews the respondent is asked at the end how s/he experienced the interview, whether topics were left unaddressed that s/he feels would have needed dealing with, whether s/he has any recommendations. Many researchers – especially if the interview dealt with potentially emotional issues – leave a list of organizations the respondent can contact if s/he feels s/he would need assistance, or would like to go over issues again with a professional. In that build-down phase, distance is resumed, so the 'moving-away' phase also serves to prepare for ending the interview.

Note that in topical interviews, the interviewer assumes a more formal role; there are more prescribed beginnings and endings. In that sense, the topical interview is clearly less naturalistic, less of a natural conversation than the unstructured interview, even though the interviewee clearly has much room for answering.

Topical interviews may also be held not with one, but with a set of respondents. One variety of such an interview is the *focus group* – although it must be said that some research methodologists would not agree with the hermeneutics to subsume the focus group under 'Interviews'. In a focus group, a set of specialists (usually therefore a purposive sample, see section 3.3.2) is asked for its knowledge and views on a particular topic, and in many cases also for a solution or recommendations. In a focus group, diverging views or opinions of the group members may be resolved or contrasted, and in that sense a focus group is a very efficient way to get an overview of viewpoints quickly. Often, professionals such as lawyers, youth workers, accountants or attorneys are asked to participate in focus groups. Focus groups need pleasant, versatile and analytical chairpersons or moderators, who should ensure not only that all relevant topics are covered, but also that shy participants are not overwhelmed by the more vocal and self-confident ones.

Topical interviews, like unstructured interviews, may be taped and transcribed – and are perhaps more often transcribed than unstructured interviews as they are less lengthy – in order for the raw material to be used for analysis. Also for topical interviews, the researchers may after conclusion of the interviews quickly make a summary of the answers, as taking notes may disrupt the flow and naturalness of the interviews. Again, after transcription or conversion into summaries, the interview material can be analysed using any of the techniques for qualitative data analysis described in chapter 7. Just like for unstructured interviews, for an interview to be transcribed it should be taped, to which respondents have to consent and which some respondents may not like. In that case the only resort is to make summaries quickly afterwards and/or take notes during breaks or write memos shortly afterwards.

(3) *Interview with questionnaire*

Many researchers – especially when they conduct quantitative research – prefer interviews using a questionnaire format to unstructured or topical interviews. Questionnaires have a fixed set of questions, which are asked in exactly the same order, whether or not a respondent at question 13 brings up an issue that is not addressed until question 36. The pre-set order must be followed. Obviously, if a respondent does not have children, the questions about those children's ages and gender, etc. do not apply, and may be skipped, but regardless of such 'inapplicable' questions, all questions are posed in exactly the same standardized order and format to all respondents, in exactly the same fashion. Where in unstructured and topical interviews the interviewer has much more freedom to adapt or rephrase questions, or address issues in any order that appears apt, with questionnaires it is as if the researcher's role is now increasingly standardized and automated, made uniform.

Such standardization serves to minimize distortion through interviewer behaviour or wording of the specific questions. By ensuring that each interviewer gives exactly the same introduction to the questionnaire, gives out informed consent forms in exactly the same order, has pre-fab answers to frequently asked questions, poses each question in exactly the same manner and in an identical order, this aims to rule out or minimize interviewer influence over the respondent's answers. Phrased differently, the aim of all this standardization is to ensure that the interviewer is but the vessel through which the respondent's properties, experiences, attitudes or feelings are transmitted. The interviewer functions as the medium through which the respondent's answers are passed on, and s/he should not influence the nature of those answers. Formulated differently again, if respondents' answers differ, we want those differences to be attributable to respondent differences only, and not to interviewer particularities. Standardization essentially serves to eliminate the interviewer him- or herself.

Interviews with questionnaires or question schemes thus standardize the situation in which the questions are posed. Given such standardization, it is possible to either allow respondents to answer the questions in any format they like (by providing so-called *open-ended questions*, see section 4.3), or to also standardize the answering options of the respondents (by supplying so-called *closed-ended questions*, see also section 4.3), in which case a limited set of possible answers is provided by the researcher, which the respondent has to 'tick' to confirm. In the first case we would label the interview as a *semi-structured interview*, the criterion being that the interview situation has been standardized, but the respondent is still free to answer any way s/he sees fit. If however only closed-ended questions are provided, we label the interview as *structured*, also referred to in the literature as *completely structured*. When an interview situation is completely structured, not only is the setting constrained, but also the behavioural options of the respondent.

When a researcher or interviewer administers the questionnaire and poses the questions, this is called *face-to-face* interviewing. It is also possible to have respondents fill out the questionnaires on paper, on a laptop or via the internet; we call these self-administered questionnaires. We discuss these interview modes below.

(4) *Self-administered questionnaire*

Obviously, respondents who can read and write may fill in questionnaires by themselves. This has a huge financial advantage (no interviewer needs make an appointment, travel, sit in), but comes at the cost of no one being able to explain possibly unclear questions, nor to use probing, or to aid in filling out the questionnaire when needed. Another disadvantage is that – particularly for more lengthy questionnaires – it is more likely that respondents will give up when filling it out takes too long.

Self-administration of questionnaires puts heavy demands on these questionnaires: on clarity, layout and attractiveness. Questionnaires must be tested and piloted extensively before they can be used in a real-life setting, as no amendments can be made once the respondent has to do the job all by him- or herself. If questionnaires are unclear, it is likely that respondents will not want to continue, generating missing data or in the worst case nonresponse. It is then also more likely that respondents will get confused and write down answers that are technically or practically impossible, such as having had 33 children, or writing down that they have never been in contact with the criminal justice system, but later writing that their last incarceration was from 2007 to 2009. Such impossible combinations of answers are sometimes jokingly referred to as 'pregnant grandfathers'.

(5) *Self-administered computerized questionnaire*

In recent years, ICT and the internet have grown tremendously in importance for research. While researchers not only write all their articles now on computers with word processing packages, computers (and the internet) are increasingly used for data collection too. Paper-and-pencil questionnaires have become almost completely replaced by e-versions, which can be filled out on a laptop or via an app on a smartphone. The computer is important for several reasons.

A first reason is technical. Using special software (an example of user-friendly software is LimeSurvey) one can programme questionnaires. This means that not only the text of all the questions is entered into the computer, but that the questionnaire itself is programmed in the sense that on the basis of the answers given, questions are skipped. This rids the respondent from tedious instructions such as *'If you filled in 'yes', please move to question 28'*. If someone has filled in that he is male, the questions on pregnancy are skipped automatically by the computer. This is much easier and pleasanter for respondents, speeds up the entry process, and if the questionnaire is programmed well, 'pregnant grandfathers' cannot occur. Arguably, such programming on the other hand makes correction of errors harder: if a respondent has filled in that he has never been sued, the programmed questionnaire will not lead him to the questions on this, and a previous mistake cannot be corrected in this fashion anymore. The respondent is also not triggered that s/he may have made an error in filling out a previous question.

Programming can be done in different ways. It is possible to demand that respondents fill in all previous questions before they are allowed to move to a next screen with questions. The software will then refuse to proceed unless answers to all questions have been entered. While this in principle ensures that answers to all questions are obtained and no so-called *missing values* are accrued, one may doubt whether such a strict protocol is conducive to validity of the answers. If respondents do not want to answer a certain question but the software blocks progress, they might simply fill in a nonsensical answer, just to be done with it and get on with the questionnaire. In that case, one has *an* answer but it may be doubted whether that answer is of any value. Or, worse, respondents who do not want to fill out certain questions might just bin the whole questionnaire, thus generating nonresponse, which is perhaps even more problematic (see section 3.6). It may therefore be preferable to give the respondent a gentle reminder that a question has not been answered yet, and program the questionnaire such that it asks whether s/he would be so kind as to do this after all. If a respondent again tries to proceed without answering, one could then simply allow respondents to do so. Some questionnaires have special options to respond *'would rather not answer'*, which might be a solution to this, although some respondents also do not like to explicitly acknowledge that they do not want to answer a question.

A second reason why the use of software and computers is so important in empirical research has to do with validity. If questionnaires are administered face-to-face it is possible to let the respondent fill out questions about 'sensitive issues' by him- or herself. The interviewer then walks through the entire questionnaire until a set of questions arrives for instance about offending, and asks the respondent to fill out those questions by him- or herself. The laptop is turned around and the respondent fills out the block of questions about the sensitive topics, after which the laptop is returned to the interviewer. It is generally assumed that this method yields better, more truthful answers and thus more valid and better quality data. Obviously, enhanced veracity of answers rests on the assumption that the respondent trusts that the interviewer cannot read back what s/he has filled in.

If one has designed the questionnaire such that it is impossible to page back to previous answers, respondents will likely more easily admit that they embezzled money than if they have noticed that everything can be read back. This would plead against a scroll-back-and-repair option. On the other hand, being able to scroll back and change previous answers is handy if respondents realize that they filled out questions wrongly. It is hard to say which is best.

A third reason why computers are so useful in data collection is that if answers are filled in on the computer, whether that be on a laptop or via the internet, the so-called 'data entry' phase can be skipped. Data entry is the phase where handwritten questionnaires, or handwritten notes, are transformed into variables on a computer, that can then be analysed. In general, doing so costs time, and builds in an extra layer in the data collection phase that is also an additional opportunity for mistakes to be made. Data entry by hand is fairly mind-numbing work, so mistakes in the transferral of the written material to the computer may occur. Some research firms have software to e-read filled-out questionnaires, but also that is an additional step in the process from answers to variables. Computers and especially the possibility of web-based administration of questionnaires save money and yield more reliable data.

A last reason is that computers generate – in general, though not for all respondents it must be said – a stronger sense of confidentiality and privacy. Computers are non-judgemental, while interviewers may very well be feared by respondents to be so. Questionnaires filled in within the privacy of one's own home, not in one's own handwriting, where shameful words need not be spoken aloud, may for that reason reduce the tendency that many respondents have to give answers that appear acceptable, normative, 'normal', referred to as *social desirability bias*. Thus, the use of computers or web-interviewing may also for that reason increase validity.

The computer and computer software can be used in a variety of ways. Almost all larger research departments and firms these days program their questionnaires. The programmed questionnaire can then also be administered through a telephone interview. The interviewer calls up the prospective respondent, and asks whether s/he is willing to be interviewed, after which the interviewer, sitting behind a computer screen, reads out the questions over the telephone and fills in the answers. This is called Computer Assisted Telephone Interviewing or CATI. The situation where a face-to-face interview is conducted and a laptop is present on which answers are entered, in part possibly by the interviewee him- or herself, is called Computer Assisted Personal Interviewing or CAPI. If the respondent fills in the questionnaire on a computer entirely by him- or herself, this is called Computer Assisted Self Interviewing or CASI. If respondents fill out questionnaires at home (or elsewhere) via the internet, this is called Computer Assisted Web Interviewing or CAWI.

4.3 Design of interviews, questionnaires and questions

4.3.1 Interview design

As discussed in section 4.2, interviews generally follow a certain 'intimacy curve'. By that we mean that interviews generally start with easy questions that build rapport, set the interviewee at ease, ask after simple unintrusive facts, such as age, profession, marital status and the like. Rapport-building questions should be inviting and pleasant, and should entice the interviewee to relate some facts, start talking about issues related to the interview. They could also be pleasant introductory remarks, such as: 'I haven't been to this neighbourhood for a long time, it has really changed a lot!'. Introductory questions mainly function to get the interviewee speaking and to start conversation, to establish a pleasant atmosphere. After informed consent is given, generally factual issues are addressed first. The list of factual questions should not be too long, as rattling off such facts may also be distancing and may in fact undo the pleasant, conversational atmosphere in which the interview started.

To make it easier for respondents to talk, so-called *generative questions* may be asked. Examples are *tour questions*, such as: 'Can you describe for me how a typical management team meeting looks?'. Respondents can be asked for elucidation, such as: 'You just said that you never discuss incoming mail, why is that?', or for historical perspectives ('Since when is it that you only meet once every two weeks?'). Next, hypothetical questions can be quite useful ('Suppose that you had only half an hour for your management team meeting, what would be the item you would definitely not skip?', or 'Suppose you were in complete control of your job, what activities would you give prominence?').

The opposite of generative questions are directive questions, in which an answer to a specific question is sought. The most directive type of question is the closed-ended question (see below in section 4.3.3), where a respondent can choose between a limited number of alternatives for an answer. Directive questions can also be posed to elicit reactions, for instance to pictures or video clips. Devil's advocate questions are useful to obtain additional insights into people's views, for instance by saying 'You just said that you are overwhelmed by red tape, but if I were an outsider I could say that that is all in your own hands as you are the director.' Asking people to reflect on mistakes they made or actions they regret also rank as directive questions. Such questions (similar to devil's advocate questions) may be threatening for some respondents, and they should be posed with caution. One way to be cautious and not to offend the respondent is by posing a confronting question as something said by others ('Some people might say that your answer is self-serving because...').

To wrap up, it is always wise to ask interviewees whether there is any topic that was not addressed but that should have been mentioned, or a question unasked that should have been asked. Tracy (2013) suggests – for studies in which some of what respondents said will be quoted – to ask interviewees under what name they would like to appear in the report. This assures respondents once more of the anonymity promise, and also give a gentle indication that the interview is drawing to a close. Tracy (2013) lists all these types of questions and has further useful suggestions.

As already mentioned above, interviews should not last too long. Interviewees may otherwise become bored or tired, and the quality of their answers declines. Crucial questions should not be asked at the beginning or end, but perhaps somewhere midway through the interview.

4.3.2 Questionnaire design

Designing *questionnaires* is a science or an art by itself. Most questionnaires start, like interviews, with relatively simple, 'getting-to-know-you' questions, such as questions about age, marital status, place of birth, etc. *Screener questions* may follow, which for instance ask whether the respondent was ever sued or whether the respondent was ever the victim of an accident, after which follow-up and more in-depth questions appear. After that phase, where the key issues are addressed, questionnaires next round off in the sense that they attempt not to end abruptly, but move back to a less personal layer, for instance asking about the aftermath or future expectations.

Questionnaires are recommended to end by asking the respondent whether s/he has anything to add to the interview, whether s/he has missed anything that should have been asked, remained unattended to, etc. If the questionnaire focused on possibly sensitive or emotional issues, such as victimization, the end of the questionnaire should always provide a telephone number or e-mail address in case the respondent wishes to talk about the study topic with someone else or needs help.

Before the questions proper of the study start, the questionnaire should introduce the study clearly. The introduction should state what the research question is, what the purpose of the study is, who finances the study. The introduction should also state that anonymity, confidentiality and untraceability are promised and guaranteed: all information divulged by the respondents will be treated confidentially, and remains with the researchers only. When the report of the study is published, no names of respondents should appear, and the findings should be written up such that no outsider or insider can trace the findings back to individual respondents. For example, if a study were to report on a 16-year-old red-haired sex offender with a drug-addicted father with a wart on his nose from a small village in the Netherlands, most of the 2,000 inhabitants of that village would know who that sex offender is.

The introduction should also state that consent to participate can be withdrawn at any time. The latter is not only part of the formal requirement that respondents must give *informed consent* but will likely also make it easier for respondents to agree to participate: it shows that they have control and can withhold permission again when they want. Giving an average expected duration for the interview is also helpful, as the respondent then knows what time investment s/he is agreeing to. Specifying an expected duration also prevents respondents getting restless when the interview takes longer than they had anticipated. Many introductions end by stressing that participation is very important for the research to get a full and complete picture; it is wise to also explain in what way society benefits, or how people like the respondent benefit, to encourage the respondent to agree to participate. In interviewing victims or detainees, it may be important to stress that neither the study nor the researcher or interviewer can do anything for an individual participant. Often a sentence or two will be added to the effect that the research hopes to contribute to a better understanding of the topic under study, to aid for instance in shaping the lives of family members of detainees, to give policy recommendations, and the like.

An interview is a gift, from respondent to researcher. To make respondents' task pleasant, to facilitate them to consent at all, questionnaires should be easy to fill in, as short as possible and attractive. Questionnaires should – whether they are administered with paper and pencil or are e-questionnaires – be designed such that respondents can easily see where they are, when the next question is coming, and – when the questionnaire is administered electronically – have an overview of how far along they are in filling it out; most questionnaire software have the option to show a bar that shows progress in percentage points. A printed questionnaire of 50 densely printed pages with font size 10 lettering is not going to generate valid answers – or only from a small masochistic subset of sample members. Designing your questionnaires badly results in nonresponse – and thus bias in your sample – or sloppy answers – and thus compromised validity. Not doing a good job here will only come back to bite the research in the end. The researcher proposes but the respondent disposes.

In research practice, telephone interviews should not be (although this is but a rule of thumb) much longer than 10–15 minutes. Face-to-face interviews should (but this is again a rule of thumb) not stretch beyond one and a half hours. If they do, respondents tend to tire, and their willingness to answer decreases, thereby also affecting validity. This is the reason that the central research question should be posited not at the very end of the questionnaire or interview, but somewhere around to a little over midway through: at that point in the interaction or the questionnaire, maximum intensity or depth has been built, and respondents are not tiring yet.

Questions are best clustered by topic. It costs mental energy to flip from one topic to the other, and respondents prefer to see or hear announced what the next set of questions is going to be about. Clusters are therefore best introduced by small sentences like 'We would now like to ask you something about your school years', or 'The following set of questions focuses on to the period before you started working for your current employer'.

The context in which questions are asked may affect the manner in which respondents respond to those questions. If questions about the behaviour of respondents' children are framed as pedagogical issues, then the responses will likely differ from when they are asked against a setting of parenting 'styles'. Similarly, the sequence in which questions are asked affects responses. This is another reason why there is so much focus on standardization in interviewing, so that each and every respondent can be assumed to have undergone the same influence from the questioning sequence. Small changes in the order in which literally the same questions were asked, or the context in which these were posed, have been associated with differences in prevalence rates.

Each newly designed questionnaire should be tested ('piloted') before being administered as part of the study. Piloting involves testing administration of the questionnaire, checking whether it takes as long as assumed, and assessing that respondents find the questionnaire clear, pleasant, never offensive and that they understand the questions.

4.3.3 Types of questions and question design

In section 4.3 we briefly discussed various types of questions that can be asked to prompt or seduce the respondents to talk, so-called generative questions such as tour questions or hypothetical questions. This section deals with the more technical aspects of question design for questionnaires.

Designing such *questions* for questionnaires – so at the more rigid, prescribed end of the spectrum – is something not learned in half an hour. As every experienced researcher will tell you, even questions that appear at face value completely clear and unambiguous may turn out to be multi-interpretable when administered to actual respondents. As these are questions for use in a questionnaire, in many cases researchers will not be present to elucidate bits and pieces that turn out to be obscure. Questions should therefore be crystal clear once they are printed on a questionnaire or are 'live' online. Just as questionnaires should be piloted in a real situation, so should questions be, scrupulously, one by one. Researchers should sit down with volunteers who resemble the intended respondents and fill out the questionnaire with them, or have them fill it out, and check per question whether the respondent believes s/he understood the question, how s/he understood the question, whether the question was experienced as pleasant, not too intrusive, etc.

A number of general rules help in designing good questions, and we will briefly mention the most important of them. Questions should:

(1) *Be clear*

This may seem like a superfluous statement, but there should really be absolutely no ambiguity left in the question, no words that may have various meanings, etc. Also, questions should ask after concrete phenomena. A question phrased like: 'Are you afraid to be victimized?' is not clear and pointed enough, as it is unclear to what kind of victimization it refers. Respondents may for instance not be afraid to become a victim of a crime, but may be afraid to suffer an accident.

(2) *Not have (double) negations*

It is well known that double negations are confusing for most people and therefore also for respondents. Questions like: 'Do you disagree with the Christian party's standpoint that women should not be allowed to vote?' are therefore an absolute no-no. Some respondents already have trouble dealing with (single) 'negatively' formulated statements, and it may therefore be best not to phrase questions in the negative – although this has the side-effect that all questions may become 'unidirectional' and therefore not stimulating respondents to think well about their answers.

(3) *Not be double-barrelled*

A double-barrelled question asks two questions in one. Respondents then obviously cannot know which question to answer to. Such a question would be: 'Would you vote for Joe Biden because of the economy?' The answer 'no' can pertain to not voting for Biden, or voting for Biden but not because of the economy.

(4) *Not be suggestive*

Questions should always be formulated neutrally and not lead the respondent to believe that one answer or the other is the 'correct' one.

(5) *Have answering options that are mutually exclusive and exhaustive*

This rule applies only to questions that are closed-ended. In a closed-ended question the interviewee can select from a limited set of answers only. The first requirement (be mutually exclusive) above entails that respondents know which category to tick for their answer. If for instance boxes 1 and 2 that one can tick 'overlap' (1 = before I went to secondary school, 2 = before I turned 10), respondents who experienced an event at age 9 may not know which one to choose. The second requirement (be exhaustive) has the desired effect that every respondent will be able to find a category for his answer, for example: 1 = before age 12, 2 = between ages 13 and 18, and 3 = after age 18). To ensure that this requirement is met, many questions have an 'other, namely ...' category, which ensures that if a respondent does not find his or her answer among the pre-given categories, s/he can resort to this one. Arguably, literature study and pre-testing of the questionnaire should ensure that only a small proportion of respondents need to use this 'other' category.

(6) *Minimize the risk for response styles to affect answers*

This rule is particularly relevant to questions that use rating scales for answers. Such questions usually have the format that respondents are confronted with a statement, and then are asked to tick on a scale ranging from 1 to 5 (or sometimes 1 to 7), whether they 1 = 'strongly disagree' with the statement or, 2 = 'disagree', 3 = 'do not disagree, do not agree', 4 = 'agree', 5 = 'strongly agree'. Rating scales are very often used and efficient. In general, rating scales employing 5 to 7 categories are used; a finer grid such as with 9 or 11 categories does not give qualitatively better answers as the substantive labels then differ only marginally.

Figure 4.1: Example of rating scales

Below you will find a number of statements. Please indicate by circling the numbers on the rating scale to what extent you agree with each statement. The example below shows what the numbers on the scales mean, and how to enter your answer.

1	(2)	3	4	5
strongly agree	agree	neither	disagree	strongly disagree

How strongly do you agree with the following statements?

1. My daily mood is influenced by fear of tort claims

1	2	3	4	5

2. When deciding on a patient's treatment, I often think of my liability for damages

1	2	3	4	5

For an example of such rating scales, and a brief instruction for respondents to fill out the rating scales, see Figure 4.1.

Rating scales however have the unfortunate side-effect that they may elicit *response styles*, such as the tendency to always give neutral answers (always ticking a '3'; referred to in the literature as the *error of central tendency* or as 'fence sitting'), or the reverse (ticking '1's or '5's; referred to as *extreme response bias*). Other commonly occurring response styles are so-called *acquiescence bias*, or 'agreement response bias', by which is meant the tendency to agree with every statement. To detect this response style, it is advisable to phrase some questions in the negative, and some questions in the positive – which is as the attentive reader may note counter to the recommendation made above not to formulate questions negatively. Some respondents try to weed out any inconsistencies in their answers: they check their answers to make sure that their answers constitute

Figure 4.2: Example of answering categories to prevent socially acceptable answers

How often do you wash your hair?
(please tick a box)

- ☐ never
- ☐ less than once a month
- ☐ between once a month and every two weeks
- ☐ between every two weeks and every week
- ☐ several times per week

an intrinsically logical set. This is called the *logical mistake*. Fairly rebellious tendencies can be encountered too, such as filling out answers in systematic fashion (page 1 incurring only '1's, page 2 a series of '2's, etc.), or with nice visual patterns (zigzaggingly, or Christmas-tree like).

Clearly, when response styles are present, answers may become almost useless: respondents then have not filled out what they really think or believe. One way to prevent such styles affecting the validity of the data is to impress upon respondents not to think very long and fill in the answers quickly, to state that it is the first impression that counts, that there is no 'right' answer, etc. Another option is to trigger respondents by formulating questions positively or negatively – as explained above (which does not really prevent response styles affecting the answers, but enables the researcher to detect them). A third option is to choose the labels to the categories of the rating scale such that ticking a visually neutral category amounts to a not at all neutral answer. For instance one could label '5' as 'I brush my teeth once a week' (with 7 = 'never', 6 = 'once a month', 4 = 'once every 3 to 4 days', 3 = 'every other day', 2 = 'every day', 1 = 'twice a day or more often'). See Figure 4.2 for a similar example.

Other researchers try to prevent the error of central tendency by offering not 5 or 7 categories (and thus a neutral category '3' or '4') but an even number of categories (4 or 6) – so that the respondent has to 'choose sides'. This may force some respondents to reluctantly do so – others may simply not fill out the questionnaire anymore. It may be advisable to offer respondents an escape by also providing a 'do not know' category to tick. See Figure 4.3.

Because of the possibility of one or more of these styles blurring the answers and affecting validity, some researchers pose their crucial questions several times in a questionnaire, each time slightly differently, to be sure to obtain the information

Figure 4.3: Example of rating scales with 'escape' category

Below you will find a number of statements. Please indicate by circling the numbers on the rating scale to what extent you agree with each statement. The example below shows what the numbers on the scales mean, and how to enter your answer.

1	2	3	4	☐
strongly agree	agree	disagree	strongly disagree	don't know

If you do not have an opinion or are uncertain about your opinion, please tick the 'don't know'-box as follows: ☑ don't know

How strongly do you agree or disagree with the following statements?

1. Sexual harassment at work can only be countered by tough sanctions

1	2	3	4	☐
strongly agree	agree	disagree	strongly disagree	don't know

2. Playful sexual remarks are innocent and part of a pleasant work environment.

1	2	3	4	☐
strongly agree	agree	disagree	strongly disagree	don't know

they are after, or at the least to detect that response styles are affecting respondents' answers.

(7) *Minimize the risk of socially desirable answers*

Many respondents have the tendency to give answers that are socially acceptable, afraid to be judged as deviant or weird, or unwilling to share attitudes they know would generally be regarded unfavourably. If one were to ask respondents 'Are you a bigot?', or 'Do you perform unnecessary medical procedures under fear of tort claims?' it is not likely that many would say 'yes'. If one wants to know whether respondents have politically incorrect views, whether they exhibit socially undesirable behaviour, it is therefore wise to ask this in a circumspect way, in which negative labels (such as 'bigot') are avoided but a number of different questions are drawn up to measure the various dimensions or aspects of for example bigotry, phrased as factually and neutrally as possible (such as: 'Do you agree with the standpoint of Mr Wilders that immigration to the Netherlands should be stopped?'). Social desirability is believed to pose less of a risk when questionnaires are self-administered (CASI or CAWI). Special social desirability scales have been developed that can be included in questionnaires to see to what extent a respondent's answers may have been distorted by a his or her tendency to give socially desirable answers (an old and well known example is the Marlowe–Crowne Social Desirability Scale (Crowne & Marlowe, 1960).

(8) *Operationalize the constructs for the respondent*

Questions should always contain a clear *operationalization* of what the researcher is asking. One respondent may have quite a different idea of what entails, for instance, discrimination or victimization than another. When using generic terms, the researcher leaves it to the respondent to operationalize the construct. And the researcher does not know how exactly the different respondents did that. Similarly, if a question is 'Is your medical practice affected by liability risk?', the researcher should specify what s/he understands 'affected' to be. Van Dijck (2016) reviewed the evidence on negative defensive medicine, and operationalized this as "situations where physicians no longer perform risky (but desirable) operations due to liability concerns, refer risky patients to other doctors, or stop seeing certain patients". Questionnaires to investigate whether physicians exhibit such behaviour should then quite literally mention these aspects, by phrasing questions such as: 'Have you ever/in the past year not performed a risky operation that you deemed necessary, out of fear of tort claims?', 'Have you ever/in the past year referred patients to other doctors out of fear of tort claims?' and 'Have you ever/in the past year stopped seeing patients, out of fear of tort claims?'. Van Dijck showed that the empirical evidence for such 'negative medicine' is in fact quite limited.

Questions should all in all be as factual, clear and as precise as possible, be phrased neutrally, not be double-barrelled, never be leading. One can choose – as explained above – closed-ended questions where the interviewee can only select from a limited set of answers, or open-ended questions where the interviewee can answer freely. In general, open-ended questions are supposed to be beneficial for validity, as respondents can respond in a multitude of ways – at substantially increased cost to the researcher however as all the different answers must generally be coded afterwards into meaningful categories. Conversely, closed-ended questions give better reliability, and save costs.

4.4 Interviewing: skills and approach

Not everyone can conduct each kind of interview. Interviewing is a skill that needs – for most – at least some training. In such a training, prospective interviewers acquire skills for probing, are trained in responding to different 'types' of interviewee, practice paraphrasing, summarizing, responding to questions about the research aims, procedure, etc.

For some studies, researchers have to pick their interviewers in the sense that interviewee and interviewer 'match'. In general, especially for sensitive topics, females are best interviewed by females. Many male interviewees also prefer to be interviewed by females. In some cultures, the age of the interviewer is also an issue to address, with interviewees preferring older interviewers. Especially traumatized respondents, such as victims of abuse, may not want to be interviewed by very young students. Sometimes respondents are best interviewed by someone with a similar social class or profession, for language, cultural or other reasons. Examples exist however of studies where the opposite turned out to be true: in the Netherlands in a study on domestic violence, many interviewees stated that they preferred to be interviewed by someone who did *not* have a similar migrant background; the reason being that they were afraid – given their closely knit communities – that any 'dirty laundry' might be exposed.

When approaching respondents in person, interviewer dress and appearance are important. These should be tailored to the 'type' of respondents one is approaching. If drug addicts are to be studied, it is perhaps not wise to appear in suit and tie. If corporate lawyers are to be interviewed, it may not be wise to turn up in torn jeans. Interviewers should dress, speak and behave according to presumed interviewee expectations and according to the setting the interview will be conducted in. In general, overdressing (professional dress and behaviour) is better than underdressing (joviality, informality). After all, the interviewer conducts the interview in a professional, formal role.

The first few seconds of approaching respondents are crucial. Even if respondents have been sent letters beforehand, many will not have read or taken note of those letters, and the research and its purposes must be explained at that first encounter during the first few instant when the respondent opens the door. This means that the timing of home approaches must be carefully chosen, during the daytime to start with, for those who are employed outside of the home perhaps very early evening, which however incurs the risk of ringing the doorbell when the family has just sat down to dinner – immediately generating annoyance. Contact attempts late at night are not welcomed by respondents in general – and thus also increase the risk of refusal – and may even be risky for interviewers. When meeting with busy managers or corporate lawyers, interviewers should be well on time. They should stick to the time the interview was announced to take, and preferably end a little early.

Almost all that was written here for home or office approaches goes as well for approach by telephone, where – while dress and smiles and general composure do not count – timing does, and voice and pleasantness of wording, and sensitivity to the respondent's answers and any hesitance are all the more important.

The careful approach of potential respondents is so crucially important because insensitive behaviour will quickly generate refusal, and thus nonresponse, leaving one with a likely non-representative sample. Once a sample member has opened the door, contact has been established and the sample member is no longer a 'non-contact' (see section 3.6). During the first few seconds that then follow, agreement to cooperate must be secured. Once a respondent has said 'no', it is very hard to turn that into a 'yes'. Therefore, if sample members hesitate, it may be best – and a lot depends on the interviewer's ability to correctly read verbal and non-verbal signs – to hand out the already sent out letter, or a short introduction to the research once more, and propose that the interviewer return at an agreed day and time so that the hesitant sample member can quietly think it over. It is advisable to leave a card with a name and telephone number, and an e-mail address and an attractive website with background information, so that the potential respondent can get more information or call to cancel.

If respondents are not at home (or do not open the door), they should be approached again, at different times of the day and week, to maximize the chance that one finds them home. While three attempts are customary in most studies, for some respondents up to eight attempts are used (Van der Geest, Bijleveld, & Verbruggen, 2013).

Approach via e-mail should similarly to approach in person be correct and brief, with a clear and attractive, colourful outline which has been piloted to ensure that any kind of respondent can quickly see what is asked and can easily consent. It is customary to send a number of reminders at pre-set intervals, such as after 10 days, after 20 days and 30 days.

Obviously, one can also conduct a survey of offices (instead of persons) or waiting halls in courts, assessing how these have been designed, furnished, staffed. In that case, observation rather than interviewing may be chosen, although the observations may be supplemented by interviews with officials, secretarial staff, etc. It may also be the case that the research subjects are too young to be interviewed, or that the factors we are interested are better observed than asked after, such as boardroom behaviour. Or we may have designed our study such that we will be extracting information from documents such as court files or newspaper clippings. We will discuss these other data collection modes below.

4.5 Observation

When we observe behaviour, we can do so either in a non-participatory or participatory fashion. When our observations are non-participatory, we are an outside observer to the behaviour we are interested in. We can only observe from the outside what people do. Examples are studies where researchers scrutinize managers' behaviour during boardroom meetings for the interaction between them, for instance to understand the manner in which hierarchy is built in small groups. The observers do not participate, and ideally speaking they should be as *unobtrusive* as possible. This is because if the data collection method is obtrusive (if the 'subjects' of the research are aware that they are being studied) this might affect respondents' behaviour. They might show more socially acceptable behaviour, or might on the contrary become more braggish. When research is obtrusive, it is generally not possible anymore to observe the behaviour we are interested in its natural form. Therefore, it is generally considered best if the objects of study are not at all aware of the fact that they are being studied.

Obviously, this may conflict with the requirement of informed consent (see section 4.2). Wanting to be as unobtrusive as possible (and therefore preferably 'undercover'), but at the same time conforming with research ethics, may generate a dilemma. Should not the researcher immediately tell his or her research subjects that s/he is not one of them, but is studying them? And if s/he does not do so immediately but only after a while, is this not also a breach of research ethics?

Many researchers in fact do tell the people they want to study that they are a researcher. In many cases where the objects of study are aware that a researcher is in their midst, time and good participatory behaviour may ease away any tensions or distance between the researchers and his research objects. Flood (2005) describes how when he first met the lawyers in the Chicago law firm that he was to study, someone shouted "Here's the company spy!" The gradual development of trust is essential, he writes, to overcome such an odd and uneasy start to a research project. In a previous study on clerks, Flood had spent many hours boozing away with staff, to be one of them, even though his body was not used to handling such amounts of alcohol (and did not suffer it very well he reports). Staring & Kroese (1991) report how, when they did ethnographic fieldwork in a men's prison in the Netherlands, at first the prisoners regarded them warily and were non-committal. After an incident, that the researchers witnessed, it was decided by the research team to keep the knowledge of that incident to themselves. While the prisoners knew that the researchers had this inside information, they now saw that the researchers did not tell on them. This gained the prisoners' trust, and after the incident Staring and his colleagues gradually gained access to prisoners, and were able to communicate relatively freely and openly with them.

Some qualitative researchers argue that observation does not enable you as a researcher to *understand* why humans behave as they behave. Observation places you outside the context within which your research subjects are living, behaving, making decisions. Only observing their movements does not make you understand the constraints people live under, the pressures they experience. Observation thus, according to their reasoning, generates data that are limited in validity. To understand what drives your research subjects, it would be necessary to *be* one of the group that is being studied, to undergo what they undergo and to experience from the inside what the research subjects experience. While this is never completely realizable (the researcher will be a researcher, will generally be different, will after the study return to his or her own realm) a number of researchers strongly advocate the use of so-called *participant observation*, also referred to as *ethnography*, for the study of particular (sub)cultural groups. While participant observation and ethnography are generally associated with fieldwork in disadvantaged communities, they are important methods for the study of segments of society that the researcher does not easily have access to and has little knowledge of, such as corporate culture.

The manner in which data is collected using ethnographic methods does not differ much from data collected during in-depth or unstructured interviews (see section 4.2). Just like in unstructured interviews, memos are generally written down unobtrusively in between observations and conversations, as are field jottings. Longer summaries (field notes) are compiled once the researcher is away from the field. Memos, field jottings and the more elaborate field notes are the rough material on which data analysis will be carried out. Such analysis generally starts immediately after interviews or observation have taken place; researchers then write so-called *analytic memos*. We return to these topics in chapter 7.

With the advent of ICT, behaviour can increasingly easily also be observed indirectly (and unobtrusively). Lindegaard and her co-authors (2020) observed the behaviour of shoppers on a busy Amsterdam shopping street during the first COVID wave in the Netherlands. Drawing on video footage, they investigated, amongst others, how often shoppers violated the 1.5-meter distance rule and what factors were associated with such violations. They found that violations of the 1.5-meter distance directive were commonplace, and that crowding was strongly positively associated with the rate of social distancing violations, suggesting that distancing violations may potentially be regulated through pedestrian movement management. They also found that face-masks were not associated with social distancing behaviour, alleviating the concern that face-masks may lead to less adherence to social distancing measures.

Malsch and her co-authors (2015) analysed written reports and audio- and video-tapes of police interrogations. In the Netherlands, criminal judges generally try cases on the basis of a written case file. They therefore rely heavily on written reports. The researchers were interested to find out to what extent the written summary of an interrogation corresponded with what had actually been said during an interrogation. They analysed a comparison of the recordings of 55 interrogations (both audiovisual and filmed) and the ensuing 55 written statements as they had been added to the case file.

They found that written statements contained 2–37% of the recorded interrogations. This means that the written statements are a very compact summary of what was said during the interrogation: even though the main questions posed during interrogations are generally discernible (in 63% of cases), only 25% of follow-up questions are recorded in the written statements. Other relevant interactions (remarks, statements, conversation between police officers, emotions) are recorded in only 25% of cases. Pressure on the suspect is hardly ever written down. Confrontations with incriminating material are also often omitted. Suspects' statements are often altered in the sense that the spoken words are transformed to written language; this makes the suspect appear more certain of his or her case than s/he is. Non-verbal expressions (such as 'coughs', 'swallows' or 'looks away') are less often included in the written statement; when they are, this is generally perceived as incriminating the defendant.

The use of existing video or audio material has methodological advantages over collection 'in the wild'. Much more than when data have been built from memos or field jottings, it is now possible to investigate the reliability of the data. As we described earlier, different raters can (independently) rate the same material, after which it can be assessed whether they arrived at the same coding. If the codings are virtually the same, we say that there is good *interrater reliability* (see also section 2.6.1 and section 4.6).

4.6 Data collection from documents

4.6.1 Coding schemes

Much of what was said for the design of questionnaires and questions also applies if we want to extract information not from human beings but from 'documents': files, radio programmes, newspaper clippings, registrations held by courts, and the like.

This material is often *raw*, meaning that it has to be transformed into analysable material. If a researcher has chosen to quantify the material, then a scoring list is often used – essentially the equivalent of a questionnaire except that it is administered not to a person but to a document in the broadest sense. The list contains not questions but variables, meaning that the scoring list basically has very brief indications of the variables such as 'IQ' or 'Number of children'. Again, the same options of open-ended and closed-ended entries exist. Scoring lists are generally a mixture of open-ended and closed-ended entries. For instance, when analysing court files, a large number of variables will be very short indications of the property that needs to be scored, like 'Does the defendant have a criminal record' or 'Did parties attempt mediation beforehand?'. But the scoring list may also have an open-ended entry that asks the scorer to describe briefly the nature of the claim, the facts that are uncontested between parties, and other more qualitative information that is less easily captured in variables, in an open space of about half a page.

The 'patient' raw data material has the pleasant property that it is possible to perform the data collection operation several times, checking whether different scorers or raters generate the same data. To do so – and this is often done at the beginning of the data collection phase – two or more raters are handed the same material, and they are asked to fill out the data collection forms. After scoring these independently, the scoring results are compared. If they are exactly the same, we say that there is perfect *interrater reliability* (see also section 2.6). Often that is not entirely so, and we then first inspect where differences emerged and discuss whether these can be prevented by a stricter, more precise *scoring protocol*. Next, a new test round of scoring is held, where again scores are compared between raters.

We may express the extent to which raters agree in various measures, such as the percentage agreement, or the correlation coefficient, Cohen's kappa or, where there are more than two raters, the intraclass correlation coefficient (ICC). As a rough indication, a percentage agreement of 80% and over is generally considered good, below 67–60% as not good enough. Measures such as the kappa-coefficient are stricter as they correct for the fact that if we filled in random data on the data collection forms, we would also by chance get some agreement (see also section 2.6.1). The scoring protocol is for that matter an integral part of the data collection instrument.

Augusteijn (2022) analysed the court rulings of all cases of sexual abuse published on the Netherlands Council for the Judiciary website `rechtspraak.nl` from 1 January to 1 October 2021 in which a victim had claimed immaterial damages. A total of 250 rulings were scored by herself and a number of assistants. Interrater reliability was nearly perfect, as all variables were very factual with little room for interpretation or ambiguity. Augusteijn used a scoring instrument that had closed-ended and a few open-ended entries. One of its pages (with fictitious data) is given in Figure 4.4.

Figure 4.4: Scoring list for court rulings file

Case number	ECLI:NL:RBAMS:2022:9999
Short description of the criminal case	Defendant has sexually abused his nephew for a period of 5 months
Amount of claimed compensation (numeric)	€10,000.-
Standpoint of defense on the claim	X Reject 0 Partially award 0 Fully award
Standpoint of prosecution on the claim	0 Reject X Partially award 0 Fully award
Type of sexual crime	0 Rape X Assault
Pervasiveness of the criminal act	0 Attempted rape 0 Touching 0 Kissing 0 Sexual acts by hand X Sexual acts performed orally 0 Vaginal penetration 0 Anal penetration
Age victim	0 <12 X 12-15 0 16-17 0 >18
Vulnerable victim	0 Yes X No
Unconscious victim	0 Yes X No
Care or dependency relationship	X Yes 0 No
Abuse of authority or trust	X Yes 0 No
Repeat victimization by same offender	X Yes 0 No
Multiple offenders	0 Yes X No
Violent acts	0 Yes X No
Particularly harmful consequences	X Yes 0 No
Particularly threatening or humiliating	0 Yes X No
Sex of the victim	X Male 0 Female
Known offender	X Yes 0 No
Previous consensual sexual relationship	0 Yes X No
Drug or alcohol use victim	0 Yes X No
Resistance	0 No resistance X Freeze 0 Resistance
Sex worker	0 Yes X No
District criminal court	X Amsterdam (FI) 0 Den Haag (FI) 0 Gelderland (FI) 0 Limburg (FI) 0 Midden-Nederland (FI) 0 Noord-Holland (FI) 0 Noord-Nederland (FI) 0 Oost-Brabant (FI) 0 Overijssel (FI) 0 Rotterdam (FI) 0 Zeeland-West-Brabant (FI) 0 Amsterdam (A) 0 Den Haag (A) 0 's-Hertogenbosch (A) 0 Arnhem-Leeuwarden (A)
Awarded compensation (numerical)	€ 7,500.-
Argumentation decision on claim by court	In view of the foregoing, the Court is of the opinion that the claimed non-material damage is partially admissible. All things considered, the court considers the claim to be equitable up to an amount of € 7,500.- and will therefore allocate this amount.

Croes & Van Os (2012) investigated changes in the costs of legal procedures for private citizens in the Netherlands. One of the questions they were interested in was whether Dutch citizens had seen their costs increase over the past years. In the Netherlands, about 40% of citizens are eligible for government-funded legal aid. Citizens are

Figure 4.5: Percentage of cases with contribution required for subsidized legal aid

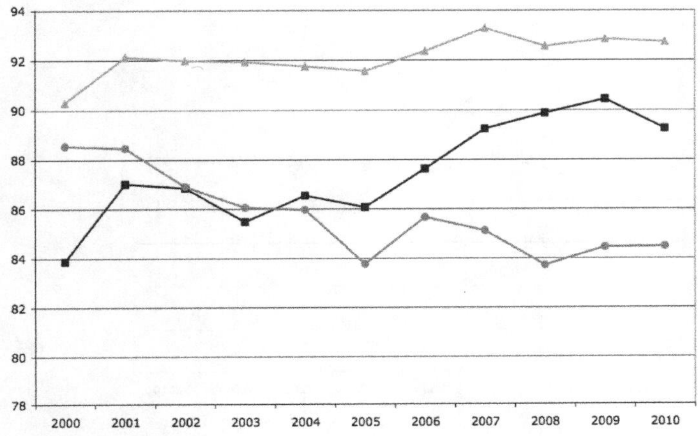

Source: Croes & Van Os (2012) (triangles: commercial law; circles: family law; squares: admin. law)

however in general required to contribute to such costs, according to a fixed tariff based on their income and wealth; those below a certain threshold do not need to contribute.

In their study, Croes and Van Os first showed, using existing registrations from the Netherlands Council for the Judiciary, that the percentage of cases in which such a contribution was required changed over the years. As Figure 4.5 shows, the percentage grew for disputes within the domain of commercial law, increased most for disputes within administrative law, but decreased for family law disputes. The figure also shows that in a very large percentage of cases (the lowest being 85% for family law, the highest 93% for commercial law) such a contribution is required.

Next, using data from the Netherlands Council for the Judiciary and Statistics Netherlands, they calculated how high this contribution was on average over the investigated years. Figure 4.6 gives the average amounts, not corrected for inflation. The figure shows how the trends for commercial, family and administrative law are quite similar: the average amounts grew until 2005, after which they all decreased again. The authors do not discuss why that decrease occurred so markedly similarly. One reason may be that, as the authors also report, the Dutch government from 2005 subsidized mediation for those qualifying for legal aid subsidies, to a much lower tariff however (51 euros for the first four sessions, and an additional 51 euros for a larger number of sessions for those above a certain income), as a cheaper alternative to dispute settlement via the courts – but additional study would be needed to verify this. The figure also shows how average contributions are always highest for commercial law and lowest for family law.

The authors write that, in addition to being entitled to government-sponsored legal

Figure 4.6: Nominal contribution paid for government-subsidized legal aid

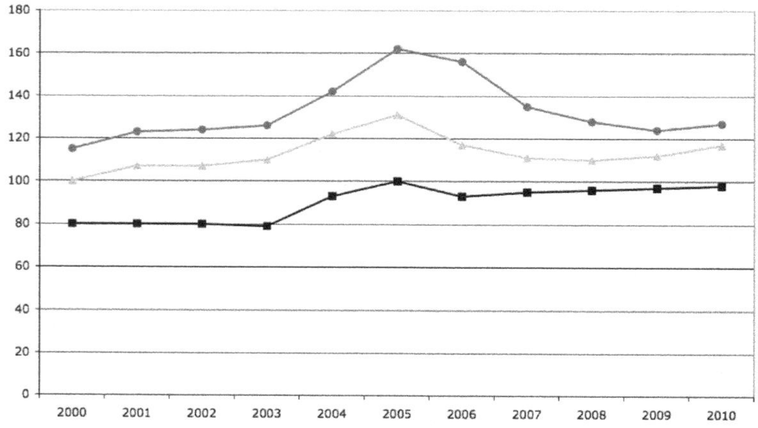

Source: Croes & Van Os (2012); (triangles: commercial law; circles: family law; squares: admin. law)

aid, many citizens have taken out insurance against legal costs. They report that 42% of families have such insurance. All in all, only 27% of Dutch citizens have to pay the full costs of legal procedures, either because their income is too high to qualify for government subsidies in legal aid, or because they are uninsured against legal costs.

4.7 Relative strengths and weaknesses

In general, the more open and qualitative a data collection procedure is, the higher we may expect the validity of the data to be, and the deeper our understanding of the phenomenon under study. Unstructured and topical interviews, as well as ethnographic and participatory methods, give respondents the chance to venture all that is relevant in their eyes, as well as topics the researchers had not thought about and could thus never have been provided as a question or an answering option in a questionnaire. Participant observation and ethnography enable you as a researcher to see the world, as it were, through the eyes of your research subjects, and to understand from within why they act the way they act, to contextualize their behaviour and to infer the meaning of their surroundings to their lives. Participant observation – the observational parallel of the unstructured interview one could argue – gives a deeper understanding of the phenomena under study than observation, as it were, from the outside.

Structured interviews with closed-ended questions on the other hand, such as web-based apps, reduce the answering options of respondents, which makes the researcher's life easier and reduces costs and effort. They tend to make for greater reliability. The 'harnessed' nature of the data collection method however also means that respondents cannot respond how they would really like to respond – and thus validity may suffer.

As said, the more 'open' and qualitative data collection methods can be very strong on validity, but it may be harder to achieve reliability. A study by Lindegaard et al. (2016) shows however that this need not always be the case: as these authors describe, they coded and independently re-coded a large number of CCTV fragments that they had used to analyse public confrontations and bystander behaviour, showing how the reliability of their codings was well above commonly used thresholds. The coders had all used the same previously developed coding scheme (using therefore an 'etic' coding method, see chapter 7), with pre-set categories, which likely had strongly enhanced reliability. Of course, they were able to do this as they had 'patient', archival material, which they could observe and re-observe as often as they liked. In the case of ethnographic fieldwork, where one single researcher is immersed in the research setting, observing and talking and making notes and memos now and then, such independent re-coding would be practically impossible.

Open interviews and participant observation make high demands on the skills of fieldworkers. They must have excellent social and verbal skills, be malleable, flexible, adaptable to unexpected situations. They must be able to let different kinds of people speak about sometimes touchy subjects, express feelings and probe areas these people themselves perhaps had not ventured yet – and do so in such a way that it is not an unpleasant experience for the interviewee. They must be able to interpret what respondents voice, to elicit meaning from respondents' words. Such interviews take high-quality skills, and therefore extensive training. Researchers must also be able to compile field notes or memos that enable complex qualitative analysis later on. Not everyone can be taught the trade.

Because qualitative data collections are almost always more costly, in general smaller samples are investigated. Qualitative data collection puts high demands on interviewer skills. The more quantitative data collection methods are generally cheaper, and generate data with higher reliability. Preliminary research and good piloting is necessary to achieve good validity here too, as once the study has gone ahead there is no possibility to modify instruments. Larger samples can generally be studied, and when samples have been adequately drawn, generalizable statements can be made. The choice for one for the other method generally depends heavily on the research question, and the research setting and resources.

Chapter questions

1. List the continuum of interview modes with their respective advantages and disadvantages (section 4.2)

2. What is social desirability bias, what quality parameter does it threaten and how is it best prevented? (section 4.2)

3. Give three approaches to prevent response styles occurring (section 4.3)

4. List the differences between observation and participant observation, and their relative (dis)advantages for gathering reliable and valid data (section 4.5)

Chapter 5

Measurement design

5.1 Introduction

In the literature, a research plan or research design is generally described as the plan that details the steps that must be taken to be able to answer the research questions. A research plan is therefore a kind of 'road map', a protocol that describes the various steps to be set for conducting the research. The plan cannot foresee what the findings will be, but it can outline that a pilot study (see section 2.5) should be conducted and that based on its findings, the questionnaire and strategy to approach the sample members may be adapted. It will also specify whether it is necessary to have the plan itself reviewed by an *ethics committee* (see section 2.8) and will reserve time for approval by that committee. A research plan outlines what sample shall be drawn, what data collection strategy or instruments employed, what 'design' will be used (for instance, whether a control group will be studied, whether ethnographic data collection methods will be employed, whether respondents are to be studied repeatedly, etc.). A research plan generally also outlines the analysis methods: even though the data have not been collected yet, because of the research plan we will know what the data structure will be (we know the approximate sample size, we know the types of variables, we know whether respondents were interviewed repeatedly or not). This means that the research plan can – and should – also contain an analysis plan. Finally, it should contain a outline over the months that the study will run, showing the various activities (such as 'getting IRB approval', 'drawing sample', 'interviews', 'analysis', etc.) and a budget.

The part of research design that this chapter will be dealing with is the 'design'-part of the research plan, the research design 'in a narrow sense'. This part of research design is also often referred to as the 'measurement design', which is how we will in this book from now on refer to it, to distinguish it from the research design in a broader sense. The measurement design lays out the structure within which measurements are going to be evaluated. This will likely sound pretty vague, so let us give a few examples.

Suppose we want to find out whether the number of prosecuted cases of rape has increased since a law change in the Netherlands in 1991. In that year, the criminalized behaviour in the legal definition of rape was broadened. The relevant sexual behaviour was extended from 'sexual intercourse outside marriage' to 'the sexual penetration of the body'. The new law thus clearly entails a much wider range of sexual acts, so it might be expected that the number of police-recorded cases of rape would go up accordingly: rape before 1991 did not legally exist within marriage, men could not be raped, and rape could be carried out only with a male sexual organ. Now, to answer our research question we take the numbers of rape cases recorded by the police before and after the law change in 1991. And it might be the case that we indeed see that the numbers increased from 1991: let us say that 3,000 cases were registered in 1990 and 3,150 in 1991. Our problem now is that while we have ascertained that an increase occurred, we do not know whether that increase occurred *because* of the law change. It could be that rape was on the rise anyway from a number of years back, and that the increase from 1990 to 1991 is not a deviation from this pre-existing trend. Or the increase could be part of natural fluctuation. Phrased differently, we observe a rise, but it is difficult to attribute the rise to the law change. Our design (where we observe before and after the law change) does not allow us to make such causal statements.

Let us discuss a second research question. Suppose we want to know whether physical maltreatment of children by their parents increases the risk that these children themselves will later become violent as well. Suppose that we have designed our study such that we investigate a group of adults who were maltreated when they were children, and a group of adults who were not maltreated as children. Now we have what is called a *comparison group* (the non-maltreated). Having a comparison group is a powerful feature of this design. It enables us to see whether we find more violence in the group of adults who were maltreated as children than in the group who were not exposed to such maltreatment. (Note that this is a measurement design we could not possibly have chosen for the first example: the law change took place for the entire Netherlands, and there is therefore no comparison group.)

Suppose now, for the child physical maltreatment example, that we find that the adults who were maltreated as children are indeed more violent: they have for instance been more often convicted for violent offences (leaving aside whether this is a valid measure of violent behaviour). Do we now know they are more violent *because* they were physically abused as children? Even though we have a comparison group that was not abused and our evidence is therefore clearly stronger than in the first example, still there are alternative explanations for the finding. It may that the abused children inherited their violent temperament from their abusing parents. If that were the case, then it would not make a difference whether children were actually abused or not as the temperament is passed on from generation to generation anyway. Or it could be that the children learnt a certain behavioural repertoire from their parents, by witnessing their parents solving conflicts or venting their anger through physical violence.

Clearly, several so-called *confounding variables* or *confounders* – variables that covary with both the childhood violent victimization and the later violent temperament – also explain the association we find between having been physically abused and later violence. All in all, using this design we cannot determine whether it is experiencing physical abuse to which later violent behaviour can be attributed.

Suppose as a last example that we want to know whether an intervention reduces anti-social behaviour. Now we can build an even stronger design. We can sample a group of anti-social persons, divide them in two, and give (administer) the intervention to one group, and some other likely non-effective intervention, such as watching a soap series, to the other group. How do we compose those two groups? If we let our anti-social respondents choose which group to belong to, we are actually opening the door to confounding. An obvious confounder is namely 'motivation to change': the respondents who are eager to change their anti-social behaviour will likely choose to belong to the group that receives the intervention, and the unmotivated respondents will watch the soap series. If the group with the intervention turns out to be less anti-social after completion of the intervention, then this could be due to the intervention itself. But it could also be due to their different mindset, their higher motivation to change.

What we should do to prevent this – and this 'trick' is likely known to most readers – is let *chance* determine who ends up in which group. If we let chance determine who receives the intervention and who does not, it is not possible that there would be a third factor, a confounding variable, that could also explain the association between the intervention and anti-social behaviour. As only chance played a role in deciding who will undergo the intervention, there is simply no property that can be identified that is associated with receiving the intervention. Therefore, any difference between the group that underwent the intervention and the group that did not can only be explained by the intervention itself – and chance.

These three examples represent a spectrum along which designs can be ranked. The spectrum represents the strength with which statements can be made about causality, or the confidence with which we can attribute the outcome (the rise in rape cases, the prevalence of a violent temperament, a change in anti-social behaviour) to the factor we are studying. This spectrum is discussed in more detail below.

Many of the designs we discuss here are designs for quantitative studies, predominantly studies for assessing causality. Thus, in many of the examples we discuss we will speak about the effect of a certain factor X on an outcome Y. The designs we discuss will be assessed particularly for the strength with which they are able to make causal statements regarding the effect of X on Y. Design issues play less of a role in qualitative studies, as causal inferences are generally not aimed for in the same manner as they are in quantitative studies. In qualitative research, causal inferences are generally derived from context and meaning, and are generally less unifactorial. In quantitative research, we often conduct studies where we are interested in the effect, in isolation, of one or more factors X on one outcome variable Y. Qualitative studies would be employed where we want to unravel more complex multifactorial mechanisms, which cannot be reduced to a bare $X \rightarrow Y$ scheme, such as shown in Figure 5.1.

While we discussed the selection of research units in chapter 3, the choice of measurement instrument in chapter 4, and will discuss the choice of the measurement design in this chapter, it does not follow that decisions about the research plan are or should always be made in this order. In fact choices of sample, measurement instruments and measurement design are often made in an iterative process. This is because the possibilities for sampling influence the design choices, and the design that is desired given the research question also in a sense narrows the options for or dictates that certain instruments should be used.

Suppose, as an example, that we want to investigate whether and how mediation helps divorcing parents to conclude the divorce process swiftly and without conflict.

A quantitative design to investigate causality is then likely not called for. Practically speaking, we might be able to find data on a number of couples who enlisted the help of a mediator. We would then want to talk with the former partners to reconstruct what was discussed in various mediation sessions, how any potential conflicts were de-escalated, through what steps mediation was able to steer the process and let the divorcing partners construct their divorce settlement. We might learn how mediation only helps in certain settings, with certain partners. We might also uncover that in some divorce constellations mediation in fact produces worse outcomes than settlement through a family judge. The picture that we would be able to sketch would be complex, layered and contextualized. A quantitative design of the type that we will be discussing in this chapter would – practically speaking – never be able to produce such findings: the sample size is too small, and any effects depend on the type of conflict, whether custody of underage children is an issue, etc., something for which our quantitative designs are too simplistic.

In addition to such issues, time and money greatly constrain the types of design that can be chosen. If time and/or money are short, we may not be able to survey as many people as we would like, or we might not have the time or resources to develop and pilot a tailored data collection instrument. Also, it must be conceded, researcher preferences and skills play a role as well. Thus, the order in which design issues are decided upon could very well differ from the sequence in which they are presented here, and the outcome may be decided by practical constraints as much as methodological desiderata.

All the examples we have discussed so far describe essentially evaluations or assessments that are carried out *after* an intervention has taken place. Such evaluations are for that reason regularly referred to as *ex-post evaluations*. Naturally, for policy makers and drafters of laws, it is not attractive to wait until after the implementation of laws, measures or policies to hear whether they produced the expected outcome. It is good practice to attempt to estimate before implementation has even started what the likely effect of the interventions will be. Such as evaluation is referred to as an *ex-ante evaluation*. Obviously, it is impossible to assess the impact of an intervention before it has taken place, so such ex-ante evaluations rely heavily on earlier evaluations, literature review, and may employ with scenarios or simulations.

Suppose that the Council for the Judiciary has decided that in all so-called 'unilateral' divorce applications (in which only one partner files for divorce, which may be taken as an indication of conflict), a specially trained family judge will be appointed to prevent the case from escalating and to make for a smooth conclusion of the case. What impact would that have? Would the costs outweigh the benefits? Researchers could perform an ex-ante evaluation in various ways. They could conduct a literature study, investigating the impact of similar measures applied in different jurisdictions. They could interview staff at courts who already have some experience with the impact of special judges for such potentially conflictuous divorce cases. That staff might tell them that in the cases that they witnessed over the past X years, time until divorce settlement was cut by half. And the Council of the Judiciary might have statistics on the number of divorce cases that take an excessively long period of time to conclude. The researchers could then calculate the additional costs of employing such a highly trained judge, the saved costs because cases are decided upon much faster, and multiply the

Figure 5.1: Representation of relation between independent and dependent variable

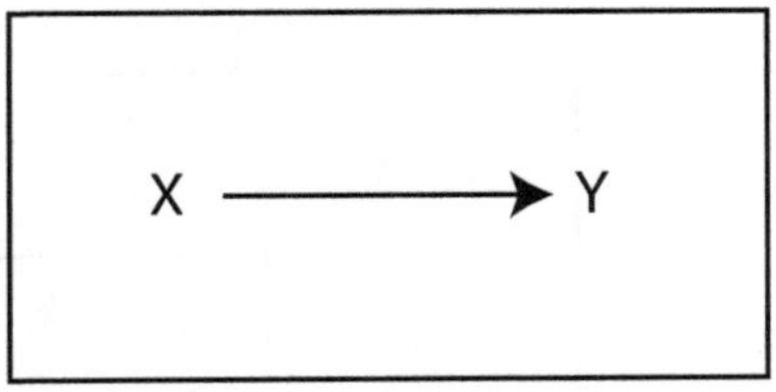

difference between the two by the number of likely cases in which these special judges' skills will be employed.

Note that such a study – while grounded in empirical observations – is still built on assumptions. It may be that once the measure is implemented, fewer conflictuous divorce cases are filed. Then, too many judges would have been trained. It might also be that more conflictuous divorce cases are filed, resulting in a shortage of trained judges. Other unexpected things might happen. It is important to realize that an ex-ante evaluation is always an estimate, an expectation. The proof of the pudding is in the eating, as the saying goes, and that saying applies very much to legal and policy interventions. The number of instances where interventions had a different impact than had been reckoned with are numerous. Sometimes this was because the ex-ante evaluation had failed to take – foreseeable – factors into account, which can be labelled as a failure to design the ex-ante evaluation properly.

5.2 Dependent and independent variables

Many of the designs we discuss in this chapter are quantitative designs for causal inference. Using the cleverest possible design, we want to make as strong as possible statements about causality. This means that in our datasets we will have variables that we think of as 'causes' and variables that are considered 'effects'. For the purposes of this book, we will defy epistemological critique and equate variables that we consider causes with the term *independent variable*. The variables that we consider effects we denote as *dependent variables*. We represent the relations between these variables as in Figure 5.1. It is a convention that dependent variables are denoted as Y. Independent variables are often written as X (which we will do too in this book). When there are several independent variables, they are denoted as $X_1, X_2, X_3 \ldots$.

Obviously, dependent variables can be influenced by more than one independent variable, and independent variables (in the sense that they influence the Y variable) can themselves be influenced by other independent variables again. See Figure 5.2, where on the right-hand side the variable Z is both a dependent (predicted by X) as well as an independent variable (predicting Y).

Figure 5.2: Representation of more complex relations between independent variables and dependent variable

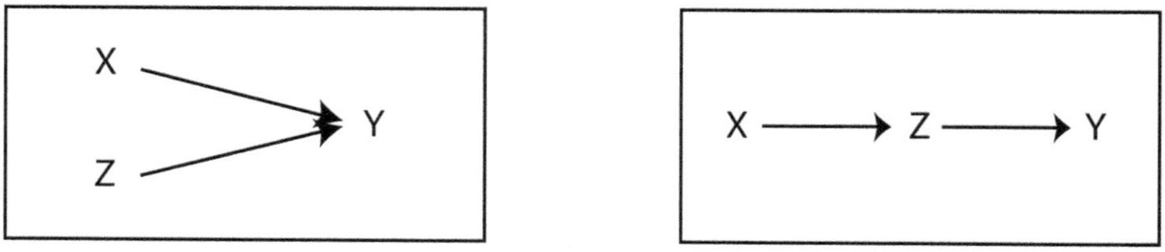

5.3 Causality

As said, in this chapter we will be discussing measurement designs, focusing specifically on the strength with which they allow us to make statements about causality. Before doing so, we will give a brief exposé of causality.

For X to be the cause of Y, three conditions must be met:

(1) *X precedes Y*

(2) *X correlates with Y*

(3) *there is no alternative explanation for the correlation between X and Y*

Obviously, condition 1 is logical, as we generally do not believe that causes occur after their effects. Condition 2 implies that we require that X and Y are empirically associated before we accept X as a cause of Y. Condition number 3 is crucial, as it requires that any empirical association cannot be explained by a third factor.

What is meant by this is the following. For instance, we may perceive that the number of firefighters at a fire is strongly associated with the ensuing damage. But do the firefighters *cause* that damage? The firefighters come before the eventual damage, the two are correlated, so the first two conditions for causality are met. However, and obviously, that damage is not caused by the firefighters, but both (firefighters and damage later on) are determined by the magnitude of the fire: when a large fire has erupted, many firefighters are dispatched and the damage will likely be large. We call this a situation of *spurious association* or spurious correlation: the number of firefighters and the damage are associated – not because they are themselves causally connected, but because they are each causally connected to the same, underlying *third factor*.

In this example, the magnitude of the fire is an alternative explanation for the association between the numbers of firefighters and the damage, a third factor, also called a *confounder* that blurs our analysis of the findings. Of course we would not be easily led to believe that firefighters damage fire scenes. But what of the association between (moderate) alcohol consumption and the risk of breaking your leg during skiing? A

Figure 5.3: Spurious association between number of firefighters and damage

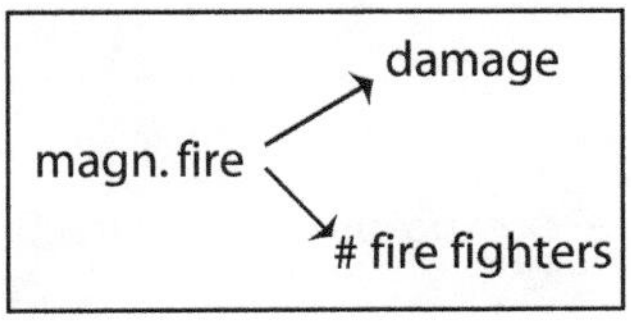

Figure 5.4: Model for the relation between alcohol consumption and risk of breaking legs

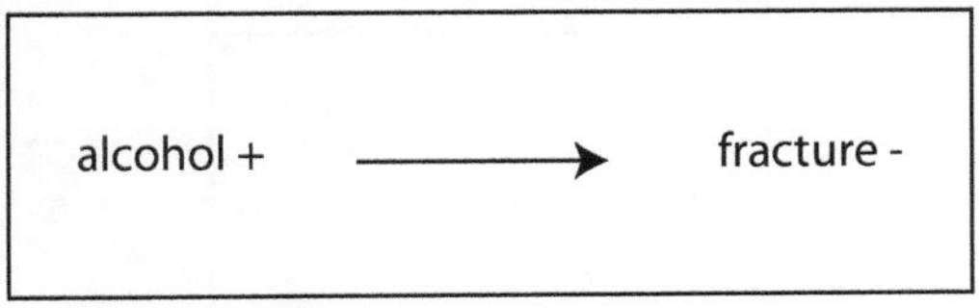

Dutch researcher a number of years ago published a study in which a clear negative association between these two variables was proven: people who drank a number of alcoholic beverages during the day, had a significantly reduced risk of fractures while skiing. The researcher said that this confirmed his theory that alcohol relaxes people's muscles, and that those who drank some while skiing would be more relaxed skiers; if they fell, they would do so in a less cramped and more supple way, thus reducing their risk of falling awkwardly and breaking something. See Figure 5.4.

After publication of the results, other researchers remarked that perhaps the association was due to the fact that people who drank more simply skied less, and thus were exposed for fewer hours per day to the risk of falling and breaking their bones. Re-analysis of the data (investigating the association between alcohol and fractures separately for those who skied 1 hour, 2 hours, 3 hours, etc. per day) proved that this was indeed the case. See Figure 5.5.

Such painful mistakes are every researcher's nightmare. Hard thinking and the exploration of all thinkable alternative scenarios that may explain the association hopefully prevent the most blatant mistakes. However, clearly we can never be sure that we have ruled out all the gazillion theoretically possible alternative explanations for the association between X and Y (condition 3). Therefore, whenever we observe an association between X and Y and even after we have ruled out all alternative explanations we could think of, still we cannot be completely sure given a correlation and the right time order that the association between X and Y is causal. Formulated differently, correlation is a necessary but not a sufficient condition for causality.

Figure 5.5: True relation between alcohol consumption and fracture risk, including exposure time

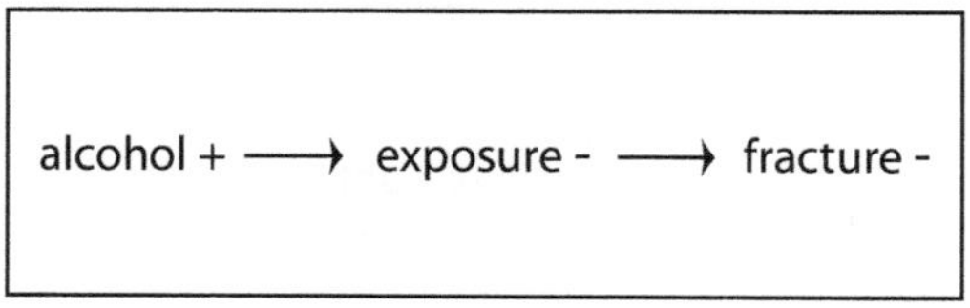

Figure 5.6: Well-being scores before and after therapy 'intervention'

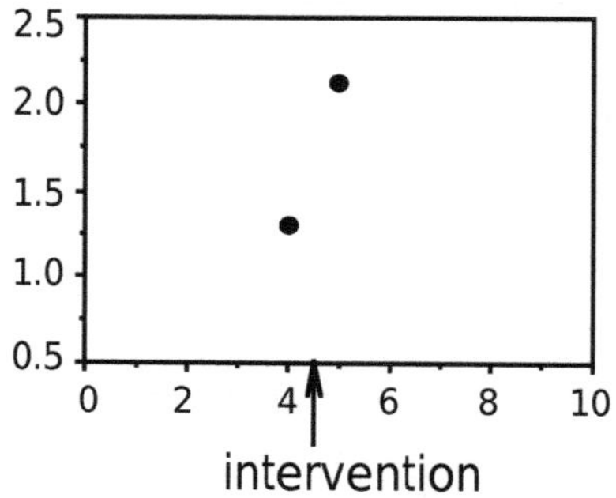

5.4 Interventions and change

Suppose that we believe that therapy increases people's well-being. We have a variable X – reflecting whether or not someone had therapy – and a variable Y – measuring well-being. If therapy works as we believe it does, then people would score lower on well-being before therapy than after. See Figure 5.6, in which we sketch a hypothetical situation where the intervention (therapy X) was administered between month 4 and 5, and where it can be seen clearly that the scores for well-being (Y) are higher after therapy than before. This is consistent with our hypothesis. We might be tempted to conclude that therapy is effective.

As argued above, we know that we cannot be sure that this improvement is *attributable* to the therapy. The increase in well-being could simply be part of a general trend: see Figure 5.7(a) where it can be seen that a steady growth in well-being set in well before therapy was administered, and that this smooth increase occurred seemingly unperturbed (perhaps there is a small additional lapse from time point 4 to 5). It could also be that the change is not more than a chance fluctuation, see Figure 5.7(b).

Figure 5.7: Development of well-being scores from month 1 to 10

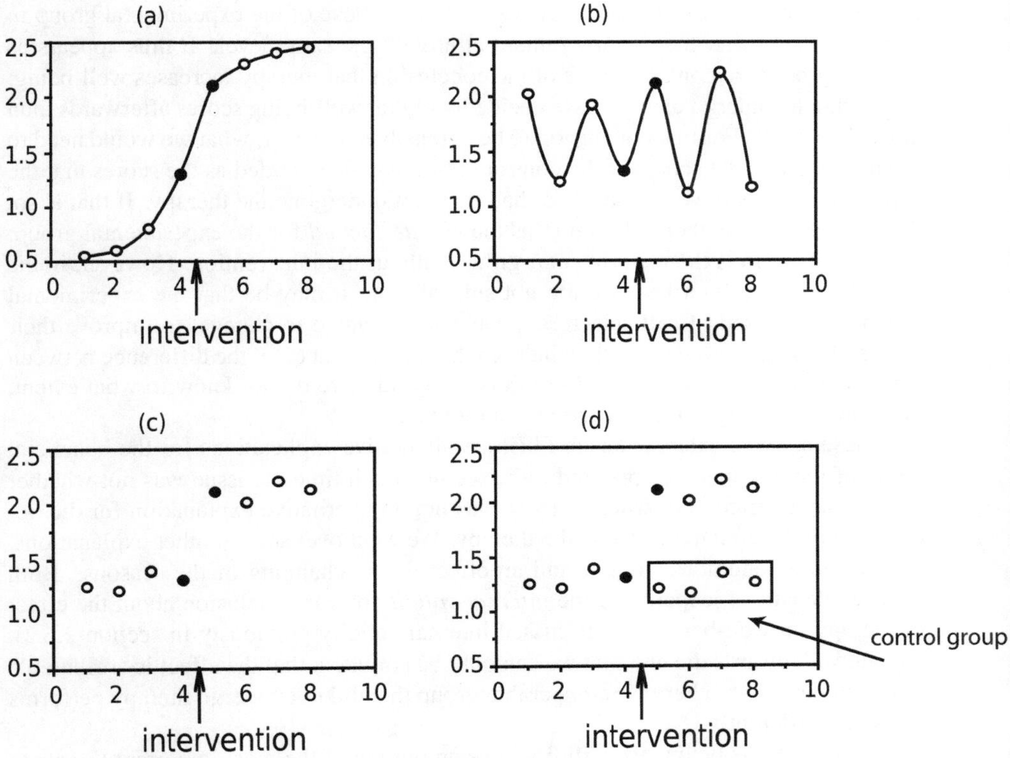

Here it can be seen that the change from month 4 to month 5 is within the bandwidth of normally occurring fluctuation; in all likelihood, if the therapy had been administered between month 5 and 6 we might even have witnessed a decrease in well-being.

The graph in Figure 5.7 appears to offer the most support for an effect of therapy X: the scores hover around 1.3 before the therapy is administered, and leap to a stable level of around 2.2 afterwards. The change cannot be explained by factors such as autonomous growth or random fluctuation.

We are however still unsure, also for the situation in Figure 5.7(c), whether the change is attributable to the therapy. Suppose that we have our data from the Netherlands and that months 1, 2, 3 and 4 were very rainy, drizzly, dreary months, and that from month 5 the weather cleared and summer set in, so everyone's well-being shot up? If we wanted to know whether the increased well-being is due to the therapy or due to other factors, ideally we would like to have comparison data from a group of people who are otherwise similar (a so-called *control group*) so that they were similarly under the influence of the weather or any other factors that impacted their well-being, and who differ from the group that received therapy (the *experimental group*) in that they did *not* get therapy, and differed from the control group *only* in that respect.

Such a situation we have sketched in Figure 5.7(d). Here we see that the control group's scores (we assume that they were equal to those of the experimental group in months 1 to 4) after the therapy remain at around the same level. It thus appears as if we may be more confident here of the conclusion that therapy increases well-being: those who do undergo therapy have decidedly higher well-being scores afterwards than those who don't. For that conclusion to be defensible, however, what we would need to be sure of is that the scores of the control group may be regarded as the scores that the experimental group would have had, had they not undergone the therapy. If that is so, the control group is then referred to as the *counterfactual* for the experimental group: the control group is the-experimental-group-without-the-intervention. However, in the situation we just described, we are not sure of that. It may be that the experimental group is composed of self-selectors, people who wanted to change, to improve their lives and who therefore elected to undergo therapy. In that case, the difference between the experimental and the control group is likely due (we do not know to what extent, but at least partially) to this difference in motivation.

These stylized examples each illustrate alternative explanations for the beneficial effect of therapy that we appeared to be seeing. Each time the issue was not whether where was an effect, but whether there was not an alternative explanation for the occurrence of the effect, other than the therapy. We went over several other explanations, such as an autonomous 'trend', and an effect of the changing of the seasons. Both these explanations jeopardized the *internal validity* of our conclusion about the effect of therapy on well-being (we discussed internal validity previously in section 2.6.2). We showed towards the end that we can only be confident that the effect is attributable to the therapy if an otherwise comparable group that did not undergo therapy performs markedly differently.

In the sections below, we will first give an outline of the most important threats to internal validity. Their discussion will be brief and summary. After that, we will rank-order designs by strength and discuss three main classes of designs, which correspond to the examples we started this chapter with. We will show that, if designs become 'stronger' in the sense that they allow for more confident statements about causality, this is because threats to validity have been ruled out.

5.4.1 Threats to internal validity

(1) *History*

Suppose I offer therapy to citizens who are afraid of armed violence. I offer my therapy to a group of 100 volunteers, all with a reasonable to serious fear of armed violence. I neatly measure their fear of armed violence before (my pre-measurement, also called *pre-test*) and after (my post-measurement, also called *post-test*) the therapy. I notice to my dismay that in the very same week in which I give my volunteers the therapy, a huge shootout occurs at a secondary school. Every citizen's fear of armed violence goes up, including that of my volunteers.

Figure 5.8: Control for threat *history* through use of control group

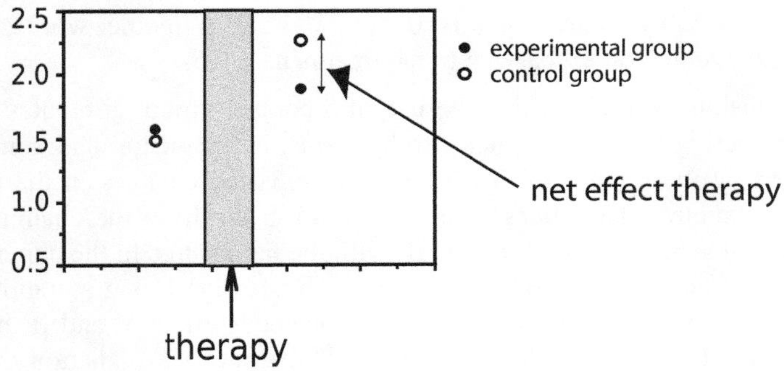

This external event – which influences the scores on the dependent variable – is often referred to as *history*.

It is defined as a threat to internal validity because it jeopardizes the conclusions that can be drawn about the effect of the intervention under investigation. As it is confounded with the intervention (it occurs around the same time and influences fear scores too), it affects the *internal validity* of the study: I may not conclude that the increase in fear scores (Y_2 - Y_1) is attributable to the intervention (X), as there is now a third factor (the shootout) that is an alternative explanation for the increase in fear levels.

Because of this external event, I now can judge no longer the effectiveness of my therapy. Maybe my volunteers' fear levels would have been much lower if that shootout had not occurred! If I only compare the pre- and post-therapy scores of my volunteers, there is however no way I can find that out. Obviously, I would have had no problem if I had included a comparison or *control group* in my study. The control group would then to have been comparable to the experimental group (the group undergoing the therapy). They should differ only in that these volunteers do not get the therapy. If we let chance decide who becomes a member of the experimental and control group, we are certain that there are no systematic differences between the two groups. Any differences between the two groups can then be attributed (and attributed *only*) to the therapy. There is then no alternative explanation – except chance – for differences between the two groups.

See Figure 5.8, in which the solid dots represent the scores for the treated (experimental) group and the open dots those for the control group. The figure shows that the two groups are approximately equal at pre-test and that indeed the scores for the experimental group went up, from about 1.5 to about 1.75. The scores in the control group went up much more, however, from about 1.5 to about 2.25.

Given that – if we have designed our study well and assigned respondents randomly to groups – the control group equals the experimental group without the treatment, i.e. the control group behaves how the experimental group would have behaved had they not received the intervention, we may conclude that the gain in fear generated by the treatment is -0.5 (1.75 − 2.25). In other words, we may state that the reduction in fear due to the treatment is 0.5.

The conclusion we draw is that the use of a control group eliminates the risk of history acting as a confounder. Both groups, experimental and control, are influenced by the same historical events. Comparing changes in the two, we can simply subtract any changes in the control group from the changes in the experimental group, and we will be left with the net change in the experimental group, net of any perturbances we are not interested in. Using a control group therefore means that we may – if cause X precedes effect Y and if there is a correlation between X and Y – state that no alternative explanation exists for the association between X and Y and that therefore X causes Y. The use of a(n equivalent) control group is one of the most powerful aspects of experimental designs. It means that experimental designs are strong on *internal validity*.

(2) *Maturation*

The threat we sketched previously in Figure 5.7(a) is referred to in the literature as *maturation*. Here it is not the intervention but an autonomous trend that generates the change from pre- to post-test. An often-used example is that of maths training. If I were to offer a new kind of maths training to school pupils, I would likely find that their maths skills go up from pre-test to post-test. This may be due to the maths training. But it may also be due to the fact that students mature over the course of a school year. Part of the effect may be due to the training, part may be due to that ripening or maturation.

Only by working with a control group can I determine what part of the improvement is due to the training, and what part of the improvement would have occurred anyway. Using a control group I can determine the change that the experimental group would have shown had it not received the new maths training:

$$\text{change}_{\text{control group}} = \text{autonomous trend}$$

The change in the experimental group is now due to that autonomous trend plus the effect of the maths training:

$$\text{change}_{\text{experimental group}} = \text{autonomous trend} + \text{effect maths training}$$

Comparing the two changes (for each group the difference between post-test and pre-test) gives:

$$\text{change}_{\text{experimental group}} - \text{change}_{\text{control group}} =$$

(autonomous trend + effect maths training) – autonomous trend =

effect maths training

We can write this more generically as follows. If E_1 is the average score at pre-test in the experimental group, and E_2 the average score at post-test, and if C_1 is the average score at pre-test in the control group, and C_2 the average score at post-test, then we can write the design for this study schematically as:

$$\begin{array}{lcl} E_1 & \ldots\ X\ \ldots & E_2 \\ C_1 & \ldots\ldots\ldots\ldots & C_2 \end{array}$$

with X the intervention. This design is officially referred to as the *untreated control group design with pre-test and post-test* or as the *randomized controlled trial* or RCT, and in other literatures often as 'classical experiment'. Given that the change in the control group ($C_2 - C_1$) represents the change in the experimental group had the intervention not been administered, the change in the experimental group ($E_2 - E_1$) minus the change in the control group is the net effect of the intervention:

$$\text{net effect X} = (E_2 - E_1) - (C_2 - C_1)$$

Had we not used a control group, we would have been able to see only the gross effect of the intervention $E_2 - E_1$, being the combination of the effects of the maturation and the maths training, without being able to separate the two.

(3) *Testing*

It is known from the literature that administering tests or questionnaires by itself changes people's ideas, skills, and thus possible scores on the next administration of that same questionnaire. A relative of the author once had to be operated, and was asked, before receiving the anaesthetic, to fill in a small test. After waking up she filled in the same test. To the surprise of the researcher, she had better scores – a few hours after the anaesthetic – than before. She, being a well-trained social scientist explained to him that this was due to *testing*, the phenomenon that people's scores are affected by the completion of tests: she simply learned from filling out the test the first time.

As the attentive reader will have gathered, this threat to validity is also effectively countered by using a randomized control group. If testing affects the scores, then it will do so equally in the control and experimental group and we can again find the net effect of the intervention by comparing the changes in the control and experimental group.

(4) *Instrumentation*

By *instrumentation* is meant that apparent changes from pre- to post-test may actually be generated by changes in the measurement instrument. Thus, one observes a change in respondents' scores from pre-test to post-test, but the different scores are not due to people changing, but due to the instrument changing from pre-test to post-test. If one could, one would likely always keep one's instrument identical across multiple waves of the same study, across respondents, etc. But sometimes this is not possible: political parties have changed from one wave to the next, the meaning of religion and church attendance has changed from 1950 to the present, and the like. Again, this threat of instrumentation is countered by using a control group. If instrumentation affects the scores, then it will do so equally in the control and experimental group and comparing the changes between the control and experimental group will again give us the net effect.

The first four threats that we discussed are therefore all effectively countered if we use a control group. In each instance, the 'distortion' occurs in both the control and experimental group and any threat is simply subtracted by computing the net effect $(E_2 - E_1) - (C_2 - C_1)$. It may be that several threats occur simultaneously, or that other disturbances also affect the data – but all of that does not bother us, as the design is such that we will always be able to distil the net effect of the intervention:

$$\text{change}_{\text{experimental group}} - \text{change}_{\text{control group}} =$$

$$(\text{history} + \text{maturation} + \text{testing} + \text{instru.} + \text{any other} + \text{effect intervention}) -$$

$$(\text{history} + \text{maturation} + \text{testing} + \text{instru.} + \text{any other}) =$$

$$\text{effect intervention}$$

For the threats to internal validity we subsequently discuss, the use of a control group as such is not always sufficient. These threats either bear on other issues that may affect the usefulness of a control group, the choice and retention of group members, or they deal with more practical issues, such as whether control and experimental group members know of each other's existence.

(5) *Selection*

We say that *selection* is a threat to internal validity when the experimental and control group have not been put together randomly. Whenever that is the case, we cannot rule out that a third factor (the factor that influenced who became a member of which group) can also (partly) explain the difference between the experimental and control group.

Selection definitely occurs if one lets sample members decide themselves whether they want to be a member of one group or the other. It may also occur if we work for instance with existing school classes. Even though it is hard to envisage how exactly conclusions would be affected, knowing that there are other systematic differences between the groups (for instance, different teachers) is sufficient to be aware that internal validity is compromised.

If the control and experimental groups have not been formed by a random process, it may happen that one or more of the threats discussed above occurs in one group but not in the other. If my fear of armed violence experimental group is based in Alkmaar, and my fear of armed violence control group in Alphen aan den Rijn, where a massive shooting incident took place in a shopping mall in 2011 just when I was offering my therapy, it is likely that this history type of effect plays a larger role in the control group than in the experimental one. This might then even make us overestimate the effect of the therapy to combat fear of armed violence.

(6) *Attrition*

As we discussed in section 3.6, attrition is generally non-random: those who drop out of a study generally have different characteristics than those who remain. In the context of experimental design, attrition or drop-out (also called *experimental mortality*) may cause groups to become incomparable, as attrition may differ from one group to the other. This means that if we start out with two comparable groups, control and experimental, beautifully formed by chance, attrition will generally cause these groups to become non-random. Attrition is reported to occur more easily in the control group as respondents are aware that they have not been included in the group that receives the experimental intervention. Then, the same problems as outlined just above under 'Selection' emerge.

(7) *Insufficient separation between groups*

Suppose that we are conducting a study within a large firm. We are trying to train employees to work more efficiently. Now, we try to evaluate the training according to the state of the experimental art – that is, we have formed an experimental and control group from employees within one and the same firm. However, having trained the experimental respondents, there is a risk that the training in a sense 'seeps through' to the control respondents: they meet each other afterwards at the coffee machine, in the elevator, over lunch. Control employees might even witness the experimental employees employ all these handy tricks, and decide that they want to become as efficient.

We call this situation one of *insufficient separation between groups*. Because the intervention also reaches the control group, leaks to the control group members, we are likely to underestimate its effect.

A solution is hard to find in this case. Forming a control group out of employees from, say, a different branch will make the control and experimental group less comparable, and thus generate other problems.

(8) *Perceived differences between groups*

Continuing from the example we just discussed, it might also occur that a certain envy is generated by this design. Suppose that the experimental respondents are trained in a nice location and share fancy lunches together, while the control group respondents have to plod on in the same old dreary office. Examples have been reported where the control respondents gave up doing their job decently altogether (resulting in the effect of the training being overestimated), as well as the opposite where the control respondents work so hard to show off that it would have to be concluded that the training was useless (thus meaning that its effect is underestimated).

(9) *Regression towards the mean*

To give an example of the last threat that we discuss, suppose we want to investigate the effect of, again, a maths training. We have a group of children who have had consistently low scores on maths tests, and these form our experimental group. Of course, we know we must have a control group as well, so we administer a maths test to all other children in the school, and we take the children scoring lowest on that test as our control group. Regression to the mean is now likely to occur. But what do we mean by that? It is best understood as follows.

It is likely that in our lowest scorers who formed the control group, a few scored low on the test just because of some quirk, they had an off-day, a headache, they were madly in love. They were not consistently low scorers, otherwise they would have been members of the experimental group.

Now if we compute the scores of this group on the post-test, it is likely that some of those accidentally low scorers will at post-test no longer have their off-day or their headache or bout of love-sickness. They will score higher at C_2 than at C_1. Their scores have regressed ('gone back') to the group mean. This means that we – in this example – will underestimate the effect of the maths training.

Regression towards the mean regularly occurs, also outside the context of experiments. It was first described by Francis Galton, half-cousin of Charles Darwin, an extremely broad scientist and an avid traveller to some of the remotest corners of Africa.

5.5 Types of (experimental) designs

Other types of measurement designs than the ones we discussed are possible too. For example, we may interview a sample of respondents once, and ask them for their opinion about a number of topics. Such a design does not allow for causal statements. The designs we discussed so far all have in common that they are structured such that we can make statements about the causal effect of an independent variable on a dependent variable. We have a pre-test and a post-test, which means that we measure at least twice, and always have a comparison to gauge our results. Whenever we want to make causal statements about the effectiveness of an intervention, an experimental design is needed.

Experimental designs vary – as elaborated above – by the strength with which they allow to make causal statements. We saw that designs without a control group are vulnerable to threats of internal validity. Including a control group is already a huge improvement. The strongest designs are, however, those that have randomly formed experimental and control groups. In that case, it can be excluded that any systematic difference between the groups can explain differences between the groups: as the groups were formed randomly, there are no systematic differences – except the intervention. A difference in scores can therefore be tied to the intervention, and to the intervention only.

In criminology, the so-called *Maryland Scientific Methods Scale* or MSMS (Sherman et al., 1998) is often used as a reference to gauge the strength of particular designs.

It has five levels. The levels can be summarized as follows:

(1) At this level a correlation has been established between an intervention and a dependent variable at a single point in time.

(2) A temporal sequence between the intervention and the outcome has been observed, or there is a comparison group without demonstrated comparability to the treatment group.

(3) A comparison between two or more comparable units of analysis, one with and one without the intervention.

(4) Comparison between multiple units with and without the intervention, controlling for other factors, or using comparison units that evidence only minor differences.

(5) Random assignment and analysis of comparable units to intervention and comparison groups.

While the first level is fairly vaguely described, level 2 describes a design where a control group is present, albeit an incomparable one. Sherman et al. (1998) use as a rule of thumb that designs below level 3 are unfit for evaluation research. Any design that does not meet the criteria of level 3 or higher should therefore be disregarded for causal inference. Level 3 describes a situation where a reasonably comparable control group is present. Level 4 describes the situation where the experimental and control groups differ only slightly. At level 5, we have a truly randomized design, an RCT. This means that the Maryland Scientific Methods Scale rejects for causal conclusions all studies without a well-comparable control group.

In a completely randomized design, the researcher exerts control over all aspects of measurement: s/he assigns respondents to groups, (often although not always) administers the intervention, and conducts the measurements. Designs with non-randomized control groups (levels 2, 3 and 4) are in the literature referred to as *quasi-experimental designs*. In a quasi-experimental setting, there is less control: while the researcher may still administer the intervention and conduct the measurements, s/he works with existing groups, such as classrooms or companies.

Both the experimental and quasi-experimental designs look schematically as follows:

$$
\begin{array}{lcl}
E_1 & \ldots\ X\ \ldots & E_2 \\
C_1 & \ldots\ldots\ldots\ldots & C_2
\end{array}
$$

but differ in the nature of the control group (randomized or not). The MSMS disaggregates quasi-experimental designs into those with very well comparable control and experimental groups (level 4), those with comparable control and experimental groups (level 3), and last those with actually quite incomparable control groups (level 2).

Other types of designs than the randomized controlled trial are possible. The following is called the one-group pre-test-post-test design:

$$E_1 \ \ldots\ X\ \ldots\ E_2$$

This is the design that we depicted in Figure 5.6. It is as we showed a weak design. A better design is the so-called *time series design* that we depicted in Figure 5.7(a), as with this design we will be able to detect maturation, as well as testing and instrumentation. It does not control for history occurring simultaneously with the intervention:

$$E_1 \quad E_2 \quad E_3 \quad \ldots \quad X \quad \ldots \quad E_4 \quad E_5 \quad E_6$$

If the intervention in such an 'experimental-group-only study' is not administered by the researcher, the study is denoted as an *observational* or *passive observational study*: the researcher does not administer the intervention and does not assign respondents to groups; all s/he can do is observe the data.

Luckily, some intermediate solutions are possible that improve upon the situation of having only observational data. One such possibility is to seek, for every member of the 'experimental group', one or more observational units that are seemingly identical to the experimental group unit – but for the 'intervention'. For instance, if we were studying complicated divorce settlements, we might want to investigate whether mediation helps to conclude cases more swiftly than normal. Obviously, we are unable to randomly assign cases to mediation or not, as this is something that is up to the parties to decide. Some former couples have decided that they may seek mediation, while others have not, and we can only observe this happening. We can, however, for each couple that used mediation, try to find a similar ('matching') couple – in terms of relevant dispute and divorce characteristics – that did not use mediation. If the mediated and non-mediated are similar with regard to a host of pertinent characteristics (financial claims, presence and age of children, employment of spouses, other relevant circumstances of the case), we could compare differences between the similar cases settled with and without mediation, and see whether the mediated cases were indeed concluded faster. Such a design is called a *case-control design*. The procedure that we apply to arrive at such a design is called 'matching'.

Matching is very broadly used when it is impossible to randomize the intervention we want to assess the effect of. It definitely improves upon the strength of our conclusions, but does not eliminate confounding. For instance, if we were able to match perfectly on a certain number of background variables, we would be sure that the experimental and control group are identical on those variables, and that any differences between the two are therefore not attributable to these factors anymore. However, we are still unsure whether there are not other, unmeasured ('covert') factors that we have been unable to match on, that are confounded with the 'intervention' we are studying. This is a first disadvantage of matching. Second, it should be noted that matching does not by itself eliminate confounding on the matching factors (for more on this, see Pearce, 2016). A last and more practical disadvantage of matching is that if we want to match on a large number of characteristics (which we would always want to do because then we eliminate the risk that these factors blur our conclusion on the relation between the intervention and the independent variables), it may quickly become impossible to do so. It may simply be impossible to find a matching case that is identical as to type of conflict, age of partners, presence and age of children, socio-economic status of parties, and so forth. Innovative methods such as propensity score matching (see Bijleveld et al., 2015) provide tools to deal with this, but even so matching remains a second-best solution that one resorts to only when one has no other option. This is unfortunately often the case, including in empirical legal research.

5.6 Longitudinal and cross-sectional designs

Whenever measurement units are observed repeatedly, we call the study *longitudinal* to denote that it stretches over time and, crucially, is designed to measure change. Longitudinal studies are often contrasted with cross-sectional studies, where measurements are made at one point in time, and the aim is not to observe or explain change.

Longitudinal designs can be classified into prospective and retrospective designs. Of the two, the prospective design is by far the strongest one. We will illustrate this with an example. Suppose that we study a sample of male child sex abusers. And suppose that we note that almost all of these sex offenders were themselves sexually abused as a child. We might then be tempted to hypothesize that child sexual abuse is a risk factor for sex offending against children. This statement is however based on *retrospective* data: because of our design, we only observe those who became a sex offender, but not those who were abused but did not become a sex offender. If we want to be sure that sexual abuse victimization is a risk factor in the aetiology of sex offending, we would have to investigate a sample of sexually abused children (as well as, preferably a sample of not sexually abused children), following them into adulthood. This is what is referred to as a *prospective* study, prospective because measurements are not obtained looking back, but looking 'forward', so to speak. The big advantage of this prospective design is that we will also be able to see the negatives: the number of children who have been abused who do not become sex offenders.

While prospective studies are methodologically much stronger than retrospective studies, they are – not surprisingly – much more costly and may take a very long time to complete. Prospective research is much more expensive as it takes so long: it is extremely costly in terms of database maintenance, follow up of sample members, and staff costs. It often takes too long for policy purposes too.

5.7 Vignette studies

A special type of RCT is the so-called *vignette study*. In a vignette study hypothetical cases (or 'vignettes') are offered to respondents. The properties of these cases have been altered purposely from case to case, with the relevant properties thus, as it is called, manipulated.

De Keijser & van Koppen (2004) used such a vignette study. They investigated whether in the sentences that judges mete out in the Netherlands these judges show evidence of so-called 'compensatory punishment'. The authors report that many lawyers are convinced that judges tend to give more lenient punishment in cases where proof is not very strong: the idea is that judges 'compensate' for the fact that the evidence is not overwhelming by giving shorter sentences. It would be very hard to investigate this assertion in real court cases as so many factors play a role in judicial decision making that could act as confounders. The authors therefore constructed three types of court

Table 5.1: Results of experiment on compensatory punishment

crime	proof	sentence in months	t-value
serious assault	strong proof	28.7	1.85 (ns)
	weaker proof	32.9	
burglary	strong proof	5.4	0.66 (ns)
	weaker proof	5.7	
simple assault	strong proof	3.1	1.40 (ns)
	weaker proof	2.7	

ns = not significant

cases, a simple assault, a serious assault and a burglary case. They changed the cases such, that for each type of offence there was a description where the proof was sufficient (otherwise judges would acquit) but not overwhelming, and one case where proof was very strong. In this manner, the authors *isolated* the factor they were interested in: strength of proof. Each time the case description was identical, the only aspect that varied was how strong the proof was. Changes in sentence length could therefore be attributed only to strength of proof.

In total 36% of judges that were asked to participate consented. Each judge was randomly given one case with strong evidence and one case (with another offence, otherwise judges would understand what the authors were after) with weaker evidence. The results of their study (with the properties of the fictional cases and average sentence length in months) are in Table 5.1.

The authors concluded that their experiment did not show any evidence of compensatory punishment. They also note, however, that the cases they presented judges with are 'artificial' cases and lack the depth and complexity of real court files (De Keijser & van Koppen, 2004). They therefore do not want to rule out that in reality compensatory punishment occurs (see also section 5.8 below). With these reservations, the authors concede that while the internal validity of their vignette study is high, external validity may be less.

5.8 Pros and cons of various designs

The experimental designs we discussed above, particularly the completely randomized design or RCT, are in a sense the gold standard of all evaluation research. We reiterate – possibly to the boredom of the reader – that only this design gives us hard evidence of causality. That being said, and being true, experimental designs have their drawbacks too.

First, experimental designs score high on internal validity, but their so-called *external validity* – the extent to which these findings are replicable in other settings – is disputed. A situation where a researcher divides two groups randomly in two is hardly a 'naturalistic setting' and examples have been reported in the literature where an effect of an intervention could be proven in a lab setting – but not outside in the 'real world'. This *external validity* is therefore a special kind of generalizability – not from a sample to the population, but from one setting to another setting. This weak point of experiments is also referred to as lack of *ecological validity*. Thus, even when conclusions are as 'hard' as cast iron within the research setting, they will be of little use if in real-life applications they would not emerge. This has led some scholars to prefer more naturalistic experiments over more controlled ones.

The ecological validity of controlled experiments may be compromised by several factors. One such factor is the so-called *Hawthorne effect*. This effect is named after a factory in the US where the effect of lighting on worker performance was investigated. The (possibly apocryphal) story goes that whichever way the lighting in the factory was altered, work performance always improved. This finding was explained by supposing that performance went up because the workers knew they were being investigated.

Another such threat to external validity is the *placebo effect*, also well known from pharmaceutical research. By this is meant that just from receiving some medicine (whether it has active ingredients or not) patients report feeling better. This effect can easily be countered by offering control respondents an intervention that has all the looks of the experimental intervention, but lacks the relevant elements. Thus, if we wanted to investigate the effect of a training video on secondary school students' bullying behaviour, we would, to counter the placebo effect, have to offer the control group a video too, although on an unrelated, neutral topic.

The last threat to external validity we will discuss (a few more have been listed in the literature) is the so-called 'Biotex' effect (Bijleveld & Van der Geest, 2021). Now this may seem an odd name, as Biotex is a special kind of washing powder which Dutch housewives love because after soaking hopelessly dirty clothes in it for a while, these become sparkling clean when washed in the washing machine afterwards with regular detergent. This Biotex effect has also been observed in experiments, in the sense that an effect of the intervention can only be demonstrated after respondents have been 'sensitized' to the intervention by a pre-test. Of course, in the real world, the intervention would generally not be administered after a pre-test and then the effect would not emerge. This threat can be detected by adding a second control and experimental group to the experiment and not administering a pre-test for these additional groups.

Secondly, not all interventions can be – as it is sometimes phrased – manipulated by a researcher. It is impossible to randomly assign child maltreatment or heroin use. The impact of such events can generally only be studied non-experimentally in naturalistic, observational settings. And in this, science is sometimes aided by natural events or manmade interventions that make it possible to study the effects of the upheaval they cause. Such occurrences are called *natural experiments*. We discuss such natural experiments in somewhat more detail in the next section.

5.9 Natural experiments

Titiunik (2021) ranks natural experiments, in terms of the extent to which they can provide proof of causal effects, in between the RCT and a quasi-experimental study. In an

RCT the researcher has *assured* through some sort of randomization procedure that observation units in the experimental and control conditions do not differ systematically – in other words, that only chance differences exist. In a quasi-experimental study, the researcher has not formed the groups, a different entity has done so, and as such we cannot be sure that the groups have been randomly formed and we must therefore reckon with the possibility that confounders obscure our picture.

In a natural experiment, according to Titiunik (2021), the treatment assignment mechanism is neither designed nor implemented by the researcher, is unknown to the researcher, but is probabilistic by means of an external event or intervention. It is generally assumed that that external event leads to random assignments of persons to groups. Because the researcher does not exert control over the randomization, such assignment is referred to as 'as-if' randomization: we can only assume that assignment was indeed random. One important additional condition for such an observational study to be classified as a natural experiment is that the respondents who are 'assigned' to the experimental and control groups do not exert any control over this assignment: they also must be unaware of the mechanism, and they should be unable to anticipate the intervention.

Natural experiments are often found upon the introduction of administrative or legal changes; often the 'collateral', unintended effects of such laws are studied employing the fact that the 'intervention' may be considered to qualify as 'as-if' random.

An example from life-course criminology illustrates such a natural experiment. In the Netherlands, all men born in 1959 were exempted from military service. The Dutch government had introduced this one-year exemption as it could not handle the large numbers of men who were being drafted. If one wanted to study the impact of military service on life outcomes such as marriage chances or earnings, one could not do that validly by comparing the outcomes of men who have served and who have not: medical and psychological checks for admission into service are likely confounded with characteristics that are associated with these life outcomes as well. However, as none of the men born in 1959 were drafted, through an entirely random mechanism, and as there is no reason to suppose that the cohort born in 1959 differs systematically on any relevant characteristics from men born in 1960 or in 1958, Van de Weijer & Bijleveld (2016) could exploit this random intervention and compared the criminal records of men born in 1959 (of whom no one had been drafted) with those born in 1960 and in 1958 (of whom some were drafted). They found no difference in the percentage of men who had a criminal record for these birth years, meaning that the military service did not impact criminal careers. They did however find that men who had not been drafted were more likely than those who had been drafted to follow in their father's footsteps, that is, to also become an offender if their father was an offender. The authors interpret this as suggesting that military service may 'break' the intergenerational cycle of transmission of criminal behaviour.

A famous example also using military records is the study by Angrist (1990). Research using administrative records had shown that men who had served in the Vietnam war earned less than men who had not served in the Vietnam war. The issue at stake was whether that was so *because* they had served in the war. Again, because various characteristics of the men could co-vary with both the choice to sign up or not and with lifetime outcomes such as earnings, it is hard to attribute any lower earnings to the military service in Vietnam. However, five draft lotteries had been held during the Vietnam war period, from 1970 up to 1975. And within these years, a number of cohorts could be identified that had groups of drafted and non-drafted men, formed randomly. Angrist showed, using Social Security administrative records, that the earnings of white veterans within these groups were approximately 15% less than the earnings of comparable nonveterans.

Natural experiments are also found when disasters occur. One such disaster was the so-called 'Hunger Winter' in the Netherlands, the 1944–1945 winter that was extremely cold and in which particularly the west of the Netherlands under Nazi occupation suffered severe food shortages. In the winter and spring of 1944, after a railway strike, the Nazi German occupiers limited rations such that people received as little as 400–800 calories per day. It was known that babies born during or right after this period had lower birth weights. Researchers studied the long-term consequences of this famine in people born or conceived during the Hunger Winter. The design appears to meet, to a large extent, the criteria for a natural experiment: the treatment assignment mechanism is neither designed nor implemented by the researchers, is an external intervention, that is unforeseeable and outside of the control of the subjects of the intervention. One could of course argue that the experimental group misses out on parents who managed to leave the west of the country (although that was very hard to do), and that children born earlier may have been exposed to the famine too. The design ranks, all in all, with its 'as-if' randomization, somewhat below an RCT in terms of strength to prove causal relations.

The researchers studied three groups of people. Firstly they studied children born during the Hunger Winter or right after (and thus conceived during that period), who could be called the 'experimental' group; these children had been found through the registries of the midwifery schools in Amsterdam and Rotterdam, and the delivery ward in the Leiden University Academic Hospital. These were therefore children born in the west of the country where the famine was worst. A second group consisted of children born in the same clinics, but in 1943 or in 1947, so before or after the Hunger Winter; this group served as a control group of children born in the same location, but not exposed to the famine. See for more on the samples Rooseboom et al. (2006).

A subsequent study showed that women exposed to the famine during mid- to late gestation had babies with significantly reduced birth weights. Babies whose mothers were exposed only during early gestation had normal birth weights. However, the latter grew up to have higher rates of obesity than those born before and after the war and higher rates than those exposed during mid- to late gestation, with the difference in weight on average almost 5 kgs. At ages 56 to 59, both men and women exposed to famine during the early stages of gestation performed worse on a selective attention task (De Rooij et al., 2010). Thus, the studies have found both physical and mental long-term health consequences.

Natural experiments have not been employed often yet in empirical legal research. One set of studies on sex discrimination cases is discussed in detail by Erikson (2022). These studies all investigated the effect of the presence of a female judge in sex discrimination cases, i.e. cases where discrimination against an individual is claimed because of gender identity, including transgender status, or because of sexual orientation. The author studied a database of 435 sex discrimination cases, containing US Appellate

Court decisions from 1995 to 2002. These are cases where a decision is arrived at by a panel of judges. And one reason why the impact of the gender of the judges can be studied using these data is that judges should be assigned *randomly* to panels: there are therefore no systematic differences between the judges that may co-vary with the types (and therefore possibly the outcomes) of sex discrimination cases.

Earlier research had found that male judges were about 10% more likely to side with a female plaintiff if they served with a female colleague on the panel, a finding that was highly statistically significant (see Erikson, 2022). The author, before embarking on his analyses, tested first whether assignment of judges to cases could actually be assumed to be random ('as-if' randomness). For that, he investigated whether male and female judges differed in terms of the earlier verdict in the case they were assigned to. He found that that was not the case, so that random formation of panels with male and female judges could be assumed.

Erikson (2022) next improved on previous research with two additional control steps. First, he compared cases with an all-male panel (about two-thirds of the panels) with cases where the panel contains a female judge, each time within the same time period. This rules out the alternative explanation that more female judges sit on panels in more recent years, and that any difference in favour of sex discrimination plaintiffs is actually a period effect (judges become more responsive to sex discrimination cases in more recent years). Erikson also compared only pairs within the same appellate circuit to rule out any confounding on this variable. Second, he compared panels (with and without a female judge) pairwise, with the judges in the pairs of control and experimental panels having the same distribution of political affiliations. This is to rule out the alternative explanation that it is not a judge's female gender which impacts judgments in sex discrimination cases, but the fact that female judges more often vote Democrat.

Erikson also exploited an attractive property of the data, namely that male judges sometimes sit on panels with only male judges and sometime on panels with a female judge as well. Erikson could therefore investigate not only effects across panels of judges, but also *within* judges over time, in longitudinal fashion. He investigated judgments of male judges before and after having served with a female judge, and found that male judges after having served on a panel with a female judge do not become more likely to vote in favour of plaintiffs in sex discrimination cases. Erikson's study (2022) confirms earlier research, but he reports a larger effect size, of around 13%. It should be noted that Boyd, Epstein, & Martin (2010) found such gendered judicial effects also (but only) for sex discrimination cases. These authors therefore conclude that in the USA the presence of women in the federal appellate judiciary rarely has an appreciable empirical effect on judicial outcomes.

5.10 Further reading

The 'classic' read on experimental designs is Cook & Campbell (1979), with Shadish, Cook, & Campbell (2002) its successor. Farrington (2003) is a lucid and much cited piece on standards for evaluation research, mostly focusing on crime and criminal justice.

Chapter questions

1. What are the necessary and sufficient ingredients for a randomized controlled trial? (section 5.4.1)
2. Argue what confounders can be detected in a design with only pre-test and post-test (section 5.4.1)
3. Why are history, maturation and testing all eliminated as confounders in a design with randomly chosen experimental and control groups? (section 5.4.1)
4. Argue why selective attrition is more likely to occur if no placebo is included in an experiment and why that constitutes a threat to internal validity (section 5.4.1)
5. Argue whether a vignette study meets all the criteria of a randomized controlled trial (section 5.8)
6. Do the same for a natural experiment (section 5.9)
7. What is meant by 'as-if' randomness? (section 5.9)
8. Argue whether the introduction of a new law constitutes a natural experiment (section 5.9)

Part III

DATA ANALYSIS

Chapter 6

Quantitative data: univariate and bivariate analysis

In this chapter, we start with more formal notation for key concepts such as variables and respondents. Next, in section 6.2 measurement levels are discussed, which are important for understanding the information content of variables, and necessary to take into consideration for choosing one's analysis technique. Subsequently, we discuss a number of descriptive measures for univariate analysis, such as the mean and the standard deviation. We continue with measures to describe the association between variables, that is to say, bivariate analysis. We discuss two important classes of measures to investigate association: through correlation coefficients and through the analysis of cross-tabulations. We give some examples of graphs that can be used to display findings attractively. In section 6.4.3 we sketch univariate and bivariate analysis of duration variables, such as time to settlement of disputes.[1]

6.1 Analysis units versus variables

When we carry out research we usually – as stated on a number of occasions above – collect information on entities (citizens, lawyers, villages, yoghurt desserts, light bulbs, court cases) and we generally do so with regard to a number of their properties (religious affiliation, population structure, creaminess of texture, lifetime, time to completion). The entities are in methodology-speak called 'respondents' or 'analysis units'. Although the term 'respondents' is a universally used term, as the examples show, respondents can also be non-people, such as files that contain information, or structures such as buildings, or conglomerates such as cities, occurrences such as charges or victim impact statements, or even household appliances.

Often, when we are not studying persons, we indicate the entities as the entities they are or simply as 'analysis units' or 'replications' – as 'respondent' then has an

[1]This section can be skipped by readers with no particular interest in the analysis of such variables as it is not essential for understanding the subsequent chapters.

odd feel to it. Thus we say that we have studied bankruptcy with 200 replications over bankruptcy cases, or that we have studied the life-time of 500 light bulbs. In general, the number of replications over entities is indicated with the symbol 'N'. In the bankruptcy cases we just gave, N equals 200, and for the light bulbs N equals 500.

What we are interested in is the properties of these entities: respondents' political affiliations, profession, age, gender, income, intelligence, result in the half-marathon. When the entities are not people, we are still interested in their properties, such as time to failure of light bulbs, amounts paid out to creditors in bankruptcy cases, creaminess for yoghurt desserts. These properties are called *variables*. Thus creaminess is a variable, as is lifetime for the light bulb and amount paid out in bankruptcy settlements. We may measure more than one variable per respondent. In general for the light bulb, we would not have a lot to measure other than lifetime, as light bulbs are fabricated in identical fashion, although we might want to measure weight, and the time when the bulb was produced (it might be that bulbs tend to be less solidly produced and to function for a shorter period when the machines need oiling or maintenance and repair). In general, whenever we are investigating 'richer' phenomena, such as court cases, we tend to register more than one variable.

Indeed, often we are not only interested in one, but in several properties of our units of observation. This is so because generally we not only want to describe a variable, but also to describe its association with other variables, or even *explain* it. We might for instance want to know what factors determine amounts paid out in bankruptcy cases, or what the profile is of bankruptcy cases in which we typically find suspicions (or proof) of an *actio Pauliana*. The number of variables measured is generally referred to as 'k'. In some cases of social research, several hundreds of variables may be measured depending on the research question at hand and the richness of the available material.

Variables are usually, if we write things more formally and mathematically, given symbols – such as X instead of 'age' or Y instead of 'amount paid out'. When we have several variables, they are generally indicated with a subscript, such as X_1, X_2, X_3, etc., to indicate the first, second and third variable. As we have often at least several replications over respondents, the respondents can also be indicated with an index. The notation then becomes in purely abstract notation X_{ij}, with X_{ij} indicating the score of the i-th person on the j-th variable. See Table 6.1, which has data for four respondents on three variables: age, gender and type of legal dispute the respondent is involved in.

Table 6.1: Example of notation of variables and respondents

respondent (number)	age	gender	type of legal dispute
John (1)	46	male	unemployment benefits
Beth (2)	30	female	tort
Pete (3)	45	male	bankruptcy
Mary (4)	21	female	medical malpractice

In Table 6.1, X_{11} is 46 and X_{12} is 'male'. Pete's score on 'age' is X_{31}, being the score of the third person on the first variable, and Mary's score 'female' is indicated as X_{42}, and X_{43} is 'medical malpractice', being the legal dispute Mary is involved in.

6.2 Measurement levels

6.2.1 Nominal to absolute measurement level

Variables can have varying information content. When a variable measures age, for instance, the values of that variable contain a lot of information. If one respondent is 50 years old, and another is 25 years old, we can safely say that the first respondent is twice as old as the second. And whether we measure age in weeks, or years, or seconds, that conclusion remains the same. If however our variable measures religion, we can say no such thing. If a first respondent has the category 'Buddhist' and the second has the category 'Christian', the only inference we can draw is that the second person's religion is different from the first person's. We cannot say that the first person has more or less of the property 'religion' or that the second has twice as much, or half, the religion that the second one has. The only information content that the variable 'religion' has is equality and inequality: we know whether our analysis units have the same or a different score on that variable, but we cannot order the categories, let alone infer whether the categories are a multiple of each other. The information content that categories of a variable have is commonly referred to as a variable's *measurement level.*

In general, five measurement levels are distinguished, which can be rank-ordered as to the information content of the categories. These measurement levels are: *nominal* measurement level, *ordinal*, *interval*, *ratio* and *absolute*. We will discuss each of them in turn.

(1) *Nominal measurement level*

At the nominal measurement level ('nominal' from the Latin *nomen* meaning 'name'), the categories of the variables are nothing more than distinct categories, which have no other relation than that they are different. The variable 'Type of legal dispute' is such a variable. The legal disputes could be coded as 1='unemployment benefits', 2 = 'tort', 3 = 'bankruptcy', and 4 = 'medical malpractice'. But they could also have been coded as 100 = 'unemployment benefits', -12.2 = 'tort', 27 = 'bankruptcy', and 0.004 = 'medical malpractice'. The numbers have no other meaning than to distinguish the different categories. As such, it would not make sense to compute a mean, or some such statistic.

As such, a nominal variable is a variable that classifies the respondents into distinct sets of different classes. Other examples of nominal variables are 'type of court', 'hair colour', 'gender', etc.

(2) *Ordinal measurement level*

When we move up to the ordinal measurement level, the categories of the variable reflect an *ordering* – the name 'ordinal' says it. This means that if John has score '1', Pete has score '2' and Mary has score '3', John has the least of property that the variable measures, next comes Pete, and Mary has the most. If the property is for instance likeability, this means that John is the least likeable, next Pete, and that Mary is the most likeable of the three. As the variable is an ordinal variable, John, Pete and Mary could however as well have had scores of -187, +2 and 236,000. As the scores of an ordinal variable reflect an ordering only, from these values we would also draw the same conclusion: John is least likeable and Pete follows him, with Mary having the highest score and therefore being the most likeable.

An example of such a variable is the ordering of winners in a half-marathon. In that case we would know that Jet ended first and Klara second and Bibi third, but we would not know their actual times. It could be that Jet ran in 1:59:03 and Klara in 1:59:59, and Bibi in 2:11:04, in which case Jet and Klara are very close and Bibi came in quite a bit later. However, it could also be that Jet ran in 1:52:45, Klara in 2:13:33 and Bibi in 2:13:58, in which case Klara and Bibi ended with only a small difference and Jet was way ahead of these two. That information is not contained in an ordinal variable, however.

Ordinal variables are encountered often in so-called 'preference judgements', for example when respondents are asked to say which of certain foodstuffs or smells they like best, which one comes next, which afterwards, or to compare such items pairwise (i.e. A against B, A against C, A against D, B against C, etc.).

When variables are ordinal, special techniques must be used to analyse them. Clearly, also for ordinal variables computing a mean score is not informative. What we could do, obviously, is compute a mean *rank* score, and carry out our computations on that in a sense derived variable. Such approaches will be discussed below in section 6.3.1.

(3) *Interval measurement level*

Moving up the measurement level ladder, we arrive at the interval level. When a variable has been measured at interval level, we can compute a mean score, and get a meaningful summary of the scores on that variable. As such, the category values of an interval level variable contain more information than just equality and difference (which a nominal variable had) or ordering (which an ordinal variable had).

If a variable is an interval variable, we know that the intervals are equidistant: the difference between a score of 4 and 5 is just as large as the difference between a score of 1 and 2 or between 3 and 4. Examples are rating scales, where we ask respondents to rate to what extent they agree with a certain statement, for instance on a scale from 1 to 7 or 1 to 4.

Does this mean that if person A has scored '10' on the interval level variable and person B has scored '5', that we may conclude that person A has twice as much of the property the variable is supposed to measure? This cannot be done because an interval level variable has no *fixed origin*.

Let us explain this with an example. Temperature can be measured in degrees Celsius but also in degrees Fahrenheit. Suppose that on one day it is 24 degrees Celsius in Amsterdam, and 48 degrees Celsius in Khartoum. While 48 is twice 24, it does not make sense to say that it is twice as warm in Khartoum as in Amsterdam, because those temperatures could be equally well have been measured in degrees Fahrenheit (namely as 118 and 75 respectively) but would then have a very different ratio. That this is so is because Celsius and Fahrenheit have different points of origin.

(4) *Ratio measurement level*

A ratio measurement level variable is a variable that does have a fixed origin. Examples are weight or price. Prices for instance may be given in US dollars, British pounds or euros, so the scale may vary. But if something is twice as expensive in dollars, it is also twice as expensive when the price is calculated in euros. And a product that is free is free in whatever currency prices are given. This means that from a ratio variable onwards, we can make statements such as 'product A is twice as expensive as product B'. The same goes for height, which may be expressed in yards or metres, but also here little John is half his father's height, regardless of the metric in which these heights are measured. This means that we may – formally speaking – change the scores in the following manner: $X' = aX$.

(5) *Absolute measurement level*

Once we have arrived at the highest measurement level, a variable's value contains all information there is. This also implies that we can no longer alter or transform the scores without affecting the meaning of the score: the scores we have measured are the final, ultimate, only measurements.

An example of an absolute variable is a variable that measures the frequency of occurrence of some phenomenon, for instance the number of children that respondents have. If someone reports that she has four children, we cannot transform this to eight children, or two. She simply has four children and that's it.

If we summarize the above, we note first that the various measurement levels are ordered in the sense that as we move up from nominal to absolute, variable values contain increasingly more information at each subsequent level. At nominal interval level, a variable does not do more than disaggregate the respondents into different categories. Once we are at ordinal level, these categories are ordered; we now know who has more and who has less of the property that the variable measures. At interval level, the ordering becomes more structured, and we may transform the data to present them on a different scale. Once at ratio level, the information content of the data is already so high that the only transformation that is allowed is multiplication or division. At absolute measurement level, the scores are exactly the information content of the variable and may thus not be altered any more.

The terminology employed here is commonly used. We may also encounter nominal variables as *categorical variables*; sometimes the same is said of ordinal variables.

By contrast, interval and ratio level variables are often referred to as *continuous* variables; they are also encountered under the label *numerical* variables. Variables with only two categories are labelled *dichotomous* variables.

6.2.2 Implications for analysis

Now why is it important at all to know what measurement level a variable has? It is important because the measurement level dictates the analysis method that can be used. To give a very simple example: if we have measured a variable at nominal level, it does not make sense to compute a mean score: there is for instance no such thing as a mean 'religion'. Conversely, if we have measured a variable at ratio level (for instance 'age'), there are more efficient ways of describing the measurement than through a frequency tabulation that gives the number of cases with ages 18, 19, 20, ..., 65.

This applies to the choice of very simple descriptive statistics, as well as to the choice of more sophisticated methods. Knowing the measurement level is therefore important to be able to decide what methods can be used to summarize and analyse the data.

The interval measurement level, in a sense, constitutes a watershed, as from interval measurement level onwards we can use standard quantitative statistical techniques. Ordinal variables need special methods and so do nominal variables. Dichotomous variables (variables with just two categories) are a special case, as technically speaking they are equivalent to interval variables, but in research practice they command special analysis techniques. Examples of such variables are 'gender', 'agree–disagree' judgements, 'guilty–not guilty' verdicts, etc.

6.3 Describing the variables

Suppose we interviewed 100 secondary school students. We asked these students to tell us whether they committed during the past school year any of the three following offences: theft, assault, or vandalism. We noted the gender of these respondents, the type of secondary school they are in, and we asked them how much pocket money they received.

If we want to report on our findings, we need to summarize them. What the reader would want to know is things like: how many students committed an offence last year? How many property or violent offences were committed on average? Did students differ a lot in how much pocket money they had?

If we want to provide the answers to such questions, we need simple summarizing measures. Such summarizing measures come in two classes. The first are *measures of central tendency*, which tell us what scores respondents tend to have, what the average of the students is. Second, what a reader would want to know is whether all respondents tended to score on or around the average, or whether there was quite a bit of fluctuation in respondents' scores. In other words, the reader would want to have a measure of *variability* as well.

These measures, measures of central tendency and of variation, are labelled 'statistics', not because they incorporate complicated statistical reasoning, but because they in the etymological sense summarize a set of numerical values into one number: a statistic.

In the following we will discuss both groups of measures: measures of central tendency and measures of variability. With such measures we do a *univariate analysis*: we present the results for just one variable.

6.3.1 Central tendency: the mean, median and mode

If we want to give the reader an overview of our findings, we generally start by giving mean values, or so-called measures of central tendency. The average or 'arithmetic mean' is the run-of-the-mill average that everyone employs automatically when we ask after his or her average grade or alcohol consumption. In formula it is written as:

$$\sum_{i=1}^{N} \frac{X_i}{N},$$

which is nothing more than the sum of all observations X_i from the first to the N-th respondent, divided by the total number of respondents N – or our standard run-of-the-mill mean. The average or mean is the most often used measure of central tendency. It is attractive because it is easily and intuitively understood by readers. The mean is written as $\bar{X}$, as M_X, or simply as M.

A disadvantage of the mean is, however, is that it is sensitive to so-called outliers, i.e., extreme scores. Suppose for instance that we have a list of observations 1-2-5-7-3-6-6, of which the average is 4.29. But suppose now that the highest score was not 7 but 27 – an extreme score. The average would then suddenly be 7.14! The value 7.14 is obviously not a good summary of the scores. In fact, all scores but the extreme 27 lie below that summary value. This means that the reader does not get the right impression, a good overview of the scores 1-2-3-5-6-6-27.

In such cases, the *median* is a good alternative. The median is that number below which 50% of the values lie (and above which thus also 50%). It is that number that cuts the distribution of scores in two. In the example we just gave, the median is equal to 5, with three values below, and three values above it. Note that the median is indeed insensitive to outliers: whether the highest score is 7, 27, or 27,000, the median remains 5. The median is therefore a good measure of central tendency whenever there are outliers, or whenever the data have a skewed distribution. In empirical legal studies, we often encounter skewed variables, such as amount of damages awarded or sentence length.

Lastly, for summarizing the scores on a variable, the *mode* may be used. The mode is the score that occurs most often (as reflected in 'modal'). The mode is not often used as the only measure for central tendency, one reason for which may be that distributions may have more than one mode (they are then called bimodal as opposed to unimodal). Suppose for instance that in the example of the 100 students given above, an equal number were to own up to vandalism and property offending: we would then report two modes.

6.3.2 Measures of variability

Central tendency is not the only relevant measure to summarize the distribution of scores. In practice, we do not only want to know what the average number of offences was, but we would also want to know whether all respondents scored the mean or close to the mean or whether on the other hand there was a lot of variation in scores. In practice two measures are used to express such variability. The first is the *variance*, often used in computations but not aiding the reader so much in understanding what is going on. The second is the *standard deviation*, which is more insightful to gauge the extent to which respondents vary around the mean. We will detail them both.

The first measure is the *variance*; it is denoted with the symbol s^2. The variance is computed as the mean sum of squared deviations of the individual scores from the mean.[2] If you do not understand this right away, that illustrates why the variance is of limited conceptual use. A problem with the variance as a measure of variability is namely that because of the squaring of the differences between means and scores, the relation with the original scaling of the variable is gone. It is hard to interpret the number that is generated by the formula.

For that reason, in most situations, the so-called standard deviation is used, which is simply the square root of the variance:

$$s = \sqrt{s^2}.$$

The main advantage of the standard deviation compared to the variance is that it is, because of the square root, expressed again in the original scale of the variable. This means that the standard deviation can easily be interpreted. If for instance the mean number of offences of secondary schoolers is 1.3 and the standard deviation is 0.7, this can be rephrased by saying that on average the secondary schoolers varied by 0.7 offences around the arithmetic mean. It can also be envisaged as the scores hovering – on average – between 0.6 and 2.0. The advantage of the standard deviation is that it gives you a 'feel' for how much fluctuation there was. The standard deviation is often abbreviated as 'sd' or 'SD'.

[2] s^2 is computed as:

$$\sum_{i=1}^{N} \frac{(X_i - \bar{X})^2}{N-1}.$$

In this formula the following happens. For each respondent i we take his or her score X_i and compute how much it deviates from the mean $\bar{X}$: $(X_i - \bar{X})$. We square all these deviations and then add them up (if we not square them first, they would always add to zero). The sum of squared deviations, which is in the numerator, reflects how much people vary around the mean: if everybody had scores really close to the mean (a case with little variability), the sum of the squared deviations would be small. As people's individual scores are further away from the mean, the deviations become larger, the squared deviations do so too, and so does the sum. So, the numerator is small when the scores cluster around the mean, and it gets larger as they are further away from that mean, which reflects that overall they vary more. Next, we divide that sum by the number of respondents minus 1: (N-1). This serves to standardize the measure: if we did not do so, the variability would become higher with sample size, which would be strange.

6.3.3 Graphs for visualizing the variables

As stated, the mean is meaningful only for variables from interval level up. The median can be used for rank-ordered variables, and variables from interval level up. The mode can be used for any kind of variable. If we want to give an indication of the variability in scores, the standard deviation is generally used, but again this is only for variables from interval level up. So, what if we want to give an overview of variables that are at lower than interval levels, such as a nominal level variable?

There are two approaches to describing the distribution of scores for such variables. The first is through simple *frequency tabulation*, such as that produced in any computational software package. See Table 6.2, which gives an example of the distribution over the categories of the variable 'employment status' from a study among 240 volunteers. The first column gives the values of the categories, the second gives the absolute numbers, the third gives the percentages. So we can deduce from Table 6.2 that a total of 240 volunteers took part in the study, that almost two-thirds were employed, and two in nine were students, of whom half had some kind of employment. Almost 10% were retired, a few unemployed and one person did not want to give their employment status.

Table 6.2: Frequency tabulation of employment status

employment status	number	percentage
employed	154	64.2
working student	27	11.3
student	28	11.7
retired	23	9.6
unemployed	7	2.9
other	1	.4
total	240	100.0

A second option for describing nominal data is through the use of graphs. See Figure 6.1, which is an example of a so-called *pie chart* for the same data as in Table 6.2. In a pie chart the data are represented as a pie, and the chunks represent the proportion of cases scoring in each of the respective categories. The data were collected in a study on office misbehaviour (Wesselius et al., 2023). Pie charts are very easily understood by readers, including the non-academically trained, and informative at a glance. Pie charts are often used when the various categories to be represented graphically are categories of a nominal variable.

Graphs have the huge advantage that they are inspected quickly and in general also understood well by readers. In more lengthy, dry texts, they have the added advantage that they in a sense 'break' the text, making the look of the pages more lively, and thus adding to comprehension and retention of the material.

Figure 6.1: Pie chart of employment status

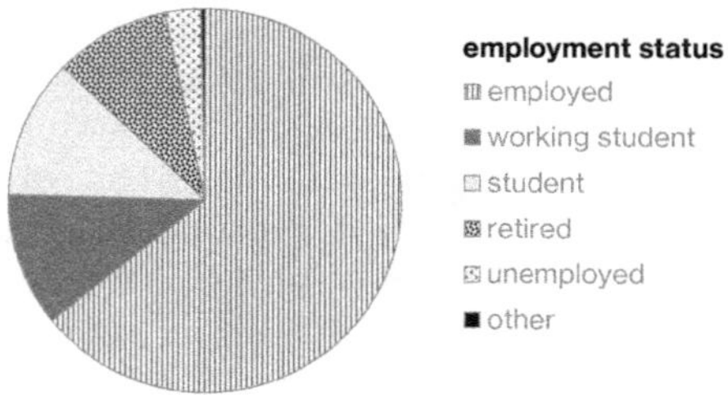

Figure 6.2: Bar chart of employment status

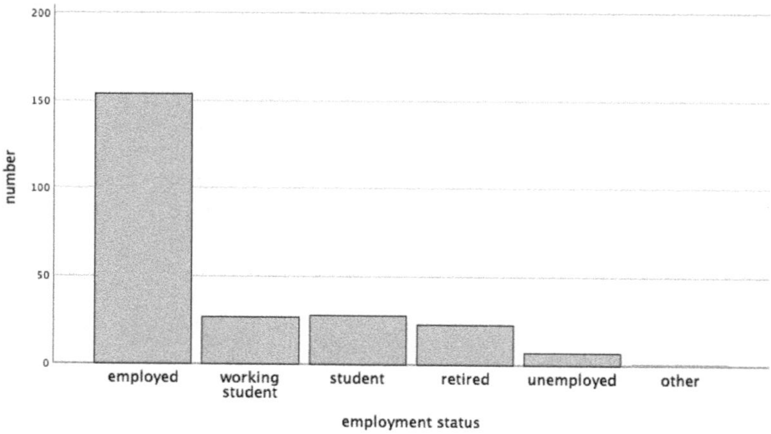

A second way to graphically display these data is by using a bar chart. An example is given in Figure 6.2, in which the categories of employment status have been ordered along the x-axis, and the y-axis gives the number of cases for each category (obviously, the percentage could have been taken just as well). In a bar chart, the categories of the variable along the x-axis are unordered, indicated by the fact that the bars are not connected.

When a variable has been measured at interval measurement level or higher, we generally use means and standard deviations to summarize the variable for the reader. However, also for ordered or continuous variables, graphs would have the advantage that they are easier to inspect and interpret. In addition, they can show how a variable may have a *skewed distribution*, something which means and variances do not show. See Figure 6.3, an example of a so-called *histogram*, that shows the distribution of the age of respondents in the vignette study on office misbehaviour mentioned before (Wesselius et al., 2023). Mean age is 38.24 (sd = 16.62, skewness = 0.738), but the

Figure 6.3: Histogram for distribution of age in 5-year categories

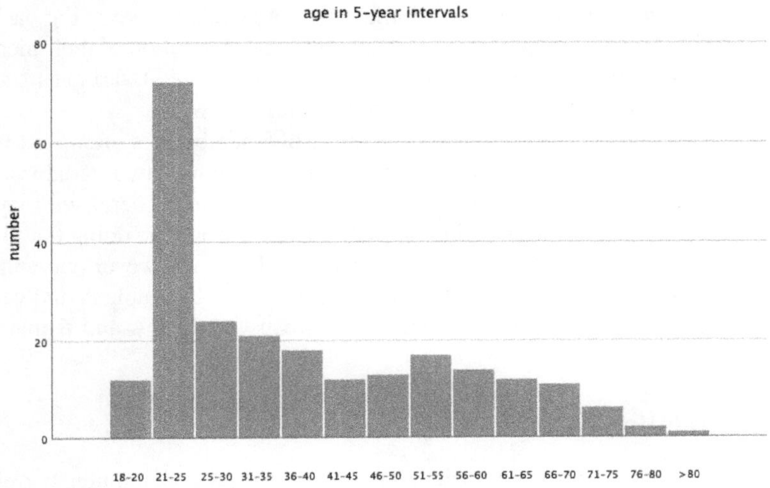

graph is much more informative. Age, categorized into 5-year intervals, is clearly quite skewed because of a large number of respondents in the 21–25 age range, and numbers tailing off towards the right. The graph also shows that there are actually two peaks: in addition to the peak in the 21–35 age range, there is also a peak between 51 and 55 years of age. The data collectors in this research were students, and they likely, as the authors report, sampled persons from their own network as well as from that of their parents.

6.4 Describing the association between variables

So far, we have talked about ways to describe the variables that have been measured. Such descriptions generally entail properties such as the mean or standard deviation, or distribution – either through frequency tabulations or using graphs. But often we want to go further and we want to investigate not only variables one by one, but to look as well at how variables are interrelated. We might want to assess for instance whether older citizens have more trust in the criminal justice system than younger citizens, or whether judges' gender matters in the assessment of sex discrimination claims.

We need tools to summarize such interrelations, just like the tools of mean (or median) and standard deviation for summarizing central tendency and variability. Many of such tools are available. In general, they are called coefficients of association or coefficients of correlation. What tool is appropriate in a given situation depends on two criteria. Firstly, it depends on the *measurement level* of the variables. If we want to report on the association between two continuous variables, a different measure must be employed than if we want to investigate the association between two nominal variables. Secondly, the choice of measure depends on the *distribution* of the variables. If this is for instance very skewed, different association measures are recommended.

While there is a host of different measures to represent association or correlation, measures are generally interpreted in a similar way. As such, not knowing each and every one of them in detail does not in practice hamper interpretation of their meaning. The class of coefficients for the association between two nominal variables stands a little apart however, so we will treat those in more detail below.

When we investigate the association between two variables, it is often said we are carrying out a *bivariate analysis*: we present the interrelation of two variables. This is different from the univariate analyses we just talked about. There, we may also analyse more than one variable. But then, in each case, we would be doing that for one variable by itself; it is a variable by variable analysis. Below, however, we will each time investigate the variables in conjunction. As such, it is not variable A and variable B we are investigating; rather, it is the relation between variables A and B that is the object of interest.

6.4.1 Correlation coefficients

The most often-used measure for association is the Pearson product moment correlation coefficient. Often, when speaking of 'the correlation', people refer to this correlation coefficient,[3] with the coefficient for the correlation between X and Y written as r_{XY}.

To understand what the correlation coefficient expresses, it is easiest to use scatterplots, that is, plots of the scores of the respondents on the variables X and Y. To make these, we take the score on the X variable as an X-coordinate, and take the score on the Y variable as the Y-coordinate. The scores on the variables X and Y then become points in a two-dimensional space. In Figure 6.4 we give four such *scatterplots*.

The first scatterplot depicts a situation of moderate to strong positive association. When X is high, Y tends to be high too; when X is low, Y is also generally low. The second (upper right) scatterplot depicts essentially the same situation but now the cloud of points has become much narrower. For this plot as well, if we know that the score on X is high, we know that the score on Y will likely be high too, but we know that now with a much narrower margin: while in the upper left plot, there could still be quite a range in possible values for Y given a certain X, the picture has become much 'sharper' in the upper right one. Knowing X, I know within a fairly narrow band what Y will be. The thick Cuban cigar-shaped cloud in the first picture points therefore to a weaker

[3] In formula the Pearson product moment correlation coefficient is:

$$r_{XY} = \sum_{i=1}^{N} \frac{(X_i - \bar{X})(Y_i - \bar{Y})}{(N-1)s_X s_Y},$$

which is translated in words as: the correlation coefficient is the sum of the product of each respondent's score X_i in deviation from the mean of that variable X and each respondent's score Y_i in deviation from variable Y's mean, divided by the product of the respective standard deviations of X and Y, times a correction factor for sample size. This may not all be immediately obvious to the reader, so we will now first look at the correlation in a more intuitive way, and then investigate whether this formula indeed gives us a quantity that corresponds to our intuitive idea of association.

Figure 6.4: Scatterplots for associations of various direction and strength

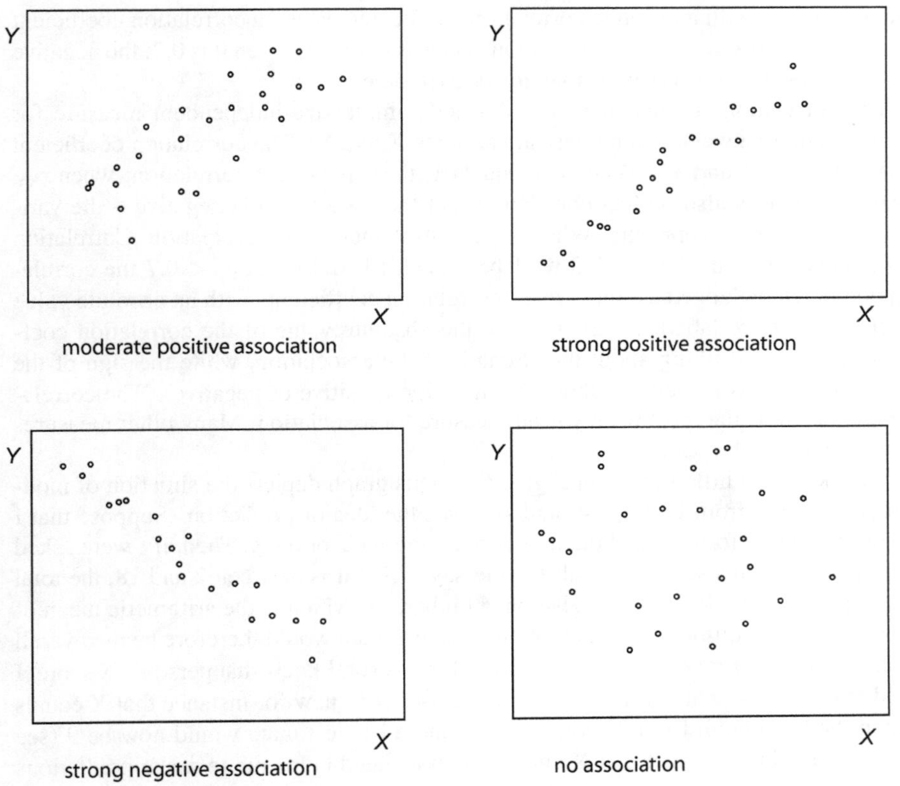

association between X and Y. As the cigar becomes slimmer and turns into a ladylike thin cigar or even cigarette, the association becomes stronger. If the cloud of points form a straight line, the association is perfect. The third picture (bottom left) gives a situation of strong negative association – in fact it is the exact mirror of the upper right one. So the association is just as strong, only in the reverse direction: if the score on X is high, the score on Y will likely be low, and vice versa. The last picture gives the situation of almost no association: knowing X does not tell us anything about Y.

Thus, in a situation where people with higher than average scores on X also have higher than average scores on Y and vice versa (those with very low scores on X also have very low scores on Y), we would say that X and Y resemble each other; they are similar. In that case everyone would say, without needing to do any computations, that these two aspects are correlated. And we would expect r_{XY} to turn out to be high. That is exactly what r_{XY} does.[4]

[4] To understand how the formula works, suppose that a particular respondent i's score is much higher than the mean on X: $X_i - \bar{X}$ will then be high. And suppose that that respondent i's score on Y is also much higher than the mean on Y: $Y_i - \bar{Y}$ will then also be high. Simply said: this respondent scores higher than

Now what if we have the opposite situation? That is, people with higher than average scores on X have lower than average scores on Y (and vice versa). Now X and Y are not similar, they are each other's mirror in a way: X is the opposite of Y.[5] In that case, we end up with a negative correlation coefficient. When a correlation coefficient is negative, say r_{XY} = -0.7, the association is just as strong as when it is 0.7; the negative sign indicates that the variables now mirror each other.

The correlation coefficient is a scale- and sample size-independent measure for the association between two numerical variables X and Y.[6] The correlation coefficient varies between -1 and +1. When r_{XY} equals 1, there is perfect correlation; when r_{XY} equals -1, there is also perfect correlation, but the association is negative – the variables are each other's opposite. When r_{XY} equals 0, there is no association. Correlation coefficients between -0.3 and 0.3 we label 'weak'; if $0.3 < |r_{XY}| < 0.7$ the correlation coefficient is judged as 'moderate'; correlation coefficients with an absolute value larger than 0.7 are labelled 'strong'. So, the absolute value of the correlation coefficient tells us something about the strength of the association, while the sign of the association tells us something about the direction (positive or negative). The correlation coefficient is the most widely used measure for association. Many other measures are variations on the structure of r_{XY}.

We take this a little further in Figure 6.5. This graph depicts the situation of moderate association from Figure 6.4, and sketches the idea of prediction. Suppose that I do not have any information about a person's score on Y or on X. Then, if I were asked to predict a person's score on Y, all I could say is that it is between 2 and 18, the total range of the scores. I could also give one number, 11, which is the arithmetic mean of Y. Without any additional information, my best estimate would therefore be the overall mean of Y (see Figure 6.5 along the y-axis). If however, I knew that person's X score, I could make my estimate of Y much more precise! If I knew for instance that X equals 8, then the bandwidth for Y becomes 6–11, and a best estimate would now be 9 (see Figure 6.5). Thus, the fact that X and Y are associated helps me to make predictions

average on X and higher than average on Y. The product of these two terms – that is in the denominator of the formula – will then for this respondent also be high. If this applies to all respondents, i.e. that those who score higher than average on X also score higher than average on Y (and vice versa: those who score lower than average on X also score lower than average on Y), we get for each respondent a large product term $(X_i - \bar{X}) \times (Y_i - \bar{Y})$ and summing all these product terms a large value in the denominator, and thus eventually – after the further divisions in the denominator – a large value for r_{XY}.

[5]In that case, in the formula, each case where X_i is higher than the average and $X_i - \bar{X}$ is positive will then couple with the situation that Y_i is lower than the average and $\bar{Y}$ and $Y_i - \bar{Y}$ is negative. Their product will then be negative. Then, the sum in the nominator does not become a large positive number, but a large negative number.

[6]The correlation coefficient has a term (N-1) in the denominator to correct for sample size – if sample size increases or decreases the correlation remains equally strong (why that term is N-1 and not simply N is discussed in more depth in statistics textbooks). Secondly, the denominator contains terms for the standard deviation of X, s_X, and the standard deviation of Y, s_Y. Why this is necessary is best understood as follows. Suppose that we are investigating whether shoe size X and height in metres Y are associated. Suppose that we have computed a correlation coefficient and that that coefficient equals 0.95, meaning that shoe size and height are correlated positively and (very) strongly. Suppose now that we decide to measure height not in metres, but in centimetres, or inches. Intuitively, this should not change the association between X and Y. However, if we change the values for Y – moving from metres to centimetres – they would be multiplied by a factor 100, and the r_{XY} would also become 100 times as high! Dividing the denominator by the standard deviations solves for such undesirabilities.

Figure 6.5: Relation between association and prediction

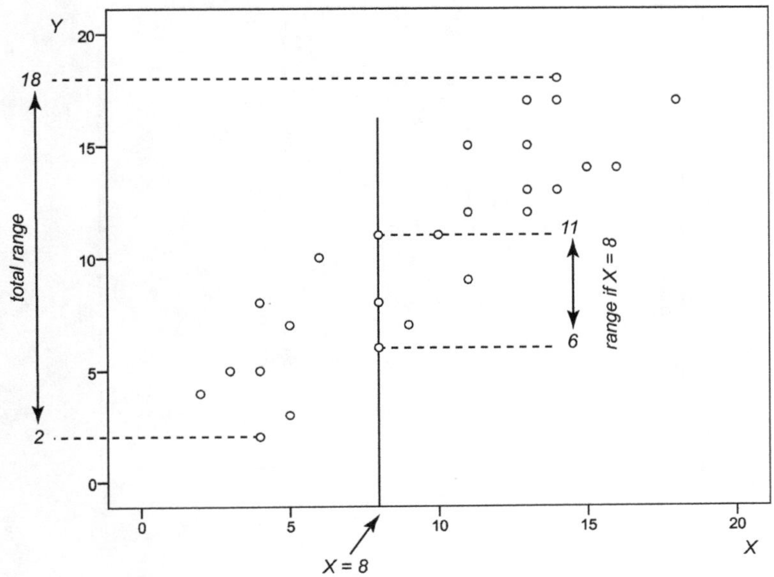

about one variable, using information from the other. Knowing X tells you something about Y.

Now, we said above that a cigar-shaped cloud like we have in Figure 6.5 is indicative of moderate to strong association, and that as the cigar becomes slimmer the association becomes stronger. If that is the case, then we would expect our prediction to improve as an association gets stronger. Imagine, therefore, in Figure 6.5 a similarly positioned but slimmer cigar. Again, suppose that I know that X equals 8. Now, however, because the cigar is slimmer, the possible range for Y is narrower: it is possibly 8–10 instead of the wider 6–11 that we had. If I were required to give one number again for Y, again I would estimate Y at 9. So, a stronger correlation between X and Y does not lead to a different estimate for Y on the basis of X, but it leads to a *more certain* estimate, reflected in the smaller bandwidth of the possible values for Y.

There are two important issues to heed when using the Pearson product moment correlation coefficient. The first is that the correlation coefficient is a measure for *linear* association. The Cuban and ladies' cigars we drew were all clouds around a *straight* line. But what if we have the situation as depicted in Figure 6.6? In this case there is a – strong – *non-linear* association: if we know X we can predict within a fairly narrow bandwidth what Y is. However, if we were to compute the correlation coefficient for these data, it would turn out to be almost zero. That is not a wrong result, as the Pearson product moment correlation coefficient is a measure of *linear* association – and indeed there is no linear association here. However, from that we cannot conclude that there is no association at all. Other measures would be needed to

Figure 6.6: Non-linear association between X and Y

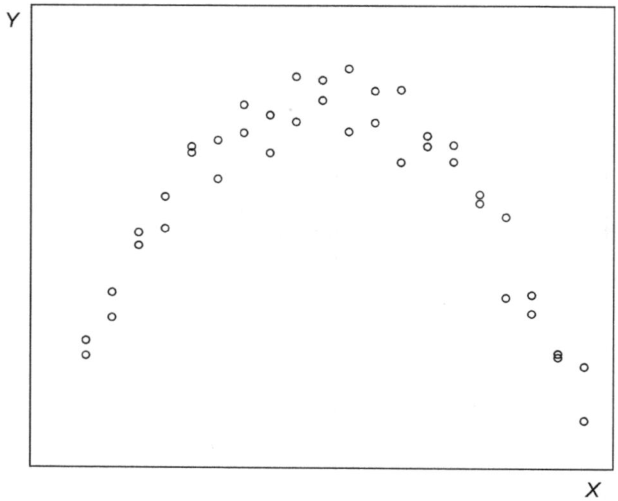

capture the non-linear association. Several such measures (the best known is probably η) are discussed in standard statistics textbooks. For now, it is sufficient to know that the ordinary correlation coefficient is useful for assessing linear association between continuous variables only.

Eyeballing the graphs is important for the second issue too. The correlation coefficient is namely sensitive to so-called *outliers*. See Figure 6.7, in which an example is given of a sample in which the scores on X and Y are negatively associated: a cloud of points in the lower left corner forms a ladies' cigar, tilted to the left, indicative of a (fairly strong) negative correlation. However, because there is one person who combines a huge X with a huge Y, the correlation coefficient if we were to simply compute it would come up strongly positive here. That correlation coefficient is, however, based on just one out of N sample members, so not a result one would want to report like that. Inspecting the scatterplots therefore also prevents mistakes one could make if one were to simply – blindly – compute the correlation coefficient. Outliers like the one depicted here are generally removed from quantitative analysis: they are considered an anomaly that distort our view of the general picture.

Most researchers compute their correlation coefficients with a software package or a calculator. Understanding the formula for the coefficient is noble, but not crucial. What is however crucial is to understand the scatterplots we discussed and to realize how much can be gleaned from them. Anyone – including the maths-averse – can read from a simple scatterplot whether there is a linear or a non-linear association between X and Y. Also, anyone can see whether the association is positive or negative. Lastly, anyone can get at least an idea of the strength of the association. It is only when we want to have an exact number that we need to resort to computations. All the other

Figure 6.7: Outlier

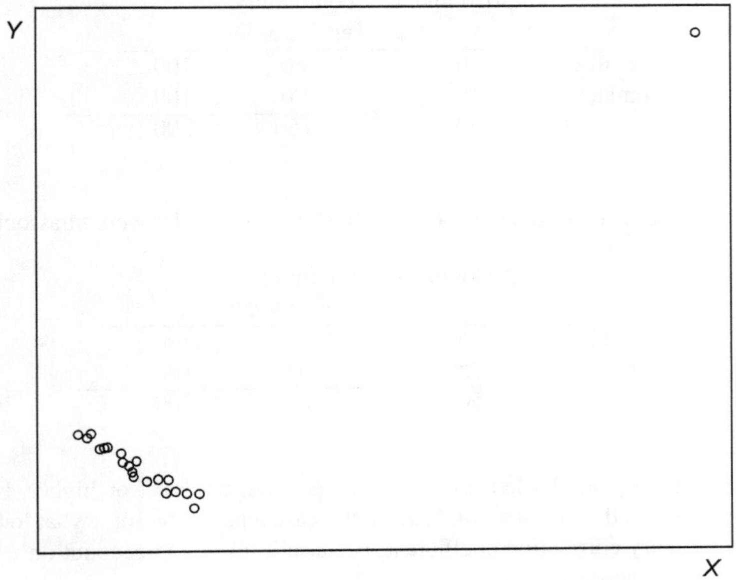

much more relevant and much more interesting stuff we can all do by simply eyeballing the graphs.

6.4.2 Other measures of association

As we said earlier, the ordinary Pearson product moment correlation coefficient is but one measure of association: for the linear association between two continuous variables that – we hinted at this but did not make it explicit – are distributed pretty 'normally'. The moment one of the variables is not interval level or higher, if the association is not linear, or if one of the two variables has a 'funny' distribution (like a skewed distribution), we must resort to other statistical measures. This is important to know.

We will however not discuss all those measures: mainly because it is all pretty tedious and not really necessary for our purposes, as most coefficients are interpreted along similar lines. The reader who needs to decide which coefficient to use can look up the various options in a textbook, for instance Hinkle, Wiersma, & Jurs (2003). We only briefly mention two other fairly commonly used correlation coefficients.

The first of these is Spearman's ρ (or 'rho') for variables X and Y both measured at ordinal level. Spearman's ρ varies – just like the ordinary correlation coefficient – between -1 and 1, and the interpretation given to these numbers is also identical.

The second is Kendall's τ (or 'tau'), which is a measure for the association between two ordinal variables. It is less often used for ordinal variables than Spearman's ρ. It

Table 6.3: Observed frequencies of sentence type and gender

	imprisonment	community service order	
males	40	60	100
females	10	90	100
	50	150	200

Table 6.4: Expected frequencies if sentence type and gender were unassociated

	imprisonment	community service order	
males	25	75	100
females	25	75	100
	50	150	200

is however regularly used when the variables are interval level or higher, but their distribution is skewed. The value of 'tau' in that case tends to be somewhat lower than that of the ordinary correlation coefficient, because it takes into account only ranking information of the scores.

When we are interested in the association between two nominal or categorical variables, numerous measures are available. Each has weaknesses and strengths. In research practice, however, two are most often used: the χ^2 (or chi-square) and the odds ratio. The first is not really a measure of association (although it is often interpreted as such); it is a statistical test, which does not actually tell us how strong the association between the two nominal variables is, but rather how likely our data is to be found if the variables were unassociated. The second tells us something about the strength of the association between two dichotomous variables (i.e. variables with two categories each only). It expresses this association in terms of risk. We will first discuss the chi-square (or χ^2), which is very often used. The examples that we use are, for ease of explaining, simple two-way tabulations; for the chi-square, all computations can be simply extended to variables with more categories.

Suppose therefore that we have measured two nominal variables for a number of respondents, and that our findings are as given in Table 6.3. In this table we see that a total of 200 respondents have been investigated: the sample consisted of 100 males and 100 females. Of these 200 respondents, a quarter, or 50, were sentenced to imprisonment, and 150 received a community service order. Now the question is: are the two variables we are investigating here associated? Are gender and type of sentence associated? In other words, does it make a difference for sentencing whether a respondent is male or female? We can see without any computational fuss that this is the case. Of the women, only one in ten was sentenced to imprisonment, while for the males this was 40%. Clearly, gender matters. But how strong is the association? Can we express that in a number, a statistic?

For that, the observed frequencies (Table 6.3) are compared with the frequencies we would expect to find if the two variables were not associated. In Table 6.4 these are given: we see that if gender played no role in sentencing we would expect to find equal proportions of men and women sentenced to imprisonment (25) and to a community service order (75). Formulated differently, with the data as in Table 6.4, knowing what someone's gender is does not give you any information on the type of sentence they likely received. For computing the chi-square, the differences between the observed and expected frequencies are used.[7]

As the chi-square is computed as a sum of squared values, its lowest possible value is zero: a value of zero indicates that the frequencies are exactly as expected under the null hypothesis (see chapter 8) of no association. We then conclude that the association between the two variables is insignificant. The higher the chi-square that is computed, the more likely it is that we can conclude that the two investigated variables are associated. Almost all software packages that compute the chi-square also generate the significance level. At this point we reiterate that the chi-square can be computed for nominal variables with more than two categories (for instructive purposes we used only dichotomous variables here). Attention should be paid to whether the cells of the cross-tabulated variables are adequately filled: if the sample size is small or too many expected frequencies are low, the test does not perform well and other tests may be recommended (such as Fisher's exact test).

In our example, the chi-square value equals 24, which is highly significant ($p <$ .001). The significance of the chi-square is in research practice often equated with the strength of the association between the two investigated variables. In that sense, formulations of the χ^2 are often slightly sloppy.[8] While this may seem nit-picking, it should be noted – as we will discuss in chapter 8 – that significance also depends on sample size. So, if we have a very large sample, a tiny value for the chi-square test may also emerge as significant even though the association between the two nominal variables may be weak.

Various measures are available that do give an indication of the strength of association between nominal variables – just like the correlation coefficient does for continuous variables. Probably the best of these, under some conditions, is the so-called *Cramer's V*, which gives us a number between 0 and 1, with 0 reflecting no association, and 1 perfect association (meaning that from the score on one nominal variable,

[7] The chi-square is computed as:

$$\chi^2 = \sum_{i=1}^{k} \frac{(O_i - Ei)^2}{E_i},$$

with k the total number of cells, O_i the observed frequency in the i-th cell of the cross-tabulation, and E_i the frequency we would have expected in that cell if – in this example – gender and sentence type were unassociated, as given in Table 6.4. The chi-square then becomes:

$$\frac{(40–25)^2}{25} + \frac{(60–75)^2}{75} + \frac{(10–25)^2}{25} + \frac{(90–75)^2}{75} = 24.$$

[8] A second manner in which wording of the test is generally sloppy, is that most researchers speak of the value of the χ^2, while the statistic computed is written with a Latin letter X as X^2, and in the hypothesis the Greek letter χ is employed.

Table 6.5: Observed frequencies of sentence type and gender

	imprisonment	community service order	
males	40	60	100
females	10	90	100
	50	150	200

the score on the other nominal variable can be predicted perfectly). Other measures are also available, such as the ϕ-coefficient for two-by-two tables, or λ.

However, whichever measure one uses, it is important to realize that we should always inspect the cross-tabulation to understand what the substantive interpretation should be. As the correlation coefficient deals with continuous variables only, it is easy to interpret: if the coefficient is high and positive, high scores on X imply high scores on Y. For nominal variables, the interpretation is not immediately obvious. In our sentencing and gender example, the χ^2 tells us that the two are associated but it does not tell us whether that means that being a man increases the likelihood of imprisonment, or whether it is being female that increases the likelihood of imprisonment. So, we always need to refer back to a cross-tabulation to be able to interpret the association between the two nominal variables. We refer the reader to a statistics textbook such as for instance Hinkle, Wiersma, & Jurs (2003) for more information.

For dichotomous variables, another very often used measure to inspect association is the *odds ratio*. The odds ratio is not easy conceptually, but very easy in use and interpretation. The reasoning behind it is best explained with an example. Suppose that we have the same data we had before. See Table 6.5, which is repeated here for inspection purposes but is the same as Table 6.3.

The reasoning of the odds ratio is as follows. In the example, we have data on gender and sentence type. For females the probability of receiving a prison sentence is 0.1, and the probability of a community service order 0.9. This means that for females the probability of being sentenced to a community service order is 9 times that of a prison sentence. For males, we can apply the same reasoning and then we find that the probability of receiving a community service order is 1.5 times that of a prison sentence. The odds ratio now is the ratio of these two ratios or odds,[9] which equals 6.

How can we interpret this? The literal interpretation is that the ratio of imprisonment to community service order is for males 6 times that for females. This is hard to master conceptually, and a jumble of words. In practice the two terms in the nominator and denominator are perceived of and formulated as 'risk'. The odds ratio is conceptualized as a ratio of risks (or indeed 'odds'). In practice, interpretation is unproblematic with formulations such as: 'the risk of imprisonment for males is 6 times the risk for females'.

9

$$OR = \frac{\frac{\text{male imprisonment}}{\text{male community service order}}}{\frac{\text{female imprisonment}}{\text{community service order}}} = \frac{\frac{40}{60}}{\frac{10}{90}} = \frac{\frac{1}{1.5}}{\frac{1}{9}} = 6.00$$

Note firstly that a risk is not a chance: risks can be larger than 1 while probabilities are always between 0 and 1. Secondly, it is important to note that if there were no difference in risk between males and females, the odds ratio would be 1 (not 0!). Compare again the data in Table 6.4. This table reflects the situation where there is no relation between gender and sentence type – in other words, for the scores on sentence type it does not make any difference whether someone is male or female. Thus, we would also expect no difference in the odds. And if we wanted to compare the risk for men and women for this dataset, we would indeed arrive at an odds ratio of 1.[10]

So, an odds ratio equal to 1 means no difference in risk, and an odds ratio larger than one means an increased risk. Obviously, if we had in our example in Table 6.5 reversed men and women in the equation, we would have arrived at an odds ratio of 0.1667,[11] and we would have reported that females have a 6 times *lower* risk of imprisonment. So, with the odds ratio, it is important to keep in mind how this risk is specified (i.e. what is in the nominator and what is in the denominator). Also, because of this, an odds ratio of 2 (twice the risk) reflects just as big a difference in risk as an odds ratio of 0.5 (half the risk).

Now what is generally perceived as an increased risk, or as a not-so-strongly increased risk? Just like for the correlation coefficient, here also there are rules of thumb. In general, an odds ratio larger than 2 or smaller than 0.5 is judged to constitute a sizeable risk increase or decrease. This is a rule of thumb though, and for some research situations an odds ratio of 1.3 may already be judged to constitute a relevant increase in risk. It is also possible to test whether an odds ratio differs significantly from 1.

In an exploratory study, Tollenaar (2018) investigated differences between culpability as assessed by municipalities and as assessed by administrative courts when deciding on administrative fines in the Netherlands. Data were collected from the website `rechtspraak.nl`, the official website of the Dutch judiciary, using the search terms *bestuurlijke boete* (administrative fine) and *verwijtbaarheid* (culpability) for cases dealt with by the Centrale Raad voor Beroep (Central Appeal Tribunal) from late 2014 to mid-2017. This led to a usable sample of 125 cases in which an administrative body – municipal or judiciary – had imposed a fine and an administrative court had later judged culpability in the case.

Tollenaar first described how many citizens had defended themselves by stating that they were not, or only to a limited degree, culpable. Second, he found that many administrative authorities had assumed that the transgression was intentional (28% of cases). Third, Tollenaar notes that administrative courts often judged the behaviour to be non-intentional, but instead constituting normal culpability (70%), or reduced or in fact no culpability (16%); the percentages for the municipal authorities had been 50% and 9% respectively. The data are in Table 6.6.

10

$$OR = \frac{\frac{\text{male imprisonment}}{\text{male community service order}}}{\frac{\text{female imprisonment}}{\text{female community service order}}} = \frac{\frac{25}{75}}{\frac{25}{75}} = 1.00$$

11

$$OR = \frac{\frac{\text{female imprisonment}}{\text{female community service order}}}{\frac{\text{male imprisonment}}{\text{male community service order}}} = \frac{\frac{10}{90}}{\frac{40}{60}} = 0.166667$$

Table 6.6: Positions of the administrative authorities and court judgment

Degree of culpability	Position of administrative authority	Judgment of administrative court
Intentional	28%	6%
Gross negligence	11%	7%
Normal culpability	51%	70%
Reduced culpability	8%	14%
Absence of culpability	1%	2%

Source: Tollenaar (2018)

Next, Tollenaar sets out to explain this difference. For this, he compares the judgments of the administrative authority against those of the courts on a case-by-case basis. He notes that in 62% of cases, the court and administrative authority judge identically. In 38% of cases they judged differently, and the court always found lower culpability.

Tollenaar identifies two possible explanations. The first is a temporal one: he states that it may have taken the administrative authority a while to absorb new rules that took effect from late 2014. The data do not support this explanation, however. It is not the case that differences were larger after the new rules took effect. A second explanation is that smaller municipalities may have lacked the knowledge and expertise to apply previous judgments of the Central Appeal Tribunal. Tollenaar states that this is a much more likely explanation, as the Association of Netherlands Municipalities, which normally supports municipalities with the implementation of new regulations, only issued a position paper in April 2017, well after the new rules came into effect.

Additional analyses lend further support to this explanation. Disaggregating the cases by whether they had been dealt with in first instance by a municipal administrative body or by a national administrative agency, it became clear that decisions made by the national agency had much more often been upheld by the courts (88%) and rarely altered (11%). For the municipalities this pattern was reversed: a majority of cases were altered by the courts. See Table 6.7.

The odds ratio equals 8.83 (computed as the odds of confirmation versus alteration for national agencies, divided by the odds of confirmation versus alteration for municipalities), showing how indeed the risk that the court confirms is very much increased in national agencies as compared to municipalities.

These results do not prove that it is municipalities' lack of expertise that causes the difference. Tollenaar argues that municipalities and national agencies typically deal with different, likely not well-comparable cases: municipalities decide mainly in social benefits cases, while national agencies decide in employee insurance schemes. Second, municipalities must pay social benefits out of their municipal budgets, which may be an incentive to educate offenders about the need to observe the relevant provisions.

Last, we note that the sample of cases does not constitute a representative sample of all cases in which administrative fines have been imposed, as not all citizens who are

Table 6.7: Type of administrative authority and court judgment

	National agency	Municipality
Court confirms	88%	48%
Court alters	11%	53%
$\chi^2 = 19.79, p <.001$		

Source: Tollenaar (2018)

handed such a fine will object and take their case to court. It also does not constitute a representative sample of all cases that were decided by the courts.

6.4.3 Graphs for describing the association between variables

What we said in section 6.3.3 about the ease of visual representation for simple descriptives – such as the distribution of a variable – also applies when it comes to investigating the association between variables. Here also, graphs are an efficient tool to make the reader see and interpret association. Given however that association is investigated, graphs are bound to be more complicated. We already showed a number of scatterplots in section 6.4.1, and stressed how important it is not to rely on computations only, but to actually inspect the data. Doing so will reveal non-linear associations and outliers. This means that the use of graphs is not only pleasant for readers, but supports the analysis as well.

Another way to graphically display association is by using a special kind of bar chart, a so-called *stacked bar chart*. See Figure 6.8, in which we show several things, with the data again stemming from the study on office misbehaviour. Firstly, we show how many respondents did and did not personally know someone who had experienced office misbehaviour. The graph shows that approximately 100 did, and 140 did not. Next, the graph also shows that the majority of those who knew someone who had experienced office misbehaviour was female, while for those who did not know such a person the distribution was approximately even. There is all in all a clear association between the two variables.

When a variable is at interval measurement level or higher, we can also visualize association. Using a so-called *clustered histogram*, we can inspect whether the distribution of one variable differs by the categories of another variable. See Figure 6.9, in which we depict scores on a dependent variable, disaggregated by age category of the respondents.

Figure 6.9 breaks up the distribution of age into two groups: one below 40, and one above 40. We see that the distribution of agreement is mirrored: the distribution in the younger group is right skewed and in the older group it is left skewed. Again, this pattern is much easier to grasp and understand for readers than the same data in a table would be.

Figure 6.8: Example of stacked bar chart for type of abuse and recidivism

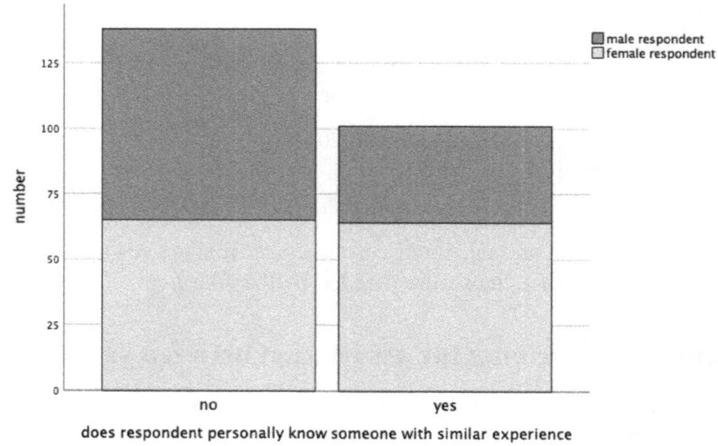

Figure 6.9: Clustered histogram for distribution of ratings by age group

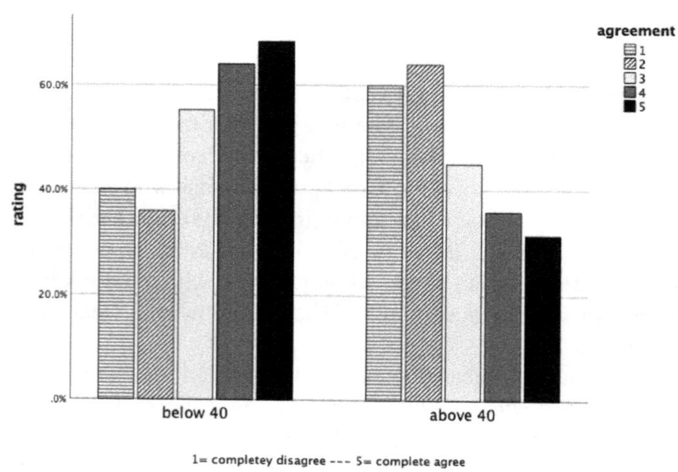

6.5 Duration variables: survival analysis

In some types of research, we encounter special variables. The properties of these variables are such that we cannot do regular computations with them. One example of such a special variable we encounter regularly in empirical legal research is a so-called *duration variable* or a *time-to-event variable*. This may sound fairly obscure, so let us illustrate what we mean through an example.

Suppose we want to study recidivism in released prisoners. We want to assess how long it takes, on average, for prisoners to recidivate in the sense that they are re-sentenced to imprisonment and return to prison. Now let us assume that we have a sample of 10 prisoners who were released on various days over the course of one year. The day that a prisoner is released we count as day zero, and from that day onwards we start counting. For a prisoner who is reconvicted and is re-imprisoned after 30 days, we set the variable 'recidivism' we are interested in at 30; another prisoner, back in prison after 90 days, gets a value of 90 for the variable 'recidivism'. If we were to calculate the average time to recidivism for these two prisoners, we would arrive at a value of 60 days. And if we have another two prisoners who are reconvicted and returned to prison, one after 120 days and the other after 320 days, the mean time to recidivism for all four would be 140 days. So far, so good, it appears.

But what are we to do with six other prisoners who did not recidivate within our observation window of one year? If we report that average time to recidivism is 140 days, we are well off the mark; we do not reckon with the fact that there are six others who did not recidivate for all those 365 days we observed them... The average of 140 days is not a good summary of what happened. Should we then set the recidivism time for these six at 366 days? This is also not a good solution as that is not what happened; it is in fact quite likely that some will not recidivate at all, or possibly only after a very long time. And suppose that one prisoner dies after 200 days, not having recidivated. Do we remove this prisoner from our dataset? That would also be distorting as then we are omitting someone who did not recidivate and are then left with a more 'serious' subsample.

Survival analysis is a technique that can deal with these issues. It is a method that is very often used in epidemiological research, where for instance survival after treatment for a certain disease is studied. Survival analysis is encountered under different names, such as *event history analysis* or *failure time analysis*. The dependent variable in survival analysis is survival time (in epidemiology real physical survival, so time until death) or time until a certain event takes place. That event can be recidivism or time until a court case is dispositioned. Survival analysis is also used in other disciplines, such as in demography, where it can be used to study survival but also time until divorce.

Survival analysis has a method to deal with the specific properties of the time-to-event variable. A first property is that the values of this variable can only be positive (prisoners cannot return to prison before they were released). This by itself does not generate massive issues, as it is not problematic to compute averages for variables with positive values only. What is problematic though is the phenomenon we just described. As we conduct our study over only a certain stretch of time, we do not have values on the duration variable for those who do not recidivate before the end of our observation period. While we know that they did not experience the event we are interested in, we have no way we can attach a value to their duration variable.

The duration variable is for these persons, as it is called, *censored*. It may be that they do recidivate at some point after our study has ended, but we do not know whether that is the case, or when. This phenomenon is also referred to as *censoring*. Survival

Table 6.8: Months, recidivism and censoring, number of persons *at risk*, event chance, survival chance and cumulative survival chances

month	event	*at risk*	P_t(event)	P_t(survival)	S_t
1	-	5	0.00	1.00	1.00
2	recidivism	5	0.20	0.80	0.80
3	-	4	0.00	1.00	0.80
4	censoring	4	0.00	1.00	0.80
5	recidivism	3	0.33	0.67	0.54
6	recidivism	2	0.50	0.50	0.27
7	-	1	0.00	1.00	0.27

analysis can deal with this censoring. What it does is to incorporate the measures for all those who have not recidivated into the analysis, until the point where we are unable to observe them anymore, either because our window of observation ends, or because they have died or emigrated or moved out of our sight in some other way. This may sound pretty abstract, so we will demonstrate survival analysis using a small example.

In its simplest form, survival analysis computes a function of survival against time. The curve of this function (the 'survival function') shows, for every observation point in time, the percentage of respondents that has survived until then, that is, that has not experienced the event we are interested in. As said, our respondents can be people and the event can be criminal recidivism, or disease, or employment after obtaining a law degree. But our 'respondents' can also be court cases or tort claims, and then we would be interested to see how soon these are dispositioned or settled in some way.

Let us construct a very small example of five fictitious persons who were sentenced to community service. We want to analyse how soon they recidivate. The day community service is completed is day zero, after which the clock 'starts ticking'. We observe these five persons for seven months. At the start of the first month, nobody has recidivated yet. All five respondents are, as we say, *at risk* of experiencing the event. Suppose that nobody recidivates in the first month. The chance of survival is then 1, and the chance of recidivism 0. See the first row of Table 6.8.

At the beginning of the second month, all five respondents are therefore still at risk; each of them can still undergo the event. Now suppose that in month 2, one person indeed recidivates. This respondent then has not 'survived'. The average survival chance in month 2 P_t(survival) is then equal to 0.8 (and the chance of undergoing the event P_t(event) is therefore equal to 0.2). At the beginning of month 3, we are therefore left with four persons who are still at risk of experiencing the event; see the third column of Table 6.8. The last column of this table gives the so-called cumulative survival probability S_t, the proportion of respondents who have survived until time point t. S_t is calculated as $S_{t-1} \times P_t$(survival). One of the assumptions of survival analysis is that the survival chances are independent across the time intervals, so that we may multiply them, to end with a proportion of survivors.

Now suppose that in month 3 no one recidivates. The chance of undergoing the event is then 0, and the survival chance 1. The cumulative survival probability remains at 0.80. In month 4, a respondent emigrates; this means that we will not have information on this respondent's recidivism for the coming months, hence we now have censoring. At the end of month 4, the cumulative survival probability is still 0.80. However, at the beginning of month 5, we have only three respondents who are still at risk. While the emigrated respondent may undergo the event, we have no way of registering this as the respondent has disappeared from our sight.

In month 5, a second respondent recidivates. The chance that the event occurs is in this month P_5(event) equal to 0.33: one out of three respondents at risk has recidivated. The survival probability P_5(survival) is therefore equal to 0.67. The cumulative survival probability S_5 now equals $S_4 \times P_5(\text{survival}) = 0.80 \times 0.67 = 0.536$. Note how the cumulative survival probability incorporates the effect of censoring: even though two out of five respondents have recidivated, we do not calculate the cumulative survival as 0.60 but arrive at a lower figure of 0.54, because we now take into account that one respondent has 'disappeared' from our calculations. See Table 6.8.

At the beginning of month 6, only two persons are still at risk of undergoing the event. If in that month one person recidivates, the probability of undergoing the event is in that month 0.50, the survival chance is the same, and the cumulative survival probability is 0.27. At the beginning of month 7, only one respondent is still at risk.

The cumulative survival probabilities constitute the survival function. Figure 6.10 shows the survival function from the example we just discussed. As we are dealing with a small number of respondents, the curve is quite jagged; if we analyse larger samples, the survival curve will be smoother. This curve is also called the *Kaplan–Meier curve* (Kaplan & Meier, 1958). It is customary to indicate with a small cross or dot when censoring took place (see the little cross for our emigrated person in month 4 in Figure 6.10).

Using survival analysis, it is also possible to compare the survival curves of one or more groups. Suppose for instance we have two groups of former prisoners, one that had a normal incarceration regime, and another group that was administered a special training to facilitate reintegration. We would expect those who had undergone the training to recidivate less. We would expect their survival curve to differ from the survival curve of the regular prisoners. If that is the case, we may conclude that there is an association between the reintegration training and recidivism: those with the training have different patterns than those without the training.

Bruns, Pullmann, Wiggins, & Watterson (2011) investigated the King County Family Treatment Court (KCFTC), an effort to address the special needs of families involved in the child welfare system due to child abuse and neglect charges related to parental substance abuse. Family treatment courts (FTC) were modelled on drug treatment courts, but differ in their aims. While drug treatment courts aim to keep offenders free from the influence of drugs and alcohol so that they do not have repeat involvement with the criminal justice system, FTCs aim to strengthen family bonds, and promote children's health and safety. The child welfare system is involved in the judicial process, and court-appointed special advocates may be enrolled. The authors studied a host of outcomes for one of these courts, the King County Family Treatment Court.

For this, they collected data on a total of 258 parents, of whom 76 were KCFTC participants, and 182 were parents in principle eligible for KCFTC but were not admitted for various reasons. This means that we have a quasi-experimental design, with

Figure 6.10: Kaplan–Meier survival curve

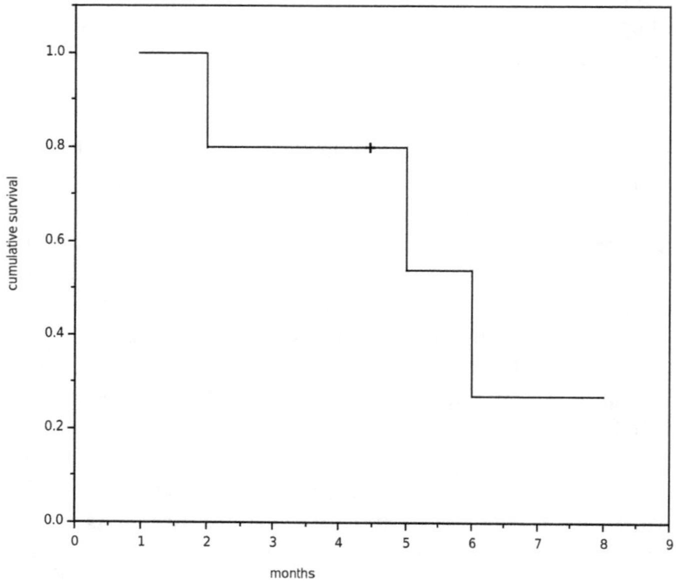

some doubt on whether the KCFTC and non-KCFTC parents were comparable (in fact, the groups were indeed not comparable as the KCFTC parents had fewer risk factors). The authors investigated a large number of questions, of which we will focus on two, namely whether – as compared to the control group – KCFTC parents were admitted to treatment more quickly than the comparison group, and whether the involvement in the child welfare system of children of KCFTC participants ended sooner.

For the first question, the authors conducted a Kaplan–Meier survival analysis. The dependent variable is here 'time until admission to treatment'. The survival curves are depicted in Figure 6.11, with the top curve representing the comparison group and the lower curve the KCFTC group.

If we inspect the figure, we see immediately that the survival curve for the KCFTC parents is always (much) lower than that of the comparison group. For instance, after 100 days, we see that only approximately 30% of KCFTC parents has survived, that is, have not undergone the event. This means that after 100 days or about 3 months, 70% of the KCFTC parents are enrolled in treatment. The comparable figure for the control parents is 70%, meaning that only 30% of control parents are in treatment after 100 days. This difference remains, and even increases. For instance, after 200 days, a little over 15% of KCFTC parents have not experienced the event, so that 85% are enrolled in treatment; of the control parents, a little over 40% are by then enrolled in treatment. The figure shows two more interesting things. First, we see how enrolment in treatment stagnates for both groups. After about a year we see no real improvement anymore: within the KCFTC parents about 10% do not enrol anymore, and within the control

Figure 6.11: Kaplan–Meier survival analysis of days until treatment entry for all parents

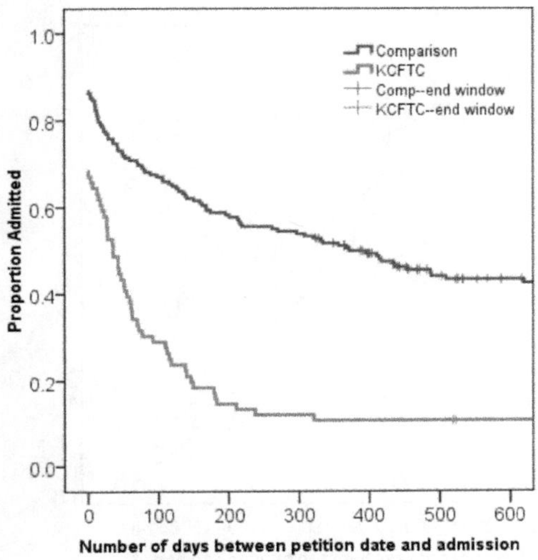

Source: Bruns et al. (2011)

parents this is a little under 50% – a huge difference. Second, we see how from the start KCFTC parents were already doing better (underlining that the two groups were not randomly chosen). On the day the 'clock started ticking' for the survival analysis (the day a so-called 'index petition' was handed in), a little over 10% of control parents were already following treatment. KCFTC were from day 1 already faring better: 30% were already enrolled.

For the second question, the authors also conducted a Kaplan–Meier survival analysis, with as the dependent variable now 'time until child is no longer involved in child welfare system'. The survival curves are depicted in Figure 6.12, with the top curve again representing the comparison group and the lower curve the KCFTC group.

Here, the interpretation is identical. After developing similarly to the comparison children for the first 200 days, their survival curves start descending faster, meaning that more of them leave the child welfare system. While the differences are less marked than in the previous picture, the KCFTC children are also here doing consistently better. After 500 days, 40% of KCFTC children have left the child welfare system, while 75% of control children are still in the child welfare system. In this figure, we see a similar 'stagnation', which turns out to be much less favourable for the control children. Towards the end of the evaluation period, it appears that 40% remain 'stuck' in the sense that they seem unable to leave the child welfare system, but for a few who did so

Figure 6.12: Kaplan–Meier survival analysis of length of time until child's end of involvement in the child welfare system

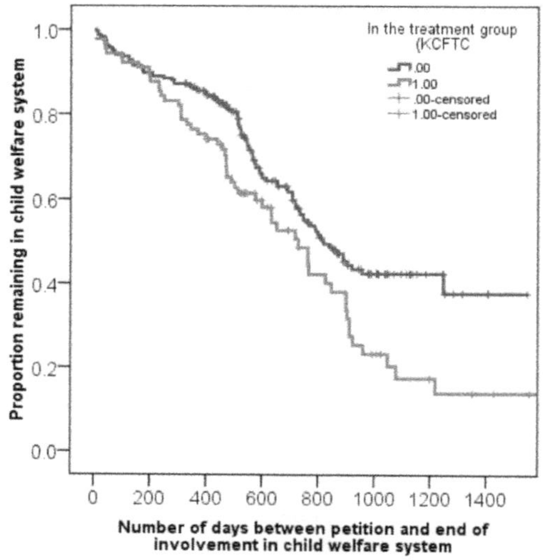

Source: Bruns et al. (2011)

eventually. This applies to a much smaller percentage of KCFTC children, just a little over 15%. All in all, a – roughly speaking – 25% difference between the two groups.

Do these results mean that we can be sure that these differences are attributable to the KCFT Court? Strictly speaking not, as parents were not allocated to the Court randomly. As the figures also showed and as other tables in the report indicate, there is reason to suspect that the KCFTC parents and children were doing better from the outset. To eliminate such *confounding*, the authors performed a number of supplementary statistical analyses. The findings from these analyses also pointed in the direction of the FTC special courts indeed having a beneficial effect.

Numerous extensions of survival analysis exist. We showed only examples where the survival curves of two groups are compared (for instance KCFTC and non-KCFTC). Other comparisons are possible too; it is for instance also possible to investigate not just the occurrence (or not) of one event, but the occurrence of several events (for instance settlement, withdrawal, judgment). An accessible introduction to survival analysis is Allison (1984); a more elaborate classic is Kalbfleisch & Prentice (2002).

6.6 Wrapping up

In this chapter, we introduced concepts such as respondents, variables and measurement levels. We gave a number of statistics to summarize variables, such as the mean for central tendency and measures for variability. After such univariate statistics, we discussed bivariate measures, such as the correlation coefficient for numerical variables, the χ^2 for nominal variables and the odds ratio for dichotomous variables. We also illustrated how to use graphs to visualize such bivariate associations. We discussed a special kind of analysis, survival analysis, for a dependent variable that is a time-to-event variable. Even though we each time gave the formulas in footnotes for the measures we discussed, we also stressed that these formulas are not necessary to understand how the statistics work, nor needed if one has a statistical software package at hand (even Excel will do quite a few statistics).

Chapter questions

1. What are the five measurement levels? (section 6.2.1)
2. Describe in what ways they are ordered (section 6.2.1)
3. Argue why outliers are particularly problematic for measures of association and central tendency for interval level variables (section 6.3)
4. List the measures of association that are available for nominal, ordinal and interval level variables (section 6.4)
5. Under what conditions can the Pearson product moment correlation coefficient be used? (section 6.4)
6. What is meant by censoring in duration variables? What complications does it cause? (section 6.5)
7. Argue whether regular correlation coefficients could be used if a duration variable had no censoring (section 6.5)

Chapter 7

Qualitative data analysis

7.1 Introduction

In chapter 2 we very briefly touched upon qualitative research. We presented it – simplifying matters somewhat – as juxtaposed with quantitative research: where quantitative studies describe a limited number of issues, in isolation, for a large number of people, qualitative research describes many issues, in their interrelatedness, in a specific context, for a not necessarily representative set of people. This means that, where quantitative research often isolates variables and studies the impact of these on other variables, in qualitative research pre-defined variables or factors are less often studied. In fact, a qualitative approach is generally chosen because the factors of interest need to be studied within a specific context, or in their complex or layered interrelation with other variables. Also, many qualitative researchers argue that human behaviour cannot be understood 'from the outside', but that we need to know the *meaning* that events and behaviour have in order to be able to understand why people behave as they do. To uncover meaning, persons need to be queried repeatedly or deeply, or observed within their natural habitat, necessitating naturalistic and participatory approaches to data collection. Context and meaning are key concepts in any qualitative study.

This has important implications for the type of data that are gathered and the manner in which these can be analysed. As qualitative researchers argue that behaviour is understood best within its context, it is not strange that qualitative researchers rarely use standardized, 'pre-fab' instruments, because, given that each context is unique, such standardized instruments are inherently useless as they might easily skip essential elements of the context. Therefore, more often than not, qualitative researchers actually start their analysis from the physical world and human behaviour as observed in it. The data themselves can be the starting point of analysis, and meaning and structure may be derived from the data and not imposed upon it as a *Fremdkörper*. Some grounded theorists even go as far as to do their literature review only once all the data have been collected.

This – for a quantitative scholar 'topsy-turvy' – approach is given the epistemological outlook of qualitative research inherently logical. Phenomena can only be understood after the researcher has grasped the meaning of behaviour, of symbols, happenings, occurrences. Hence the strong emphasis of qualitative research on embeddedness, on immersing oneself as a researcher in the world of those who are to be studied – in corporate culture, in the lives of recipients of welfare – and the extensive use of open or in-depth interviews, in order to *understand* in the research why decisions are taken by municipal staff as they are, or whether welfare recipients perceive administrative procedures as fair. For that matter, as we stated in chapter 2, qualitative research is also referred to as *interpretative* empirical, with quantitative research conversely labelled as *analytical* empirical; parallel labels are *inductive* for qualitative research and *deductive* for quantitative.

It must be noted, as we also said in chapter 2, that this contrast between qualitative and quantitative research is slightly overdone and overly simplistic. The two are not completely different, irreconcilable approaches to empirical legal research. In practice, many studies combine qualitative and quantitative elements. Much qualitative research is not entirely 'grounded', but works from theoretical assumptions, or employs existing legal categories or theoretical constructs. Nor is quantitative research entirely inductive, as often exploratory, more qualitative phases are built into the research design. This means that there is no watershed between qualitative and quantitative research, and that qualitative and quantitative analysis methods are not in entirely different leagues. Qualitative researchers also aim to describe prevalent or dominant patterns, or are seeking relations between variables. As we will see below, some analysis methods for qualitative data may be in fact entirely quantitative.

7.1.1 The iterative nature of qualitative research

Regardless of the above, the more 'prototypical' qualitative analysis methods can be contrasted with quantitative methods as on average less prescribed, less 'recipe-wise', and more iterative. This also holds true for qualitative data collection procedures, which are generally not often very closely prescribed and are instead flexible and adaptive. Especially ethnographic researchers generally start by interacting with the people they aim to study, and may draw up hypotheses as they go along. They may ask as many questions as they need to understand the phenomenon they are studying. As they do not know beforehand what will cross their path, these interviews are far from pre-designed questions administered by web survey: they must take place in preferably face-to-face settings, where researchers are able to note facial expressions, hear inclinations and deflections of voice, see emotion or boredom in people's faces.

In some qualitative approaches, a participatory stance is taken, where researchers attempt to view the world from their research participants' perspectives. They cannot, goes the reasoning, really understand their respondents' predilections, motives, constraints, unless they are able to – in a sense – lead their lives with them. An example of such a study is the famous criminological study on gang life and the urban poor in Chicago by Venkatesh (2008), which has been immensely important for theory formation on the pathways in and out of gang membership. The study by Flood (2005) similarly was one where the researcher attempted to immerse himself in the corporate world he studied, and was in that sense ethnographic: Flood was even hired by the firm that he studied, sat in on meetings and joined office parties, like a regular employee.

We discussed at length in chapter 4 how qualitative data collection generally occurs in open or topical interviews, and how the data that results from such fieldwork generally consist of transcriptions of interviews, field notes and analytic memos. Qualitative data can also consist of documents or video material (or even movies, advertisements, YouTube uploads or Instagram pictures). What all these data have in common is that they are generally (highly) unstructured. In order to make sense of them, to analyse them and arrive at conclusions, we must therefore structure the material, reorganize it so that an overview can be made. Then we will be able to see the woods for the trees, and structure may emerge and the research questions be answered.

In qualitative data analysis, that process is often iterative. By that we mean that analysis does not take place in one pre-designed sweep as it does in quantitative data analysis, but that the researcher in fact iterates over explanations of the data. It is possible, after coding textual material and analysing the codes in a second step, to return to the original codes and modify them, and then re-do the analysis step. The qualitative researcher may in each step visit the raw material, draft an analysis or explanation, revisit the material and check – looking at all the transcripts and notes and memos – whether that analysis is tenable or needs to be adjusted, adjust the hypothesis, then revisit the data to see whether the adjusted hypothesis now holds, etc., until a conclusion is reached that is satisfactory and is in line with everything that is in the data.

The research cycle that was introduced for quantitative research in section 2.2 and that is travelled through only once for a quantitative study may in fact be traversed in as many loops as are needed for answering the research question in qualitative research. This can even go so far that hypothesis formulation, data collection and analysis are interwoven, and are performed iteratively, with as many waves of data collection and analysis as necessary. Researchers then collect data, analyse the data and arrive at a tentative conclusion (for example written down in analytic memos) and then return to the field, collect new data and test their tentative conclusion against new information that was gathered. Once such iterative loops do not lead to adjustment of the conclusions (no new insights are gathered from additional interviewing or observation), it is said that *saturation* has been reached (see for a classic reference Glaser & Strauss, 1967). This process, where one samples respondents up to the point where adding new sample members would not change the conclusions, is referred to as *theoretical sampling*. It is often used when purposive samples are drawn. At the point where the researcher decides that data collection can be stopped and saturation has been reached, it is then also said that high *theoretical validity* has been achieved.

It is generally advised to test this to the limit in the sense that researchers are encouraged, once their preliminary interpretation of the data has been formed, to actively seek out cases for inclusion in the sample that do not seem to match the tentative conclusions. This practice of deviant or negative case analysis could be regarded as an aberration if one were to strive for randomness of selection research subjects. It can, however, also be regarded as a kind of quota or stratified sampling, where one aims to have sufficient spread in the sample over possible subgroups of respondents.

A related issue is the analysis of outliers. These can be regarded as deviant cases: they do not fit the general pattern. In quantitative analysis these are generally seen as a nuisance. One should in quantitative analysis scan for such outliers, and if they appear they are often ignored in analysis. They are regarded as an anomaly, as exotic and not indicative of a relevant pattern for the majority of the investigated sample. Contrarily, in qualitative analysis it is considered imperative to include these outliers. They are perhaps even regarded as the canary in the coal mine, as specific cases that may indicate where the extracted pattern or devised theory is simply not ready yet, which may lead to a major improvement of the conclusions that have been reached so far. Qualitative researchers attempt to incorporate such cases to the very end, revisiting their theoretical framework and analysis to see whether the outlier can be made to fit, or whether one needs to conclude that it does not fit after all. Flyvbjerg (2006) is an interesting read on the usefulness of the study of such outliers, or more broadly case studies, that may put one on the path to discovering a black swan. All in all, sampling and analysis may be interwoven in qualitative research. We will for that reason sometimes in this chapter on data analysis also discuss data collection issues.

One important implication of this is, as discussed, that in qualitative research, we often do not work with just one research cycle, but in a sense a (sometimes very long) corkscrew of mini-research cycles. A qualitative study is therefore by itself a spiral of small research cycles. By the time the explanation or interpretation of the phenomenon under study converges, and does not change anymore with new respondents or data added, nor even with negative cases added, the research ends and conclusions can be drawn. Qualitative research unfolds all in all quite differently from the quantitative research mould. It is for qualitative research generally much harder, therefore, to predict what a sufficient number of sample members will be, how long the study will take, and therefore to budget costs. It must be said that also this depiction is slightly overdone, as in the real world also qualitative researchers must draw up budgets and plan their studies.

Before we start our discussion of qualitative data analysis, it should be noted that there appear more different takes among qualitative researchers than among quantitative researchers on what suitable or preferred methods are for specific analysis questions. As qualitative research may study idiosyncrasies, many qualitative researchers are also bound to adhere to their own, or special analytic 'culture'. Textbooks on qualitative research are for that reason often an amalgam of various methodological approaches and 'schools', working from different epistemological stances. While there is fairly general agreement among quantitative researchers on how a regression analysis should be carried out (although at times there can be wide-ranging differences too on the 'right' approach for answering a specific quantitative research question!), there does appear to be less agreement among qualitative researchers on what suitable methodological approaches are. Given the scope of this book, it will be impossible to address all these different schools and traditions and nuances. What we will do is discuss a number of analytic approaches and tools that are shared among most qualitative scholars.

7.1.2 Modes of qualitative data collection and analysis

As we discussed in previous chapters, qualitative data collection methods can consist of various types: ethnography, where the researcher in a sense immerses him- or herself in the world of the objects of study and where a combination of approaches is generally used (interviews, observation, dialogue, documents), interviewing, where generally open or in-depth modes of interviewing or narratives are used, and observation, where the researcher does not take part in any social interaction with the research subjects (the researcher is in a sense a 'fly on the wall', not participating, unobtrusive and only registering behaviour). As we discussed briefly, the use of documents or secondary material, such as published court rulings, where essentially the researcher also 'observes', can be considered a separate source. Under such 'patient' sources, we also classify blogs, videos, films, advertising material, diaries and the like.

These modes can be thought of as being on a continuum of 'participation' or 'immersion': the most participatory method is then ethnography, where the researcher may him- or herself even 'become' the instrument as we said; interviews assuming a middle position, where the researcher plays a role in what is said as s/he poses the questions, decides on what to probe, registers emotions (or not), so that the researcher influences to a certain extent what behaviour and verbal utterances the respondents show; and observation, under which also falls the study of documents, as the most 'unparticipatory', where a researcher need not even have any exchanges with the respondents.

On the other hand, these three modes of data collection can also be ordered differently, on a continuum of 'naturalness' with which study participants may be expected to behave. Interviews are then the mode in which respondents' behaviour would be least natural, ethnography would assume a middle position as the researcher will collect data such that the study participants can go about their ways as normally as possible but the researcher remains a stranger in their midst, and observation (under which again the use of existing materials) would be the data collection mode (especially when unobtrusive methods are employed such as through CCTV cameras, the 'fly-on-the-wall' mode) where respondents can behave as naturally as possible. Figure 7.1 depicts this in schematic fashion.

All analysis of qualitative material, whether gathered using ethnographic methods, interviews or observation, can be carried out employing a '*formal* mode' and an '*informal* mode'. By the formal mode, we mean methods to structure and analyse the material using tools and methods that are interchangeable between researchers. A researcher can employ for instance first-level coding and second-level coding using the tools that we point out below. However, during data collection, informal methods may also be used. By these we mean for instance that researchers may also pick up implicit information that is unique to one particular researcher, such as a specific response that fieldworkers encountered upon entering gang turf, or a response by an interviewee that may be tied to characteristics of the researcher.

Such information can definitely be used in analysis: in fact, some parts of texts or of interviews may even give you as a researcher a particular feeling, or even a sensory experience such as nausea or a shudder, which may offer important clues for analysis. And such sensations should therefore definitely be employed in analysing the material. During coding (formal mode), researchers should then ask themselves: why does this particular sentence or expression affect me so much? Pondering such particularities that may be tied to yourself as a data collector or researcher is important, and qualitative researchers should indeed in this sense be sufficiently 'reflective'. The term 'positionality' is often used to denote how researchers can and should reflect on their gender, social class or specific privileges that impact data collection and other research methods.

Figure 7.1: Schematic representation of three modes of qualitative data collection

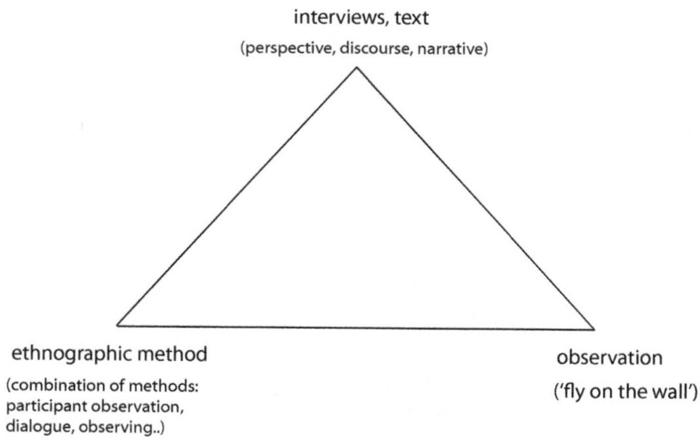

Clearly, such information picked up that is related uniquely to the researcher is less easily exchanged with or found by other researchers. A particular response may be tied to a researcher's gender, so that a researcher with a different gender would not even pick up the cue, or responses may be due to cultural differences or preconceptions. Researchers may use meta-information that they happened to pick up or gather during the fieldwork or in other phases. Using such informal modes of analysis is part and parcel of qualitative analysis. All in all this means that qualitative data analysis is influenced by personal experiences and individual characteristics of the researcher. This makes it inherently more difficult to achieve reliability. In the following we will mainly focus on the more formal modes of data analysis.

Qualitative data is usually massive and unstructured. Qualitative data analysis therefore generally consists of two steps: one to order the unstructured data, and a second to analyse these ordered data in order to answer the research questions.

7.2 Coding qualitative data

As said, before the analysis of qualitative data can start, the data have to be ordered in a manageable format. Data can be interviews, transcripts, minutes of board meetings, court verdicts, plea bargains, newspaper reports, notes, or even pictures or videos. They have to be transformed into a format that is analysable. If the data are not written text yet, they are generally textified, that is, turned into written text. Interviews are transcribed for that: all that is said is literally typed up, sometimes including coughs and 'ehhrmms' (see section 4.2).

Most researchers these days use software to order and analyse their data. CAQDAS (computer-aided qualitative data analysis software) is the generic name for these packages. They all have in common that they make it possible to structure and restructure the data, regroup fragments, attach codings and subcodings to text blocks, and look for patterns in the data. Such software is almost necessary to get an overview of the often massive amounts of material (transcripts of interview can easily add up to hundreds of typed pages). A veteran programme is ATLAS.ti (`atlasti.com`), which has been around for many years and is available for many platforms (Mac, Windows, and even a smartphone version is available). Friese (2019) offers an accessible and hands-on manual for coding using ATLAS.ti. Other packages are NVivo (`qsrinternational.com`) and MAXQDA (`maxqda.com`). In addition to tools for coding, most commercially available packages also aid in aggregation and visualization of the data. Quite a number of free packages are available as well, but these generally offer coding only; an exception is qdap (the acronym for Quantitative Discourse Analysis Package), an R-based package that offers word extracting, statistical analysis and visualization (see `cran.r-project.org/web/packages/qdap/index.html`).

However, for analysing small bits of data, such a package is not necessary. Especially for the first sweeps in coding, when the aim is to get a feel for the data, the text may simply be highlighted with felt pen, or some first coarse coding done by hand.

7.2.1 Description: first-level coding

Analysis generally starts with first-level coding, also referred to as primary-cycle coding or first-cycle coding. In the analysis of qualitative data, one is generally faced with an immense amount of unstructured, 'raw' data. The goal of analysis is to get an overview, to describe what is there, and to find relationships between pertinent constructs, or to detect logical schemes. In order to be able to do so, the data first has to be reduced to manageable shorter units. This is what the first-level phase is about: in the first phase of coding the aim is to develop a list of codes under which the information in the data can be subsumed and therefore ordered. The code list should capture the relevant issues that are there in the data. All the written material should, formulated differently, be classified under a number of codes, after which the codes can become the focus of analysis.

But this may still sound somewhat mysterious, because what is a 'code'? Saldana (2013, p. 3) defines a code as:

> *"A code in qualitative inquiry is most often a word or short phrase that symbolically assigns a summative, salient, essence-capturing, and/or evocative attribute for a portion of language-based or visual data. (...) The portion of data coded during first-cycle coding processes can range in magnitude from a single word to a full paragraph, an entire page of text or a stream of moving images."*

First-level coding is therefore a first, descriptive step. In first-level coding one reads through all the data and attaches codes to relevant parts of text. Here one essentially tries to attach labels to chunks of the data, to group sentences or pieces of text under various descriptive headers. First-level coding is in a sense quite 'flat' and easy as it is descriptive, one only codes *what* is in the data. The aim is essentially to arrive at a sort of inventory of the information content. Pieces of text (or other coded material) are grouped under the codes that are homogeneous: they all refer to the same phenomenon, meaning, interpretation. Segments under the same label refer to the same issue, segments under different labels refer to different issues. Coding is therefore a process in which one identifies similarities and differences in the information content of the data. Every relevant segment of text should be coded (and may in fact also receive two or three codes).

Coding can be done on the basis of an existing list of codes ('top-down'), or it can be done in a more 'grounded' way. In the first approach one would for instance be testing a theory that uses particular constructs, or searches for specific legal arguments used in rulings: encountering these known categories, they are marked and labelled as such. When, on the other hand, coding is done in a more grounded way, one scrutinizes the data for categories or themes that emerge from the data. Coding using existing categories is also referred to as 'etic' or 'deductive' coding; coding employing categories as they present themselves from the data is also referred to as 'emic', 'open' or 'inductive' coding'. Deductive coding, with a set list of codes, is arguably easier to replicate by other coders and reliability is therefore sooner achieved (see section 2.6).

It is difficult to pinpoint exactly how one determines codes inductively. The most basic technique is essentially reading and eyeballing the data: reading the material once, twice or even a third time, and noting phrases or words that 'appear' to be 'key'. Another observational technique to extract themes from transcribed text is to focus on repetitions: when you interview people repeatedly, or groups of people, there will be issues that recur. These may be 'fairness' or 'respect' or 'class differences'. Apparently, as such themes emerge so often, they are important, they clearly constitute a relevant issue. Metaphors may often signal so-called 'themes'. Quinn (1996, in Ryan & Bernard, 2003) studied American marriages. She noted that respondents often used metaphors to indicate that marriage is intended to last: interviewees would state that a marriage was like 'the rock of Gibraltar' or was 'nailed in cement'. Apparently, this lastingness was a dominant issue. The term 'theme' is often used interchangeably with the word 'code' in inductive coding.

In spoken and written texts, transitions such as new paragraphs or a pause in speaking often indicate that a new theme is coming. And what may be equally important, is to not only search when identifying themes for what is there, but also for what is *not* there. Silences in interviews, looking away, can be as telling as words. Information that is missing, gaps, things left unexplained may be important clues. Ryan & Bernard (2003) give the example of interviewees who did not respond that they disapproved of government policy, but simply went silent if a question to this effect was asked. Attaching a theme becomes more slippery here, however, because how can one interpret something that is not there? And how can one be sure that the interviewee is silent because s/he disagrees with government policy? Maybe the interviewee is simply fed up, or thought the question trivial.

We illustrate the first-level coding process using data excerpts from a study by Bijleveld et al. (2022). Employing vignettes, the authors asked respondents to what extent they considered fair (on a rating scale) a sentence of eight years for a perpetrator who had committed war crimes. In the vignettes the authors randomly varied – amongst others – whether the perpetrator had apologized or not, and whether the perpetrator was a commander or a foot soldier. After respondents had indicated whether they believed the sentence was just right, too short or too long, they were asked to elaborate on the reason for their answer. Figure 7.2 gives an illustration of the type of data the authors gathered, and a first round of coding made by the authors.

Because the authors had randomly varied aspects of the vignettes, they first searched for mention of these aspects. They therefore scanned the comments for mention of the apology made (or not made) by the fictitious perpetrator, and for mention of the rank of the perpetrator. In addition, they also employed inductive coding in that they searched for other arguments that respondents thought pertinent. In this study, a mixture of deductive and inductive coding was therefore used. Given that the authors interviewed 570 respondents, the example with 14 motivations can give only a glimpse of the coding process. Even so, what we see is that from the list of given codes, apologies were often mentioned: seven times in all, of which five times that no apology had been given by the perpetrator and twice that an apology had been given. Also twice it is mentioned that the sentence should be long because the perpetrator was a commander in charge. Once it was mentioned only in interaction with the apology: the apology is regarded as insincere because, as a commander, the perpetrator was in charge.

The respondents also gave other arguments, not related to the manipulated factors, for the sentence being too short (mostly) or just right. Seven times it was mentioned that the crimes were too serious for the sentence. Other arguments emerged for favouring a longer sentence: deterrence was mentioned, and the fact that the offender needs more time to rehabilitate, or justice for victims. We also see in Figure 7.2 how the coder was hesitant at times, unsure what code to use. For instance, the second respondent mentioned that the perpetrator should be tried for war crimes in a similar way that Nazi commanders were prosecuted, but the coder did not know yet under which header to capture that part of text.

This brings us to the fact that coding is seldom finished in one round. Researchers generally attach codes to the various segments of text in their data in a first sweep, and then revisit the data and check and change the codes somewhat. Software is very helpful here. Using packages like ATLAS.ti, one can reorganize the data to show all text that was given a certain code, to review. Review of the codes should verify that the text fragments are homogeneous and fitting. It could then emerge that some text fragments actually do not fit under a given label. Or that two subcategories exist within a larger category. During such review rounds, or during later analytic phases, it may also become apparent that two different codes actually describe the same phenomenon: the codes can then be lumped under a new header. For the example we gave above in Figure 7.2, the codes could for instance be regrouped into arguments in favour of a longer sentence, or arguments why the sentence was just right, or why it should be shortened.

Some researchers even go back, after a first analysis has been conducted, to the original text and apply new codes, and then re-do the analysis. Some in fact very quickly start coding once the first data is in. And they may then also go back to their codes and modify them after more data has been collected, and may go back again and

Figure 7.2: Descriptive codes vignette study of international sentencing

I believe it is just because his crimes against civilians were heinous. He also did not exhibit any sort of remorse nor did he apologise, demonstrating that he does not see the error of his actions. As such, 8 years is quite necessary for him. However, it is already 10 years after the fact, and thus I did not give a score of 5 to include the long delay of the sentence, to signify that it is already quite late for this.	*too serious crimes* *no apology* *fair trial*
He may have been carrying out orders from even higher superiors (or doing them on his own which is worse) but that does not excuse his behaviour. After the second world war, Nazi commanders were also prosecuted for their crimes and I think in this case it is similar in that David should also be given a higher sentence.	*duress* ~~*serious crimes?*~~ *consistency?*
The sentence is way too short for having committed two deaths and tortured civilians.	*too serious crimes*
I think 8 years is enough in a sense because it is a reasonable amount of time, but I don't think it serves as justice for the victims. He did apologise to the victims so that's a step in the right direction	*no justice for victims* *apology*
I think that 8 years is very little for him having committed essentially a war crime with the torturing of civilians and the death of two people. Although he apologized we are not even sure whether he meant the apology because why would he have committed those acts as a Commander?	*too serious crimes* *apology* *sincerity unsure because commander*
8 years is too less for what he did. It doesn't change a person to lock him/her up for only 8 years	*too serious crimes* *no effect on offender*
Prison is necessary only when there is a big threat, which it doesn't seem to be here	*incapacitation unnecessary*
I believe that 8 years was unjust. Eight years is not enough for at least two deaths of innocent civilians.	*too serious crimes*
He was in charge and in the position to have avoided this.	*commander position*
Because he shows no remorse even after 10 years. Should be more, especially as the commander.	*no apology* *commander position*
No, the time period is not reflective of the death and trauma for the survivors. Nor is it adequate rehabilitation time for someone who does not show remorse.	*too serious crimes* *no rehabilitation* *no apology*
It is too short and thus does not set enough of an example as a deterrent for others who could commit such crimes in the future. He shows lack of remorse.	*no deterrence* *no apology*
He should have received a harsher sentence to reflect the severity of his crimes	*too serious crimes*

make new choices again given additional data that they encountered or more recent interview material that has been added. First-level coding is all in all more often than not an iterative process. Spencer, Ritchie, & O'Connor (2010, p. 229) stress that in the final stages of this first-level phase – which is essentially a data management phase where the original data are summarized and synthesized in order to reduce the amount of material and retain the essence of what was there – three requirements apply. First, key terms, phrases or expressions should be retained as much as possible. Secondly, interpretation should be kept at a minimum. Thirdly, phrases that do not appear to make sense or appear irrelevant should not be dismissed: their relevance may appear at later stages.

So in this coding phase, scholars often attach to the various relevant parts of the text labels that summarize, capture or indicate what is being said or written. The coding process is therefore definitely more than simply organizing the text: coding does always imply some interpretation and therefore analysis. Because labels can also narrow one's vision, some researchers prefer not to attach their own labels, but the very words that the interviewees use to code fragments. In doing so, one postpones the interpretation, reduces the risk of tunnel-vision or imposing pre-set notions. Such coding is called *in vivo* coding. Obviously, by using *in vivo* codes one remains closer to the original text, and retains the actual language used; however, in the choice of fragments, some organizational choices are arguably made which means that some interpretation is effectively there.

Obviously, if one were to strictly apply *in vivo* coding, one could end up with thousands of codes. This can also happen when one applies selected labels, as coding can be done in a very detailed way, giving each part of a sentence its own label. This is referred to as 'fractured' coding, and the process as 'splitting'. The advantage of this kind of fine-grained coding is that all nuances and little fragments are preserved and remain highlighted. Obviously, the downside is that the codings may become too fine-grained to be able to see much: there may be too much detail, one does not see the wood for the trees. Because the aim of the first-level coding is to reduce the amount of information, by combining text fragments into categories, this defies the purpose. In practice, researchers who start out with very detailed coding are for practical reasons often forced to lump categories together.

Some researchers on the other hand start out by using fairly coarse, general labels; this is referred to as 'lumped' coding. Those who start out more coarsely will quickly disaggregate labels into different, more specific labels. But how many labels should one use? There are not more than rules of thumb on how many codes should be developed. The number of codes firstly depends on the richness and breadth of the material. If the respondents all mention the same arguments, a small number of codes will do. If there is a lot of variability in people's answers, one would likely have to employ more codes, and many more so if *in vivo* coding is used.

Using a software program, it is technically possible to develop a list with 500 different codes. However, this list will likely be too large to be able to get an overview of what is there in the data, as so many codes are conceptually unfeasible. It is therefore, to get a grasp of the material, to be able to get an overview, much better not to work with too many codes. In the literature, a maximum of 100–200 codes is regularly mentioned, although in practice much lower numbers are encountered. An extensive and thorough guide to coding is Saldana (2013).

The codes that are given should be described and documented, and explained what kinds of text are given that label. Most researchers therefore draw up – just like during fieldwork – a certain diary-like record of all choices and alterations they made during coding and why, and an *analytic memo*. This is not only for the researchers' own pleasure but intended to contribute to transparency of the analysis process and thereby reproducibility and replicability.

7.2.2 Analysis: second-level coding, patterns and typologies

After the raw material has been coded, analysis proper starts at the stage of second-level coding. Here researchers will interrogate the data with the research questions in mind. Here meaning has to be extracted, from the manner in which codes co-occur, or by looking at the profiles of respondents who give certain answers. There are various ways in which analysis can be carried out in this second phase, depending on the type of data available and the research questions that need to be answered.

Whichever approach one uses, it is customary to use *exemplars* or *vignettes* to present the findings, that is, parts of interviews or delineated portions of text or other material, collected during fieldwork, that are exemplary for what the researcher believes has been found. In some cases, respondents formulate so succinctly and precisely, or a life-story of a respondent in a sense illustrates the themes so well, that these are reproduced *verbatim*. Vignettes do the same thing, but are artificial exemplars in the sense that the researcher has constructed them. Note that the term 'vignette' has a different meaning here than it had in chapter 5.

It is at this second-level analysis stage that theoretical sampling may be employed: as meaning and interpretation emerge from the material, a search for empirical data that do not match the emerging interpretation can aid to strengthen the interpretation (when it turns out such 'negative cases' cannot be found) or broaden the scope or generalizability by extending the theoretical findings. Throughout the second-level coding, researchers should also keep a diary-like record of the interpretations that emerge, the choices that were made. Such a diary, which we already briefly mentioned in section 4.2, is referred to as an 'analytic memo'.

Numerous textbooks have been written on the analysis of qualitative data. While relatively extensive as regards first-level coding, textbooks are less explicit when it comes to the analysis phase. This partly because analysis is generally of itself fairly particular or idiosyncratic. Some textbooks recommend that the reader simply starts at it, and Friese (2019, pp. 5–6) describes holistic analysis as follows:

> *"Take a printout of one or more transcripts. In summer, look for a delightful place outside; in winter, find a cozy spot in front of the fire. Have something to eat and drink and then spend some time reading your data from beginning to end in sequential order, reminding yourself of the interview situation or other contexts. Do the same with videos or other type of data you may have. There is no need to sit in front of the computer all the time. Reading the data via a different medium, such as on good old-fashioned paper, is likely to give further insights."*

This sounds woolly and far from concrete. While numerous approaches can be distilled from textbooks, we will describe four main approaches to the analysis of qualitative data after they have been coded at first-level. These are: interpretative coding, pattern analysis, axial coding and typologies.

Interpretative coding
A very illustrative example of interpretative coding is the analysis by Lindegaard et al. that we described previously in section 4.5. Lindegaard and her co-authors (2016) coded the behaviour of all people (victims, bystanders and perpetrators) present in a number of robberies from CCTV fragments. They coded numerous fragments of the video images in very general, descriptive and as neutral terms as possible, looking at the movement of people's limbs, the direction they were looking, whether they stood still. Codes given in the first-cycle coding phase were for instance 'hands at waist', 'pushing victim', 'touching arms of bystander'. Alongside to these behavioural categories, they also noted where the robbery took place, how many people were present and other situational characteristics.

In a subsequent coding step, Lindegaard and her co-authors *interpreted* these behavioural codes and attached labels to them that were not descriptive anymore but captured what that behaviour meant in that particular situation. They coded for instance whether the behaviour constituted resistance by a victim, or whether offender behaviour constituted a threat or actual violence. If a supermarket employee raises her hand, this can be because she puts her hands up as a sign of submission, but it could also be an attempt to grab the weapon of the robber (meaning taking control). This means that the authors must decide what the function or intention of the behaviour was.

The authors had set out to know what precursors predicted whether a robbery would turn violent. In a subsequent step, they therefore investigated whether there was a specific pattern or sequence of acts by bystanders, victims and robbers that often led to violence, and whether there were specific patterns or sequences that were associated with a robbery ending non-violently. Their analysis therefore also involved a search for patterns, over the time elapsed – often minutes – that the robberies took.

Pattern analysis
A second approach to analysing the first-level codes is through a search for patterns. It may be that to answer the research question we want to know whether, for instance, certain legal arguments are always used in conjunction: whether respondents who attach prominence to one aspect of sentencing tend to also answer in a particular way with respect to other aspects. This may sound pretty vague, so we illustrate it with an example. In the study by Bijleveld et al. (2022), the authors coded the arguments respondents gave for their assessment of the sentence length.

The authors noted that apologies offered by the perpetrator did not in general lead respondents to opt for a shorter sentence. A total of 54 respondents indicated that the absence of an apology should imply a long(er) sentence: "Lack of remorse deserves longer sentence", "Because [the perpetrator] does not show remorse and the crime is severe, there is a need for an appropriate punishment", "[The sentence is] long, but since not apologised it's suitable", "[The perpetrator's] lack of empathy and apology should also add time". However, an apology by the perpetrator much less often made respondents propose a shorter sentence or deem the sentence too long (13 times): "[The perpetrator] showed remorse, asked for forgiveness and recognized [the suffering of the victims]", "Too short for two deaths, although the apology helps", "[It is] already ten years later, [the perpetrator] offered his excuses and has also built a new life".

The authors also analysed the data quantitatively, which revealed that apologies significantly impacted respondents' preferred sentence lengths. The qualitative analysis now clarified how this impact was in fact non-linear, and adds on to the existing literature on the relationship between apologies and sentencing. That is, while the existing legal and empirical-legal literature on international criminal justice (Hola, Bijleveld, & Smeulers, 2011; Tudor, 2008) points to apologies and remorse as mitigating factors in sentencing, this study showed that for ordinary citizens it is the *absence* of apologies that may be considered an aggravating factor.

Note that pattern analysis may also entail simply tallying the occurrence of arguments. Wijntjens (2020) investigated, in a study of in case law that we return to in section 10.3, whether apologies were regarded by judges as constituting an admission of culpability. Wijntjens scrutinized almost 600 rulings and found that apologies were decisive in the ruling in only a little over 1% of cases. It is here that we see how qualitative analysis can very well incorporate quantitative analysis methods.

Pattern analysis can be greatly supported by software such as ATLAS.ti. The program has features to search for and investigate the co-occurrence of codes, whether certain codes follow each other, whether one code always encompasses another, etc. It is also possible to search for differences, such as whether people with certain educational levels, or different migration backgrounds regard the justice system differently. For more on this, see Friese (2019, chapters 6 and 7).

Axial coding

Axial, or hierarchical coding is the third approach that we describe for analysing the first-level codes. Axial coding is in a way the reverse of the first-level coding process. While in first-level coding one attempts to break up the text into a large number of codes, at this stage one tries to combine these codes into overarching dimensions or axes (hence 'axial' coding). With axial coding, central, overarching codes or constructs are identified that bind or encapsulate the first-level codes. The codes that are arrived at in axial coding are often elevated to the (somewhat confusingly labelled) higher status of 'category'. Axial coding is also sometimes referred to as hierarchical coding.

One way to do this is to reorganize the text fragments (and this is again where the qualitative data analysis software packages come in so handy) so that text that has similar labels is regrouped to appear together. One can then re-read all (parts of) sentences and see whether new, conceptual 'umbrella' concepts describe data under one label.

Figure 7.3 gives a worked example on data as were collected in the study by Bijleveld et al. (2022) that we used previously for illustration purposes. In the figure, the first-level codes and second-level, axial codes have been entered. In this example, three axes have been identified, of which one is eminently clear: 'Utilitarian' indicates whether someone employed arguments that indicated whether a shorter or longer sentence would 'work' for some reason (such as protecting society, rehabilitating the offender). The two other axes are less clear (and would likely be altered or removed in a next analytical run over the data). One of these is labelled 'Normative' and connects to the seriousness of the crime and what – given that seriousness – a suitable sentence would be. A third refers to justice, whether the sentence would be just. Justice can refer to victims, but it also does so twice to the perpetrator: whether it is fair to punish someone after such a long time, and whether the perpetrator did not commit the crimes under duress, although the respondent rescinds that argument in the same sentence. The codings show once more how second-level coding may require a number of iterations to arrive at a satisfactory analysis.

Typologies

While pattern analysis can be regarded as an analysis at the level of the variables, a similar kind of pattern analysis can also be conducted but now at the level of the respondents or sample units. Then, one is interested to find out whether certain combinations of codes, or profiles, can be distinguished that classify the sample members into groups. Such profiles define what are called 'typologies'.

In constructing typologies one divides the sample into a small number of groups, of which each and every member belongs to one and only one subgroup. Typologies are an organizational tool to divide or sector the real world, and thus to describe and understand it. Ritchie, Spencer, & O'Connor (2010) give an example of parents who had children with learning disabilities who had continued to live in the parental home. The authors of the study had constructed four typologies, using two dimensions or 'axes' along which parents could be ranked. The two axes were first the recognition of the need to find alternative arrangements for the child and second the immediacy of action by the parents. This resulted in the following groups: evaders (parents who felt their children need not leave the home), delayers (parents who knew their child had to leave the home eventually but did not take action yet), debaters (parents described as torn between the need for change and the difficulty of implementing it) and action-takers (parents who saw the need for change and who had already started preparations for it).

Typologies are often constructed with the aid of underlying axes, resulting in four or more typologies. We will return to the construction of typologies in section 10.2. The concept of typologies is fairly strict in the sense that it is required that each and every member must be fitted into one group and one group only (like a taxonomy). It is also fairly strict in the sense that people cannot have partial profiles: they cannot belong to two typologies at the same time. On the other hand, members within the typology groups need not all be identical; some variability is regarded as natural.

7.3 Content analysis

Content analysis is the broad generic name commonly attached to the analysis of large volumes of existing text documents. Content analysis in fact comprises a fairly broad class of analytic techniques that aim to analyse texts to reveal what information they contain. Both quantitative and qualitative approaches are viable to do so. Content analysis can be carried out using first- and second-level coding of the transcribed material, methods that we discussed just now. Often, and especially when the material to analyse is voluminous, special software is used to carry out the analysis of the qualitative material. Automated procedures for content analysis are increasingly used.

Although the category is broader, content analysis has often been used to reveal the meaning or symbolic or covert intent of communications, whether these be written,

Figure 7.3: Descriptive and axial codes in vignette study of international sentencing

I believe it is just because his crimes against civilians were heinous. He also did not exhibit any sort of remorse nor did he apologise, demonstrating that he does not see the error of his actions. As such, 8 years is quite necessary for him. However, it is already 10 years after the fact, and thus I did not give a score of 5 to include the long delay of the sentence, to signify that it is already quite late for this.	too serious crimes no apology fair trial	NORMATIVE UTILITARIAN? JUSTICE PERPETR.
He may have been carrying out orders from even higher superiors (or doing them on his own which is worse) but that does not excuse his behaviour. After the second world war, Nazi commanders were also prosecuted for their crimes and I think in this case it is similar in that David should also be given a higher sentence.	duress ~~serious crimes?~~ consistency?	JUSTICE PERPETR.
The sentence is way too short for having committed two deaths and tortured civilians.	too serious crimes	NORMATIVE
I think 8 years is enough in a sense because it is a reasonable amount of time, but I don't think it serves as justice for the victims. He did apologise to the victims so that's a step in the right direction	no justice victims apology	JUSTICE VICTIMS
I think that 8 years is very little for him having committed essentially a war crime with the torturing of civilians and the death of two people. Although he apologized we are not even sure whether he meant the apology because why would he have committed those acts as a Commander?	too serious crimes apology sincerity unsure because commander	NORMATIVE
8 years is too less for what he did. It doesn't change a person to lock him/her up for only 8 years	too serious crimes no effect on offender	NORMATIVE UTILITARIAN
Prison is necessary only when there is a big threat, which it doesn't seem to be here	incapacitation unnecessary	UTILITARIAN
I believe that 8 years was unjust. Eight years is not enough for at least two deaths of innocent civilians.	too serious crimes	NORMATIVE
He was in charge and in the position to have avoided this.	commander position	NORMATIVE
Because he shows no remorse even after 10 years. Should be more, especially as the commander.	no apology commander position	NORMATIVE?
No, the time period is not reflective of the death and trauma for the survivors. Nor is it adequate rehabilitation time for someone who does not show remorse.	too serious crimes no rehabilitation no apology	NORMATIVE UTILITARIAN
It is too short and thus does not set enough of an example as a deterrent for others who could commit such crimes in the future. He shows lack of remorse.	no deterrence no apology	UTILITARIAN NORMATIVE
He should have received a harsher sentence to reflect the severity of his crimes	too serious crimes	NORMATIVE

oral, in images or even iconic representations. Once all such communications have been coded, that is, once descriptive, first-level codes have been assigned, one starts to search for meaning in the coded material. Analysing transcriptions of for instance boardroom meetings in law firms, one can note what is said, literally – which is what is summarized in the first-level codings – but one is mostly after more, such as the meaning and impact of communication, or the symbols behind expressions, tones or gestures, the meaning that people attributed to events. In the literature, numerous labels are given to the methods to do so. Essentially what one does in content analysis is uncover themes in the qualitative material (and possibly sub-themes), selecting from all themes the ones that are relevant for answering the research question, connecting these themes in a meaningful way so as to answer the research question, and, lastly, linking the findings back to theory. In that sense, it does not differ in a fundamental way from the coding and analysis of regular interviews or field notes.

In content analysis, quantitative methods are employed relatively frequently. The qualitative material is then quantified, and analysed using regular quantitative methods. In such a quantitative content analysis in its simplest form, one could for instance count the frequency with which certain words appear (such as 'solution' or 'conflict') in tort cases, or how often victims in criminal cases are referred to as 'vulnerable' or similar words. Quantitative analysis can be made more interesting by not only looking at means or percentages ('univariate analysis'), but by combining occurrences of words. One would then look at relational patterns: do for instance lawyers use different adjectives for male than for female clients? In a sense, one then carries out a bivariate analysis. In multivariate varieties one can look at combinations of words or phrases and contexts. Some such content analysis methods are quantitative – from basic to quite 'hard-core' – and others are qualitative and flexible – and hard to describe in a recipe-like manner.

Schmader, Whitehead, & Wysocki (2007) carried out a more quantitative analysis of qualitative material. They analysed letters of recommendation for male and female biochemists. Using special software for text analysis (Linguistic Inquiry Word Count (LIWC) Pennebaker, Francis, & Booth, 2001), they analysed how often particular words appeared in letters of recommendation as gauged against the total number of words in the recommendation letters. These words were: achievement words (e.g. goal), communication words (e.g. talk), positive emotions (e.g. happy), negative emotions (e.g. worthless), tentative words (e.g. perhaps), and certainty words (e.g. always). In addition, they studied the appearance of, amongst others, 'grindstone traits' (such as hard-working), ability traits, and standout adjectives (such as 'great' or 'brilliant').

The study showed that letters for male and female candidates were quite similar in terms of the various word counts, but that recommenders had used significantly more standout adjectives for male candidates as compared to female candidates, even though objective criteria showed no gender differences in qualifications.

See Hsieh & Shannon (2005) for a more in-depth discussion of qualitative content analysis, and see the short, pragmatic and very readable overview of the analysis of themes in qualitative analysis by Ryan & Bernard (2003).

7.3.1 Systematic case law analysis

Systematic case law analysis is a special kind of content analysis, of particular relevance to ELS scholars. On systematic case law analysis Hall & Wright (2008) state:

> *"Using this method, a scholar collects a set of document opinions on a particular subject, and systematically reads them, recording consistent features of each and drawing inferences about their use and meaning. This method comes naturally to legal scholars because it resembles the classic scholarly exercise of reading a collection of cases, finding common threads that link the opinions, and commenting on their significance. But content analysis is more than a better way to read cases. It brings the rigor of social science to our understanding of case law, creating a distinctively legal form of empiricism."*

In systematic case law analysis, one selects a sample (or an entire population) of document opinions or court rulings, reads and codes the material, and searches to answer the research questions. Very often the first-level codes have been derived in a dogmatic analysis, using standard legal research methods. The codes are then analysed in the second cycle using empirical, qualitative or quantitative methods, to answer the research questions. Systematic case law analysis is therefore also regarded as a hybrid, in between dogmatic and empirical analysis; in section 10.3 we present an example of case law analysis that focused on argumentation schemes employed by judges. However, in its design, systematic case law analysis follows the lines of a regular content analysis, with the raw data simply case law rulings.

Systematic case law analysis is a very promising type of empirical legal research. With the advent of digitalization, a wealth of case law has become easily available. Software packages facilitate the automated analysis of textified material. Some software enables the analysis of parts of texts or entire text documents.

Mascini & Holvast (2023) carried out a systematic case law analysis to investigate the relationship between the level of experience of law clerks and the confidence that is expressed in the writing style of their drafted judgments. Based on US research, concerns had been voiced that the delegation of drafting duties to law clerks "transforms the judge from a draftsman to an editor" (Posner, 1985, p. 104), which would render opinions and judgments less appealing and candid than if the judge had personally written them. Assuming that in many cases final judgments are based on edited versions of drafts made by law clerks, the hypothesis that the authors tested was that law clerks with more experience would write judgments with greater confidence than less experienced clerks.

Mascini and Holvast downloaded all administrative court cases published in the Netherlands in 2020 (N = 4,642) from the website of `rechtspraak.nl`, which publishes a selection of judgments. As they show, their sample, while large, amounted to not more than 5.9% of all administrative court decisions in that year. Their dependent variable was confidence, that is writing style of the judgments. The latter they operationalized as having three dimensions: judgment length, level of standardization, and number of legal references. They expected that experienced law clerks would draft shorter judgments that were less standardized and had fewer legal references. Given the number of judgments, these three dimensions were extracted from the court files in automated fashion. Judgment length was measured by simply counting the number of unique characters in each judgment. Standardization was measured with machine learning techniques using Doc2Vec (Le & Mikolov, 2014), software that can calculate the similarity between entire documents. The number of legal references was measured by counting the number of references to case law and legislation – which could be easily retrieved from a linked data portal of the Dutch government – or in case these were references to previous ECLI cases, by using pattern matching. While the data are qualitative, the authors made use of automated extraction methods and software to quantify their dependent measures of interest. From other sources, the authors had obtained data on career length of clerks.

In their analyses, the authors controlled for a number of possible confounders. These were firstly judges' career length (supposing that more experienced judges might depend less on clerk drafts), complexity of the case (which might arguably affect judgment length as well as possibly standardization), and court level (expecting that judgments from first instance courts would be more elaborate than from appellate courts). They ran separate regression analyses, predicting each of the dimensions of writing style separately, in which they each time also included the other writing style dimensions, as these were correlated.

The authors showed that – in line with their hypothesis – law clerks with more experience co-signed judgments that were less standardized, and contained fewer legal references. However, the judgments were not shorter. The authors are not entirely sure to what this can be attributed, as they attempted to control for case complexity. The study shows, according to the authors, that it is important to replicate empirical legal research across various jurisdictions as the findings from one jurisdiction (USA) clearly may not hold elsewhere (the Netherlands). The authors recommend to replicate this research in still different areas of law as well as in jurisdictions that employ a scribe model of clerking, and to investigate the role of other factors such language proficiency to predict writing style characteristics. They also recommend to test the confidence hypothesis on a less heterogeneous set of cases, to reduce the risk of confounding with factors such as case complexity.

We give an extensive example of systematic case law analysis in section 10.3, to which we refer for more illustration.

7.4 Analysing other material

Qualitative research can use a wide variety of materials to analyse. Materials can be primary (when the researcher has gathered them him- or herself) or secondary. In the latter case, the material can be documents (such as discussed under content analysis), but news items can be analysed as well, as can movies, memes, ads or song lyrics. While the analysis of some of these materials may be slightly different, in the end some 'textification' of the materials is generally derived, after which the materials can be analysed by regular methods, using first-level and second-level coding. While there may therefore be slight differences with the steps as we discussed them here, the basic principles are the same.

This is less easily said when the materials have been gathered during participant observation. Here, it is likely that interviews and conversations, observations and text materials, video images and even music comprise the documents on which analysis should take place, but much of the information that will be relevant for information is likely stored in the researcher's head. It is then much harder to describe how analysis should proceed, what the steps are, and how one arrives at conclusions, as much of the material may be tied in with the researcher's experiences and perceptions.

Formulated differently, in such participant observation, the researcher him- or herself has become the data collection instrument, or even the data. While qualitative data analysis is already by nature contextualized, this is even more strongly so in the case of ethnographic research. It is then extremely difficult and even undesired to outline beforehand the steps to be done for the analysis of the data. While the descriptions of first-level and second-level coding were already quite dense, this becomes impossibly so for ethnographic analysis. Apart from generic principles, not many guidelines or specific procedures can be outlined. Especially for such data, it is immensely important to document precisely in analytic memos what steps were taken, what insights presented at what moments etc.

7.5 Reliability and validity in qualitative analysis

Qualitative methods come in many forms and shapes. Some are described with very little guidance: reading the data, over and over again, until you 'see' the themes. Others are more prescribed, such as when deductive codes are used, or when the occurrence of words is tallied in texts.

We stated in section 2.7 that, relatively speaking, quantitative studies tend to be stronger on reliability and qualitative studies may be stronger on validity, but that was perhaps a fairly vague statement, as there is such variation within qualitative research. Some of the studies that we touched upon, such as the studies using CCTV images by Lindegaard and her colleagues (2016), and systematic case law analysis are examples where reliability is in fact easily achievable because the material to be analysed is 'patient' and can be coded, the codebook refined, and re-coded until interrater reliability is reached.

One can assess interrater reliability by hand, inspecting the codes attached to textual units by different coders and decide whether these are identical or substantively different, both the textual units as well as the codes. The coding by the second coder should of course have been done 'blind', independently of the first coder. Software packages for qualitative data analysis also have options for automatically computing interrater reliability.

Such automated assessment of reliability is a meticulous business, however. Within ATLAS.ti one can compute Krippendorff's α (see section 2.6.1), but ATLAS.ti does so using exact text fragments. That is to say, if one compares one piece of text that has been labelled with code X and a second chunk of text that includes a few more words grouped under the same header X, the program will not identify this as a 100% match. The program works with exact 'textual units' and exact labels, and is merciless on textual overlap: it has to be exact. This means that for determining reliability of interpretative codes one often resorts to doing so oneself, identifying and evaluating each other's attached codes and textual units.

When material is less easily accessed by others than the researcher him- or herself, such as when ethnographic or participatory methods are used, it is important that researchers themselves scrupulously check and re-check the quality of the data and their interpretation. As mentioned previously, an analytic memo is a must, in which the researcher notes all decisions taking during analysis. If it is not possible to compute quantitative measures such as the kappa-coefficient, qualitative researchers should assess the consistency of the fieldwork, whether analysis was conducted systematically and in a reproducible manner. The findings of such a scrutiny cannot be captured in a simple number but should constitute a convincing account.

Miller (2013) showed how much the outcome of qualitative research can depend on the person of the researcher, and one could say, in methodological terms, how difficult it is to achieve reliability. Using two cases (one a fictional description on what happened in a police station when a woman tried to report a crime, the other an actual description of gang violence at an American secondary school by a gang member) she asked 31 qualitative scholars working in criminology to each, independently, retrieve the most important 'themes' (i.e. the topics that are meaningful elements of the text) from the transcript. Miller found that there was not a single theme retrieved from the raw material that was brought up by more than 50% of the scholars. While Miller acknowledges that analysis of qualitative material may differ across scholars and that such divergence is not worrisome per se, she states that when scholars diverge so much on what can be seen as the rough data – the themes that are relevant – reliability may indeed be at stake (see section 2.7).

Validity is equally important and also – like in quantitative research! – not easy to prove with a simple check. Also here, the researcher should question him- or herself, and provide a convincing account of why the conclusions drawn from the research are valid. Lewis & Ritchie (2003) give a few examples: whether the sample was not biased, whether the observation or interview method allowed for a full view on the phenomenon under investigation, whether the categories and axes chosen reflect the meanings of the study participants and the meaning that is there in the material, and whether the interpretation and conclusion are supported by the data. The constant comparative method and deviant case analysis are tools to assert this. For more, see Lewis & Ritchie (2003).

7.6 Wrapping up

As we saw, the analysis of qualitative data can take many shapes. We gave an overview of the gamut: from hands-on coding of field notes, ethnographic observation, the coding of transcribed interviews or of CCTV images, to the analysis of textified material using software packages, to content analysis using automated data extraction and coding, on which quantitative analyses are performed. Qualitative data analysis is all in all a short label for a very broad set of analysis methods.

Qualitative analysis methods for ELS is also a rapidly developing field: the availability of software and digitalization of legal data has given content analysis and systematic case law analysis an enormous boost. For lack of space we left out exciting new methods such as network analysis, in which networks of verdicts or legal opinions are researched in order to uncover authoritative verdicts or changes in dogmatic reasoning. For more information on these developments, see Van Kuppevelt, van Dijck, & Schaper (2020), for a more technical comparison of such content analysis methods see Dyevre (2021), and for network analysis software, see `maastrichtlawtech.github.io/case-explorer-ui/#/`.

7.7 Further reading

We have in this chapter only touched upon qualitative data analysis. There are many more different qualitative approaches, schools and types of analysis that can be employed than we described here. We refer to textbooks on qualitative research for more examples than we gave in our cursory overview of qualitative data analysis. Classics are Stern (1995) and Glaser & Strauss (1967). Chapters 8, 9 and 10 in Ritchie & Lewis (2010) give a readable overview of analysis methods. Webley (2010) discusses qualitative methods specifically for empirical legal research. An often referenced textbook on qualitative research in general is Denzin & Lincoln (2011), and a fairly practical one on ethnography is Hammersley & Atkinson (2007). A concise and accessible textbook is Tracy (2013). We already mentioned Friese (2019) as an accessible and hands-on manual for coding using ATLAS.ti; Saldana (2013) gives an elaborate and accessible overview of the coding process in all its facets.

Chapter questions

1. Argue whether the different modes of qualitative data collection have implications for data analysis (section 7.1.2)
2. Why and when is *in vivo* coding warranted? What are its disadvantages? (section 7.2.1)
3. What requirements apply to the final stages of the first-level coding phase? (section 7.2.1)
4. What are analytic memos intended to contribute to? (section 7.2.2)
5. Argue why content analysis is often regarded as a hybrid of qualitative and quantitative research (section 7.3)
6. Give two aims of the use of deviant case analysis (section 7.1.1 and section 7.5)
7. Describe whether reliability and validity are assessed differently in qualitative and quantitative research (section 7.5)
8. Argue why systematic case law analysis is also regarded as a hybrid between dogmatic and empirical analysis (section 7.3.1)

Chapter 8

Inferential statistics

This chapter takes statistics one step further, from descriptive – which we dealt with in chapter 6 – to inferential statistics. Inferential statistics are necessary whenever we want to *infer* something from a sample, that is, declare the findings from that sample applicable to a larger set of units, a population. Whenever we use inferential statistics, we do this because there is uncertainty. We have studied a subset of the total universe we are interested in. We want to conclude something about that total universe, but as we have sampled only a fraction of it, we cannot be sure that we know exactly what is going on in that larger universe. So our statements about the larger universe are always uncertain.

How to deal with that uncertainty is what inferential statistics is about. In the following, we will introduce the basics of statistical testing. In doing so, we discuss hypotheses, testing, distributions and the power of tests, dealing with fairly abstract theoretical as well as practical issues. We end with a short paragraph that discusses some basic issues in estimation.

As we will hopefully be able to show, the rationale behind statistical testing is not difficult or ungraspable for the mathematically insecure. In fact, statistical reasoning is quite logical and of the kind that we apply in day-to-day situations. While we will try to keep the formulas and calculations to a minimum, we do need to show some formulas in order to explain the reasoning that is formalized in the procedures and formulas, and to show that they indeed function as we would expect them to. We encourage the reader to take these parts in his or her stride, and if necessary to jump over the formulas if they distract from the main thrust. While it is not necessary to understand or work with these formulas when using statistical testing, it is important that you do understand what testing is about, what it means when you say something is significant, what a confidence interval says, and what the power of a test is and how that relates to sample size. We will highlight these key take-aways in the questions at the end of the chapter.

8.1 Statistical testing

Thus far, whenever we mentioned inferential statistics we did so pretty vaguely and in an off-hand manner. It is now time to become more precise. In the following sections we will explain – again starting with logics and employing ordinary wording as much as possible – how inferences are made in statistics, and how uncertainty is quantified using statistical techniques.

Let us assume that we have a representative sample. Given that the sample is representative, we may after calculating various properties of the sample, such as the mean, median, variance, association between two variables and the like, declare those sample results applicable to the population. We could find that civil law judges have higher IQs than criminal law judges, or that female victims sue for larger amounts of compensation for pains and damages than male victims. However, even though we just stated that such inferences are defensible, we obviously are not *certain* about such generalizations.

Could our finding not simply be attributable to chance, a random result, coincidence? Because our sample was drawn randomly, we may consider it to reflect the population, but even so, uncertainty does remain. After all, we have not observed each and every population member, and there is and remains always a chance that our findings, such as differences between civil and criminal law judges, between female and male victims, hold for the sample but that patterns are quite different in the population...

In order to deal with this uncertainty, we generally use statistical tests. There are very many different kinds of tests. The basic rationale of these tests is however always the same. And this rationale is not difficult, as it follows the kind of reasoning each of us applies in everyday life. We will give examples of that below.

8.1.1 Day-to-day statistical reasoning

Suppose that you go out to dinner at a nice new little restaurant around the corner from your house. The meal tastes wonderful, you're having stuffed calamari. That night, however, you wake up feeling all queasy, and after a while, you have to throw up. The food clearly didn't agree with you. Now, there's stomach flu going around, so you simply assume that that must have been it, and leave it there. A few months later, you invite a friend for a meal at the same place. Again, the food is wonderful, you're having a salad and beef stew. That night, to your surprise the same thing happens as last time, and when you meet your friend the next day, you find out that she has also been hanging over the loo getting rid of the restaurant food. Now you draw your conclusion: this is a bad restaurant. The first and the second time you went out for dinner at the restaurant under the assumption that they would be serving good food. Now you cross out that assumption, you reject it, and conclude that it is a bad restaurant. A very logical, intuitively reasonable conclusion.

Suppose, in a second example, that you are walking along one of the grotty shopping streets of Amsterdam, the Kalverstraat. About halfway, you spot a man, dressed in a suit, who tells you: 'I have ten dice. If I toss the dice and if for each of the ten dice, six spots come up, you pay me 100 euros. Anything else I toss, I pay you 100 euros'. You start calculating fast. The chance that this man will toss ten times six spots is really very small, actually it is $(\frac{1}{6})^{10}$ so the chance that you will make 100 euros is actually almost 1, namely: $1-(\frac{1}{6})^{10}$! You take the bet.

What happens next? The man tosses ten times six and you have to pay him 100 euros. What do you infer from this? Now most people respond here by saying that the man is a cheater, but that answer is incorrect. What you conclude would be that the dice are loaded, or 'iced'; they've been tampered with. In your calculations you did not reason from the assumption that the man was honest, but that the dice had equal chances of 1, 2, 3, etc. spots coming up. However, the chances of this outcome if the dice are fair are so incredibly extremely small that you now conclude that you cannot reasonably stick to your initial assumptions and keep on believing that they are fair. Whether that is because the man has tampered with them or knew they were loaded is irrelevant.

Are you *certain* of your conclusion that the dice are loaded? 'No', is the right answer here, you are not 100% certain. You have not conducted a physical investigation of the dice, you have not inspected their weight per side on a weighing scale. You have only observed their behaviour, from which you infer something about their properties. Actually there is a theoretical possibility that someone would toss ten times six spots in one toss – but the chances of that happening are really too small. It is really 'too coincidental'. And so you conclude: the chance that this toss is the result of chance is so terribly small that I dare conclude that the dice are not fair.

If we translate this example into statistics-speak, we would say that you accepted the man's bet working from the so-called *null hypothesis* or H_0:

$$H_0 : \text{the dice are fair.}$$

After the experiment, where the man tossed six spots for each of the ten dice, you reject the null hypothesis and instead accept the alternative hypothesis H_A, also referred to as H_1:

$$H_1 : \text{the dice are loaded.}$$

As said, you are not *certain* that the alternative hypothesis is true. However, given the null hypothesis, the dice-tossing results are so unlikely that you dare to switch to the alternative hypothesis.

If the null hypothesis is true, you draw the wrong conclusion. The chance that in that case you do so is however very small, namely:

$$(\frac{1}{6})^{10} = 0.00000001654,$$

or a little over one-and-a-half-millionths of a percent.

Statistical reasoning runs along exactly these lines, relatively common reasoning sets that all of us employ. In that sense, statistics is not difficult and intuitively understandable. We will now discuss statistics more formally.

8.1.2 More formalized statistical reasoning

In the examples above, we discussed two situations. In each, we had first made an assumption about the state of the world: we assumed that a restaurant served good food, and we assumed that ten dice were fair. Next we witnessed occurrences that were fairly unlikely if our assumption were true. We therefore each time concluded that the assumption was untrue, and opted for the reverse scenario: the restaurant does not serve good food, the dice are loaded.

We noted that in each instance we were not entirely certain of our conclusion. We had not subjected the cooking pots of the restaurant to bacterial tests, we had not fine-weighed the dice. We had a number of observations, a sample, and we drew a conclusion from what we saw. This means that there is a chance that we make the wrong decision. We may decide that the restaurant serves bad food, while it actually is a really clean place and we were simply both times unlucky to have fallen ill right when we went there to eat. The same goes for the dice.

We work from an assumption on the state of the world, our H_0 or null hypothesis. This null hypothesis is generally formulated as 'nothing out of the ordinary', such as 'there is no association between X and Y', or 'the IQ of law students is not different from that of psychology students', or 'the dice are fair'. Next, the researcher gathers some data. Then, it is calculated how likely it would be to find these data if the null hypothesis were true. If the results are very unlikely, the researcher decides to abandon the null hypothesis and instead assumes that the alternative hypothesis is true.

Now, if the likelihood of finding the results if the null hypothesis were true – as we say *under* the null hypothesis – is very small, and smaller than a certain threshold value, we say that the finding is *significant*. Formally speaking, the risk of making the wrong decision – or more precisely, the chance of accepting the H_1 when H_0 is true – is called α. This mistake is called a *Type I error*. But, for rejection, how unlikely then under the null hypothesis should the results be? Is 1% enough, is one millionth of a percent enough? Would a 10% chance of finding these results of still do to switch from H_0 to H_1? How small should α be?

In essence, this depends on the researcher. What this chance namely amounts to is the chance to reject H_0 while H_0 is true, and thus the chance to be wrong. It therefore depends on the researcher what risk s/he is willing to take, that is, whether s/he finds a certain α an acceptable risk. As a convention, researchers generally set their α at 5% or 0.05. This rule of thumb means that we find it in general acceptable, as researchers in academia, to abandon our initial assumption 'nothing much is going on' and instead assume that 'something special is going on', for instance that there is an association between X and Y, or that law students are indeed smarter than psychology students. We generally accept a 5% or a one-in-20 chance of 'crying wolf' when in fact nothing is out of the ordinary. This 5% (called 'α') is called the *significance level.*

This is however a convention, and other criteria play a role as well in deciding what an appropriate significance level would be. Suppose for instance that we are not talking about restaurant food or about dice and 100 euros, but about the decision whether a sex offender in a treatment institution for compulsive sex offending should be allowed to go on unsupervised weekend leave. Here the null hypothesis is:

$$H_0 : \text{the sex offender is still dangerous}$$

and the alternative hypothesis is:

$$H_1 : \text{the sex offender is not dangerous anymore.}$$

Suppose that some risk taxation instrument indicates that the sex offender is not dangerous anymore. Obviously, such risk taxation instruments are not infallible, and suppose therefore that the chance that while the offender is still dangerous the taxation states that he is not were 5%. Would we find that an acceptable risk here too? Would we find it acceptable that out of 20 sex offenders thus released on weekend leave, one would still be dangerous and thus perhaps commit a new sex offence? Given the seriousness of the consequences, we might decide here that we must scale down the chance of making a wrong decision, perhaps to 1% or even 0.1%.

Setting the significance level that low has its disadvantages, however. If we set α smaller, this implies that the likelihood that H_1 is accepted becomes correspondingly smaller. Eventually, with decreasing α (implying we have ever smaller chances to wrongly reject H_0) we might simply in practice never reject H_0 anymore. This means that we will then never decide that H_1 is true. Obviously, if H_1 were true, our test with its very, very small α will hardly ever make us state that H_1 is true, and will thus not allow us to detect that H_1 is true. Formulated differently, if we are afraid to make one kind of mistake, we may in fact be increasing the chance that we make a different kind of mistake.

Above, we said that α is also referred to as the 'Type I error'. This suggests that there might also be another type of error. This is exactly the kind of mistake we just discussed: the mistake of not stating that H_1 is true when it is true. This type of error is named the *Type II error*. While the Type I error is the error of stating that something special is going on when everything is as it is supposed to be, failing to note that something out of the ordinary is going on is a Type II error. The probability of making this mistake is labelled β.

The possible outcomes of a statistical testing procedure are summarized in Figure 8.1. Two possible states can be true: either H_0 is true, or H_1 is true. There are two possible decisions we can take: either we decide that H_0 is true, or we decide that H_1 is true. This gives a matrix with four possible situations. See Figure 8.1.

If H_0 is true, and we decide so, we are doing things right: we take the right decision. If however H_0 is true but we state that H_1 is true, we make a Type I error. Moving to the top right of the matrix we have the situation where we also make a mistake: here H_1 is true, but we fail to acknowledge this – this is a Type II error. In the bottom left of the matrix we are doing things right again: H_1 is true, and we acknowledge this.

Note that in all the text above, we have always made *conditional* statements. We have said that *if* such-and-such is the case, *then* the chances are.... Thus, we have never said that the chances of making the wrong decision are x% or y%. We can in fact never say that, because we do not know whether H_1 or H_0 is true. Thus we only say that *if* H_0 is true, *then* ... Given that we are only making conditional statements, we cannot only give the chances of making mistakes (α and β) but also the chances of making the right decision. If namely H_0 is true, and if the chance of making the wrong decision (Type I

Figure 8.1: Overview of testing

	H_0 true	H_1 true
"H_0 true"	OK	Type II error (β)
"H_1 true"	Type I error (α)	OK

error) is α, it follows that the chance of making the right decision is 1–α. Similarly, if H_1 is true, and the chance of making the wrong decision (Type II error) is β, it follows that the chance of making the right decision is 1–β.

Because the hypothetical situations H_0 and H_1 are constructed so differently, with H_0 the 'normal situation' and H_1 the exceptional case where something really special is going on, the Type I and Type II errors are also fundamentally different mistakes, and of fundamentally different importance. While not a perfectly applicable analogue, the example of a fire-alarm serves the purpose of explaining why.

Suppose that my house has a fire-alarm. If that fire-alarm also rings when someone is frying eggplants in my kitchen, it is set too lightly, it is too sensitive. Such false alarms (where I have to run upstairs and slam the alarm with a newspaper to silence it) are annoying – they are the analogue of the Type I error: much ado about nothing. Clearly this is something we do not want. The fire-alarm can, however, make a different kind of mistake too. If its sensitivity is too low, there is the possibility that it will not detect a fire. This is the analogue of a Type II error: not detecting when something out of the ordinary is going on. Clearly this type of mistake is not just annoying, it is unacceptable and in fact potentially deadly.

The example shows the different nature of the two types of errors. They are not simply each other's mirror image; they are of a qualitatively different nature. Ideally one would want the chance for Type I error as well as the chance for Type II error to be as small as possible. Obviously, they are linked. If I level up the sensitivity of the fire-alarm, it will detect a fire sooner, but also more often give false alarms. If I decrease the sensitivity, I will have fewer false alarms, but the chance will be increased that a real fire is missed. The situation in testing is just like this: if I lower α, this increases the β, if I allow α to be bigger, this generally decreases β.

Before we move to the finale of this section, we zoom in on a particular area of the matrix in Figure 8.1. The lower right corner denotes the situation where something out of the ordinary is going on (H_1 is true) and where the test is able to detect that. The chance that this happens if H_1 is true, is $1-\beta$. In terms of the fire-alarm, this is the chance that the fire alarm starts screeching when there is a fire. In statistics this chance, $1-\beta$, is generally referred to as the *power* of the test. Ideally, we would want the power of any test, just like our fire-alarm, to be really good. However, while we can ourselves decide how high we want to set the α, this is not generally possible for β and thus also not for $1-\beta$.

In general, the power of a test is reduced as samples become smaller, and is increased as samples become larger. This is only intuitively logical, because when our samples become larger we inspect a larger part of the population and therefore must be able to better discern what is going on. For more details we refer to statistical textbooks, such as Hinkle et al. (2003).

All this sounds – hopefully – pretty straightforward. But is testing always possible? Can things go wrong when we test? Yes, they can. Firstly, it may be the case that the sample we are working with is simply too small to generate meaningful results. When samples are too small, almost no difference or association will turn up as being *significant*, i.e. no test will decide that H_1 is true instead of H_0. Tests are then simply unable to detect what is going on, they have too few observations to confidently draw conclusions, and will then always opt for 'nothing out of the ordinary'. Small samples are therefore of little use, statistically speaking, and samples of about 30 are generally regarded as at the absolute lower limit. From sample sizes of about 100 onwards, statistical tests can be carried out with more confidence and stronger conclusions drawn – for reasons to be detailed below.

Secondly, testing may be hampered if the data are very noisy. Any association or difference (see also above section 5.4) in a sense 'disappears' in the noise. Tests then cannot detect differences anymore; these are masked by the large variability in the data. Lastly, it may be the case that the assumptions of the testing procedures have been violated. By the latter we mean for instance that a statistical test assumes that the data are normally distributed, and generates significance levels based on that assumption – but the data are differently distributed, rendering the tests invalid. Such issues are detailed in statistics textbooks and are beyond the scope of this book.

8.2 Distributions and tests

In the above examples, we were mostly pretty vague. We spoke of 'unlikely' and 'too coincidental' mostly, and only in the example with the dice did we give exact chances for the occurrences under the null hypothesis. We did also announce that we would become more precise later on, and this is the paragraph where we will do so. Again we start with an example.

One crisp autumn morning, the sun barely risen and the air damp and foggy, I step out of my kitchen door to collect the windfall from my apple tree, when suddenly I spot in my back garden a huge dead heron. Yuck. It lies sprawled across the grass. Even though my garden is not large, this poor beast appears to almost stretch the entire

Figure 8.2: Normal distribution of wing span of *Ardea cinerea*

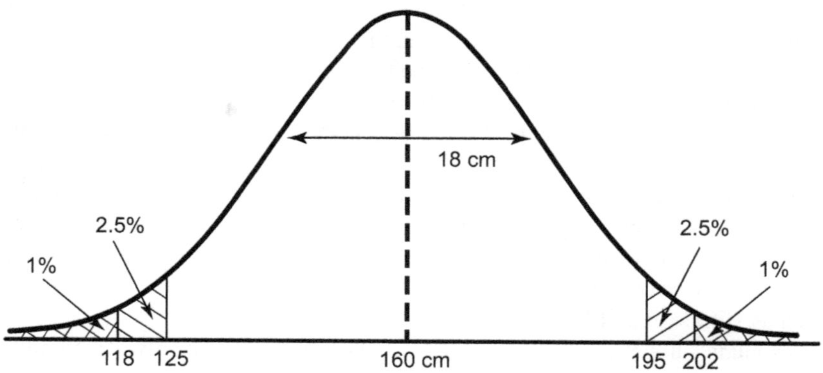

breadth of the garden and it does look like a lot for a heron! I am convinced it is a huge beast, it must be one of the largest of its kind, I think, that has crashed in my garden.

I measure the dead heron's wing span. It is 2 metres and 3 centimetres. That really seems like a lot. This heron must belong to the top 1% largest of its kind! I look up *Ardea cinerea* (the Latin name of the blue heron): it appears that the wing span of this type of heron is 'normally distributed' with an average wing span of 1.60 metres and a standard deviation of 18 cm. What does that tell me?

Figure 8.2 graphically depicts this information: it is a picture of a normal distribution with a mean of 160 cm and a standard deviation of 18 cm.

This figure illustrates firstly that a wing span of 160 cm is the most frequent: the peak of the distribution is at 160 cm. This is because the y-axis reflects the number of herons for the various wing spans X. With most herons having a wing span of 1.60 metres, as we move to smaller and larger wing spans, we see that the numbers tail off. Fewer and fewer herons are encountered as we move to more extreme values. In the picture, it is also shown that, on average, wing span deviates 18 cm from this average of 160 cm. The standard deviation is 18 cm. We see also that the distribution of wing span is symmetrical: the distribution has exactly the same shape on the left- and right-hand side of the average. What, however, does it mean when it is said that wing span is 'normally distributed'?

The normal distribution is a distribution that is often encountered in the natural world. Many properties of living beings are normally distributed: height, intelligence, whale teeth size, etc. All these properties have in common that they cluster around a mean. The normal distribution is also referred to as the Gaussian distribution, or more popularly as the bell curve[1].

[1]The normal distribution can be described by its *probability density function*

$$p(x) = \frac{1}{\sigma\sqrt{2\pi}} exp^{\left(\frac{-(x-\mu)^2}{\sigma^2}\right)}$$

Figure 8.3: Area under the curve

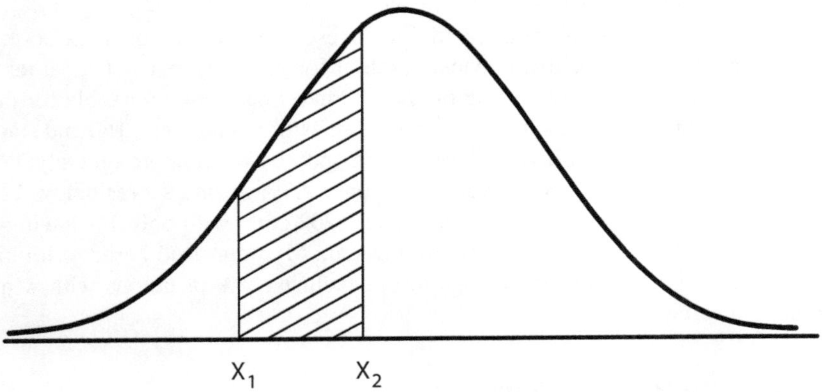

This probability density function is bell-shaped (hence the 'bell curve'), being more or less attenuated depending on the standard deviation. For now, it is enough to know that the height of the curve (the value on the y-axis) reflects the number of cases with a certain value X on the variable, the so-called *density*; the density is a mathematical concept best understood as – but not equal to – a frequency-like measure. The density has however nice properties that make it possible to translate the properties of the curve directly into statements on chances and probabilities. The probability that a variable assumes values within a certain range, say from X_1 to X_2, is equal to the *area under the curve* of the probability density function between X_1 to X_2. See Figure 8.3, where this has been indicated.

This property is very useful as it enables us to make lots of inferences. Firstly, because the distribution is symmetrical, we know that the chance that a randomly selected heron's wing span is more than 160 cm is equal to 0.5. For the same reason, the chance that a randomly selected heron's wing span is less than 160 cm equals 0.5 as well. Because chances are always between 0 and 1, and the sum of all possible outcomes equals 1, the total area under the curve must be equal to 1, and the mean neatly chunks that area into two – because the distribution is symmetrical, necessarily equal – parts. Note that the chance that a heron's wing span equals exactly 160 cm is not defined: chances are defined as areas under the curve, and the point 160 has no breadth and therefore no area defined under it. This means that we can only determine the likelihood of a *range* of outcomes, say a value being between values 160 and 180, or between $-\infty$ (minus infinity) and 140 cm.

The normal distribution has a number of useful properties. As said, firstly, it is symmetrical. This has the nice advantage that we know that the probability of a heron having a wing span larger than 160 cm is equal to the probability of a heron having a wing span smaller than 160 cm. Secondly and most importantly, because it is possible to compute the probability that a variable assumes values within a certain range A to

B, we can also compute the chance that an observation from a normal distribution is higher than a certain value, or lower than a certain value. This is exactly what I wanted to do for my poor, magnificent, dead heron: I wanted to know what the chances are that a heron has a wing span between 203 cm and ∞.

While it is possible to do these computations oneself, many statistical textbooks, online gadgets and statistical software packages do it for you. Using a statistical textbook (e.g. Hinkle et al., 2003) or surfing on the internet, I can look up a table for the normal distribution and find that – for this normal distribution with mean 160 and standard deviation 18 – 95% of all herons have a wing span between approximately 125 and 195 cm – with only 2.5% above 195 cm and only 2.5% having scores below 125 cm – and 98% having a wing span between 118 and 202 cm – with only 1% having a wing span above 202 cm and only 1% below 118 cm. My poor dead heron, with his wing span of 203 cm, thus indeed belongs to the exclusive 1% of herons with wing spans of 202 cm and more.

8.2.1 Standard scores and testing

If we work with scores such as the wing span of the dead heron discussed just now, the values of the variables we are working with are often *standardized*. We do this because – while the raw scores are relatable – it is not easy to get a feel for how deviant a score is. We devoted quite a number of paragraphs in the previous section to revealing whether the dead heron was extraordinarily big or not. Formulated differently, working with raw scores it is hard to get a 'feel' for the distribution of the variables. I had no clue whether my dead heron with its wing span of 203 cm was really so extraordinary. If we however turn raw scores into standard scores, we much more easily grasp how far from the mean and therefore how deviant scores are.

Standardization usually is done by subtracting from every score the mean, and then dividing the result by the standard deviation:

$$\frac{\mathrm{X_i} - \bar{\mathrm{X}}}{\mathrm{s_X}}.$$

The resulting values are called standard scores, or standardized values, denoted by z or z_{X}. Standard scores always have a mean of 0 and a standard deviation of 1. The resulting normal distribution of these scores is now called the *standard normal distribution*.[2]

A standard score of 2 already is quite informative: it tells me that on this variable the respondent deviates twice as much as average (namely twice the standard deviation) from the mean. A standard score of -.5 tells me that this respondent is in fact much less 'deviant', the score is only half a standard deviation below the mean. The standard normal distribution is given in Figure 8.4.

In this figure, the mean is at 0, and as scores become lower or higher, they are rarer. In the limiting case (when X approaches either ∞ or $-\infty$), the curve approaches

[2] The probability density function – given that μ equals 0 and σ equals 1 – simplifies to:

$$p(\mathrm{x}) = \frac{1}{\sqrt{2\pi}} exp^{-\mathrm{x}^2}.$$

Figure 8.4: Standard normal distribution

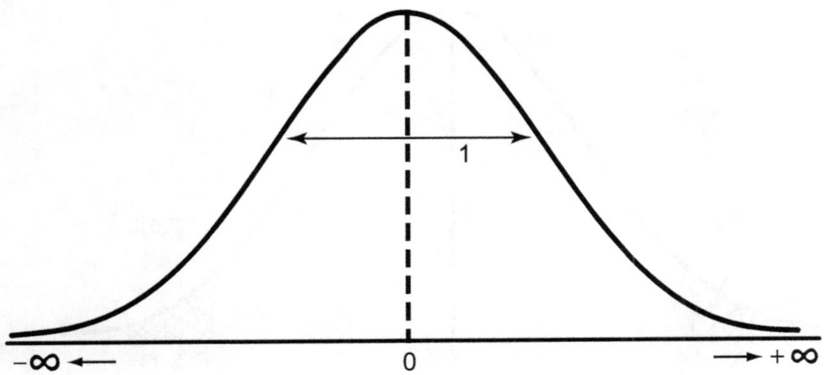

the x-axis. The curve never reaches the x-axis, it creeps closer and closer. The area under the curve equals 1. The area above 0 equals .5, and the area below 0 equals .5 as well. Tables in any textbook will list the chances of finding observations above certain values. For instance, such tables will tell you that the area beyond 1.99 equals .0233 or 2.33%. This tells you that the chance that a respondent has a standard score higher than 1.99 equals .0233. Because the distribution is symmetrical, the chance that a respondent has a standard score lower than -1.99 is then also 2.33%. The more extreme the score, the less likely it is to find respondents with such scores.

Now how does this translate to testing? Suppose that we have two hypotheses, of which H_0 is:

H_0 : Law students are as bright as psychology students,

and the alternative hypothesis H_1 is:

H_1 : Law students are not as bright as psychology students.

Suppose further that I have measurements of the IQ of a random sample of law students and of the IQ of a random sample of psychology students. On average, the IQ of psychology students is 122. The standard deviation of their IQs is 2. For the law students, I also have measurements of IQ in exactly the same manner. I find that the law sample's IQ is on average 127. Clearly, this is higher. But is this result so striking, so significant, that I dare to decide that the law students have an IQ that differs significantly from the IQ of the psychology students? Could this not simply be a chance result, coincidental? How likely is it that if the law students are actually no different, that by chance I could end up with these results in my sample? This likelihood, this chance, is exactly what the statistical test will tell you.

We go about finding the answer as follows. Our null hypothesis is the hypothesis that states that there is no difference, nothing is out of the ordinary, there is nothing

Figure 8.5: Standard normal distribution with critical standard scores

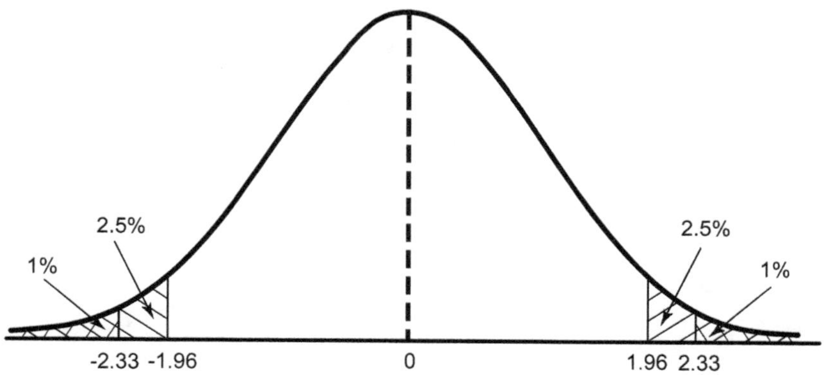

special going on. So our null hypothesis is that law students stem from the same population as psychology students, namely a population where the mean IQ equals 122, so $\mu_{IQ} = 122$. We also assume that in the population of law students the standard deviation of IQ is 2, like we measured for the psychology students. So $\sigma_{IQ} = 2$. The hypotheses are now:

$$H_0 : \mu_{\text{IQ law students}} = 122,$$

and

$$H_1 : \mu_{\text{IQ law students}} \neq 122.$$

Note that in the hypotheses, which specify the properties of populations, we use Greek letters. Before we do the testing, first the raw scores are rewritten as standard scores:

$$\frac{X_i - \mu}{\sigma} = \frac{127 - 122}{2} = 2.5.$$

Now, this value of 2.5 is a z-value, a standard score. This means that we can – assuming that the data we are inspecting are normally distributed – look up what the chances are that a z-value exceeds 2.5. Tables with z-values are in the appendices of any statistical textbook, and can also be found on the internet; see for an application `psych-www.colorado.edu/~mcclella/java/normal/normz.html`. Looking up the z-score, we find that if the z-score were 2.33, the area under the curve beyond 2.33 equals 1%. With the value of z equalling 2.5, the area under the curve therefore sums to a little under 1%. This means that the chance that, if I draw this sample from a population with a mean of 122 and a standard deviation of 2, the chance that I find this result of 127 is a little under 1%. A wee chance. See Figure 8.5.

If we translate this into words, we say that *if* H_0 is true, the chance of finding this result is about 1%. This is pretty unlikely. Not as unlikely as the 0.00000001654 in the dice example, but even so only a one-in-a-hundred chance to find this result if H_0

Figure 8.6: Normal distribution with critical raw values

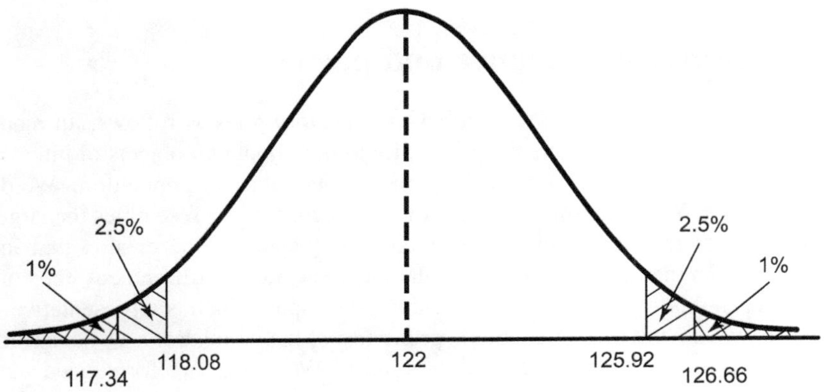

is true. So, we might decide that H_1 is true. Are we *sure* about this? No, we are not. It is possible to find an IQ of 127 in our sample of law students if they come from a population with a mean of 122. But the chances to find such a result – depending on the sample size – are actually pretty small.

So, to reject the H_0 would be a logical thing to do. There is a chance – if the H_0 is true – of around 1% that we make the wrong decision, but in general that is viewed as an acceptable risk. So, in this example, we would state that this year's law students have significantly higher IQs than psychology students.

Above, we looked at the sample mean and investigated what the chances for this result were under the null hypothesis. However, we can also work the other way round. Then, we decide first on the acceptable risk to make the wrong decision (α), draw the probability density function, and compute the so-called *critical value*: any sample mean above this critical value leads to rejection of the H_0. See Figure 8.6, in which we have depicted the critical values for this example for α's of 5% and 2%. So, if we are willing to accept a risk of making a Type I error of 5%, this means that we reject H_0 if the sample mean is above 125.92, or below 118.08. If we feel that 5% is a risk we dare not take, we set the critical value sharper, rejecting sample means only above 126.66 or below 117.34. These results are intuitively reasonable: if we want to reduce the risk of a Type I error, we reject only from values further away from the mean; we need scores that differ more from the postulated population mean. See Figure 8.6.

This is a very summary description of the procedure of testing. We have discussed only the normal distribution. There are numerous other distributions, of which we name the t-distribution, the F-distribution, the χ^2-distribution. They generate different numbers and are applied slightly differently, but the principles are identical: if the value exceeds a critical value, the H_0 is rejected. There are also distribution-free tests. We will leave such other tests mostly undiscussed, as they are not essential for the purposes of this text. Suffice it to say that the rationale of testing, the choice of hypothesis, the procedure of rejection or acceptance are all substantively identical: any differences are in the mathematics. See for more information on testing any statistical textbook, for instance Hinkle, Wiersma, & Jurs (2003, chapters 14, 21 or 22).

8.3 Sampling, significance and power

If we summarize what we have described so far, the story goes as follows. In many research situations, we do not have the possibility to investigate all objects of interest. Instead, we investigate a small part of that entire collection, that population. We do that in a clever way. We make sure that the part that we investigate resembles the larger universe it comes from: we pick the sample members by chance. This ensures that any differences between the sample and the population are accidental differences, they are not systematic. In this way, we arrive at an unbiased sample, which is representative.

Obviously, we are not certain about the properties of the population: we have studied only a part. How do we deal with this uncertainty? We do that in a formalized way. This formalized manner of thinking is intuitively logical and reasonable. Because of the particular rules and calculations we follow, it becomes statistical reasoning. What we do is to calculate what the chances of finding our observations are, if a certain assumption about reality were true. If these chances are very small, we switch to the alternative assumption about reality. We then say that the finding is *significant*.

Significant is a term we use in our daily lives as well, it means something like 'important' or 'meaningful'. In statistics, it has this particular meaning: the chances of opting for the alternative scenario if the regular situation were true. In general, we work with significance levels of 5% or 1%, depending on sample size and other considerations. We then say that we 'set α at 5%' or that such-and-such finding is significant 'at the 5% level'.

We want our chances of making a wrong decision to be as small as possible. Deciding that the alternative scenario is true while the regular scenario holds is one type of mistake. As we describe the regular scenario fairly precisely under H_0 (e.g. $H_0 : \mu = 122$), we can make fairly exact calculations as well. If we assume that the data are distributed in a certain way (normally, or F-distributed, or χ^2), or if we know what the chances of a certain number of spots are when we toss dice, we can therefore compute exactly what the chances are that a certain extreme result appears. This means that we can always ourselves determine α. It is for us to decide, and we can actually decide exactly, what risk we are willing to run of making a Type I error.

However, as described earlier, there is a second kind of mistake we could make. We could also on the basis of the empirical results in our sample decide that there is no reason to reject H_0 while in fact H_1 is true. Then we would make a Type II error. The chances for that we call β. Now, while we can set the α, we cannot beforehand design the test in such a way that we have an acceptable β. Why is that so?

The reason that we cannot pre-determine the β the way we can choose our α is because the alternative hypothesis actually comprises a range of options. In other words, while H_0 gives one and only one μ (such as 122 in the example above), under H_1 the μ can assume many different values: 121, 180, 85... So how are we then to compute what the risk is to make a Type II error? We cannot.

Figure 8.7: Distribution of coping skills under H_0 and H_1 with α=1%

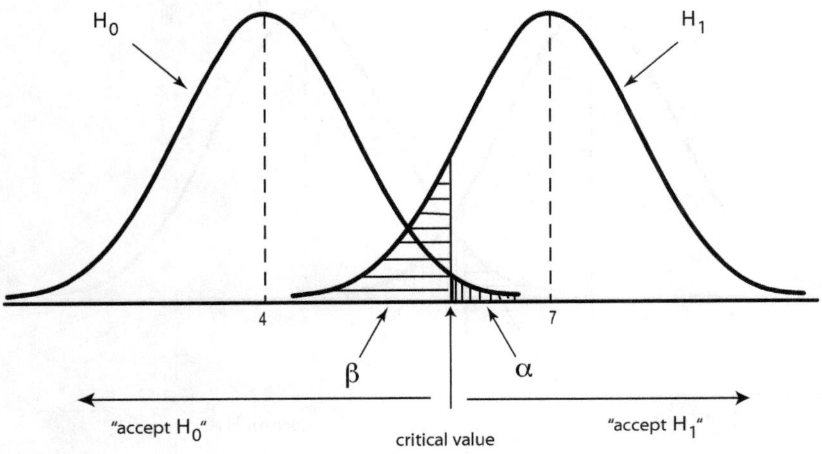

What we can do, however, is pick a certain alternative μ, and compute – for that alternative μ – what the chances are that we would actually miss discovering that H_1 is true. Let us illustrate this with an example. Suppose that we are looking at the coping skills of ex-detainees. While they were detained, their coping skills were 4 on average. We have trained all these detainees to increase their coping skills. A coping skills level of 7 is sufficient for normal societal functioning, while 10 means excellent societal functioning. So, obviously, we would be really pleased if the training we gave our detainees increased their skills to a level of 7: that would mean they did really well. This also means that we would be really unhappy if we were to test the trained ex-detainees, but our test was unable to pick up this relevant difference. Figure 8.7 depicts the testing situation where α has been set at 1% but where in reality – but we don't know this – μ equals 7.

Figure 8.7 shows the α as the area under the H_0 curve beyond the critical value, as an area that has vertical stripes. The area under the H_0 curve to the left of the critical value is the chance that I accept the null hypothesis if H_0 is true. As the total area under the curve is 1, or 100%, and as α is 1%, this chance is therefore 99%. The second curve, on the right-hand side, is the situation when actually H_1 is true. We do not know whether this is the case, but *if* it is the case then this is how the coping skills scores of our ex-detainees would be distributed, around 7, and with a normal distribution. Looking at the curve for H_1, we can see that the chance that we miss discovering that H_1 is true is equal to the area under the H_1 curve to the left of the critical value (the area with horizontal stripes). This is where we end up when we find a not very unlikely result in our sample and therefore see no reason to reject the H_0. If H_1 is true, then the chance that we make the right decision, that we decide in favour of H_1, is equal to the area under the H_1 curve to the right of the critical value: this is the

Figure 8.8: Distribution of coping skills under H_0 and H_1 with α=5%

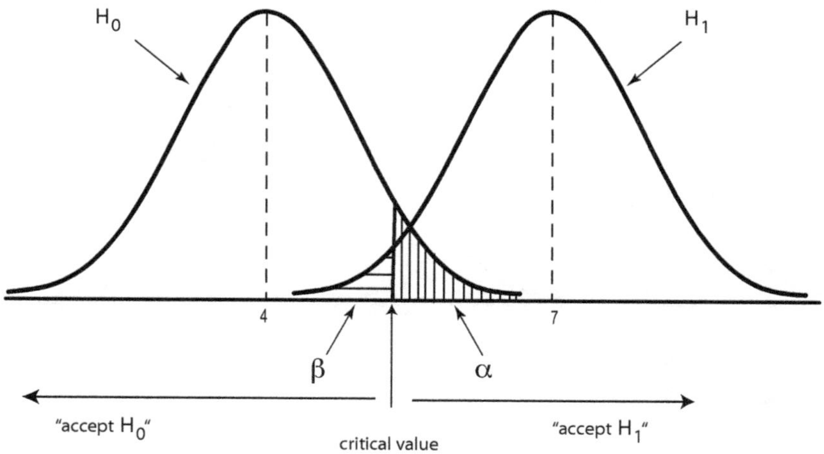

chance that we decide for H_1 if H_1 is true. This is the power of the test.

The power in this example would be – eyeballing the graph – somewhere in the range of 80–85%, so a four-in-five chance if H_1 were true, that our test would lead to the right conclusion. In general, this is considered a reasonable power. If, however, we decide that that is not enough, that we want to have a higher chance of discovering that H_1 is true if it is, then – all else being equal – we can achieve this by relaxing α. If we decide that 5% is also acceptable as a chance for making a Type I error, this reduces the Type II error, and increases the power. This illustrates that α and β are connected, although not by some simple straightforward formula. In general when one decreases the chance of one type of error, the chance of the other type goes up, and vice versa. See Figure 8.8.

While the chance of a Type I error is determined by the researcher, and generally set at a value between 5% and 1%, the chance of a Type II error, β, and therewith the power 1–β, cannot be pre-set. This is due, as we stated, to the fact that the alternative hypothesis covers many possible values for the property we are studying. What we can do is deduce what the power would be for one particular value of the parameter of interest where the H_1 is true.

We showed how increasing the α decreases the β. So, to increase the power, one has to accept paying the price of a higher chance of the other type of mistake, which is not very attractive. We gain in one area but we simply pay in the other. Is there then no other way to increase the power? For sure there is, and that manner is intuitively understandable. Obviously, if we increase our sample size and investigate a larger chunk of the population, we will have more information, so it can only be that we get better estimates, that we observe more sharply what is going on, what the properties of the population are. Inspecting a larger sample must therefore reduce the chance that we make mistakes. It would be highly illogical if this were not the case. Below, it will be illustrated using formulas that this does indeed happen: if sample size increases, the chances of errors go down, so that with a given α the power increases. Larger samples have more power.

Several tools are available to aid in choosing the necessary sample size for a certain desired power level. One such tool is G*Power, available as freeware online: the researcher needs to input the test s/he wants to perform (such as a test for the difference between means), chosen α-level, the effect size that the researcher wants to be able to detect and the desired power level. The tool will then return the required minimum sample size. See for quick introductions `stats.oarc.ucla.edu/other/gpower/` and `psychologie.hhu.de/arbeitsgruppen/allgemeine-psychologie-und-arbeitspsychologie/gpower.html`; for more background see Faul et al. (2009).

8.3.1 Hypotheses revisited

In the previous section, some readers may have been confused by the following. If we believe that the dead heron we found is extremely large, and if we believe that this year's law students are brighter than psychology students, why then do we have rejection regions both at the left-hand and right-hand side of the graph as in Figures 8.5 and 8.6? Given that in both cases the result in the study is higher than expected under the null hypothesis, why would I need a critical value for the opposite result? The fact that in each of the examples we have areas under the curve both in the left and the right tail of the distribution is a consequence of the fact that we are investigating a so-called *two-sided hypothesis*, in the example of the law students' IQs:

$$H_0 : \mu = 122,$$

and

$$H_1 : \mu \neq 122.$$

If we design the null hypothesis this way, it means that we expect the mean to be 122, and that if it is either very much higher, or very much lower, we reject H_0. In both cases the result is so unlikely that we no longer state the null hypothesis to be true. See Figure 8.9, which sketches the situation.

In this figure, it can be seen that the null hypothesis is rejected when $\bar{X}$, the mean IQ of law students, is either larger than 126.66 or smaller than 117.34. If H_0 is true, and the observations have therefore actually been drawn from a population with mean 122, I have when I test in this way a chance of 1% that I find a sample mean higher than 126.66 and thus a 1% chance of drawing the wrong decision. If I find a sample mean lower than 117.34, then I will also draw the wrong conclusion and the chances of that happening are also 1%. So, in total I accept, in this scheme, a 2% chance of making the wrong decision: 1% if the sample mean is accidentally very low, and another 1% if it happens to be very high. See again Figure 8.9.

Obviously, if I have strong reasons to suspect that the deviation from H_0 is in a certain direction, I do not really need the rejection area on the left-hand side. Then, if I stick to my α of 2%, the critical value from which point onwards I will reject the

Figure 8.9: Test situation for two-sided null hypothesis with critical raw values

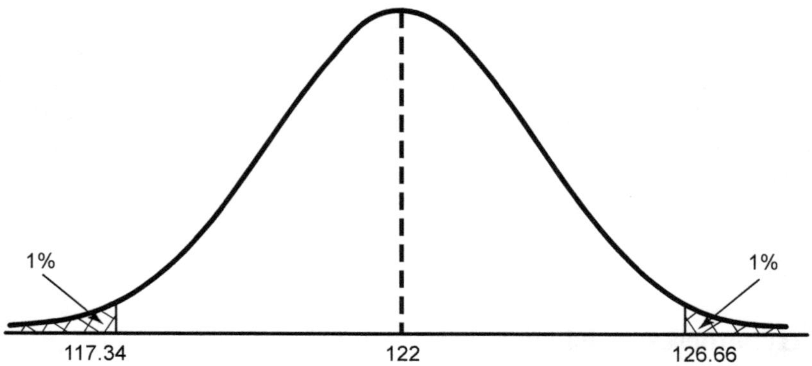

Figure 8.10: Test situation for one-sided null hypothesis with critical raw value

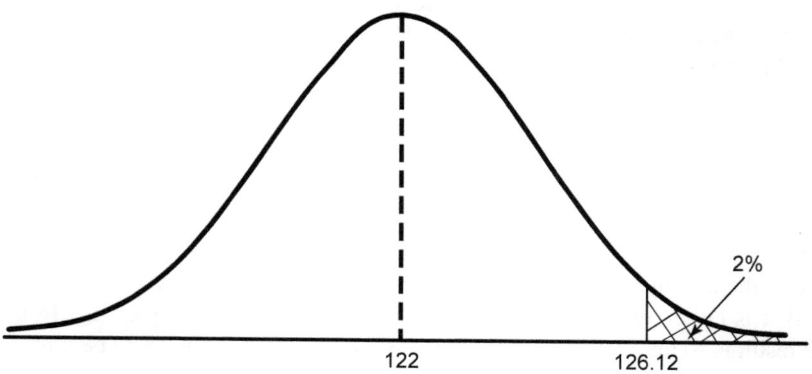

H_0 also changes, see Figure 8.10. The 2% area under the curve that was first divided between the left- and right-hand side of the curve, is now lumped on one side. The corresponding null and alternative hypotheses are:

$$H_0 : \mu \leq 122$$

and

$$H_1 : \mu > 122.$$

This type of hypothesis is called a *one-sided hypothesis*. This means that by formulating the null hypothesis as a one-sided hypothesis, the critical value is lowered. Formulated differently, if I had constructed the null hypothesis as a two-sided hypothesis and my sample mean had been 126.40, I would not have been able to reject the null hypothesis: 126.40 is outside the rejection area. I would have been really disappointed as my belief that law students are brighter was so strong and I did not see it confirmed.

If however I construct my null hypothesis as a one-sided hypothesis, and I find for the sample a mean of 126.40, I can suddenly reject the H_0! The α is the same, but in this case I reject and in the other I could not. This reeks of 'lies, damn lies and statistics', some would say, and clearly this offers possibilities for fiddling.

That is why there are clear rules for how hypotheses should be formulated. The first rule is that the hypotheses must be constructed before the data are investigated. They must be constructed beforehand, so that any post-hoc fiddling is precluded. Secondly, there is a clear rule that one-sided hypotheses are formulated and tested only when there are strong theoretical reasons to suspect that any effect will be in one direction only. Obviously, working with one-sided hypotheses has its risks too: if the sample mean suddenly does happen to be very low in the one-sided hypotheses formulated above, H_0 cannot be rejected even though it is obviously very different from what was expected.

Note that the null and alternative hypotheses must always complement each other: together they encompass the entirety of what could possibly be the state of affairs.

In the examples so far, we have always sketched the situation where one is interested in finding the mean μ of the population. It is however also possible that we would be interested to know whether two properties are associated in the population, in which case we could test whether a correlation coefficient differs significantly from zero, or whether an odds ratio differs significantly from 1.

8.4 Theoretical foundations of sampling and testing

In all the texts so far, we have been fairly sloppy, in the sense that we talked about estimation but never defined exactly what we meant by that. Also, we implicitly assumed that the sample mean $\bar{X}$ would be a good estimator of the population mean μ. We talked about normal distributions and we implicitly assumed but never explicitly proved that the sample mean itself would follow a normal distribution. Textbooks and theoretical books have been written about these issues, but much of the detail and theory there are not essential for our purpose which is giving a brief conceptual outline of statistical reasoning and methodological procedures. There is one issue that we announced we would discuss in more depth, however, and that is the issue of sample size. We said that it is intuitively clear that working with larger samples gives better results. But can it be shown that that is so? Yes, it can. What we will use for this is the *central limit theorem*, which states that as the size N of a randomly drawn sample increases, the distribution of the sample mean, regardless of the original distribution (with mean μ and finite variance σ^2) from which the sample was drawn, approximates a normal distribution.

This theorem is central to statistical testing. What it first says is that, regardless of how the original variable was distributed, the sample means of that variable – if I take care to draw large enough samples and draw them randomly – is distributed normally.

So if I would draw 100 samples from a population, each time randomly, the sample means would vary but they would follow a normal distribution. This theorem therefore is the basis for using the normal distribution to test whether a sample mean differs significantly from what would be expected under the null hypothesis.

Secondly, the theorem can be used to show that – something that is again intuitively appealing – the sample mean $\bar{X}$ is an unbiased estimator of the population mean μ.

Thirdly, the theorem can be used to show that as sample size increases, the sample mean becomes a more precise estimator of the population mean. The latter is so because the standard deviation of the sample mean, also called the *standard error of the mean*, equals:

$$\sigma_{\bar{X}} = \frac{\sigma}{\sqrt{N}}.$$

Given σ, the standard deviation of the mean of the scores in the population, $\sigma_{\bar{X}}$, therefore becomes smaller as N increases. Intuitively, this can only be so: as I investigate larger proportions of population members, my sample mean can only approach the population mean more and more. The formulas however show how fast this goes: increasing the sample size by a factor 4 decreases the variability of the sample mean by a factor 2. As samples become bigger, the sample mean fluctuates less around the population mean. In the limiting case, as N approaches the population size, the variability approaches zero.

Fourthly, the theorem underscores the importance of random sampling. If we do not draw randomly, then the theorem does not hold, and we miss out on all the associated niceties.

Lastly, the theorem states that as sample size becomes bigger, the sample mean becomes a more precise estimator of the population mean. The nice thing now is that statistical research has shown that already from sample sizes of about 30 the distribution of the sample mean is pretty normal. From a sample size of a little over 120, it is for practical purposes entirely normal. The central limit theorem is one of the reasons why we use the rule of thumb that N, the sample size, should be about 100. In that case, the sample mean is approximately normally distributed, so that we can use the normal distribution for significance testing.

The central limit theorem is, all in all, indeed very central to statistical testing. It tells us that sample means are unbiased estimators of population means, it instructs us to draw random samples, it tells us that large samples are less noisy than smaller samples, and it tells us that we can use the normal distribution to test whether a sample mean differs significantly from a sample mean expected under the null hypothesis. The central limit theorem provides a rule of thumb in the sense that samples of 30 at the minimum are – for simple testing purposes – of sufficient size.

The central limit theorem is formulated assuming that the population variance σ^2 is known. While we assumed that as well in most of our examples above, the population variance is obviously more often unknown than known. In such cases, we use the sample variance as an estimate of the population variance. In that case, however, a sample size of 30 is not sufficient and we have to test using a different distribution, the so-called *Student's t-distribution*. From samples of 100 upwards, the t-distribution is again practically equivalent to the normal distribution again, and we can use our standard testing procedure.

In summary: given that samples have been randomly drawn, if sample size is above 100, we use the normal distribution to test hypotheses on the population mean. If samples sizes are between 30 and 100, we use the normal distribution if the population variance is known and the t-distribution if it is unknown and we need to estimate the population variance from the sample variance. For samples under 30, testing becomes harder, and in practice the t-distribution is used. Also, researchers then resort to so-called non-parametric tests, statistical tests that do rely on a specific underlying distribution like the normal distribution.

8.5 Estimation and uncertainty

In the above, we have regularly spoken of estimation, of the mean of the population, of the variance of the population, and similarly we might want to estimate the association between variables. Each time when we estimate, we attempt to find the value of a so-called *parameter* in the population. The mean is a parameter, as is the variance or standard deviation. They are properties of the distribution of variables that describe or characterize that distribution. The mean tells you around what value the values cluster and the standard deviation tells you how much values on the variable fluctuate around that mean.

8.5.1 Point estimates versus interval estimates

Above we said, basing ourselves on the central limit theorem, that the sample mean is an unbiased estimator of the population mean. We write the sample mean as an estimator of the population mean as follows:

$$\hat{\mu} = \bar{\mathrm{X}},$$

where the hat above the μ tells us that we have not actually measured μ and that we do not equate μ to the sample mean, but that we employ $\bar{\mathrm{X}}$ as a mere estimate only.

Similarly the sample variance can be used to estimate the population variance:

$$\hat{\sigma}^2 = \mathrm{s}^2,$$

where again the hat tells us that the sample variance is used as an estimator of the population variance.

Now all these estimates are what we call *point estimates*. They tell us what we infer from the sample about the population, what we believe μ in the population to be on the basis of the sample information. However, in some cases we may be more certain about this estimate than in other cases. For instance, when we have investigated only a small sample, we are – with an identical value for that estimate – obviously less certain about that estimate than if we had drawn a large sample. A way to give an indication of that certainty or uncertainty is to present an interval estimate. We will discuss interval estimates or confidence intervals in the next section.

8.5.2 Confidence intervals

Many estimates in quantitative research are reported with a so-called confidence interval. What does this stand for? We illustrate it with a numerical example.

Let us assume for our law students' IQ example above that we found that the sample mean is 122.8. Let us also assume that we rejected the null hypothesis ($H_0 : \mu = 122$), that the standard deviation in the population is 2, and that we had 100 students in our sample. We work with an α of 5% and as we use a two-sided null hypothesis, the testing situation looks like it did in Figure 8.5: we have two areas of rejection, each good for an area of 2.5% under the curve. We have therefore two critical values: the critical values for the z-distribution beyond which we would reject are -1.96 and +1.96.

Our estimate of law students' IQs is the sample mean, which is as we said 122.8. Obviously, as we have drawn a sample, we are not certain that this is the mean IQ in the population of law students, it is an estimate. We can express the certainty with which we report that estimate using a *confidence interval.*

For computing the confidence interval around that estimate, we use the following formula:

$$\text{CI}_{95\%} = \bar{\text{X}} \pm z_{\text{critical value}} \times \sigma_{\bar{\text{X}}},$$

where '$\text{CI}_{95\%}$' stands for the 95% confidence interval. When we plug our data into the formula we get:

$$\text{CI}_{95\%} = 122.8 \pm 1.96 \times \frac{2}{\sqrt{100}},$$

which is equal to

$$\text{CI}_{95\%} = 122.8 \pm 0.392,$$

so that the 95% confidence interval in this example is 122.408–123.192. How do we say in words what this means? A loose, intuitive way of describing the confidence interval is as your margin of uncertainty. A more precise way is to say that we are 95% confident that μ_{IQ} is in the 122.408–123.192 interval.

Note that the value for μ under the null hypothesis that we are testing, 122, is not contained in the confidence interval we just computed. It would be very strange if it were, because we just rejected the H_0 – by which we said that we believe that the μ is *not* equal to 122. So it would be contradictory if now it were contained in our confidence interval!

Confidence intervals are regularly used. For instance, for assessing whether an odds ratio is significant, mostly its confidence interval is computed. If that confidence interval contains 1, we say the odds ratio is not significant, if the confidence interval does not contain 1, we conclude that the odds ratio differs significantly from 1.

As said, the confidence interval gives you a margin of uncertainty: wider confidence intervals mean more uncertainty, narrower confidence intervals mean more certainty. From that it follows that if we were to investigate a larger sample, in which case we would be more certain of our estimate, the confidence interval would have to become correspondingly narrower. Is that the case? We can simply check this by recalculating the interval for a sample size of, say, 144 instead of 100. The calculations then become:

$$\mathrm{CI}_{95\%} = 122.8 \pm 1.96 \times \frac{2}{\sqrt{144}},$$

so that

$$\mathrm{CI}_{95\%} = 122.8 \pm 0.327,$$

so that the 95% confidence interval in this example is (122.473–123.127), which is indeed narrower than the 95% confidence interval when the sample size was 100. Similarly, it can be computed that as sample size decreases, the confidence interval widens.

These examples have given the 95% confidence interval. It is also possible to compute a 99% confidence interval. As we are in that case talking about more certainty it is logical that with the same data the interval would become wider. If we wanted to be 100% certain, the interval would span $-\infty$ to ∞!

We have given examples where samples of 100 and over were investigated, and where the population variance was known, so that regular z-scores could be used for the critical value. If however, the population variance is unknown, and smallish samples are used, then just like for the testing situation here too for critical value a value from the t-distribution must be used.

Leaving aside the formulas and all the nitty-gritty tech specs of when to use z- and t-values, the important thing here to remember is that the confidence interval reflects statistical precision. Narrow confidence intervals reflect that we are more certain of our estimate, wider confidence intervals reflect the reverse. Confidence intervals narrow and widen with sample size, variability in the data, and the level of confidence we desire, all in a way that is intuitively logical.

8.6 Practical limitations in sampling and testing

Clearly, all the above instructs us that the ideal situation in research is to draw random samples, to ensure that these are big and then we can do some regular standard normal distribution tests, and all will be well. Is that indeed the ideal situation? Yes and no.

Obviously, if one is able to draw a random sample, and thus achieve generalizability, that is better and more desirable than working with non-random samples. However, in many situations, samples simply are non-random, either because there is no sampling frame, or because nonresponse has affected the randomness of the sample, or for some other reason. Often, we simply have to make do with such less than ideal samples. The research situation on the ground simply is not that clear cut and well-organized. The art of research then can no longer be to arrive at a technically perfect situation, but to operate sensibly and pragmatically from a technically suboptimal or defunct situation.

Secondly, large samples – seemingly paradoxically – have their disadvantages too. If I draw a sample of 180,000 persons out of the Dutch population, an approximately 1% sample, that sample size is so huge that any test I perform will turn out to be significant. The test value $z_{s_{\bar{x}}}$ is defined as

$$\frac{\bar{X} - \mu}{\sigma_{\bar{X}}},$$

but given that

$$\sigma_{\bar{X}} = \frac{\sigma}{\sqrt{N}}$$

the resulting test value z will with such a large N be divided by a very small $\sigma_{\bar{X}}$, and thus become huge. As can be seen from all the graphs shown before, more extreme values of the test statistic imply that the null hypothesis will be rejected. Thus, with such a large N, any test will turn out to be significant. This is logical, as with such a huge sample the likelihood that any results are attributable to chance is negligible. The flip side is however that testing becomes in a sense meaningless: tests will always be significant. Very tiny differences will be marked as 'significant': a correlation coefficient of 0.01 (that is: a situation where there is practically no association between two variables) will also be defined as not attributable to chance, i.e. significantly different from zero. In these situations, while there is statistical significance, there is no *practical significance.* In that sense, samples can definitely become too big.

So here too there is a trade-off. While a larger sample absolutely does give you a better idea of what is going on in the population, it makes judging how meaningful findings are harder. Small deviations from the situation under the H_0 are marked as 'significant' when they may be too tiny actually to warrant mentioning.

For that reason, the α is often set proportionate to the sample size. A regular α, for ordinary samples of, say, between 100 and 500, is generally set at 5%. Once sample sizes become really big, researchers may revert to a smaller α, say 2.5% or 1%. Conversely, if one has to work with very small samples of well under 100, researchers sometimes relax the α, and may accept 10% as a significance level. It is then the custom, however, not to speak of significance but of a 'trend'.

A second instance when there is reason to use a stricter α is when one wants or needs to perform many tests. If α is 5%, what this means is that out of 100 tests on the same phenomenon, one would expect 5% to show up significant – just accidentally, that is what the reasoning says. So if one performs 100 tests, reporting a number of these as significant doesn't really prove a lot. This is referred to as *chance capitalization.* For that reason, if one performs a large number of tests on phenomena that may be not exactly identical but nevertheless capture the same phenomenon or tap into the same association, it is customary to balance this by also reducing the α. In some contexts, this is referred to as a *Bonferroni correction.*

8.7 Wrapping up

This chapter introduced some technical foundations of statistical testing. We started out by showing how statistical reasoning is in fact quite similar to our day-to-day reasoning. Using the analogy of a fire-alarm, we illustrated how in deriving statements about reality (a population) on the basis of incomplete information (a sample), we may make mistakes: we may think that a fire is burning when it is not, or may miss a fire that is burning. Statistics help us to deal with, and quantify, the uncertainty that is inherent to sampling. We showed how the chances of mistakes (rejecting H_0 when H_0 is true or, conversely, not accepting H_1 when H_1 is true) are connected, and that only by increasing sample size do we reduce the risk of both. Hypothesis testing and one-sided and two-sided hypotheses were introduced. We briefly outlined the central limit theorem that underscores the importance of random sampling introduced earlier in chapter 3. We discussed confidence intervals as a way to express uncertainty. We ended by contextualizing the former in the sense that we discussed how in practice it is often impossible to achieve truly random sampling and how very large samples may also pose some challenges.

Chapter questions

1. What do we mean when we say that a finding is 'significant'? (section 8.1.2)
2. Describe the null and alternative hypothesis for a study in which we attempt to find out whether mediation settles divorce procedures faster than regular procedures through family court (section 8.1.2)
3. Describe the quadrants in Figure 8.1 for a COVID test: give labels to the rows and columns. Argue what you would like α and β to be (section 8.1.2)
4. Explain why α and β are 'communicating vessels' (section 8.1.2 and section 8.3)
5. What is meant by the power of a statistical test? (section 8.3)
6. What are two ways to increase the power of a test? (section 8.3)
7. Can samples become too large? (section 8.6)
8. What does a confidence interval indicate? (section 8.5.1)

Chapter 9

Quantitative data analysis: multivariate analysis

In this chapter, we will slowly shift to the more applied side of statistics and research methodology, in the sense that we will discuss multivariate models that are often used in applied research. The model that is central in this chapter, the *regression model*, tries to give us an answer to the question whether, in a certain sample, the scores on a dependent variable (an 'effect') can be predicted from the scores on one or more independent variables (the 'causes'). This means that in this chapter, we have arrived at *multivariate analysis*.

In previous chapters, we have so far discussed univariate (one-variable) analyses (analysis of the mean or median), or bi-variate analyses (analysis of correlations or odds ratios). In this chapter, we discuss two techniques with which the impact on one dependent variable of *several* independent variables is simultaneously analysed. When we use a regression model, we have several independent variables that are of interval measurement level or higher, and the dependent variable is also interval level. When we use an analysis of variance model, we have several independent variables that are of nominal measurement level, with the dependent variable at interval level

In the following, we will first expand and philosophize a little on the term 'model'. What are models, and what do we use them for in research practice? Next, in section 9.2 we will introduce the regression model, in its simple, bivariate form and its multivariate form, as well as touch upon a number of more complicated, multivariate varieties. Such models are hugely important: many of the phenomena that we study in empirical legal research are complex. In general, more than one variable or factor operates on a certain outcome, and we must then also study these phenomena in a multivariate fashion, that is, by taking into account simultaneously all factors that may be relevant.

These multivariate models come with tests and possibilities to assess model fit, i.e. measures that describe how well the model describes the data. We describe these briefly as well. We illustrate both techniques with short examples.

9.1 Models

In daily life, we frequently use models. When we buy for instance a new coffee machine, the box in which it is wrapped generally contains a drawing of the machine that indicates where essential buttons are, how to replace parts etc. That drawing does not depict every detail, colour, or curve of the machine. The drawing serves to outline the basic properties of the machine and to point out the vital buttons. It is made such that you can find your way, that you know how to operate it. As such it is a summary of the machine's appearance. It is an abstraction, in which the essentials have been maintained and nonessentials left out. This has been done so that it is easier to understand the functionality of the machine, to focus on the functions that you as a user are interested in.

For the same purpose that we use models in daily life, we also use them in academic research. Models can be models of scale, giving an overview of a lab machine. Other common models are computer simulation models. Models can also be simple drawings that outline the relations between variables; a number of examples of such conceptual models will be given below. All models have in common that they are an abstraction from reality, in which core elements have been retained. They also have a similar purpose: to facilitate understanding of the functioning or structure of the object they represent.

From the above, we can deduce a number of properties of models. First, models must have a similar structure to the object they are representing. Second, models should enable us to observe and possibly manipulate the object they represent, without interfering with the object itself however. Computer simulations of disease prevalence for instance enable us to model what happens to the spreading of the disease if half of the population is vaccinated, or 25% of the population is vaccinated, etc. We don't need to try this out ourselves: we would not want to! If we feed the right parameters into the model, the model will give us an estimate, a prediction of what will happen. Models can be physical (such as manikins) and virtual (computer models, or even mental representations).

Third, and this is exactly the reason that we work with them, it is much easier to observe the model than to observe reality. That is the crux, and what makes models so eminently useful. Reality is often complex, and hard to get an overview of its complicated intricate entirety. Models are exactly the reverse: they are simple and you can look at them from all angles, roll them around in your hands, put them upside down, whatever you wish. Without needing to worry about that complex and multifaceted reality out there, where many things are interrelated and happen at the same time, with a model we can simply manipulate one aspect – and see what happens, and next manipulate another aspect – and see what happens next. We don't need to worry about all those annoying confounders; we control them.

In summary, a model of reality is a representation of that reality that is firstly independent of it, secondly better observable, and thirdly has a similar structure.

9.1.1 Models with dependent and independent variables

In scientific research we want to – in the end – find the causes of the phenomena we are studying. We try to discover with what other factor our phenomenon of interest correlates, and – importantly – what it does not correlate with. We try to prevent our perception being muddled by any spurious associations. We try to get a grip on the phenomenon, we try to grasp what is going on and what is driving the trend we are seeing, the increase in litigation, the reason why divorce procedures take increasingly long, or whatever we are studying.

In these examples, there is each time one central property we are interested in: duration of procedures, number of litigation cases, trust in the criminal justice system. As discussed previously in section 5.2, we call such a central variable, which we in a sense want to find the drivers or causes of, the *dependent variable*. The dependent variable is the variable we are interested in, the variable we want to explain, understand or predict from other variables, the variable for which we want to know what the mechanisms are that drives it. We write the dependent variable as 'Y'. Given that the dependent variable is the variable we want to find the causes of, the so-called *independent variable* is then that cause. Defined more precisely, independent variables are variables that are not predicted by other variables, they are the external forces that exert force on the dependent variable. The dependent variable is also often referred to as the *output variable*, the *endogenous variable*, or also simply the outcome. Independent variables are also referred to as *predictors*, *input variables*, *exogenous variables*, *explanatory variables* or, even a bit confusingly, *covariates*. We denote the independent variable by 'X'.

Many of the phenomena we focus on in empirical legal studies are multi- rather than monocausal: often, more than one 'cause' or factor is relevant in explaining what is happening with a dependent variable. So, we may have more than one independent variable, with the various independent variables written as X_1, X_2, X_3 etc.

As an example we again take the theory of procedural justice (Tyler, 1990, 2008), which postulates that for citizens to perceive the outcomes of legal procedures as fair, not just the outcome plays a role, but also and perhaps predominantly the trajectory along which that outcome was arrived at. Procedural justness comprises, according to this theory, several dimensions or variables. A first is whether there were opportunities for participation by citizens, also referred to as 'voice'. A second is the degree to which participants were treated with dignity and respect. As a third factor neutrality is often postulated, that is, whether the forum that proclaimed the outcome is regarded as neutral. Other factors may be incorporated depending on the particular situation investigated. A schematic representation of such a model is given in Figure 9.1.

More complex models may also contain other variables, which play a role 'in between' the independent and dependent variable. Such 'in-between' variables are called *mediating* when they simply channel the association between the exogenous and dependent variable. Mediating variables are no more than a transmitter, they are the delivery man that brings the parcel that your aunt dispatched to your doorstep: without the delivery man the parcel would not get from your aunt to you. An often-used example is the impact of lack of sleep on task performance. When you do not sleep well, your alertness is decreased, and it is through this decreased alertness that task performance is affected.

Figure 9.1: Visual representation of model with predictors and dependent variable

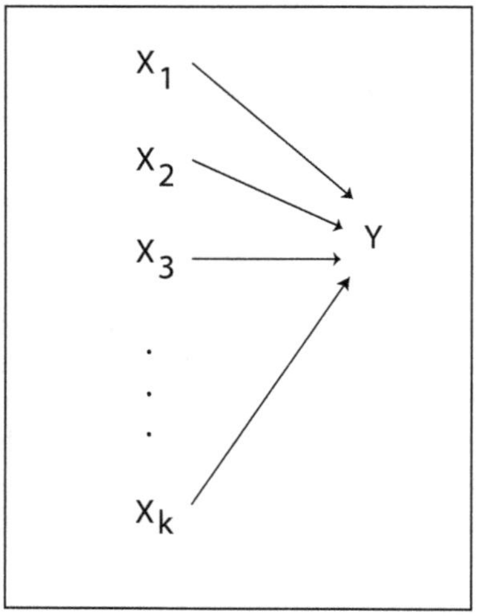

'In-between' variables sometimes do more than simply channel the impact of the independent variable on the dependent one: they may also change, amplify or suppress an effect of a certain X on Y. For instance, painkillers can be safely used at a certain dosage. However, these painkillers may have adverse side-effects in persons with a certain medical condition. That medical condition is then a moderator: it changes the effect of the painkiller. Such variables are called *moderator variables*, and these effects are more broadly referred to as interaction effects. We return to this in topic in section 9.3.3.

9.1.2 Model building

In practice, models have to be built. While a manikin can be a simplified replica of a physical entity, a model in social research practice is usually conceptual. Using data, and reasoning from theory, we try to explain some phenomenon by building a conceptual structure. We presume for instance that divorce procedures of spouses with underage children last longer than divorce procedures of spouses without children. And we also presume that divorces of spouses that have disputes about division of matrimonial property take more time than simple divorces without any financial disputes. Our model is then, very simply written:

$$\text{disposition time}_{\text{divorce procedures}} = f(\text{underage children} + \text{financial disputes}),$$

which reads like: disposition time is a function of the variables 'Underage children' and 'Financial disputes'. We can write it in a more compact way as:

$$\mathrm{DT_d} = f(\mathrm{U} + \mathrm{F}).$$

We know that disposition time will not be approximated by simple addition of these two independent variables U and F. In fact we expect that the presence of underage children (a score of '1' on the variable U) will increase DT and that financial disputes (a score of '1' on the variable F) will also increase DT. We can express this by inserting weights b_U and b_F in the formula:

$$DT_d = b_U * U + b_F * F,$$

written more generically as:

$$DT_d = b_1U + b_2F.$$

We are expecting that b_1 and b_2 will both be positive: both underage children and financial disputes are expected to increase disposition time. Before we start estimating our model, we note that – even if we are in the most favourable situation without financial disputes between spouses (a score of '0' on F) and no underage children (a score of '0' on U) – disposition time cannot be zero. There will always be a lag between the filing for divorce and the day the case is legally closed. We know that minimum disposition time is 30 days, with most cases taking 60 days or more. We accommodate for such a start 'tariff' by inserting a so-called *intercept*. The formula then becomes:

$$DT_d = a + b_1U + b_2F.$$

The value of the intercept will have to be estimated, and it will likely not be lower than 30 days. The coefficients b_1 and b_2 are called *weights*. Both the coefficient a and the b_j are *parameters*.

Now, we may try to find out whether this model actually does describe our data well. Are we able to predict time to conclusion of cases using these two variables: 'Underage children' and 'Financial disputes'? Or are our predictions very much off the mark?

As models seldom explain all 'behaviour' of the dependent variable on the first try, models are generally built step by step, in an iterative process, to try to improve upon model performance. Researchers may do so themselves. Also, one researcher may start with a model, after which the next researcher adds on to it, specifying certain relations, adding new ones, inserting better measures of certain variables, deleting or replacing old ones. In our example, for instance, it may be that the model misses out on whether a mediator was involved in the divorce process. Also, it may be the case that procedures are concluded faster in certain courts: they may be faster in courts that serve rural areas. But when divorces are more acrimonious they may take longer. Or divorces that are filed by both partners instead of unilaterally may conclude faster. Or it may be that the specific combination of underage children and high conflict is particularly obstructive (an interaction effect).

For our example we could indeed try to improve our predictions by adding such additional characteristics of court cases. We may for instance add whether a mediator ('M') was present:

$$DT_d = a + b_1U + b_2F + b_3M,$$

and next add a variable that captures the degree of spousal conflict, such as the Glasl escalation ladder (Glasl, 1977). The model then becomes:

$$DT_d = a + b_1U + b_2F + b_3M + b_4G.$$

With each variable that we add, we make the model more complicated. We do not only include more variables, but with each variable we add we need to estimate an additional parameter b_j. In general, models with more variables will better predict the scores on the dependent variable. That is logical. If we add variables, we have more information, so it is likely that our prediction improves (that it is to say: it cannot get worse). But, as models get more complicated, we in a sense pay a price for that: our model is then also less easy to understand, to grasp conceptually, and to manipulate. Of course, we could choose to work with simple, easy-to-handle models that describe reality in a few 'sound bites'. The price we pay then, conversely, is that they will describe reality less well. In that sense, there is always a trade-off. We prefer our models to describe the data as well as possible. At the same time, we want them to be as simple as possible – the latter is called the principle of *parsimony*.

The two 'bite' each other. For perfect prediction, we might want to add all the characteristics we can find. But for understanding reality, models would rather be simple. The art of model fitting is therefore to find the best balance between simplicity and prediction. We want to find the best-fitting model with the fewest variables. If we can choose between two models that predict equally well, and one is sparser than the other, we would choose the sparse, simple one. In the following section, we will discuss this a bit more.

9.1.3 Model fit

In general, simpler models are easier to work with, easier to understand and conceptualize, easier to test. However, they have less explanatory power: they are simply less well able to describe the complicated world. How well a model describes reality is often expressed in a number that represents how close the values of the dependent variable as predicted by the model are to the real, observed values. If the dependent variable as predicted by the model approaches the observed dependent variable very neatly, we say that the *model fit* – also *goodness of fit* – is high. The model that we built is then able to predict what the scores on Y are. The model then, as we say, 'fits' the data. This is what we want. We have then a model that performs well.

Complex models generally describe reality better. As we said, if we include more factors that might play a role, i.e. more variables, it is, as we said, only logical that will become better able to capture what is happening and thus to describe reality better. We then have the possibility to model lots of causal relationships, the manner in which variables mutually influence each other, or influence the dependent variable through loops, mediate and moderate, so that it is not surprising that we are then better equipped to describe all manners of behaviour of the dependent variable.

Complex models have disadvantages too. First, as already mentioned, they may become too complex to conceptualize, too complex to understand, too intricate to be of practical use. But in addition, they may also become untestable. That is because, for a very complex model, we would really need a large sample size, a lot of respondents or objects that we studied, to be able to investigate whether the model 'holds'. For the models that we discuss in this chapter, there are two general rules of thumb. The first one harks back to what we discussed in the chapter on testing (chapter 8), where we stated that for statistical testing in general sample sizes from 100 become workable. This does not mean that a sample size of 90 is useless, and as we will see, multivariate analysis can even be conducted (although with limitations) with datasets with an N a little over 60 (see section 10.4). The second rule is also best used as a rule of thumb. It states that for estimating the multivariate models we discuss in this chapter, sample size should be approximately 10 times the number of variables one wants to use.

So if we wanted to test a model with 12 variables (which is likely a quite complicated model), we would need a sample size of at least 120. It is not that the model will immediately break down if too many variables are stuffed into the model for the sample size. The software with which one runs computations will generally produce results. However, extremely complex models may also become trivial in the sense that while they might predict the behaviour of the dependent variable pretty well, they capitalize on small differences, which are of little conceptual or practical use. As such, they do not offer a lot of insight into the mechanisms we are interested in; they distract from the core issues. Formulated differently, such very complex models are not really models any more: models are supposed to be an abstraction from reality, simplified for the purposes of manipulation and easier understanding. Very complex models do not do that anymore, so they may deserve the qualification 'model' no longer.

We reiterate that we prefer models to be simple, or 'parsimonious'. It is not difficult to attain a good model fit if you use a lot variables. The art of model building is to arrive at a good fit using just a few variables, to get to the core of things, the crux of the mechanisms we are studying.

We will return to the issue of model fit in section 9.2.4, where we introduce measures that capture model fit. We will then also discuss a particular measure that not only takes into account how well the dependent variable is predicted by the model, but also gives a 'penalty' for the complexity of the model.

It should be noted that the fact that a model fits the data well does not mean that we have discovered the mechanism that drives the dependent variable, that we have discovered the causal mechanism. The Ancient Greeks believed that malaria was caused by living at low altitudes – they had observed that in the highlands people never contracted malaria. Putting these variables in a model gives a good fit: we can very well predict whether someone will catch malaria from a variable that measures whether someone lives at sea level on the Mediterranean or in the Alps. But the real mechanism is not captured. One variable is omitted: the presence of mosquitos and more precisely the presence of mosquitos that carry the malaria parasite. We can predict the incidence of malaria with a variable that correlates with the true causal agent. This we call *model misspecification.*

Models on observational data as we discussed here (malaria, disposition time) can therefore never prove causality. When models work well, when they help us to understand the world around us, we use them. If we find that they are not helpful anymore, we discard them. Models are not true or false, or just or discriminating. Models are no more than a tool for understanding the world around us.

9.2 Regression model

In this section we will discuss the regression model more formally. The regression model is a model just like the models we discussed above. It is a model in the sense that a mathematical formula is used in which one or more independent variables X_1, $X_1 \ldots X_k$ play a role, and that with these a dependent variable Y is predicted. Regression analysis can be carried out with just one predictor variable, or with several; the latter is the usual situation.

Regression models are used very often in applied social research, which empirical legal studies is. That is because many of the questions we ask centre around causality. The regression model, if specified adequately, is a suitable tool for investigating questions of causality. Regression analysis, or 'regression' for short, has been called the workhorse of social science.

Estimations will tell you what the best predictors out of a set X_1, $X_1 \ldots X_k$ are of a phenomenon of interest Y. If the model fits well – which is when X_1, $X_1 \ldots X_k$ contribute significantly to predicting Y – then it can be used to predict future Ys. It can also point us towards interventions. If we were to find, for instance, in a model in which we predict disposition time of divorce cases using a large number of input variables, that the use of mediation predicts a shorter disposition time, this might help courts decide to offer such mediation services (although it would be wise to evaluate their effect using an RCT).

9.2.1 When to employ regression analysis

Regression analysis is a feasible technique if one wants to predict one variable Y from one or more independent variables X. The X_k are regarded as the causes or determinants in the process that the regression model attempts to capture, which means that they function as the independent variables. The Y is seen as the 'effect', which means that it fulfils the role of dependent variable.

Regular, that is, linear, regression analysis can be performed if all these variables meet some requirements. Regression analysis is feasible if the dependent variable is at least at interval measurement level and if it is not too weirdly distributed. If Y were to be for instance very skewed, then regular regression analysis is not possible: the conclusions from the analysis are then untrustworthy. The X are supposed to be interval level variables too, even though some accommodations for this are possible in practice (see the example discussed in section 10.4).

We introduced the word 'linear' in the above paragraph. By that we indicate that it is assumed that the association between the variables in the model is linear. If the association is curvilinear (for instance if Y is high for average values of X, but low for extreme values of X), the regression analysis will not be able to describe that relation, as it can only fit linear relations. The model is then misspecified. In such cases, it is possible to transform the independent or dependent variable: especially when variables have a skewed distribution, some researchers regress the X variables on a logged version of the Y variable. At times one also encounters squared versions of the input variables. These are all attempts to 'fold' non-linear relations into the model.

Figure 9.2: Visual representation of association between X and Y, and prediction of Y from X

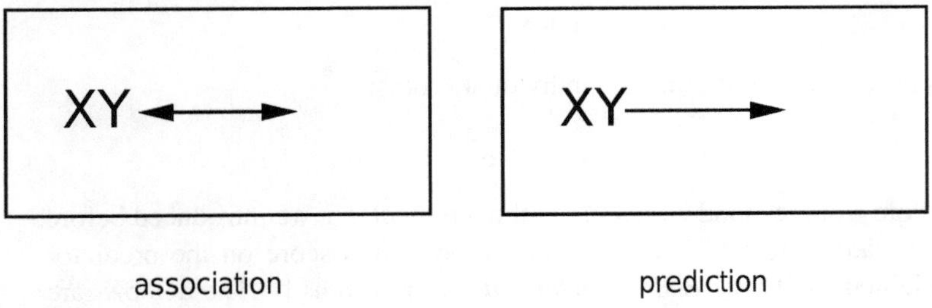

If the Y variable is not interval level, a different kind of regression analysis must be performed. For instance, if Y is a dichotomous variable (meaning it has values 0 and 1 only), a so-called logistic regression analysis should be performed. If Y is an ordinal variable, linear regression is unsuitable (even though it must be said that if deviations from linearity are not too large, most researchers simply perform regular regression analysis on the rank-ordered scores of the ordinal variable). If Y has yet other properties, other varieties are possible (see for an overview Bijleveld et al., 2015, chapter 2). We will discuss none of these in detail; for our purposes it is only important to know that it must always be checked whether Y has the properties it should have. See also section 9.2.6 below.

9.2.2 Simple regression analysis

We will discuss simple regression analysis in somewhat more technical detail, because the technique can easily be illustrated for this simple case, with just one X variable to predict Y. We then speak of 'simple regression analysis' or 'simple linear regression'. We are then essentially carrying out a *bivariate analysis*.

When we investigate the association between X and Y, we are interested in the extent to which they have something in common. We can do so through a correlation coefficient. When we carry out such a correlational analysis, X and Y are interchangeable; the analysis is symmetric. However, when we carry out a regression type of analysis, the two variables have different roles: one is modelled as the consequence of the other. The roles of X and Y are therefore not interchangeable. See Figure 9.2.

As said, the analysis we are conducting is directional. We want to predict Y, not X. Our question is not about the strength of the association between X and Y, or in the sign of that association (positive or negative), we want to know whether information on X helps us to conclude something about Y. Obviously, correlation is important. If X and Y are correlated, then it is likely that information on X also tells us something about Y. If we know that someone has shoe size 46, then that person is likely tall. The two are related, which means one can be used to predict the other. If we denote the Y predicted by the regression model as $\hat{Y}$, then the art of regression analysis is to find a

$\hat{Y}$, a predicted Y, on the basis of the regression model, that approaches the observed Y closely.

In order to predict Y from X, we construct the following linear model:

$$Y = a + b\,X,$$

which we use as follows for predicting the individual scores:

$$Y_i = a + b\,X_i + e_i,$$

where Y_i is the score from respondent i, and a is the *intercept* that we introduced before (see section 9.1.1), added to which is the same respondent's score on the predictor variable, X_1, weighted by its *regression coefficient* referred to as b. The a + bX_i are what is predicted for Y on the basis of the model. As that prediction will not always be perfect, a so-called *error term* written as e_i is defined as the difference between the actual, observed Y, and $\hat{Y}$, the predicted Y:

$$Y_i - \hat{Y}_i = e_i.$$

The error term is actually best thought of not as an 'error' in the sense of a mistake, but as a prediction error. If we attempt to predict Y from X, that prediction will not be perfect: in some instances $\hat{Y}$ will be a little too low, in other instances it may be a little too high. The difference between Y and $\hat{Y}$ is our prediction error.[1]

Let us illustrate all this with a simple example. Suppose that I want to predict someone's height from his or her shoe size. I myself am 170 cm tall and I wear a size 39. My brother is 191 cm tall and wears a size 46. If we were to concoct the following regression model – and this is a home industry example – we would be able to predict my and my brother's shoe sizes:

$$\text{height} = 53 + 3 \times \text{shoe size},$$

which means nothing more than: if I wanted to predict someone's height from his or her shoe size, I would have to start from 53 cm, and add 3 cm for every shoe size up. For myself this would become 53 + 3 × 39 = 170, i.e. a perfect prediction (so that $e_{Catrien} = 0$). For my brother the formula would be 53 + 3 × 46 = 191, i.e. a perfect prediction again, with the corresponding error term again equal to zero.

In reality, predictions will hardly ever be perfect. We illustrate this with a small real dataset, which contains shoe sizes and heights for four more people. See Table 9.1.

We see that in this dataset there is a fairly strong correlation between shoe size and height: another male has large feet (shoe size 44) and there is a shorter male with shoe size 43, but we also have a fairly tall female (179 cm) with shoe size 40, and a shorter female with shoe size 37. For these other sample members, the regression model that we just thought up will not predict perfectly. For instance, for the third respondent, clearly 53 + 3 × 40 $\neq$ 179, and for the relatively shorter male, 53 + 3 × 43 $\neq$ 180.

[1] The parameters a and b are computed as $b = r_{XY}\frac{s_Y}{s_X}$, with r_{XY} the correlation coefficient between X and Y, s_Y the standard deviation of Y, and s_X the standard deviation of X, and as $a = \bar{Y} - \bar{X}$, with $\bar{Y}$ and $\bar{X}$ the means of the variables X and Y.

Table 9.1: Dataset with shoe size, height and gender

respondent	shoe size	height	gender
1	39	170	female
2	46	191	male
3	40	179	female
4	45	188	male
5	43	180	male
6	37	163	female

Figure 9.3: Scatterplot of shoe size against height

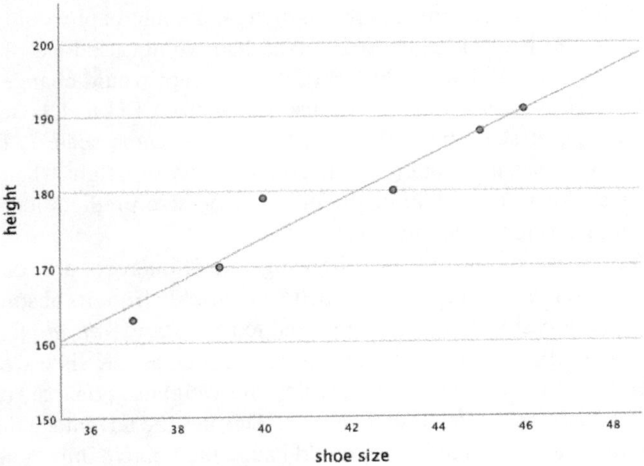

However, the correlation coefficient between height and shoe size is very high (r = .965), so while we will not get a perfect prediction, we do get a pretty nice prediction.

We illustrate this in Figure 9.3, which contains a scatterplot of shoe size against height for this dataset. We see that the dots are aligned, and we are able to fit a straight line through the dots.

If we were to estimate a regression model using a statistical software package, we would arrive at:

$$\text{height} = 58.763 + 2.874 \times \text{shoe size}.$$

The value 58.763 is the intercept a, and the regression weight b equals 2.874. The intercept can be thought of as the predicted height for someone with a hypothetical shoe size 0: if we were to expand the x-axis to the left, the regression line would cross the y-axis at 58.763. Someone with shoe size 1 has an estimated height of 61.637 cm, someone with shoe size 2 has an estimated height of 64.511 cm, and so forth. The regression weight reflects the steepness of the regression line. All predicted values fall exactly on the regression line; the observed values are in the scatterplot a little above or a little below the line. The closer the observed values are to the line, the better the line describes the true scores, and the more successful the prediction.

My predicted height is now 170.849, quite close to my true height. But the predicted height of the tall female is actually 173.723: she is therefore at 179 cm slightly tall for her shoe size – or conversely she has relatively small feet. The picture shows this too: her observed value lies indeed quite a bit above the fitted regression line in Figure 9.3 and her predicted value, on the regression line, is quite far from her observed value. That distance, the prediction error, can be envisaged as a vertical line from the observed value to the regression line. If we were to draw all those lines for the six sample members, we would see that they are all quite short lines.[2]

At this point we remark that both the intercept and the regression weight are *scale-dependent.* They depend on the scale in which we measured the variables. If we were to for instance measure height not in centimeters but in meters, the intercept would be 0.588 and the regression weight b would equal .029. And had we not used EU shoe sizes but UK shoe sizes (which are EU size minus 33), the intercept would change to 153.595 (the regression weight will not change because going from EU to UK shoe sizes does not entail a change of scale but only a shift along the same scale). The prediction is just as good, as it does not matter for the predictability of height whether we measure height or shoe size in one scale or the other: shoe size predicts just as nicely, and the line will fit just as nicely in the scatterplot.

This has one important implication. Give that the weights and intercept are scale-dependent, we cannot infer the importance of an independent variable from its absolute value. The scale-dependent regression weights are referred to as *unstandardized.* Their value will change if we use a different metric for the variables, such as UK shoe sizes, or inches or feet for height. It is possible to standardize the weights. For that, one standardizes the X and Y, which means that a will be zero. This has the advantage that, if we had more than one variable in our model, we could gauge the relative importance of the variables from the values of the standardized regression weights. The standardized b is generally written as β. Obviously, the disadvantage is that we can less easily translate the impact of the independent variables on the dependent variable.

To assess the significance of a variable in predicting a dependent variable, we use a significance test. For the example we just used, shoe size (even in this tiny example) is a highly significant predictor of height ($p = .002$). We will return to this in section 9.2.5.

Now, when does a regression analysis perform well? As said, we judge this by how close the predicted Y, $\hat{Y}$, are to the observed Y. Ideally, we would like the differences between predicted and observed values of Y to be zero, a situation of perfect

[2] By computing a and b with the formulas given in the previous footnote, the error terms always add up to zero so that the average predicted Y is always equal to the average observed Y. These formulas also ensure that a best fitting line is found, a line that minimizes the sum of the squared error terms $\sum_{i=1}^{N} e_i^2$. Formulated more wordily: using these formulas ensures that we will always find the best possible solution. The manner in which a and b are computed is called 'least squares' or 'ordinary least squares' (OLS).

predictability that is in ordinary social research practice hardly ever achieved (and if it is, is cause for suspicion and careful scrutiny of the data). So, if the error terms e_i are large – the distances between the observed values and predicted values on the regression line – prediction is not going so well. If they are small, prediction is going well. We will discuss measures that express predictability below in section 9.2.4.

9.2.3 Multiple regression analysis

Simple regression analysis is indeed a fairly 'simple' technique. If we were to employ a regression model with just one predictor, we would assume that the variable Y is under just one other external influence. For many practical situations, that is too simplistic. In empirical legal studies, we know almost for a fact that most processes are not monocausal. Mostly, various factors play a role in the processes we are interested in. So, it would seem logical to employ not one but several independent variables.

The model we then use becomes correspondingly more complicated:

$$\hat{Y}_i = a + b_1 X_{1i} + b_2 X_{2i} + b_3 X_{3i} + \cdots + b_k X_{ki}.$$

Note that, as we use k different independent variables to predict the dependent variable Y, we also have as many b-coefficients: one for each X variable. Still, we have only one intercept, the in a sense 'starting value', to which multiples of the respective X variables must be added to arrive at an estimated Y. Again, we arrive at a predicted Y value, $\hat{Y}$, and we have differences between the observed Y and $\hat{Y}$:

$$Y_i - \hat{Y}_i = e_i.$$

Also, just like the simple regression case, we hope that the e_i are small. For fitting the model, we compute an a, and we compute several b, just as many as we have independent variables. Very few researchers still compute the values of these parameters by hand[3], and software packages like SPSS, Stata or freeware like R are generally used to do so.

We will now discuss an important property of the multiple regression model. For that, it may be instructive to look at the formulas in the footnotes given, without needing to grasp them fully. It is important to note that the formula for β_1 – the standardized regression coefficient of b_1 – contains the correlation coefficient between Y and X_1, but

[3] We give the example for the case when there are two independent variables, X_1 and X_2. We give for reasons of simplicity the standardized regression weights β_1 and β_2:

$$\beta_1 = \frac{r_{YX_1} - r_{YX_2} r_{X_1X_2}}{1 - r^2_{X_1X_2}},$$

and

$$\beta_2 = \frac{r_{YX_2} - r_{YX_1} r_{X_1X_2}}{1 - r^2_{X_1X_2}}.$$

As explained above, when a regression weight is standardized, this means that the regression weight takes into account that the original variables have been standardized. The scale or unit in which they were measured therefore does not play a role anymore; they are the regression weights we would obtain if we worked with standardized variables only.

it also includes r_{YX_2} as well as $r_{X_1X_2}$. And the formula for β_2 contains the correlation coefficient between Y and X_2, but it also has r_{YX_1} as well as $r_{X_1X_2}$. Clearly, in computing the weight for estimating Y from one predictor X_1, the other variable X_2 plays a role as well – it is taken along in the formula – as does the correlation coefficient between the two predictors. Apparently, the regression coefficient for one variable X_1 is not computed in isolation. The association between the other predictor and Y, as well as the intercorrelation between the two predictors, is taken along as well. Why is this?

It is because the regression weight does not so much tell you whether some predictor variable X_k and Y are associated; rather, it tells you how much a variable X_k contributes to predicting Y, given the other variables in the model – in other words, how much a variable contributes to the prediction of Y over and above the other variables. This is a very important property of multiple regression and is exactly what makes it such a powerful technique in theory building and the search for causal relations.

To illustrate this, let us imagine the following situation. We are predicting Y from X_1. As we have only one predictor, we are performing a simple linear regression. To this model, we now add a second predictor, X_2; this predictor is however identical to X_1. As X_2 is identical to X_1, adding X_2 to the model does not improve the prediction. X_2 does not supply us with new information; all there was to know is already contained in X_1. So, essentially, to improve the prediction of Y, adding the variable X_2 is of no use. One could say, given that X_1 is already there in the equation, X_2 might just as well receive a regression weight of 0, as it cannot add to the prediction of Y. All that X_2 has, X_1 had already.

This may seem paradoxical, because, as X_2 is equal to X_1, it correlates just as strongly as X_1 does with Y, so you would expect it to play a similar role in the regression equation! However, and this is what is really important here, the regression coefficients do not tell you how strongly variables are correlated with Y, but how much each variable adds to the prediction of Y, *given the other variables in the model.*[4]

It is important to always keep in mind that the regression weights have meaning only relative to the other variables in the model. That is why in reporting on regression weights the formulation should always run like: 'Given the variables A and B, the

[4]Suppose that we have two predictor variables that are fairly similar. Let us assume that they correlate really strongly, so $r_{X_1X_2} = .9$. We also assume that both are equally strongly related to Y, such as $r_{YX_1} = .8$, $r_{YX_2} = .8$. If we would estimate two univariate models, once for X_1 predicting Y and once for X_2 predicting Y, the standardized regression weights β would in both cases equal .8. But what happens to the weights in the multivariate situation when we perform multiple regression? Now, however, let us look at the regression weight for X_1 in the multivariate situation, i.e. after we have added X_2 to the regression equation. Then:

$$\beta_1 = \frac{r_{YX_1} - r_{YX_2} r_{X_1X_2}}{1 - r^2_{X_1X_2}} = \frac{.8 - .8 \times .9}{1 - .9^2} = .421.$$

The weight β_1 is now much lower than we would expect on the basis of the bivariate model (and β_2 is exactly similar). However, this is not strange if we realize that the weight tells us how important X_1 is *given the other variables in the model*. Given that X_2 is already present, X_1 adds less, is less useful than it would be if it were on its own. In the univariate case, the regression coefficient is .8; in the multivariate case it becomes .42. This can be understood by realizing that the *unique* contribution of X_1 to the prediction is less in the multivariate than in the univariate case.

Suppose now that the r_{X_1Y} and r_{X_2Y} are exactly the same, but that the correlation between X_1 and X_2 is not .9, but .3. Then β_1 becomes .615! The association between Y and X_1 is unchanged, but because there is less overlap between X_1 and X_2, the unique contribution of each variable in the prediction of Y is larger.

variable C contributes so-and-so much to ...'. If there is strong intercorrelation between independent variables, such as in our example just now, this is referred to as *multicollinearity*. Multicollinearity is undesirable. It makes it harder to interpret the regression coefficients. In extreme situations, it can make the model unstable. Researchers should prevent multicollinearity by first checking whether the predictors they want to include do not overlap too much. Correlations above .8 are generally considered too high for variables to be included in one regression equation, and specific tests for multicollinearity (such as the so-called Variance Inflation Factor or VIF which tells you how much each independent variable overlaps with the other variables in the model) are included in most software packages. Such tests are also necessary from the viewpoint of parsimony. As stated above, we want to build sparse models, with good predictions for a small number of independent variables. It then does not make sense to build a model with lots of variables that essentially measure the same.

9.2.4 Model fit

We already introduced the term model fit, and used it mainly conceptually. But how to express the fit of a model? A commonly used statistic to express model fit is the correlation coefficient between the observed Y and the predicted Y, $\hat{Y}$. It is only to be expected that, if a model is able to predict the dependent variable well, the correlation between Y and $\hat{Y}$ will be high. This correlation coefficient is denoted with a capital R:

$$R = r_{Y\hat{Y}}.$$

As a prediction gets better, the correlation between the observed and predicted Y will also be higher. Therefore, R indeed reflects the quality of the prediction. So this is all quite logical and intuitive. Mostly, however, instead of R, its squared value R^2 is used, and is referred to as the *percentage of explained variance*. If R^2 is for instance 0.64, it is said that the regression model is able to explain 64% of the variance of Y. R^2 is regarded as a 'goodness of fit' measure.

It is hard to say what acceptable values for R^2 are. Values around 0.80 are actually exceptional in most empirical studies. Depending on the research topic, some researchers are even content with values around 0.05. Much depends on the extent to which the phenomenon under investigation *is* predictable. Some processes are more accidental, others follow certain regular rules more. In the first case, we might be happy with an R^2 of around 0.10; in the second case we would expect higher values.

Many researchers prefer to use, instead of R^2, a slightly different statistic, which not only expresses how much of the variation of Y can be explained by the model, but penalizes models that employ too many variables. It is called the adjusted R^2, and written as R^2_{adj}.[5] There are several reasons why one would want to express model fit

[5]The formula for the adjusted R^2 is:

$$R^2_{adj} = 1 - (1 - R^2) \times \frac{N-1}{N-k-1}.$$

which shows that as k, the number of independent variables, increases, R^2_{adj} decreases. The formula also shows that this is particularly the case if N is relatively small, so in small samples. The impact on R^2_{adj} of including many variables is then bigger.

using R^2_{adj} rather than through R^2. A first is that an R^2 of, say, 0.65 in a model with six variables is more noteworthy than an R^2 of 0.65 in a model with 12 variables: R^2 automatically increases when more variables are added to the model, and R^2_{adj} adjusts for that. A second reason is that we aim to build parsimonious models. A third is that models with many variables may capitalize on accidental and idiosyncratic patterns in the data, which will be difficult to replicate; we call such models *overfitted*.

9.2.5 Tests

Just like we can test whether a mean in a sample is highly unlikely under a certain null hypothesis, so we can test whether finding a regression coefficient b or standardized coefficient β with a certain value is likely or unlikely under the null hypothesis:

$$H_0 : \beta = 0,$$

with the alternative hypothesis:

$$H_1 : \beta \neq 0.$$

Note that the β in the hypothesis refers to the hypothetical distribution of the unstandardized b (or standardized β) in the population. It may be slightly confusing that we use one and the same symbol for two different entities, but because when we are testing we are referring to unknown populations, we always use Greek symbols. In the null hypothesis, it is stated that the b or β as observed stems from a population where it equals zero (meaning that it does not at all contribute to the prediction of Y). The significance test will then tell us how likely it is to find the observed regression weight if that were true. If that likelihood is very small, we reject the null hypothesis. We thereby state that the particular variable X_k contributes significantly to the prediction of Y.

For testing whether that is so, it does not matter whether b or its standardized version is investigated. In fact it would be very strange if the particular scale in which a variable is measured would make a difference for how much that variable could aid to predicting a certain outcome. If a regression weight differs significantly from 0, we state that the variable adds significantly to the prediction of Y. It should be noted that, just as in the case where we are testing means, regression coefficients will turn up as significant sooner when samples are large, and will turn up as significant less easily when samples are small.

Other tests are possible when we conduct regression analysis. For instance, we can test whether the R^2 from one model is significantly higher than the R^2 from another model. We can therefore test whether a model with a few extra variables leads to a significantly better prediction of Y. Such tests enable us to compare models with a statistical criterion. Relatedly, most statistical software packages test – before carrying out regression analysis – whether the model performs better than the so-called null model, a model with only an intercept. Only when this is the case, does it make sense to proceed and interpret the regression coefficients.

Tests are used for model building: we may want to build a sparse model, a parsimonious model, and retain only variables that contribute significantly to the prediction of

Y (see also section 9.1.2). What most researchers do is first fit a model with all predictors that would seem relevant from theory or earlier research. They then remove those predictors that do not contribute significantly to the prediction of Y, and retain only the significant predictors. Most software packages offer stepwise procedures that either remove variables one by one until only significant predictors are retained, or that build the model by adding predictors until the fit of the model does not improve significantly anymore.

9.2.6 The workhorse of multivariate analysis

Multiple regression is often named the 'workhorse' of (linear) multivariate analysis, that is, analysis of the relations between a number of variables simultaneously. It is such an immensely powerful and handy technique because it can assess the effects of a large number of independent variables on a certain dependent variable that one aims to predict. In doing so, and this is likely its most attractive property, it returns the importance of each variable *given the other variables*. Importance of a variable is therefore *conditional, net of* the other variables. This means that researchers obtain ground to make statements such as 'taking into account the impact of A, B and C, the factor D still significantly contributes to predicting Y', or: 'the impact of D on Y cannot be attributed to confounders A, B or C'. This is why multiple regression a very important tool in theory building, in testing models to explain the association between variables.

The linear multiple regression model that we discussed is but one variety in a family of regression models. Depending on the type of variable that one wants to build a prediction model for, varieties of multiple regression exist. A very commonly used other type of regression model from that family is logistic regression, an adaptation of the multiple regression model where the dependent variable is not a continuous variable but a dichotomous variable (it has only two categories, such as 'yes' and 'no', or 'pass' and 'fail'). Other types exist, such as Poisson regression (for predicting very sparse events that follow a certain distribution, such as convictions). An important variant is Cox regression (for predicting variables that reflect the duration to a certain event, such as time to settlement of a claim); we encountered the univariate version of Cox regression in chapter 6 as survival analysis.

We will end this section with a small fictitious illustration of multiple regression. We investigate possible gender discrimination at universities. It is well known, and fairly universal, that female academics earn less than male academics. The issue at stake is whether these lower earnings are due to existing differences between male and female academics, or due to discrimination. A first explanation for this disparity due to existing differences may be that women are less often associate and full professor than men. Another explanation may be that women, because they more often work part-time, publish fewer articles. Then, women academics may be on average younger, which might also explain part of the salary difference. It has also been noted that some disciplines are more gendered than others (with for instance few women in beta sciences and more in the 'soft', alpha and gamma sciences). It has in addition been suggested that women with underage children perform more household chores, so that they have fewer hours in the evenings and weekends to work on their careers. All these factors are possible confounders: they co-vary with gender and they may be the real explanation for, the driving force behind, the difference in hourly wages.

One way to solve this conundrum is to carry out a multiple regression analysis. By including all these possible confounders in a regression model, together with the variable gender, one will be able to estimate the impact of gender on hourly wages *net of* rank, number of articles published, age, discipline, caring for underage children, working part-time.

Now let us assume that we have a dataset at our disposal with data on 2,000 academics, men and women, and that we have data on all these variables. We run three analyses: one with only gender, one with gender and academic variables added (rank, discipline), and a third where we add the remaining variables to the model (number of articles published, age, caring for underage children, working part-time). It should be noted that some variables will overlap: age will be strongly associated with caring for underage children or not, as will be rank. There is therefore bound to be some multicollinearity (on top of overlap of variables with gender). But that need not bother us much: we are interested to filter out as many alternative explanations for the lower salaries of female academics. Because the sample size is so large, we will not inspect the R^2_{adj} (it is likely to be barely affected by the inclusion of more predictor variables); instead we will focus on the R^2. The fictitious analysis results are in Table 9.2.

Table 9.2: Unstandardized regression weights of gender and hourly wage in euros

Variable	Model I	Model II	Model III
Gender (0=male, 1=female)	-.28**	-.18**	-.13*
Rank (asst. ref)			
associate		.20**	.17**
professor		.30**	.25**
Discipline (beta. ref)			
alpha		-.05	-.04
gamma		-.02	-.01
No. yearly articles		.02	.01
Age			.03*
Underage children			-.06*
Part-time			-.02*
R^2	.25	.39	.47
** $p<.01$, * $p<.05$			

From these analyses, we can conclude the following. In Model I, we predicted salaries of male and female academic staff from gender only. The R^2 equals 0.25, showing that 25% of the variation in hourly wages can be predicted from an academician being male or female. This is in an absolute sense not very high, but even so remarkable: a regression model with just one variable predicting that well is rare. The regression coefficient is negative, meaning that those with higher scores on the variable gender (i.e. females) are predicted to earn less per hour. As the b is unstandardized, we may infer that for every euro that a man earns, a woman earns 72 eurocents.

Model II includes two important additional predictor variables, namely an academician's rank (likely very important as rank dictates the bandwidth of salaries) and the discipline in which people are employed. Rank is an ordered variable with assistant professor – the reference category here – the rank where salaries are likely lowest, followed by associate professor and at the top full professor. Discipline is a nominal variable (with three categories: beta, alpha and gamma). Both variables are entered as so-called dummy variables. For rank we construct two variables: the first dummy whether someone is associate professor or not and the second dummy whether someone is a full professor or not. Someone who scores '1' on the first dummy variable is an associate professor; someone who scores '1' on the second dummy variable is a full professor. If someone scores '0' on both dummy variables then that person is an assistant professor. The same trick is used for the nominal variable discipline: two dummy variables are created, one for working in an alpha discipline or not and the second for working in a gamma discipline or not. We see that indeed these two predictors are quite important: the R^2 increases to 0.39. We also see how associate professors are predicted to earn 20 cents more per euro than assistant professors, and full professors even 30 cents more than assistant professors. Discipline is not significant. We see how the regression coefficient for gender is lower than in Model I: over and above effects for rank and discipline, women now earn 18 cents per euro less than men. This means that some of the 28 cents difference that we saw in Model I was attributable to women working in lower ranks and/or in disciplines where salaries are generally lower.

In Model III, four more variables are added. We see that the R^2 again increases substantially. In this final model, we are able to explain 47% or almost half of the variation in salary with our regression model. The number of yearly articles published is not significant. Age is significant and the model shows that every year adds 3 cents to people's salary. Having underage children is also significant, with those caring for underage children earning 6 cents less than those without such care tasks. Note that both men and women could care for underage children and would then be similarly affected in their salaries. Lastly, working part-time also adds significantly to the prediction, and leads to a decrease by 2 cents in predicted salary. We note how the regression weight for gender has decreased even further: it is now -.13. We summarize this by saying that over and above the impact of rank, discipline, number of articles, age, childcare and working part-time, an effect of gender remains. The 13 cents less that women receive are on top of their rank, discipline, number of articles, etc.; the effect of gender is what remains after we have taken all these other factors into account.

Does this analysis prove that women are discriminated against? It does not. It may be that other confounders still play a role, factors that co-vary both with gender and salary, that we did not incorporate in our model. If we have indeed missed important variables, we have not specified a correct model (this is also referred to as omitted variables bias), and we should continue our search and extend and improve our model. What we can be sure of is that the 13 cents-effect that remains in this analysis cannot be attributed to any of the common explanations for the pay gap between men and women we included in our model.

9.3 Analysis of variance model

In an analysis of variance model, we also attempt to predict the scores on a dependent variable Y from the scores on one or more independent variables X. Here, however, the X are not interval variables, but nominal. This means that for envisaging the model, the same conceptual representation as that for regression analysis (see Figure 9.1) can be used, but the X variables are a different kind of variable, they have a different, nominal measurement level.

Analysis of variance is in that sense a fairly straightforward analogue of regression analysis. Very often, in addition to testing whether the independent variables contribute significantly to the prediction of Y, the impact of so-called interaction effects is assessed, the impact of specific combinations of categories of the independent variables. Analysis of variance has numerous other attractive options too, like the possibility to analyse particular designs, such as designs where respondents have been observed repeatedly, or designs where respondents have for instance been offered tasks to complete in a systematic manner.

The notation that we employ in analysis of variance is slightly different from the notation in regression analysis – independent variables are in many textbooks not written as X_1, X_2, X_3, ... anymore but as A, B, C – and the model specification appears different from what we were used to. Also, the format in which results are reported differs.

Analysis of variance is very widely used, particularly in evaluation research, such as for assessing the impact of a certain therapy. In research using so-called 'vignettes', it is the standard analysis technique: in vignette studies respondents are offered – usually in a revolving or randomized way – different alternative scenarios and asked for their assessment of a dependent variable embedded in that scenario. An example is where researchers artificially construct court files, in which certain aspects are randomized such as the sex of the offender or the type of offence – all nominal variables. See also section 5.7. Analysis of variance detects what characteristics of these court cases and the respondents best predict answers on the vignette's dependent variable.

9.3.1 When to employ analysis of variance

Analysis of variance – often abbreviated as AN(alysis)O(f)VA(riance) – is a suitable analysis technique whenever we are interested in finding out the impact of one or more (combinations of) nominal independent variables on the scores on a dependent variable. The categories of the independent variables are treated as nominal, unordered categories. So if the independent variable were to be disciplinary background, ANOVA would investigate the impact of each of the separate categories (hard sciences, social sciences, law, humanities) on the dependent variable Y.

This means that when an independent variable is an interval level variable, it is not efficient to use ANOVA. ANOVA would treat each value of the interval level variable as a separate category. If we had for instance an independent variable 'age', ANOVA would treat each and every category (18, 19, 20, ... 65) as a separate category. This would not only make inspection and interpretation quite cumbersome, but there is also loss of information, as the technique does not reckon with the fact that the categories are ordered and equidistant. So, when an independent variable is an interval level variable, it is more efficient to employ a model (such as the regression model) that treats the independent variable at the measurement level it has.

Notwithstanding the above, in some cases researchers do want to use the ANOVA model and have interval level variables that they want to incorporate in the model. If the independent variable has many categories, it is then often re-coded into a smaller number of categories such as '18–22', '23–30', '31–40', and the re-coded variable used as a nominal variable in the analysis. One important reason to do so is that one suspects that the impact of age on the dependent variable may not be linear. It may for instance be the case that one thinks that labour market orientation is pretty low when people are still studying, that it is higher as people need to find a job after graduating, between the ages of 23 and 30, but that it declines somewhat as people are in the age group where they have settled in a job, are starting a family, etc.

Analysis of variance is a technique that already gives good results with small sample sizes. Formally, it is assumed that the dependent variable Y is normally distributed. However, it has been shown that even with fairly substantive deviations from normality, the technique still performs well. It is, we say, *robust* against such deviations from normality. Analysis of variance is easy to interpret as well. For all these reasons, it is widely used. Some of the possibilities it has (like incorporating interaction effects) are also possible to include in other analysis techniques but are then less easily implemented.

9.3.2 Analysis of variance proper

In analysis of variance, we attempt to investigate whether the scores on an interval dependent variable Y can be predicted from one or more categorical variables. As said, the independent variables that we have so far named X generally appear under a different name. Variables are named 'A' and 'B', etc. – although they may be named 'Gender' or 'Type of Claim' too.

Starting with the simple example where there is just one independent variable A, its categories are denoted by α. If A has two categories, we have α_1 and α_2; if it has three categories there is α_1, α_2 and α_3. The analysis of variance model is now construed as follows:

$$Y_{ij} = \mu + \alpha_j + e_{ij},$$

in which Y_{ij} is the score on the variable Y for the i-th person in the j-th category of A, and α_j is the 'effect' of the j-th category of the independent variable. The term μ is an overall average, a sort of starting point for the building of the model, just like the coefficient 'a' in regression analysis. So, every respondent starts from the same μ. If a respondent is in category 1 of the independent variable A, then for that respondent α_1 applies, if a respondent has scored category 2, α_2 applies, etc. If the total number of respondents studied is N, then in each of the k categories of A we have n respondents (and, assuming for simplicity equal cell sizes: $N = n \times k$). In ANOVA, α is computed such that the sum of all the α's over the respective k categories or so-called 'levels' of A is zero:

$$\sum_{j=1}^{k} \alpha_j = 0.$$

Obviously, not all Y scores can be predicted perfectly in this way, so also for ANOVA, just like we did in regression analysis, we need an error term to capture the difference between the observed and the predicted Y scores. The predicted Y is:

$$\hat{Y}_{ij} = \mu + \alpha_j.$$

The error terms are defined as the difference between the predicted and observed Y, just like in regression analysis:

$$e_{ij} = Y_{ij} - \hat{Y}_{ij}.$$

And, just like in the regression model, here too the error terms add up to zero, within each cell and over all levels of A:

$$\sum_{j=1}^{k} \sum_{i=1}^{n} e_{ij} = 0.$$

How do we determine the error term in practice? Suppose that we see that $Y_{13} = 10$, and we have $\mu = 7$, and $\alpha_1 = 2$, then given that:

$$\hat{Y}_{13} = \mu + \alpha_1 = 7 + 2 = 9.$$

we know that

$$e_{13} = Y_{13} - \hat{Y}_{13} = 10 - 9 = 1.$$

In words, given that μ equals 7, and α_1 equals 2, the error term e_{13} equals 1. If we had a value of 6 for Y_{14} we would conclude that e_{14} equals -3: 7 + 2 + (-3) = 6. The estimate of Y_{13} is slightly too low and the error term is 1; the estimate of Y_{14} is too high and the error term is -3. In this manner all observations are decomposed into a part constituting the mean score (μ), an effect α_1 attributable to the fact that someone is in the first category of A (A_1), and personal deviations from the ensuing estimates captured by the error terms.

So, once we have values for μ, for the respective α_j's and for all the error terms e_{ij}, how can we determine whether the independent variable A contributes significantly to the prediction of Y? Clearly, if the respective α_j's are very large, this would more likely be the case: then, it matters a lot whether someone is in one or the other category of A. And if the α_j's are all very close to zero, it is less likely that we will find a significant impact of A, as then the predicted scores are quite close to the mean μ. We will explain conceptually the reasoning that is used to determine whether an effect is considered significant. We do this with an example.

Suppose that I have developed a calculus course for those who become fearful when presented with numbers. Before the course, the participants scored on average a '5' for calculus. After the course, they score on average a '7'. Not all had the same scores,

Figure 9.4: ANOVA example: improvement in calculus before and after course

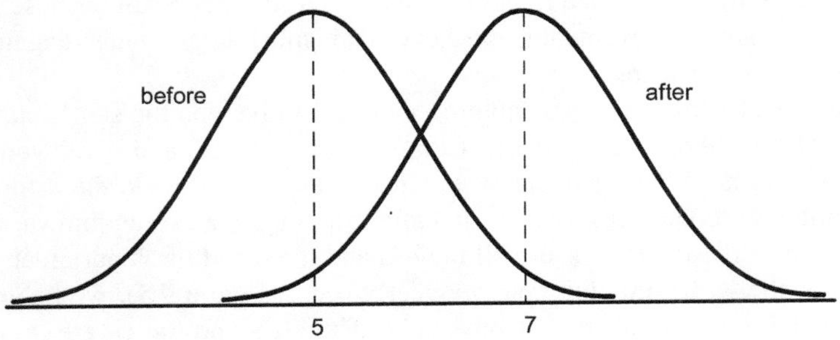

Figure 9.5: ANOVA example: calculus improvement with less variability

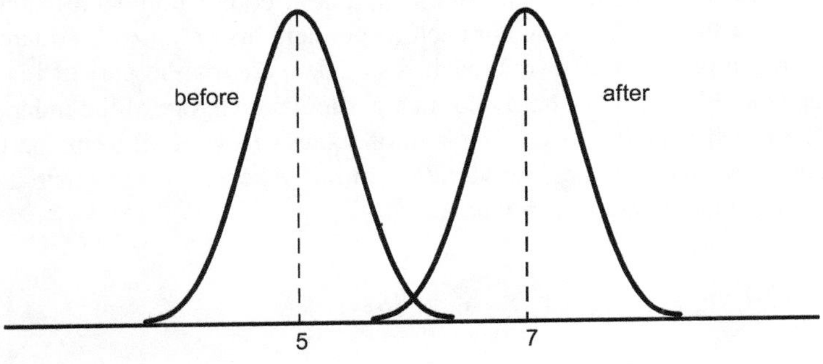

there was some variability, but we can say that the average improvement was 2. This situation is depicted in Figure 9.4.

The figure shows how indeed the average scores improved, from an average 5 to an average 7. The figure also shows that there is quite some variability: some respondents still had – after finishing the course – low scores, whereas some already had a '7' before the course started. Compare for that matter this figure with Figure 9.5. Here a situation with much less variability is depicted. Respondents here had scores that clung much more around the mean: almost all respondents had scores really close to 5 before the training, and almost all had scores around 7 after the course. The scores fluctuate much less.

Now if you were to ask someone to tell you which result s/he would find more meaningful – the one in Figure 9.4 or the one in Figure 9.5 – almost everyone would tell you – without any formulas or complicated reasoning – that Figure 9.5 is the stronger result. This is remarkable, because the net difference is the same in both examples: in both, people improved 2 points on average. However, the last figure is definitely the stronger one. Why is this so? One way of saying this is by noting that, while in the first figure some people already had good marks before the training and quite a few still had bad marks after the training, in the second figure, almost all respondents improved. In the second example, the improvement was so to speak 'en bloc' – almost all had bad marks before the training and almost all had improved afterwards. Formulated more mathematically, we find the second figure indicative of a stronger result because – even though the net average improvement is the same – it is much larger gauged against the smaller variability in the scores.

What analysis of variance does is nothing more than give you the same intuitively appealing conclusion – except for the fact that it uses formulas and gives you exact significance of results. What analysis of variance does is to evaluate the differences between a number of 'conditions' (before and after training) against random variability in the data (the e_{ij}). If we were to sum all the α's and the result turns out much larger than the sum of the e_{ij} (a situation that we clearly see in Figure 9.5), we believe the impact of A is telling, 'significant'. Conversely, if the α's and the e_{ij} are of similar magnitude, we would say that the impact of A is in fact similar to differences you might expect just by chance. This is what you see in Figure 9.4.

How then exactly do computations go? We suggested just now that one could compare the sum of the α_j with the sum of the e_{ij}, but of course both sum to zero (see above). To solve for this, in ANOVA, for each respondent his or her α_j is squared, and all squared terms summed. Recall that each respondent's α_j is the part of his or her score that is attributable to him or her being in a particular category of the independent variable A. The result is called 'SS_A', the sum of squares (SS) of all terms pertaining to the independent variable A, i.e. the variation in the Y scores that is attributable to the categories of the independent variable A:

$$n \sum_{j=1}^{k} \alpha_j^2 = SS_A.$$

Next, for each respondent his or her error term is squared and all these squared terms again summed. Recall that each respondent's e_{ij} is the part of his score that is attributable to chance. The result of adding up the squared terms is called 'SS_{error}', the sum of squared error terms, i.e. the variation in the Y scores that is attributable to chance:

$$\sum_{j=1}^{k} \sum_{i=1}^{n} e_{ij}^2 = SS_{error}.$$

The idea is that if SS_A is much larger than SS_{error}, we judge the impact of A as important. If, however, SS_A is comparable to SS_{error} or even smaller, we judge the effect of A not to be much larger than chance and therefore as not very telling.

However, before this comparison can be made, first both SS_A and SS_{error} have to be divided by the so-called 'degrees of freedom', terms that take into account the fact that SS_A will be larger if we have more levels of A, and that SS_{error} will similarly be larger if we observe more respondents. It would be an unfair comparison if we did not correct for that in some way: we might then find that with exactly the same variability, and exactly the same mean difference, one test turns out to be significant while the other does not – only because of having more or fewer respondents. Correcting for such issues, we compute the so-called mean sums of squares (MS) for both A:

$$\frac{\mathrm{SS_A}}{\mathrm{k}-1} = \mathrm{MS_A},$$

and for the error terms:

$$\frac{\mathrm{SS_{error}}}{\mathrm{k(n}-1)} = \mathrm{MS_{error}}.$$

Once these terms $\mathrm{MS_A}$ and $\mathrm{MS_{error}}$ have been computed, we have arrived at the point where we can finally do statistical testing. This is done by computing the ratio of these terms, just like we intuitively did in the figures above:

$$\frac{\mathrm{MS_A}}{\mathrm{MS_{error}}} = F_\mathrm{A}.$$

So, analysis of variance is exactly what its name says: analysis of the variance in the data, and more precisely an evaluation of the variability of the scores due to the independent variable A ($\mathrm{MS_A}$) against variation due to chance ($\mathrm{MS_{error}}$). To get exact significance statements, ANOVA tests the ratio of these terms by employing a statistical distribution, the F-distribution.

The F-distribution differs from the normal distribution, but the principle for using it in testing is the same as the principle we have been discussing all this time. The null hypothesis is that there are no differences between the levels of the independent variable (hence: *all* α_j are equal to zero), and using the F-distribution it can be inferred what the chances are of finding our results under this hypothesis. If that chance is very small, we declare the finding incompatible with the null hypothesis and reject it. We then switch to the alternative hypothesis, namely that there are categories of A that have an effect on the dependent variable. We then say that A adds significantly to the prediction of Y. Again, we can test at a 1%, 2%, 5% level; as usual we are the ones as researchers to decide what chance we feel comfortable with for taking the wrong decision if $\mathrm{H_0}$ is true.

Table 9.3: Example ANOVA results

source of variation	SS	df	MS	F	*sign*
A	48	2	24.0	15	1%
error	24	15	1.6		
total	72	17			

This F-value is the test statistic, just like the z-value was in the examples in chapter 8. How significant a certain F-value is, given the degrees of freedom for A and the error terms, can be looked up in a table online or in a textbook, and statistical software packages do that for the user. In general, the larger the value of the F-statistic, the smaller the likelihood of the result under the null hypothesis. Table 9.3 gives the analysis of variance results for a fictional example. The F-statistic is here, as we see, highly significant. Although depending on sample size and characteristics of the variables, in practice, F-statistics of around 8 and higher are (almost) always significant. (Indeed, it would be highly counterintuitive if an effect due to the independent variable that is 8 times larger than chance were not regarded as significant! This means that we conclude that there are significant differences in the value of Y between the categories of the independent variable A, meaning that A contributes significantly to the prediction of the dependent variable.

Note that we only know *that* there are significant differences between the categories of A. If for instance the dependent variable were the number of typing errors that people make, and if respondents in category A_1 consumed no alcoholic drinks, those in A_2 consumed one to two alcoholic drinks, and those in A_3 consumed three or more alcoholic drinks, we cannot conclude that people who consume more alcohol make more typing mistakes. We do not know this – we only know that differences have been measured that are very unlikely to occur by chance if it were irrelevant whether someone consumes no alcohol, one to two, or three or more glasses of alcohol. The ANOVA test tells us only that – overall – there are significant differences between the categories or *levels* of the independent variable.

As said, analysis of variance or ANOVA is widely used in many areas of social research. Numerous extensions are possible to the simplest design we just discussed. However, in each design, the principle is always the same. We inspect the variability attributable to differences between categories of one (or a combination of) independent variables. We gauge that against the random fluctuation. If the differences in scores due to the independent variable (the differences between categories of the independent variable) are much larger than the fluctuation due to chance (differences within categories of the independent variable), we conclude that the independent variable has an impact on the dependent variable.

For ease of understanding, we have here always referred to the independent variable as 'A' and denoted its corresponding sums of squares as 'SS_A'. Often, the independent variable is labelled as 'Between', as it reflects the variation between categories of the independent variable. Correspondingly, the error variation is then referred to as 'Within', as this reflects the variability within the categories of A.

9.3.3 Factorial analysis of variance

Now the same can be said for analysis of variance that we said for regression analysis: a model with just one predictor is not likely to be a model that gives very good results and is likely to be too simplistic for our purposes. So, just like in regression analysis, also in ANOVA additional independent variables are often used for the prediction of Y. One example of such a model is:

$$Y_{ijkl} = \mu + \alpha_j + \beta_k + \gamma_l + e_{ijkl},$$

Figure 9.6: ANOVA example: interaction effect

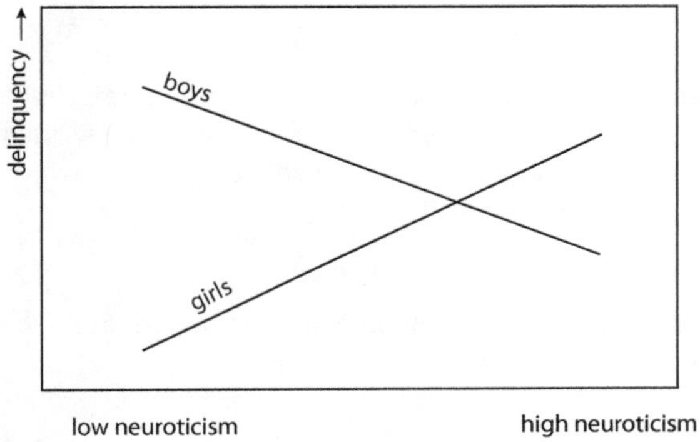

for the situation where we have three independent variables. This is called a *factorial* analysis of variance. In such a model, we measure the impact of several independent variables on the dependent variable. ANOVA has the option to not only include additional predictors, but to also investigate whether these variables *interact*. What is meant by that? Again we illustrate this with an example.

In research on delinquency it has been found that the psychological trait 'neuroticism' does not predict delinquency. Those who are highly, average, or below-average (all categorized into norm scores) neurotic all have approximately equal delinquency levels. However, if we disaggregate these findings for boys and girls, we find that for boys neuroticism is a *protective* factor: boys who are above-average neurotic have lower delinquency scores. For girls, on the other hand, we find the opposite: neurotic girls have increased delinquency scores, and neuroticism is in fact a risk factor for them. So, the overall result of 'no difference' was actually attributable to a levelling out of these opposite effects between boys and girls. There is heterogeneity. See Figure 9.6, which sketches the situation.

As can be inferred from this figure, there is only a slight difference between the delinquency levels of those who are highly neurotic and those who score low on neuroticism: if we were to average the scores, taking boys and girls together, we would find an almost horizontal line. There is a clear difference between delinquency levels of boys and girls: if we were to average the scores for boys and those for girls, we would see that boys have on average higher delinquency levels than girls. These are what is called main effects: the effects of the independent variables by themselves (here gender and neuroticism). In this example there is a clear main effect of gender. The main effect of neuroticism is minimal.

However, in the figure we see a so-called interaction effect of gender and neuroticism. For boys, higher scores on neuroticism predict lower delinquency levels. For girls it is the other way round: for girls higher scores on neuroticism predict higher delinquency levels. This means that gender affects the way in which neuroticism impacts delinquency levels: gender alters the effect of neuroticism on delinquency. When there is such an interaction effect, it is said that one independent variable *moderates* the effect of the other independent variable. Gender is then called a moderator variable. The factorial model with such an interaction effect is then written as:

$$Y_{ijk} = \mu + \alpha_j + \beta_k + \alpha\beta_{jk} + e_{ijk},$$

with α and β now referred to as *main effects* and the term $\alpha\beta$ referred to as the interaction effect between A and B. Such interaction effects are often written as A $\times$ B, or even 'Neuroticism $\times$ Gender'. A hypothetical example of a table with results for this analysis of variance is given in Table 9.4.

Table 9.4: ANOVA example with interaction terms

source of variation	SS	df	MS	F	sign
neuroticism	3	2	1.5	$F_A = 0.75$	< 1
gender	10	1	10	$F_B = 5$	5%
neuroticism $\times$ gender	36	2	18	$F_{AB} = 9$	1%
error	68	34	2		
total	107	39			

The table confirms what we inferred already from the figure. There is a – significant, it turns out – main effect of gender. The effect of neuroticism is non-significant (in fact any F-value below 1 is always non-significant, as then the variation in scores of the dependent variable due to the categories of the predictor variable is less than chance variation). The interaction effect is highly significant at the 1% level.

More complicated models are possible with interaction effects between more than two variables:

$$Y_{ijkl} = \mu + \alpha_j + \beta_k + \gamma_l + \alpha\beta_{jk} + \alpha\gamma_{jl} + \beta\gamma_{kl} + \alpha\beta\gamma_{jkl} + e_{ijkl},$$

where $\alpha\beta_{jk}$, $\alpha\gamma_{jl}$ and $\beta\gamma_{kl}$ would be labelled '1st order interaction effects', and $\alpha\beta\gamma_{jkl}$ would be labelled the '2nd order interaction effect'. Just as we had in the univariate case a test for F_A, now we have separate tests for F_A, F_B, F_C, F_{AB}, F_{AC}, etc.

Models and computations become increasingly complex with more independent variables. The principles, however, remain the same. Each time we test differences due to (combinations of) categories of variables against chance variation.

Here too, for the analysis of variance model, the same difficulties may arise that we sketched for the regression model, and for models in general. As models become more complicated, they become harder to interpret: how should we for instance interpret a 5th order interaction effect? In addition, as more independent variables and more interaction terms are added to the model, the cells along which the squared error terms are added become smaller and the error variance (the variability within the groups formed by the combination of categories of the variables) decreases too. This inflates the F-statistics. As such – to prevent opportunistic addition and spurious inflation of these F-statistics – it is the rule that independent variables and interaction terms be added to the model only when there are strong theoretical reasons to do so.

9.3.4 Tests

We discussed tests for the analysis of variance model. For each main and interaction effect, an F-test is carried out, which tells you what the likelihood is of finding the results if the data come from a population with no differences between the various categories of (the combinations of) the independent variables. As we said before, such tests tell you whether there are *any* differences between the (combination of the) categories of the independent variable(s). If you were interested in particular differences, say whether dosage p and dosage q of a drug differ significantly in migraine incidence, it is possible to carry out specific so-called contrast tests.

9.3.5 Model fit

When doing analysis of variance, it is not customary to present measures of model fit. Such measures are available, however. The most often used is ω^2, which is the analogue of R^2 in the regression situation. As such, ω^2 tells you how much of the variance of the dependent variable is explained by the entire ANOVA model. It is also possible to express the effects of the respective factors in a so-called η, with the η for each factor reflecting how much variance is explained by the respective factor.

We end this section on ANOVA with an example. Our data come from a study on workplace misbehaviour (Wesselius et al., 2023). Using vignettes, a hypothetical case was presented of an employee who sexually assaulted a colleague at a company New Year's party. The story narrated how the employee was fired by the company after complaints by the victim. Respondents were asked how 'just' they rated this outcome, on a scale from '1' to '5', with '5' indicating the respondent was in complete agreement with the decision and '1' the opposite. In the vignette, four factors had been varied: whether the perpetrator was male or female, whether the victim was male or female, whether the victim was married and had a child (an indication of the 'respectability' of the victim, following on from Nils Christie's (1986) ideal victim theory) or was single, and whether the perpetrator was a colleague or the superior of the victim. In addition to these manipulated properties, the researchers recorded the respondent's gender, age, employment status and whether the respondent knew someone who had been similarly victimized. A total of 240 respondents filled out a small questionnaire. The sample was a convenience sample.

The authors had expected that the company response (firing the perpetrator) would be rated as more just when the victim was female, the perpetrator male, the victim married and the perpetrator the victim's superior.

The authors investigated the main effects of factors they had manipulated: victim and perpetrator gender, relation between victim and perpetrator, and victim marital status. In previous exploratory analyses, they had uncovered fairly strong gendered effects, so they also included the first- and second-order interaction effects for victim, perpetrator and respondent gender. The results are in Table 9.5.

Table 9.5: ANOVA example on workplace misbehaviour

source of variation	SS	df	MS	F	sign
gender victim (v)	.934	1	.934	5.750	.132
gender perpetrator (p)	3.751	1	3.751	12.482	.153
relation	6.799	1	6.799	6.571	.011
respectability	.768	1	.768	.742	.390
categorized age respondent	14.899	5	2.980	2.880	.015
personally know victim	.554	1	.554	.535	.465
$\text{gender}_v \times \text{gender}_p$	.394	1	.394	.097	.808
$\text{gender}_v \times \text{gender}_r$	.117	1	.117	.028	.894
$\text{gender}_p \times \text{gender}_r$	.288	1	.288	.070	.835
$\text{gender}_v \times \text{gender}_p \times \text{gender}_r$	4.088	1	4.088	3.951	.048

Source: Wesselius et al. (2023)

The analysis of variance shows that three factors are significant: the business relation between the victim and perpetrator, the age of the respondent, and the second-order interaction effect between the gender of the respondent, victim and perpetrator. Of the manipulated factors, gender of the perpetrator and gender of the victim were in the anticipated direction, but the differences were clearly not large enough for the factor to emerge as significant. Respectability of the victim played only a very minor role, with differences between perceived justness for married and single victims only marginal. Personally knowing someone who had been similarly victimized also played a non-significant role.

Inspecting the significant effects, the authors report that respondents indeed evaluated the company decision as more just when the perpetrator was hierarchically superior to the victim. For age of the respondent, they inspected the category means, and found them to be almost strictly monotonically decreasing, with means as given in Table 9.6.

The authors concluded that older respondents more often disagreed with the company measure, a finding which was supported by qualitative comments that the respondents had been asked for. Obviously, ANOVA only states overall significance, but does not indicate which categories of the variable generate significant differences. From the means, it appears that there is somewhat of a watershed from age 33, and subsequent contrast tests should reveal whether that is indeed the case, that is, whether those below and above 33 indeed judge the company decision significantly differently.

The interaction effect between the genders of the perpetrator and the victim was also insignificant; this shows that specific combinations of male or female victims and perpetrators were not assessed differently by the respondents. The same goes for the other two first-order interaction effects: male and female respondents do not judge

Table 9.6: Category means for age

	mean	n
< 24	4.28	54
24 - 26	4.22	37
27 - 33	4.20	25
34 - 51	3.89	61
52 - 60	3.62	26
> 60	3.65	37
Total	3.99	240

Source: Wesselius et al. (2023)

male or female victims, or male or female perpetrators, differently. All in all, it would therefore appear that gender does not play a very large role.

The second-order interaction effect is however significant. The authors rephrase this by saying that male and female respondents do judge the different constellations of gender of victim and perpetrator differently, and they illustrate this through a graph. In the administered vignettes the male and female victims were called Matthew and Helen respectively, and the male and female perpetrators Tom and Lisa; this is how they are indicated in the graph (Figure 9.7); note that the y-axis is shortened – it starts from 3.5.

The figure shows how female and male respondents indeed attach different evaluations to the company measure to fire the misbehaving employee. Firstly, we see that male respondents agree least with the firing of the misbehaving employee when the vignette had a female perpetrator (Lisa) sexually assaulting a male employee (Matthew). The average score is lowest here. The constellation in which male respondents agree most with firing of the culprit is where a male has sexually assaulted a male.

For female respondents, the picture is quite different. For them, there is one constellation that jumps out, and that is a male perpetrator sexually assaulting a female. This has by far the highest agreement score, and the other constellations differ only marginally in how the company measure is then evaluated. For establishing what combinations of the interacting variables differ significantly, additional contrast tests would be needed.

The authors interpret this as men and women evaluating '#MeToo'-like situations differently. Supported by qualitative remarks made by respondents, they argue that men find situations with a female accosting a male relatively innocuous. Some male respondents stated that the male victim could easily have solved the issue himself, or that if the respondent himself were to receive such sexual attentions, he would be flattered. Women on the other hand disapprove particularly of 'classical' sexual harassment contexts, in which a male harasses a female, possibly as such situations are most common and realistic for women.

Figure 9.7: ANOVA example: mean justness for different gender constellations

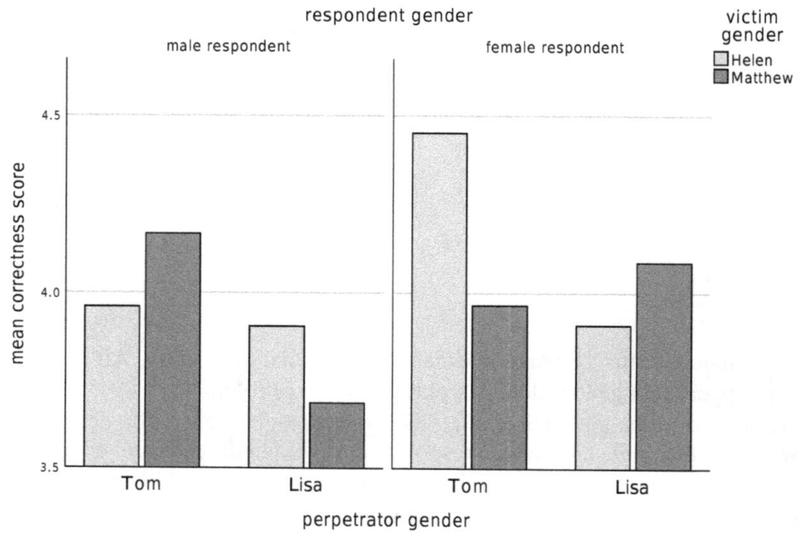

Source: Wesselius et al. (2023)

9.4 Wrapping up

It may seem odd, after the fairly different formulas, to reiterate that regression and analysis of variance models do essentially the same thing. Nevertheless, that is the case. The analysis of variance model can be seen as a more general case of the regression model, or the regression model as a special case of the analysis of variance model. We will not go into the mathematical details here, and simply note that it is important not to forget the similarities: in each case we are trying to predict a dependent variable from one or more independent variables. In each case the model is linear. While we discussed interaction terms for analysis of variance only, interaction terms can also be incorporated in regression models. And while we stated that regression models should be used when the independent variables are interval level or higher, it is also possible to incorporate nominal variables in regression models. The difference between the two techniques is in the manner in which the measurement levels of the independent variables are accommodated.

Both regression analysis and ANOVA are widely used techniques in quantitative empirical legal research, with regression analysis the more ubiquitous as it is so flexible and adaptable. Many extensions of regression analysis exist (for example, the survival models we discussed in section 6.5 also exist in regression format, so that several independent variables can be used to predict the dependent time until event). Regression analysis is also used often in content analysis of qualitative material – see section 7.3, where we discussed the study by Mascini & Holvast (2023) in which regression analyses were employed to predict writing styles. ANOVA is particularly useful for the analysis of data obtained through vignette studies in which researchers systematically manipulate factors.

9.5 Further reading

A classic (almost a Bible) on analysis of variance is Kirk (1968). For regression analysis, we recommend Cohen et al. (2002).

Chapter questions

1. What three properties make models useful? (section 9.1)
2. Give a number of synonyms for independent and dependent variable (section 9.1.1)
3. What are independent and dependent variables in the theory of procedural justice? (section 9.1.1)
4. What is the difference between a mediating and a moderating variable? (section 9.1.1)
5. List all parameters in a regression model with five predictor variables (section 9.1.2)
6. What is meant by a parsimonious model? (section 9.1.3)
7. Give two reasons why a regression model needs approximately 10 times as many replications as variables (section 9.1.3)
8. Under what conditions is regression analysis feasible? (section 9.2.1)
9. What are advantages and disadvantages of standardized versus unstandardized regression weights? (section 9.2.2)
10. What is multicollinearity and what can and should be done to prevent it? (section 9.2.3)
11. Give a number of reasons why R^2_{adj} is to be preferred over R^2 (section 9.2.4)
12. What does a large difference between R^2_{adj} and R^2 signal? (section 9.2.4)
13. What ratio is assessed using the F-statistic? (section 9.3)
14. Why is it that an F-value lower than 1 is never significant? (section 9.3)

15. What is factorial analysis of variance? (section 9.3.3)
16. Give an example of an interaction effect (section 9.3.3)
17. What are the differences and similarities between regression analysis and ANOVA? (section 9.4)

Chapter 10

Three worked ELS examples

10.1 Introduction

In this chapter we will attempt to illustrate how the methods that we discussed in the previous chapters are applied in practice. We have chosen three examples to do so, which exhibit spread over the type of methods, substantive legal domain, and type of research question.

The first example deals with social security law, which falls under administrative law. In the example we showcase a qualitative analysis of the experiences of welfare recipients who have been forced to take part in programmes that are aimed to reduce – as it is euphemistically called – their 'distance to the labour market'. These mandatory work programmes are intended to reduce dependence on welfare and to facilitate a return to paid employment. The research questions focus on whether the welfare recipients involved do experience these programmes as meaningful (or meaningless), and whether and why the programmes indeed – again in the experience of the persons involved – facilitate their return to the labour market. These questions as such belong within the third pillar of the trias ELSica that we introduced in section 1.3, the impact of laws.[1]

The second example deals with private law. In this example we illustrate the various steps in systematic case law analysis, focusing on a question that has long remained unanswered, namely whether parties who offer their apologies to victims, for instance victims of medical malpractice, thereby also admit liability in a legal sense, and thereby would weaken their position. The study neatly lays out the sampling procedure of court rulings, the doctrinal analysis of rulings and arguments used, combining this relatively standard analysis with qualitative and quantitative methods to arrive at an answer to the research questions. This study is best positioned somewhere within the first pillar of the trias, where questions are asked about assumptions in law.

The third example deals with international criminal law. This example uses simple descriptive quantitative analysis methods as well as a relatively advanced multivariate analysis to investigate whether sentences imposed by two international tribunals, the

[1] I am much indebted to Anja Eleveld who supplied much of the text for this section.

International Criminal Tribunal for the former Yugoslavia (ICTY) and the International Criminal Tribunal for Rwanda (ICTR), are predictable, or – as had been posited by a number of legal scholars – random. The study included all rulings at first instance and on appeal that had been handed down at both courts at the time the study was conducted. The research questions dealt with here are best positioned within the second pillar of the trias ELSica, the operations of the legal system.

10.2 Experiences with mandatory work programmes: qualitative analysis

In the Netherlands, as in many other welfare states, social security law contains regulations that compel welfare recipients to 'use a facility offered by the municipality, including social activation, aimed at the transition to paid work' (translated text from the Netherlands Participation Act, art. 9(1)(b)). This means that those who are receiving welfare can be forced to enrol in programmes that are intended to encourage a transition to the labour market.[2] That there can a certain degree of force is also illustrated by the fact that municipalities are obliged to cut benefits by 100% for at least one month if a recipient of social assistance benefits refuses to comply with the law.

Since the mid-1990s (the previous versions of) this regulation has been the legal basis for the obligation imposed in the Netherlands on welfare recipients to enrol in a Mandatory Work Programme (MWP). Despite the non-voluntary nature of these programmes, international quantitative studies using numerical measurement instruments have shown that MWP participants report relatively high levels of well-being (Carter & Whitworth, 2017; Knabe, Schöb, & Wiemann, 2017; Wulfgramm, 2011). Eleveld (2021) aimed to investigate this apparent paradox.

Instead of measuring well-being using one-dimensional linear measures, her study aimed to arrive at a more multifaceted and contextualized understanding of the effects of these programmes on welfare recipients' well-being against the legal obligation to participate in MWPs. Related to this, the study aimed to explore to what extent the assumption that these legal regulations will lead to welfare recipients' transition to (regular) work corresponds with MWP participants' lived experiences. Since the researcher was primarily interested in the manner in which the forced nature of work impacts MWP participants' well-being, the study primarily focused on MWP participants' meaningful (or meaningless) work experiences. As such, this study aimed to answer the following main research questions:

(1) *in what manner do welfare recipients participating in an MWP experience and interpret their work as meaningful or meaningless?*

(2) *how are recipients' interpretations and experiences related to their (subjective) prospects of transition to regular work?*

[2] This aim is elaborated in the so-called Memorie van Toelichting to the Participation Act (Kamerstukken II 2013/14 33801, No. 3, pp. 27–40), as well as in Memories van Toelichting to its predecessors Algemene bijstandswet and Wet Werk en Bijstand (Kamerstukken II 1991/92, 22545, No. 3, pp. 68–69; Kamerstukken II 1996/97, 25122, No. 3, pp. 25–26; Kamerstukken II 2002/03, 28870, No. 3, pp. 39–40).

10.2.1 Data collection

The study was conducted in three municipalities in the Netherlands to ensure spread over the Netherlands and urbanization: two medium-sized municipalities were chosen with just over 60,000 inhabitants and one large municipality with over 300,000 inhabitants. In all three municipalities, MWPs were in force. In each municipality, the researcher visited five to seven MWPs, again to ensure spread over MWPs. The MWPs for the interviewees generally entailed unskilled work such as simple production activities, call centre work, maintaining municipal green spaces, postal delivery, canteen work, serving coffee to people in a nursing home or simple administrative work. The official goal of most of these MWPs was to develop and keep up basic working skills, such as arriving at work on time, obeying an employer's instructions and so on, their work attitudes and, if possible, to further explore their work preferences.

Eleveld conducted in-depth interviews with on average two to three recipients per MWP. Participants were mostly introduced to the researcher by supervision staff at the programmes, although Eleveld also recruited some through snowballing via earlier interviewees. All in all, a total of 42 recipients of social assistance benefits who were participating in an MWP were interviewed (with approximately equal numbers per municipality). In most MWPs, recipients worked for between 20 and 32 hours a week for a minimum of three months – although often for longer. Five respondents had been participating in one or more MWPs for periods of over two years. A total of 24 women and 18 men were interviewed. Most respondents were 40 years old or over, and one-quarter had a migrant background. The interviews were conducted in 2017 and 2018. The interviewees gave informed consent to participate in the research.

Interviews lasted on average one to one-and-a-half hours. The interview format was topical, with interview topics including participants' evaluation of the MWP, their views on prospects of a paid job, relationships with colleagues and supervisors, working conditions, and the role of sanctions. The format of the interview was free-flowing, with ample opportunity for interviewees to broach new subjects and add information. Interviews were conducted by the researcher. All interviews were recorded and later transcribed, leading to several hundreds of pages of transcribed material to be analysed. For more on the data collection, see Eleveld (2021) and Dermine & Eleveld (2021).

10.2.2 Analytic methods: coding and discovering patterns

Given the large amount of textified data available, the interview transcripts were analysed using a software package, in this case ATLAS.ti. Coding and structuring the data took place over four steps, which are detailed below, after which the research questions were answered using the patterns that the coding and structuring steps had revealed.

Step 1: Descriptive (first-level) coding
In a first round, all parts of the text that directly or indirectly referred to the participants' valuation of MWP work were marked by the authors. These texts were then re-read and re-coded, predominantly using gerunds as primary codes to describe what was going on in the text (Charmaz 2012), labelled as 'Thinking along with the work programme's management', 'Feeling depressed at home', 'Rediscovering oneself', 'Learning the Dutch language', 'Feeling insecure', 'Complaining that time passes slowly', 'Enjoying

contacts with colleagues'. These first-level codes (along with subsequent second-level codes) and the original text fragments are given in Table 10.1.

Step 2: Focused (second-level) coding
In a next step, Eleveld combined the numerous primary codes[3] with similar codes, where possible simultaneously re-wording in more abstract terms (i.e. second-order categories) the descriptive codes. This entailed adding a second, interpretative layer to the relatively 'flat' first-layer codes. For example, 'Thinking along with the management' was given the second-order code 'Experiencing autonomy', attaching interpretation to the literal, first-level code. As another example, the primary code 'Rediscovering oneself' was given the second-level code 'Personal development – being yourself and knowing yourself'. While the label of this second-order code was still quite close to the primary code, in other instances the researcher actually took more liberty when formulating a second-order code. To give an example, the primary code 'Feeling depressed at home' was re-coded as 'Experiencing a more structured life', with the author motivating this through the participant clarifying his statement that working in an MWP established a basic rhythm in his life and, as such, pulled him out of a destructive situation. The example shows how coding does not amount to simply categorizing the answers, but can already entail interpreting (and as such analysing) the data.

It should be noted that, after the interviews had been read and re-read, some quotations could in fact be linked immediately to interpretive or 'second-order' interpretive codes. Here, the first-level coding step could be skipped, because the meaning of the text fragment was already clear, and a second-level code could be given right away. Examples of these secondary order codes are 'Feeling useful/contributing', 'Experiencing forced work', 'Gaining self-esteem', 'Feeling being treated inferior' and 'Lacking a prospect of future work'. These second-level codes that were found without a first step, and the original texts are given in Table 10.2.

During this process, some second-order codes were also merged. For example, the second-order code 'Feeling bored' was merged with a second-order code 'Learning nothing', as it turned out that quotations were often linked to both these codes. Re-reading such double-coded quotations (fragments of text that have been attached multiple codes) revealed that boredom was closely related to the lack of opportunities for self-development. Also, the second-order codes 'Gaining self-esteem' and 'Feeling respected' were merged, as re-reading the double-coded quotations indicated that having self-esteem was often preconditioned upon being respected. As such, merging second-order codes also constituted an analytic step.

Step 3: Axial coding
In a next, third step, a large number of second-order codes were grouped together in broader umbrella-type categories such as 'Meaningful work experiences' or 'Meaningless work experiences'. This so-called 'axial coding step', in which dimensions or axes are identified along which the second-order codes can be placed or ranked is another analytical step. Here the researcher seeks to combine or even rank the second-order

[3]We use 'primary code', 'first-level code' and 'first-order code' interchangeably, as we do 'secondary order code', 'second-level code' and 'second-order code'.

Table 10.1: First- and second-level codes and quotations

First-level code	Second-level code	Quotation
Thinking along with management	Autonomy at work	"I really like that it has yet to be set up. So that you get to think about a lot of things. It's informal"
Feeling depressed at home	Structured lives	"I couldn't bring myself to do anything. I had very heavy mental blocks"
Rediscovering oneself	Personal development-being and knowing yourself	"I also need to know where I stand in my life and that's really what it is about (...) to discovering yourself again because I was really stuck with myself
Learning the Dutch language	Personal development skills	"Also, my language improved, because at home we talk our language, Croatian and in terms of (Dutch) language I had forgotten a lot"
Feeling insecure	Lack of supervision	"When she said I can't come anymore, I said: "what are you telling me. Then my heart started beating (...) I can't manage this". She said, ask if you need help, ask Karen or the girls at the reception, they know everything. The next day I stood there alone, and I thought where to start and what to do"
Complaining time passes slowly	Feeling bored	"I have to work too many hours. Time doesn't go so fast. Half a day would be better"
Enjoying contacts with colleagues	Building & enjoying social relationships	"It was a fun group. It was like having a warm blanket wrapped around you, like coming home. You were immediately included in the group"

Table 10.2: Second-level codes and quotations

Second-level code	Quotation
Useful/ contributing	"I have no problem with having to do something for my benefits. I don't mind that. Then I still feel that I am somewhat useful. When I was still at home, I started asking myself in the morning, why do I get out of bed? I might as well stay in bed. Then you start to feel useless"
Forced work	"I'm only here to avoid a financial sanction"
Gaining self-esteem	"They kept saying:"You are doing well". I really liked that' '
Feeling being treated inferior	"Paper picking that was really the lowest point of my life I would say. I found it something I never thought I would have to do"
Lacking a prospect of future work	"It's all fun but at some point you think:"Yes, there's really no point to it all because no one will hire you". And then you stop looking at it positively. In the beginning, you're bursting with energy and really want to do it. But at some point you think: "Yes, that's it, yes" ".

Table 10.3: Grouping second-order codes related to meaningful work experiences

Subset	Second-order code
Conditions	Structured lives
	Autonomy at work/agency
Dimensions	Personal development skills
	Personal development being and knowing yourself
	Useful/contribution
	Building and enjoying social relationships
Consequences	Gaining self-esteem
	Getting social recognition

codes. What distinguishes this step from the previous steps can best be explained as follows. During the first steps, the aim is to categorize and interpret the text fragments: first using descriptive codes (codes that simply describe or summarize what is said), then using interpretative codes (codes that add meaning to what is said). In quantitative terms, one could frame these as univariate steps. In the third step, the axial coding, the researcher attempts to see how the second-order codes relate, what associations there are between them, or whether some kind of underlying or manifest structure can be discerned. Here the analysis is – one could say – multivariate (or multi-category).

In the analysis of MWPs, Eleveld did just that. She first grouped second-level codes into larger sets, or clusters of codes, such as 'Meaningful work experiences'. In doing so, she searched for codes that cluster in the sense that they refer to the same themes or general topics. After having done so, she also investigated how these codes related. Eleveld for instance discovered how the codes in the category 'Meaningful work experiences' could be distinguished into three subsets, differentiating between *conditions* for meaningful work experiences, aspects or *dimensions* of meaningful work experiences, and *consequences* of meaningful work experiences (see Table 10.3).

To illustrate findings, qualitative researchers often use exemplars. Exemplars are specific examples in the dataset that illustrate the findings (Tracy, 2020; see also section 7.1.2). To present her data, Eleveld also used a number of exemplars, one of these being a participant named Jeroen. He was a brilliant exemplar as he illustrated vividly how the four identified dimensions of meaningful work were related. He said:

> *"What I like about this work? First of all, the camaraderie and the atmosphere. I'm happy to be working again. I am among people. I like to help customers. They come to me asking questions and sometimes I am able to help them and sometimes not. I feel that I am meaningful for society. I'm not only sitting at home, alone, a loner. I am someone. I can be myself again. I can do things, have a drink with colleagues. That is fun, you are connecting with new people. And the best thing of all is that you can simply be human and be yourself."*

Table 10.4: Grouping second-order codes related to meaningless work experiences

Subset	Second-order code
Extrinsic meaningless	Bad working conditions
	No or insufficient 'payment'
	Forced to work
Intrinsic meaningless	Boring/learning nothing
	Lack of supervision
	No prospects of future work
	Feeling being treated as inferior
	Not being recognized by others

In this process of axial coding, it is possible to search for various kinds of relationships between codes. And this is also what Eleveld did. In addition to her cluster of meaningful work experiences, she had also identified a cluster of *meaningless* work experiences. Within this subset, she further distinguished between *extrinsic* meaningless work experiences, experiences to do with how the work was organized, and *intrinsic* meaningless work experiences, that is experiences to do with what according to the interviewees the work entailed in practice (see Table 10.4).

Step 4: Discovering patterns

In a final step, Eleveld analysed the patterns in the data, that is, whether some respondents had particular profiles of answering patterns. Eleveld had found that MWP work could be experienced both as meaningful and as meaningless, across various dimensions. She had also found that some interviewees experienced their work as exclusively meaningful or exclusively meaningless, but that other participants had mentioned both meaningful and meaningless work experiences. Based on an additional analysis of the data (not reported in detail here) Eleveld had also concluded that the assumption that MWP work would lead to a transition to paid work did not meet with most participants' lived experiences. On the contrary, quit a lot of them complained about the lack of future work prospects. Eleveld wanted to look for patterns in the dataset in order to understand why and how MWP participants experienced their work as meaningless and/or meaningful and how these experiences were related to their complaints about the lack of future work prospects, their personal characteristics and the characteristics of the particular MWP they worked in.

To this end, the respondents were grouped according to firstly their meaningful and meaningless work dimensions, and secondly the extent to which they complained about the lack of future work prospects. Based on these two principles, participants were allocated to five different categories. First, one group of participants was formed who referred to one of the meaningful work dimensions, without referring to any of the intrinsic meaningless work dimensions, one could say a 'positive' group. Next, from those participants who referred to both meaningful and meaningless work dimensions, first a group was formed that complained about the lack of future work prospects and second a group where participants did not utter such complaints. This aspect (whether or not participants were positive or negative about future work prospects) was of course a key variable, as the programmes had been designed to improve work prospects. The remaining participants were divided into a group that participated in the two MWPs that were – instead of supporting them to move to paid work – primarily used to punish welfare recipients (a salient characteristic as this would likely also have an association with respondents' lived experiences and future outlook) and a group comprising the remaining participants in one of the other MWPs.

Eleveld subsequently explored what characterized and distinguished the participants in each of these groups, apart from the principles that were used to form them in the first place. To this end she explored whether the categories could be connected to: 1) one or more specific meaningful or meaningless work dimensions; 2) extrinsic meaningless work dimensions (e.g. working conditions, the experience of forced work) or the nature of work; 3) a specific municipality (remember that the study was conducted in three municipalities); 4) personal characteristics (e.g. sex, age, migrant background, years of regular work experience, engagement in volunteer work, a combination of work and care); or 5) any other second-order code that had many quotations (e.g. treatment by the municipality; work identification; framing of work, work ethos; experiencing/using autonomy within work). In this step, the quotations were re-read to explore which 'emotions' were characteristic of these group members. The procedure that was employed is clearly iterative, and illustrates the fluid and flexible analysis modes that are employed in qualitative research.

Table 10.5 gives the patterns that were found. First, while participants in the abovementioned groups 1, 2 and 3 all referred to some of the meaningful work dimensions, participants in groups 1 and 3 specifically emphasized that their meaningful work experiences were related to their personal development and to gaining self-esteem and social recognition. Participants in groups 1 and 3 were also clearly more engaged in volunteer work and the combination of work and care activities, compared to the participants in any of the other groups. These participants also experienced more autonomy compared to participants in any of the other groups (despite the forced character of the MWP), either because of the (empathic) way they were treated by the municipality or because of the freedom they experienced in the MWP. All in all, these participants seemed to be less bothered by their (lack of) prospects for paid work: other issues such as self-development and volunteer work were more important to them.

Participants in these groups were also, compared to the participants in the other groups, relatively often partly incapacitated for work. In addition while participants in group 1 were relatively old (group 1), participants in group 3 had a fairly long work history. Many participants in these groups did not envisage a quick transition to paid work because of their work disability and/or old age. For them the MWP work offered rather a good alternative to sitting at home. However, participants in group 1 were generally happier with their work compared to participants in group 3 who were more critical of the MWPs but seemed to accept their situation under current conditions and sought to make the best out of it. These participants also tended to frame their MWP work as regular work.

Members of group 2 seemed to be more ambitious when it came to the transition to paid work. These participants also seemed to endorse a stronger work ethos compared to members of groups 1 and 3. However, many of them were disappointed because of the lack of skills development and the lack of clear job prospects.

Members of group 4 (who participated in the disciplinary programmes) and (to a lesser extent) those in group 5 complained about the forced nature of the work, which also influenced the way they experienced their work – as exclusively meaningless. Yet in this group the boring nature of the work (instead of the lack of future work prospects) stood out. This probably also explains why members of group 4 tended to be more resigned about their situation compared to members of group 5.

Members of group 5 were dissatisfied and sometimes even angry with their situation. Like participants in group 3, they complained about the ways they were treated by the municipality. However, in contrast to members of group 3, they were also disappointed about the lack of job prospects and the insufficient 'payments' for the work done.

10.2.3 Answering the research questions

Based on the analysis in the first three steps, Eleveld concluded that the assumption that MWP work would lead to a transition to paid work did not match most participants' lived experiences. In addition, she drew the following (broad) conclusions. First, legal regulations that compel welfare recipients to participate in an MWP imply for many of them that they are forced to perform work that they experience as meaningless – either because the work is boring, or because they do not see much prospect of a transition to paid work, or they get insufficient supervision, or they feel that they are treated as inferior or are not socially recognized in any other way.

However, second, the analysis indicated that these regulations may as well – seemingly paradoxically – increase participants' sense of agency and autonomy, especially when respondents had earlier felt they had lost control over their lives. In these instances, participation in MWPs may (also) give rise to meaningful work experiences along various dimensions (feeling useful, building and enjoying social relationships, personal development) and result in an enhanced sense of self-esteem.

Third, the analysis indicates that welfare recipients tend to experience MWP work as more meaningful when the legal regulations that compel them to participate in an MWP are implemented in less restrictive ways or when the work permits them to enjoy some autonomy and where they are less focused on transition to paid work. Under these conditions welfare recipients may focus more, through the MWP, on the development of their inner selves and appreciate their MWP participation, or simply accept their MWP participation for lack of better alternatives. However, where MWP participants expect that participation in an MWP will result in a transition to paid work, initial acceptance or enjoyment may turn to disappointment or anger, especially in the event of strict municipal implementation.

In sum, Eleveld concludes that quite a number of welfare recipients do not experience and interpret their work as meaningful. It is striking that many respondents also mentioned both meaningful as well as meaningless aspects of their MWP experiences. The legal regulations that compel welfare recipients to work in an MWP lead often to meaningless work experiences which negatively impact well-being. These regulations may, however, also give rise to meaningful work experiences and, as a

Table 10.5: Identifying patterns

Group (N)	Criteria	Main characteristics	Salient emotion
1 (N=10)	Exclusively referring to meaningful work dimensions	Focus on development inner self Positive about treatment by municipality Best option under current conditions Relatively old age Partly incapacitated	Content/ happy
2 (N=6)	Referring to both meaningful and meaningless work dimensions, including the lack of prospects of paid work	Ambitious, focus on future paid work Work is important	Disappointed
3 (N=11)	Referring to both meaningful and meaningless work dimensions, but not the lack of prospects of paid work	Ambiguous, valuing development inner self Enjoying autonomy within work Experiencing work negatively in all dimensions Best option under current conditions Partly incapacitated	Content/ acceptance
4 (N=6)	Exclusively referring to meaningless work dimensions and working in a disciplinary MWP	Work is experienced as forced work Forced character colours work experiences Feeling bored at work	Resigned
5 (N=9)	Exclusively referring to meaningless work dimensions, but not working in a disciplinary MWP	Focus on future paid work and developing skills Complaining about the bad treatment by the municipality and (to lesser extent) experiencing work as forced work	Disappointed/ angry

result, in increased well-being, especially when legal regulations are implemented in a non-restrictive way, leaving more autonomy to welfare recipients and where MWP participants do not expect that their work will lead to paid work transitions.

The analysis in addition shows that welfare recipients' experiences with MWPs depend on recipients' background and personal characteristics, and on the manner in which these programmes are implemented. The qualitative analysis showed that while programmes were designed to ease and in fact at times force welfare recipients' transition to the labour market, they appear to be appreciated most, and contribute most to well-being, when they are seen to be employed not for these purposes. This shows that recipients' interpretations and experiences are linked to their (subjective) prospects of transition to regular work, but in a sense in a reverse manner than anticipated: it is particularly the unambitious, those who do it in a sense 'on the side' and who do not have many expectations, who gain the most.

Regardless, one perhaps unfortunate conclusion from the research appears to be that the envisaged stimulus for transition to the labour market does not appear to materialize. Those employed in the programmes find them satisfying as a pastime that is better than sitting alone at home, provides activities that improve their self-image, and makes them feel useful. The programme does not appear to be perceived as an instrument for social mobility. The punitive aspects of the programmes, when experienced as such, also do not appear to serve as a push in the direction of the labour market, but to incur incapacitating emotions, such as resignation. Those who are very much focused on re-entry into the labour market are mainly disappointed.

Obviously, one question that remains is to what extent the group that was interviewed (mainly referred to the researcher by supervisory staff at the MWPs) is a special group, and whether these findings can be generalized to the entire group of welfare recipients who partake in such programmes. Given other information gathered by Eleveld from observation and from interviews with supervising staff and civil servants, it is unlikely that welfare recipients who benefited from the MWPs in the sense that they quickly found work were not sampled, as such successful transitions rarely occurred. While Eleveld had suspected that perhaps staff who referred interviewees to her might have selected relatively positive ones, this also turned out to be not the case: many referred interviewees were in fact quite negative about the programmes.

The example shows how qualitative data can be coded and combined to reveal non-linear, intricate patterns in the data, employing iterative methods. Sometimes particular choices are made by the researcher – who is immersed in and eminently familiar with the data – in a manner that would not always be replicable by other researchers. Regardless, it becomes eminently clear from the analysis that MWPs cannot be reduced to being simply 'effective' or 'not effective', and that the experiences of participants cannot be reduced to high or low scores on a one-dimensional well-being scale. Experiences are multi-layered and variegated, and depend on personal characteristics, expectations and programmatic context. Qualitative analysis methods are suited par excellence to discovering such patterns.

10.3 Apologies: systematic case law analysis

In daily life, people may suffer harm. Passengers may become hurt in traffic accidents, medical practitioners may make mistakes that disable patients, professional sports trainers may employ harsh training methods, girls raised in youth care institutions often bear the scars of sexual abuse. It happens that victims of traffic accidents, medical malpractice, sexual violence in youth care institutions, or inappropriate/transgressive behaviour seek compensation, financial or otherwise. Some of these cases evolve into disputes and are then taken to court.

Research has shown that victims generally do not just seek monetary compensation. They foremost seek acknowledgement that what happened was wrong, and recognition of the harm they suffered. Also, many victims seek an apology. In fact, it is known that if apologies are offered to a damaged party, that this speeds up the settlement of procedures, reduces the likelihood that the damaged party will enter formal legal proceedings, and contributes overall to the well-being of the recipient as well as the person offering the apology, and to a feeling of restoration after the wrongs that were done (Robbennolt, 2003, 2006; Wijntjens, 2020).

However, in the practice of compensation for wrongs suffered, many still presume that apologies entail a risk. The basis for this widespread belief, which is also prominent in the legal academic literature, is based on a number of exemplary or notorious cases, mostly similar cases that are referred to by subsequent authors, or simply cases that a legal scholar happens to know of (Wijntjens, 2020). Offering apologies is labelled by some as 'legally dangerous' (Farmer, 2015), as an apologetic statement may be admissible evidence at trial to establish liability or to prove some other element of an offence. Also, it has been noted that insurance companies may instruct the insured to be reticent in offering apologies, and to speak only summarily and with great care on what happened, with mention made of lawyers even ordering their clients to remain silent (Cohen, 1999). As a way out of this manifestly undesirable situation, so-called 'apology laws' were introduced in the USA in 1986, intended to encourage injurers to apologize, as these laws ensure that at least some types of apologies cannot be used against them in litigation. Since then, these laws have also spread throughout the common law world (Australia, Canada, England and Wales, Scotland, Ireland and Hong Kong; see Helmreich, 2012, Vandenbussche, 2018).

For the Netherlands, Wijntjens (2020) conducted a large scale study to determine to what extent this fear – of apologies amounting to an admission of liability in legal proceedings – has an empirical basis in legal practice. To investigate this, she employed systematic case law analysis. Systematic case law analysis differs from conventional legal analysis – in which issues are presented in one case or a small group of exceptional or weighty cases – in that it performs a so-called content analysis (see section 7.3) on a large group of similarly weighted cases to find overall patterns. As such, it is set up to prove a point not out of one author's rhetorical power but because the patterns that are found in case law have been uncovered through systematic and transparent analysis of the content of rulings, in such a way that the data collection, data analysis and findings are reproducible (see also section 2.2).

Systematic case law analysis, which we did rank under empirical legal studies, is therefore in a sense a particular kind of legal-empirical study, namely a study where the data are always formed by jurisprudence texts. In general, in systematic case law analysis, a representative or purposive set of rulings is sampled, the text in the dossiers or rulings coded, and the codes and relations between them analysed. In that sense, systematic case law analysis is a mixture of qualitative and quantitative analysis: qualitative methods are generally used to code and organize fragments of text, and quantitative methods may be used next to assess – for instance – how often certain evidence is regarded as admissible, or whether there is a relation between the outcome of sex discrimination cases and the gender composition of judges' panels.

In the following we will describe Wijntjens' (2020) systematic case law analysis that focused on the role of apologies in legal proceedings. In our example, we will focus on the manner in which she attempted to answer her research question, namely to what extent and in what manner apologies play a role in civil and medico-disciplinary legal proceedings.

10.3.1 Data collection

Wijntjens selected court rulings from the database of court rulings that are published online by the Netherlands Council for the Judiciary (`rechtspraak.nl`). This database contains a large number of court rulings, but not all proclaimed court rulings. For instance, all rulings by the Supreme Court are published, all rulings by the Intellectual Property Division of the Civil Sector of the District Court of The Hague, and all rulings in (attempted) homicide cases. For other types of rulings it is so far unclear how choices on publication are made. This means that it is unclear how the sample of rulings published is formed. We may not therefore assume Wijntjens' is a probability sample (see section 3.2 and section 3.3.1), and that means also that we are unsure whether the findings are generalizable. In fact, the sample cannot be regarded as more than a convenience sample.

As Wijntjens was interested in civil court rulings and rulings by disciplinary law, she first selected all rulings that were present in the database up to October 2018, the time she started data collection. To do so, she first selected all rulings present in the database under the header 'civil law': a first set already comprising a hefty 140,056 rulings!

Next, she selected all published medical disciplinary law rulings via an online disciplinary rulings database published by the Netherlands government. All rulings by the Dutch Disciplinary Committees Health Care (Tuchtcollege voor de Gezondheidszorg) are published since 2010. This resulted, at the time data were collected, in 8,283 rulings. This means that the sample she drew from this database in fact constitutes – in a statistical sense – a population (see also section 3.1), namely the entire population of all rulings from 2010 up to the moment data collection began.

To narrow down the set of documents to be studied, Wijntjens next conducted two further steps. First, she automatically searched within all digital 140,056 civil plus 8,283 disciplinary rulings for the keywords *excuse, *excuses, *regret, *apology, *apologies, *sorry and *repent. These keywords had been chosen on the basis of a study of jurisprudence on apologies, and on the basis of an earlier study by Van Dijck

(2017) on ordered apologies.[4] This reduced the set of rulings to 3,452 civil court and 872 disciplinary law rulings, and after removing some double hits to 3,117 and 821 rulings respectively. Wijntjens now had a sample of almost 4,000 rulings in which at least one of the keywords appeared.

Next, Wijntjens scanned all rulings, and judged for every case whether it was indeed relevant for her study. She decided that that was the case when it emerged from the ruling that one or more parties had offered apologies or when it was on the other hand explicitly mentioned that apologies had not been offered. It is clear that working through these almost 4,000 rulings is a massive task. Wijntjens did so using Excel.

After scanning the large set, a smaller set of rulings remained. For the civil court rulings 1,254 remained: in 915 it was written that apologies had been offered, and in 358 it had been noted that no apologies had been given (in 19 cases the text of the ruling noted both that apologies had and had not been given). For the disciplinary court cases, 644 rulings remained, of which apologies had been offered in 563 cases and no apologies had been offered in 96 cases (here in 15 cases it had been noted that apologies both had and had not been offered). This left all in all roughly 2,000 rulings.

As the example clearly shows, the case law analysis entailed trudging through a massive amount of textified material, out of which a smaller and smaller number of cases remain that are relevant for the study at hand. In the case of Wijntjens' study, the initial amount of almost 150,000 rulings was reduced to a little under 1,900 cases, a reduction by 98.72%, or, conversely, went through a funnel with just 1.28% of the original rulings remaining for coding and analysis.

Wijntjens subsequently trimmed her dataset further. She selected, within the set of cases, those cases in which apologies were not simply mentioned somewhere in the text, but actually played a role in the case. Again a smaller subset of cases contained explicit mention of the apologies made or not made that were functional in the case (this was so for 570 cases).

10.3.2 Analytic methods: coding

Next, cases had to be read and the text coded. Wijntjens enlisted support for this task. A group of Master's students aided Wijntjens in the reading and coding process. Wijntjens developed a codebook and coding scheme. To further reliability of coding, Wijntjens selected 75 rulings that were coded by herself as well as by the Master's students. In an iterative process of comparing codes, improving their codebook and re-coding new rulings, they arrived at a final codebook and final coding scheme that were clear and workable and led to consistent codes.

To assess reliability, Wijntjens then selected another 20 rulings and had these coded independently by herself and a research assistant. The interrater reliability, computed as percentage agreement between Wijntjens and the research assistant, varied between 90% and 100%, with corresponding values for the reliability measure Cohen's kappa (see section 2.6.1) between 0.62 (insufficient to reasonable agreement) and 1.00 (perfect agreement).

[4]This study by Van Dijck focused on so-called ordered apologies, cases where the injured party claims an apology, or the court orders one. Wijntjens' study in fact also focused on ordered apologies, but we do not discuss her findings on that subtopic here.

The coding scheme was a mixture of inductive and deductive coding or, in qualitative methodology-speak, emic and etic coding. Deductive codes had been taken from the academic literature and jurisprudence analysis, and were quite coarse. Inductive codes emerged during the coding process, such as apologies offered or refused, which the judge employed to judge the intentions of parties.

10.3.3 Analytic methods: classification and finding patterns

Wijntjens conducted several analyses on her data. In the first of these, she investigated the argumentative schemes that the judges used to arrive at their rulings. She assessed what role the fact that apologies had or had not been offered played in judges' argumentations. The analysis that she conducted is essentially a doctrinal analysis, assessing whether apologies played a subordinate role, a conjunct role, or a decisive role in assessing the evidence on which the conclusion about the case would be based that the judge reached.

According to her codebook, apologies played a subordinate role if they were mentioned only as a support to other, stronger evidence as indicated by the ruling. Wijntjens gives an example of a client who requested dissolution of a contract with a contractor who had agreed to improve the client's website and webshop. The judge had to decide whether the period for granting the contract had been exceeded by the contractor. The court ruled that this was not the case. In support of this opinion, it was mentioned in the ruling that this was substantiated by the fact that the client had apologized for delays he had caused.

Apologies played a secondary role if they were mentioned in conjunction with other evidence, such as in a case where a group of shareholders had asserted that a company had misled them. The court ruled that it could indeed be doubted whether the optimism broadcast by the company was justified. In the ruling, first of all, reference was made to a statement made by the then chairman of the board in an informative shareholders' meeting in which he apologized for misleading investors. Secondly, it was mentioned that even at the height of the financial crisis much remained unclear about the company's portfolio. The two arguments in conjunction formed the evidence.

Wijntjens found very few rulings where apologies were decisive in the ruling. Out of all 570 coded and rulings analysed, she found seven judgments in which the court considered that the apologies of the person causing the damage were regarded as constituting an acknowledgement of liability. This amounts to 1.2%.

Next, Wijntjes delved deeper in the patterns in the data. She outlined additional roles that apologies could play, roles that had emerged abundantly during the emic coding. For that, she selected – leaving out the seven cases in which it had been ruled that apologies had constituted an acknowledgement of liability – those rulings in which the fact that apologies had (or had not) been offered were explicitly mentioned in the ruling itself, the decision reached. For that, she zoomed in on a subset of 160 cases, in which this occurred. Table 10.6 illustrates how strongly the data were funnelled in the entire research process.

Wijntjens found that, in 111 of these 160 cases, apologies had been offered, and in 49 cases it had been noted in the ruling that apologies had not been offered. Next, she investigated what impact apologies had for the person who had offered apologies

Table 10.6: Data reduction in apologies study

Inclusion criteria	Selection method	Resulting N
all published civil court rulings on `rechtspraak.nl` as well as medical disciplinary law rulings by the Dutch Disciplinary Committees Health Care	automated	148,294
search terms *excuse, *excuses, *regret, *apology, *apologies, *sorry, *repent	automated	3,938
apologies offered, not offered or claimed	scanning	1,898
apologies functional in case	reading	570
apologies mentioned in ruling	coding	160

Table 10.7: Apologies versus outcome for apologizing party

Apologies	positive effect (N = 58)	no effect (N = 53)
No apologies	no effect (N = 16)	negative effect (N = 33)

on the outcome of the case. Where apologies had been offered, in 58 rulings it could be shown that these were to the advantage of the person who had apologized: there were instances where a sanction was moderated, where less damages had to be paid, where the judge ruled that the apology indicated good intentions, which supported offering 'second chances'. In 53 rulings the apology did not have a registered effect: examples are situations where the case was deemed too serious, or where the apology was perceived as insincere. These tallies show how in the investigated rulings apologies turn out to be beneficial in more than half of cases.

Looking at the cases where it was mentioned that no apologies had been offered, the picture was different. In 16 out of these 49 cases, the lack of an apology did not have an effect on the ruling, mostly because the judge had ruled that the case did not call for an apology. In more than two-thirds of cases, however, the absence of an apology was regarded as an aggravating factor, translating into for instance higher sums for pains and damages.

The second analysis is summarized in Table 10.7. While Wijntjens herself did not compute any statistics for these results, the frequencies in the table show how the two variables (apologies and favourableness of outcome) are clearly associated. In fact, the odds ratio for this table equals 2.257 (significant at the 5% level), which can be translated by saying that withholding an apology increases the risk of a negative outcome by 126%.

10.3.4 Answering the research questions

Wijntjens' study debunked – for the Netherlands – a persistent belief. Compiling all available evidence, her study first showed that if apologies had been given, they were mentioned in only a fraction of rulings. Her study also showed that in such cases apologies generally played no more than a supportive role in judges' reasonings. Apologies almost never played a dominant, decisive evidentiary role. Secondly, her analysis showed how apologies in more than half of cases worked out well for the apologizing party, resulting in more positive or less negative outcomes. Importantly, a failure to apologize incurred a sizeable increased risk of negative consequences. All in all, it appears as if apologizing bears little risk, and indeed may bring positive side-effects, with not apologizing a risky strategy as it may backfire.

One could doubt whether the findings – the sample of civil court rulings was as we said a convenience sample – are generalizable, in other words whether it was a particular kind of ruling that was published in the online database of rulings, and whether in unpublished cases apologies would play a different role. While this cannot be ruled out, a similar pattern as in the civil cases was found for the disciplinary rulings – which do constitute a population in a statistical sense. A second issue is that, as Wijntjens remarks, apologies may have an impact that cannot be read from the rulings: it may be that judges are influenced by the fact that one party has apologized but that this influence is not expressed in writing and therefore does not play a noticeable role in the ruling. Last, it may be that apologies have been offered, but that no note is made by the clerk of this: these cases are then wrongly classified as cases without an apology. Obviously, apologizing and not apologizing are not actions by parties that are randomly distributed over cases: we should therefore be cautious not to interpret the findings overly causally.

Regardless of these methodological issues, it does appear as if, given the beneficial effects that apologies can have in the aftermath of wrongs, there is little risk in expressing them, and it may be more risky not to do so. From the point of view of the injured party, apologies are generally welcomed. And, as Van Dijck (2017) showed, even apologies that are ordered, and are therefore not spontaneous and may even be insincere, may have a legal purpose.

10.4 International sentencing: multivariate analysis

Our third example focuses on international sentencing. Many of the institutions that deal with perpetrators of international crimes, such as international criminal tribunals and the International Criminal Court (ICC), are relatively new. Most of them therefore do not have much jurisprudence to fall back on; they do not have a legal tradition, specific legal guidance or even quantified sentencing guidelines. This raises a number of issues that relate back to fundamental principles of justice. One important such issue is consistency: similar cases should be treated similarly. Defendants with similar profiles in terms of crimes committed, role in the criminal enterprise, similar circumstances should receive comparable sentences.

As Hola (2012) discusses, consistency of sentencing should be evident at two levels: the level of the 'approach' to sentence determination (i.e. reasoning) and the level of the outcome of sentencing. As 'approach' Hola defines the manner in which sentences are determined, decisions being based on common standards or general underlying principles, uniformly applied to the facts of each case. At the second level, consistency in outcome, Hola states that comparable cases should receive comparable sentences.

The first level calls for research that investigates the manner in which standards are referred to and actually used. This would be socio-legal research in a sense, research that scrutinizes legal decisions, in which texts are scanned for active or passive reference to principles, in a sort of systematic case law analysis, and comparison of the application of such principles across cases and jurisdictions or tribunals is investigated. The second level calls for – as we will show below – fairly technical, quantitative analytic methods that are able to assess to what extent sentences are actually consistently determined, and therefore predictable.

The literature on consistency in sentencing is surprisingly sparse. What is out there has mostly focused on Anglo-Saxon countries, mainly in the context of sentencing guidelines (for example Ostrom et al., 2008), with the study on the Netherlands by Wermink et al., 2015 one exception. A few studies have focused on sentencing in international criminal law, amongst which Meernik & King (2003) on sentence lengths in general at the ICTY, Meernik (2014) on the impact of plea bargaining on sentence length, and King, Meernik, & Kelly (2016) on gendered effects in sexual violence cases.

Most studies have investigated predictability using multiple regression models (see section 9.2) and expressed predictability in R^2, the percentage of variance in sentence length that can be explained by predictor variables, variables in the model that are supposed to impact sentence length (such as number of counts, severity of crime, aggravating and mitigating circumstances and cooperation with the prosecution). If R^2 is for instance 0.50, it is said that the model is able to explain 50% of the variance of sentence length (see section 9.2.4). Most studies found R^2 to hover around 60%.[5]

Hola studied both consistency in approach (2012, chapter 2) and consistency in outcome (Hola, Bijleveld, & Smeulers, 2009) at the two international tribunals that have – still – generated the largest number of sentences in recent history: the International Criminal Tribunal for Rwanda (ICTR) and the International Criminal Tribunal for the former Yugoslavia (ICTY). It is this second study that we will focus on here. Hola, with her co-authors, studied consistency in outcome. Hola investigated the impact of a number of legally relevant factors, such as mode of individual responsibility, mitigating factors, guilty plea and the like, on sentencing outcome. She wanted to know, for instance, whether superior responsibility led to higher sentence lengths, and whether those accused of graver crimes or those with higher rank would receive longer sentences.

10.4.1 Data collection

Hola focused on the ICTY. The ICTY website has case information sheets for all cases prosecuted at the ICTY, which contain information on the indictment, the trial and the judgments. The same goes for many other international tribunals and for rulings at the International Criminal Court (ICC). Data on international sentencing are therefore generally freely available (although they may contain massive amounts of text, see for instance Chlevickaite (2022), who in her assessment of factors contributing to credibility and reliability analysed 93 ICTY, ICTR, and ICC trial judgments from 1996 to 2019, which totalled an estimated 50,000 pages).

Hola studied all 63 cases that had by the time the analysis was conducted been handed down, whether by the Trial Chamber if the case had been dealt with only at first instance, or by the Appeals Chamber if it had been decided on appeal. While these

[5]For instance, Ostrom et al. (2008) reported that R^2 equalled 67.2% in Michigan, 55.4% in Viriginia for assault and 49.3% for burglary, and a whopping 86.1% in Minnesota – which the authors qualify as extraordinary and attribute to very strict sentencing guidelines. Wermink et al. (2015) reported an R^2 of 57.4% for sentences for adults in the Netherlands.

Table 10.8: Sentence length in years, by offence, offender rank, guilty plea and mode of individual responsibility

	trial			appeal		
	average sentence (SD)	median sentence	N	average sentence (SD)	median sentence	N
Average	15.3 (10.0)	14.0	60	14.6 (8.7)	14.0	56
Crimes a/humanity	17.2 (10.2)	17.0	47	16.2 (8.9)	15.0	43
War crimes	8.4 (5.4)	7.0	13	9.1 (4.5)	9.0	13
High ranking	17.2 (10.2)	17.0	47	16.2 (8.9)	15.0	43
Middle ranking	13.5 (9.6)	10.0	25	13.3 (8.5)	10.0	24
Low ranking	13.9 (6.5)	15.0	23	14.1 (6.1)	15.0	20
No guilty plea	15.9 (10.6)	15.0	40	15.1 (8.9)	15.0	36
Guilty plea	14.1 (8.9)	12.5	20	13.6 (8.3)	12.5	20
Superiors	11.8 (10.6)	7.8	18	10.7 (6.3)	9.0	15
Perpetrators	17.5 (8.0)	17.5	20	17.3 (7.7)	18.0	18
JCE	16.3 (9.8)	15.0	22	14.6 (8.4)	13.0	19
Planners	18.5 (9.2)	18.5	2	18.5 (9.2)	18.5	2
Instigators	19.8 (15.4)	25.0	3	20.7 (12.1)	25.0	3
Orderers	21.8 (12.8)	20.0	8	16.8 (7.8)	18.0	9
Aiders	14.1 (8.4)	13.0	17	16.2 (8.5)	15.0	18

Source: Hola et al., 2009

63 cases comprised at data collection a population of cases in a statistical sense, for practical purposes it is a small sample. This limits possibilities for analysis, as we will see below.

10.4.2 Analytic methods: bivariate data analysis

Hola and her co-authors first gave descriptives of these cases. They calculated that the average number of counts for which a perpetrator was convicted equalled 4.6 (the number in first instance had been slightly higher at 5.1). Perpetrators were most often convicted for persecution (35 in total). Next, Hola described sentence length in relation to a number of legally relevant factors. Table 10.8 lists average sentence lengths (in years), as well as sentence lengths broken down by a number of categories of offenders, and by whether or not a defendant had pleaded guilty. The table gives not only means, but also median values, as the distribution of sentence length was skewed (see section 6.3.1). The table shows that sentences on appeal were on average somewhat shorter. Also, we see that crimes against humanity were sentenced more harshly, and that those who did not plead guilty received longer sentences as well. These findings are what one would expect.

There were some unexpected findings too, however: while high-ranking offenders in general received the longest sentences, the sentences for middle-ranking offenders were surprisingly low, and those of the low-ranking offenders higher again – and in fact (if looking at the median on appeal) just as high as those of the high-ranking offenders. This finding is surprising as one would expect that those with greatest responsibility for the crimes would receive the longest sentences, and those with the least responsibility, lowest in the hierarchy of culpability, correspondingly the lowest sentences.

Hola further investigated this issue by looking at the more specific modes of individual responsibility underlying an offender's conviction. She categorized these modes into Superiors, Perpetrators, Joint Criminal Enterprise (JCE), Planners, Instigators, Orderers and Aiders. Sentence lengths for these groups are also given in Table 10.8.

This categorization revealed a similar surprising finding, namely that those with superior responsibility received the lowest sentences on average, lower even than the aiders. Hola and her co-authors explain this by suggesting that superior responsibility entails the passive behaviour of a superior, such as a failure to punish or prevent subordinates from committing crimes. The omissions of superiors are perhaps perceived to be less serious than active participation in criminal activities, less serious than the activities of the executioners, those with 'blood on their hands'. However, on a bivariate level, Hola identified several other counterintuitive sentencing patterns at the ICTY, for instance that aiders and abettors (that is, facilitators of crime with arguably a very limited role in the crimes) received on appeal sentences almost as high as orderers (who are arguably more culpable due to their decisive influence on hands-on perpetrators). Thus, sentence length is likely not only a function of a perpetrator's role, but also of his or her role in conjunction with other aspects of the crime, such as cruelty or the number of counts.

This led to the conclusion that it does not make sense to investigate the effect of individual responsibility bivariately. As individual responsibility may be *confounded* (see section 5.1) with other characteristics of the cases and perpetrators, such as hands-on cruelty, one may end up with hard-to-interpret findings like the ones just discussed. Individual responsibility may in fact be confounded with various additional factors; for instance, it may also be that aiders often have in general been convicted of less serious crimes. If aiders receive on average a shorter sentence, is that because they were aiders – or because they were responsible for less serious crimes? Or do aiders receive shorter sentences because they often entered a guilty plea?

10.4.3 Analytic methods: multivariate data analysis

To disentangle all such confounding, the authors chose to do a multivariate regression analysis. In a multivariate regression analysis, one investigates the effect of each independent variable on an outcome variable, and the regression weights express the impact of the respective variables *given the other variables in the model* (see section 9.2.6). Thus, one would be able in a regression analysis to investigate the effect of being an aider *over and above* the effect of variables present in the model. The model would give the net effect of being an aider, net of whether someone had shown excessive cruelty, had confessed to his crimes, had committed war crimes, etc. The regression coefficient reflects what a variable (being an aider) adds to the prediction of the dependent variable

Table 10.9: Regression analysis of ICTY sentence lengths in years

	b	β	*p*-value
High rank	10.9	0.5	<.001
Middle rank	2.2	0.1	<.231
# Guilty counts	0.7	0.4	<.001
# Mitigating factors	-0.6	-0.2	<.025
Conviction for crimes against humanity	6.1	0.3	<.001
Instigation	7.7	0.2	<.032
Perpetration	3.4	0.2	<.079
Superior responsibility	-3.5	-0.2	<.058

$R^2 = .653$
$R^2_{adj} = .602$
$N = 63$

Source: Hola et al., 2009

sentence length given all other factors (type of crime, mitigating factors, guilty plea, etc.) in the model. This is the reason why regression analysis is a suitable technique for the question at hand, namely what the impact is of one variable on the dependent variable, controlling for any distorting effects of other factors.

Table 10.9 gives the results of the regression analysis, which was conducted using SPSS. We give only the unstandardized regression weights (see section 9.2.2 and section 9.2.6), which enable us to translate the impact of the successive independent variables on sentence length in years.

In a first step to build a final model, 14 predictors had been incorporated.[6] Even though the authors had wanted to include more predictors, the small sample size did not allow this (and 14 predictors was actually stretching it given the 63 cases). Of these 14 variables, a number were not significant (such as, perhaps remarkably, whether the defendant had pleaded guilty or not), and these were removed and the analysis re-run with a smaller set of variables, which is the final set that we will discuss here. See also 'Model building' in section 9.1.2.

However, before we discuss the results, we note that the authors had had to solve for the fact that in two instances (Stakič and Galič), life sentences had been handed down. With 'life' as the sentence length, there is no sentence length to predict ('life' being indeterminate), so that the value for the dependent variable is technically speaking

[6]One variable was added as a 'dummy variable': the variable 'perpetrator rank' had three categories and was not interval level (at most it may be considered ordinal level; see section 6.2.1). This variable was therefore included as two dichotomous variables, one indicating whether a perpetrator had high rank (1) or not (0), and a second one indicating whether a perpetrator had middle rank (1) or not (0). Such 'dummy coding' enables to include non-interval variables in the model. Significance is then assessed over the various 'splits' of the variable (here 'high rank' versus not, and 'middle rank' versus not).

missing. For this analysis, they therefore first re-coded life sentences to the expected duration of imprisonment given the convicted's age; for Stakič this led to an imputed value of 30 years, for Galič a value of 20 years. One could argue that these values are in a sense arbitrary and do not reflect that life imprisonment is intended to express a qualitatively differently sentence – much heavier – than a determinate one. In that sense, the imputed value of 20 years for Galič may be seen as too low given that for instance the average sentence of orderers at trial was already 21.8 years. The authors ran several other models, in which different imputed values for these life sentences were used. The interpretation however remained substantively the same. Given these results, the authors conclude that the findings are *robust* against different imputations of values for the life sentences. Obviously, as there were just two life sentences for which values had to be imputed against 61 determinate sentences, the results were not likely to be affected much.

The variables in Table 10.9 in the final model were all significant at the $p<0.10$ level, and therefore retained. This may appear a puzzling statement as the attentive reader will see that this is not the case for the p-value for the dummy variable 'Middle rank'. It was noted above that 'High rank' and 'Middle rank' were two dummy variables added to assess the effect of the nominal variable rank of the perpetrator. We see that the dummy variable that measured whether a perpetrator was of high versus low rank *did* add significantly to the prediction: a perpetrator of high rank was predicted to be handed down a sentence that was 10.9 years longer than a perpetrator of low rank. Perpetrators of middle rank, however, did not receive significantly longer sentences than those of low rank (the difference is indeed much smaller at 2.2 years).

After rank, instigation contributes importantly to sentence length: instigators received on average a 7.7-year longer predicted sentence than perpetrators who had not been classified such. Next, those convicted for crimes against humanity are predicted to receive a 6.1-year longer sentence, with the reference category here being a conviction for war crimes (at the time of data collection no conviction for genocide had yet occurred). In the model, perpetrators are handed down 3.4 years more than non-perpetrators, the former likely being the perpetrators with 'blood on their hands' as Hola labelled them. And, mirroring the preceding finding, superior responsibility predicts a 3.5-year shorter sentence. This counterintuitive pattern had already been observed in the bivariate tabulations, but the regression analysis shows that this is not due to any confounding with the other independent variables in the model as multiple regression gives the impact of each variable net of the other variables in the model.

Lastly, we see how mitigating circumstances and guilty counts almost balance each other out: each additional mitigating circumstance subtracts 0.6 years (or approximately 7 months) from the predicted sentence, and each additional guilty count adds 0.7 years (or approximately 8.5 months) to the predicted sentence. Said differently, if we were to have two perpetrators with exactly the same scores on all the variables, and if perpetrator A had 3 guilty counts and perpetrator B had 5 guilty counts, perpetrator B would be predicted to be handed down a 1.4-year longer sentence.

We are each time speaking about predicted sentences, because not all sentences will have been predicted perfectly by the model. The fit of the final model is .653, meaning that 65% of the variation in sentence length can be predicted from the seven variables included. The fit of the model is thus quite reasonable. We also give the R^2_{adj}, the fit measure that penalizes the inclusion of (too) many variables in the model given its N (see section 9.2.4). The sizeable drop from an R^2 of .653 to an R^2_{adj} of .602 shows that the model may indeed have been slightly overloaded.

10.4.4 Answering the research questions

All in all, the multiple regression analysis leads to a number of conclusions. Firstly, the analysis shows that the fit values of this model are adequate; they are in fact comparable to the fit values of 'national' analyses on sentencing consistency. International sentencing at the ICTY and ICTR therefore does not appear less consistent than regular national sentencing, which is a striking finding given its infancy, limited jurisprudence and the lack of sentencing guidelines. Second, the analysis showed that higher-ranking offenders did indeed receive longer sentences: in the model, being a high-ranking offender adds 10.9 years to sentence length.

The analysis also showed that the puzzling finding that those with superior responsibility received lower sentences is a true effect and not due to any confounding with the variables in the model: perpetrators with superior responsibility on average did receive a 3.5-year lower sentence, net of all other characteristics of their cases. After rank, it is those who were actively perpetrating the international crimes and the instigators who received the harshest punishments. Last, as expected, those convicted for graver crimes (crimes against humanity versus war crimes) could expect longer sentences.

Chapter 11

Conclusion: some generic methodological issues

11.1 The particular setting of empirical legal research

In this last chapter we briefly discuss two take-home messages. As we said in chapter 1, empirical legal studies are an 'awkward' field. When we conduct empirical legal research, we study the context, operations and impact of law (in its broadest sense). In doing so, we however do not use methods common in legal research, but methods that are essentially foreign to doctrinal research, and methods that very few legal scholars have been trained in.

It is quite a challenge for a lawyer to operate in this field. Empirical research methodology harbours different schools, statisticians are associated with 'lies, damn lies and statistics', and research methodology has become highly specialized. How can a lawyer, trained in doctrinal analysis, master empirical methods such that s/he can authoritatively conduct empirical research? Many lawyers profess that such research should perhaps be carried out by empirical researchers, not lawyers. Maybe lawyers and empirical researchers could collaborate.

We believe it is imperative that lawyers themselves do empirical legal studies. Only lawyers understand the law and operations sufficiently deeply and practically that they can interpret findings. And only lawyers can envisage the feedback that empirical findings can or should have on the law and the legal system. If empirical legal research were done by psychologists or economists only, it is likely that the findings would impact little on legal practice or on law: they would be a subfield of either, and law would continue to do its doctrinal thing as usual. Only when empirical legal knowledge and studies become part and parcel of legal training, and only when lawyers internalize some of the principles of empirical research, can empirical legal studies impact the law itself, a feedback loop be envisaged, and empirical research 'feed' the law.

Until law curricula train law students in research methods, only a few legal scholars will do empirical legal research, often in collaboration with interested empirical scholars. And of course, even if law students were to have training in empirical research methods, they would never have as extensive a training as psychology or sociology students: after all, they must be trained to be lawyers. But lawyers who understand the basics of the empirical language would see a wide world opening up to them and they will be able to enrich the legal discipline, and perhaps transform it.

11.2 Correlation is not causation

Perhaps the most fundamental take-home message is in the header of this section. It is the most often made mistake among all empirical researchers: mistaking correlation for causation. As explained extensively, correlation is a *necessary* but not a *sufficient* condition for causality. If X causes Y, then we would expect to find a correlation between X and Y. But that does not mean that the reverse applies too, that if we find a correlation, we may therefore conclude that X is the cause of Y.

This logical error is very often made. Researchers are often overoptimistic about the strength of their empirical evidence. They overgeneralize (declare that the findings can be generalized beyond their sample, declare that the same conclusions would be drawn in different settings). And they do not heed the rule that says that only when no third factor can explain the association between X and Y can we conclude that X is cause of Y. Researchers can only confidently make causal claims if they have been able to conduct an experiment in the methodological sense of the word. They must then have had full control over who was administered X and who was administered an equivalent placebo. This is rarely the case, especially not when we want to study the law in its naturalistic settings. This is not to say that this would be impossible; it is just not very easy to do. Just like criminologists, empirical legal scholars face the strict procedural rules of the law. They cannot, like medical researchers do, test the impact of medicines in clinical settings. While doctors are – under certain ethical guarantees – in control of the administration of medicines or procedures, legal scholars are not in control of the meting out of sanctions, or judges' decisions, or decisions reached by parties in a conflict. Independent bodies administer the law, and the legal scholar is more observer than in control.

Chance at times helps scholars, by creating settings that may function as a natural experiment, and in some cases the legal profession is eager to test procedures. But often researchers have to test hypotheses using observational designs. Caution and restraint are then appropriate when it comes to causal conclusions.

11.3 Replication, triangulation and mixed methods

Related to the above, history will show that just as in psychology, sociology and criminology, empirical legal scholars will also have to replicate studies and repeatedly deliver the same conclusions to build a knowledge base. We cannot rely on just one study to conclude that a law does or does not function, or that plaintiffs would be more content with outcomes if procedures were organized differently. When we work with samples in quantitative research as well as when we do in-depth qualitative research, we are always liable to chance, or to uncovering idiosyncrasies.

Researchers should therefore firstly very clearly report how they carried out their studies, what instruments they used, and preferably publish not only their article but also their data, so that studies can be independently replicated. Secondly, they should not rely on just one particular method or setting. Triangulation is immensely important also for this reason: for ensuring that findings have generality over different methods and setting and researchers. Progress in science does not rise from lightning-like flashes of insight, but from repeated studies with well-founded evidentiary claims that all point in the same direction.

References

Allison, P. D. (1984). *Event History Analysis*. Beverly Hills, CA: Harvard University Press.

Angrist, J. (1990). Lifetime earnings and the Vietnam era draft lottery: Evidence from social security. *The American Economic Review, 80*, 313–336.

Augusteijn, F. (2022). *Compensation for victims of sexual or violent crime in the Netherlands.* (Paper presented 7 June 2022 at the International Symposium on Victimology, San Sebastian)

Augusteijn, F., Bijleveld, C., & Pemberton, A. (2022). De praktijk van slachtofferrechten: de perceptie van professionals. Een exploratief onderzoek naar de naleving van slachtofferrechten [Victims' rights in practice: professionals' perceptions. An exploratory study into compliance with victims' rights]. *Proces, 101*, 35–53. doi: 10.5553/PROCES/016500762022101001005

Baker, S. E., & Edwards, R. (2012). *How many qualitative interviews is enough* (Tech. Rep.). National Centre for Research Methods. Retrieved from `eprints.ncrm.ac.uk/id/eprint/2273/`

Bijleveld, C., Blažević, M., Bociga Gelvez, D., & Buljubašić, M. (2022). Sanctioning perpetrators of international crimes: A vignette study. *International Criminal Law Review, 19*, 1–22.

Bijleveld, C. C. J. H., & Van der Geest, V. (2021). *Methoden en Technieken van Onderzoek in de Criminologie [Research Methods in Criminology]* (8th ed.). The Hague: Boom Juridische Uitgevers.

Bijleveld, C. C. J. H., Van de Weijer, S. G. A., Ruiter, S., & Van der Geest, V. R. (2015). *Analysetechnieken voor Niet-Experimentele Gegevens [Analysis Methods for Non-Experimental Data]*. The Hague: Boom Juridische Uitgevers.

Boyd, C. L., Epstein, L., & Martin, A. (2010). Untangling the causal effects of sex on judging. *American Journal of Political Science, 54*, 389–411. Retrieved from `jstor.org/stable/25652213`

Bruns, E. J., Pullmann, M., Wiggins, E., & Watterson, K. (2011). *King County family treatment court. Outcome evaluation* (Tech. Rep.). Department of Psychiatry and Behavioral Sciences, University of Washington School of Medicine. Retrieved from `kingcounty.gov/~/media/health/MHSA/MIDD_ActionPlan/Appendix_F_Outcome_evaluation_final_report_2_22_2011.ashx?la=en`

Cane, P., & Kritzer, H. M. (2010). *The Oxford Handbook of Empirical Legal Research*. Oxford: Oxford University Press.

Carter, E., & Whitworth, A. (2017). Work activation regimes and well-being of unemployed people: Rhetoric, risk and reality of quasi-marketization in the UK Work Programme. *Social Policy & Administration*, *51*, 796–816.

Charmaz, K. (2014). *Constructing grounded theory* (2nd ed.). London: Sage.

Chlevickaite, G. (2022). *Insider witnesses' credibility and reliability: An empirical legal framework for international criminal justice* (Unpublished doctoral dissertation). VU University.

Christie, N. (1986). The ideal victim. In E. A. Fattah (Ed.), *From Crime Policy to Victim Policy* (pp. 17–30). Basingstoke: Macmillan.

CNRS (2021). *Humanities and social sciences and the protection of personal data in the context of open science. A guide for research. Version 2.* (Tech. Rep.). CNRS. Retrieved from inshs.cnrs.fr/sites/institut_inshs/files/pdf/Guide_rgpd_2021_en_0.pdf

Cohen, J. (1999). Advising clients to apologize. *Southern California Law Review*, *72*, 1009–1069.

Cohen, J., Cohen, P., West, S. G., & Aiken, L. S. (2002). *Applied Multiple Regression/Correlation Analysis for the Social Sciences*. Hillsdale, NJ: Lawrence Erlbaum.

Cook, T. D., & Campbell, D. T. (1979). *Quasi-experimentation: Design and Analysis Issues for Field Settings*. Boston, MA: Houghton Mifflin.

Croes, M., & Van Os, R. M. V. (2012). *De kosten van procedures. Gedragskeuzen in de delta van geschilbeslechting. [Costs of procedures. Behavioural choices in dispute settlement]* (No. 12-2). Den Haag: WODC/BJU. Retrieved from wodc.nl/binaries/memorandum-2012-7-volledige-tekst_tcm28-72133.pdf

Crowne, D. P., & Marlowe, D. (1960). A new scale of social desirability independent of psychopathology. *Journal of Consulting Psychology*, *24*, 349–354.

Davies, G. (2020). The relationship between empirical legal studies and doctrinal legal research. *Erasmus Law Review*, *2*, 3–12.

De Keijser, J. W., & Van Koppen, P. J. (2004). Compensatoir straffen: Over de relatie tussen bewijs, overtuiging en straf [Compensatory punishment: On the association between proof, conviction and punishment]. In J. W. Keijser de & H. Elffers (Eds.), *Het Maatschappelijk Oordeel van de Strafrechter: De Wisselwerking tussen Rechter en Samenleving [Societal Judgments of Judges: Interaction between Judges and Society]* (pp. 133–183). The Hague: Boom Juridische Uitgevers.

Denzin, N. K., & Lincoln, Y. S. (Eds.). (2011). *Handbook of Qualitative Research* (4th ed.). Thousand Oaks, CA: Sage.

Dermine, E., & Eleveld, A. (2021). Protecting working welfare recipients through human rights experimentalism. *International Journal of Law in Context*, *17*, 529–547.

Dijksterhuis, B., & Vels, N. (2011). *HvA-LBIO-rapport alimentatieberekening: onderzoek naar de mening van burgers over de berekening van kinderalimentatie [HvA-LBIO- report alimony calculation. research into citizens' opinions on the calculation of child maintenance]* (Tech. Rep.). Hogeschool van Amsterdam. Retrieved from docplayer.nl/12715177-De-mening-van-burgers-over-de-tremanormen.html

Dixon, J. C., Singleton, R. A., & Straits, B. C. (2016). *The Process of Social Research.* Oxford: Oxford University Press.

Dyevre, A. (2021). The promise and pitfall of automated text-scaling techniques for the analysis of jurisprudential change. *Artificial Intelligence and Law, 29*, 239–269.

Eleveld, A. (2021). Applying neo-republican theory to welfare to work practices: Rules and arbitrary power in mandatory work programmes in the Netherlands. *Social Policy and Society*. doi: doi.org/10.1017/S1474746421000439

Epstein, L., & Martin, A. D. (2014). *An Introduction to Empirical Legal Research.* Oxford: Oxford University Press.

Erikson, R. S. (2022). Appellate court assignments as a natural experiment: Gender panel effects in sex discrimination cases. *Journal of Empirical Legal Studies, 19*, 423–446.

Farmer, C. (2015). Striking a balance: A proposed amendment to the federal rules of evidence excluding partial apologies. *Belmont Law Review, 2*, 243–267. Retrieved from `repository.belmont.edu/lawreview/vol2/iss1/8`

Farrington, D. P. (2003). Methodological standards for evaluation research. *The Annals of the American Academy of Political and Social Sciences, 587*, 49–68.

Faul, F., Erdfelder, E., Buchner, A., & Lang, A. G. (2009). Statistical power analyses using G*Power 3.1: Tests for correlation and regression analyses. *Behavior Research Methods, 41*, 1149–1160.

Flood, J. (2005). Socio-legal ethnography. In R. Banakar & M. Travers (Eds.), *Theory and Method in Socio-Legal Research* (pp. 33–48). Oxford: Hart Publishing. Retrieved from `johnflood.com/pdfs/Socio_Legal_Ethnography_2005.pdf`

Flyvbjerg, B. (2006). Five misunderstandings about case-study research. *Qualitative Inquiry, 12*, 219–245.

Friese, S. (2019). *Qualitative Data Analysis with ATLAS.ti* (3rd ed.). London: Sage.

Glaser, B., & Strauss, A. (1967). *The Discovery of Grounded Theory: Strategies for Qualitative Research.* Chicago: Aldine De Gruyter.

Glasl, F. (1977). *Konfliktmanagement. Ein Handbuch für Führungskräfte, Beraterinnen und Berater.* Bern: Paul Haupt Verlag.

Hall, M., & Wright, R. (2008). Systematic content analysis of judicial opinions. *California Law Review, 96*, 63–122.

Hallgren, K. (2012). Computing inter-rater reliability for observational data: An overview and tutorial. *Tutorials in Quantitative Methods for Psychology, 8*, 23–34. Retrieved from `ncbi.nlm.nih.gov/pmc/articles/PMC3402032/pdf/nihms372951.pdf`

Hammersley, M., & Atkinson, P. (2007). *Ethnography, Principles in Practice.* London: Routledge.

Heckatorn, D. D. (1997). Respondent-driven sampling: A new approach to the study of hidden populations. *Social Problems, 44*, 174–199.

Helmreich, J. (2012). Does 'sorry' incriminate? Evidence, harm and the meaning of apologies. *Cornell Journal of Law and Public Policy, 21*, 567–609. Retrieved from `ww3.lawschool.cornell.edu/research/JLPP/upload/Helmreich-final.pdf`

Henster, D. R., & Gasperetti, M. A. (2017). The role of empirical legal studies in legal scholarship, legal education and policy-making: A U.S. perspective. In R. Van Gestel, H. W. Micklitz, & E. L. Rubin (Eds.), *Rethinking Legal Scholarship: A Transatlantic Dialogue* (pp. 450–475). New York: Cambridge University Press.

Hinkle, D. E., Wiersma, W., & Jurs, S. E. (2003). *Applied Statistics for the Behavioural Sciences* (5th ed.). Boston: Houghton Mifflin.

Hola, B. (2012). *International sentencing – A game of Russian roulette or consistent practice?* (Unpublished doctoral dissertation). VU University.

Hola, B., Bijleveld, C. C. J. H., & Smeulers, A. L. (2009). Is ICTY sentencing predictable? An empirical analysis of ICTY sentencing practice. *Leiden Journal of International Law*, *22*, 79–97.

Hola, B., Bijleveld, C. C. J. H., & Smeulers, A. L. (2011). International sentencing facts and figures: Sentencing practice at the ICTY and ICTR. *Journal of International Criminal Justice*, *9*, 411–439.

Hsieh, H. F., & Shannon, S. E. (2005). Three approaches to qualitative content analysis. *Qualitative Health Research*, *15*, 1277–1288.

Kalbfleish, J. D., & Prentice, R. L. (2002). *The Statistical Analysis of Failure Time Data* (2nd ed.). New York: Wiley.

Kaplan, E. L., & Meier, P. (1958). Nonparametric estimation from incomplete observations. *Journal of the American Statistical Assocation*, *53*, 457–481.

King, K., Meernik, J., & Kelly, E. (2016). Deborah's voice: The role of women in sexual assault cases at the International Criminal Tribunal for the former Yugoslavia. *Social Science Quarterly*, *98*, 548–565.

Kirk, R. E. (1968). *Experimental Design: Procedures for Behavioral Sciences*. Belmont, CA: Wadsworth.

Knabe, A., Schöb, R., & Wiemann, J. (2017). The subjective well-being of workfare participants: insights for a day reconstruction survey. *Applied Economics*, *49*, 1311–1325.

Krippendorff, K. (2004). *Content Analysis, an Introduction to Its Methodology*. Thousand Oaks, CA: Sage. Retrieved from `books.google.nl/books?id=JRsdEAAAQBAJ`

Krippendorff, K. (2011). *Computing Krippendorff's alpha-reliability* (Tech. Rep.). University of Pennsylvania. Retrieved from `repository.upenn.edu/cgi/viewcontent.cgi?article=1043&context=asc_papers`

Kritzer, H. (2021). *Advanced Introduction to Empirical Legal Research*. Cheltenham: Edward Elgar. Retrieved from `books.google.nl/books?id=JRsdEAAAQBAJ`

Landis, J., & Koch, G. G. (1977). The measurement of observer agreement for categorical data. *Biometrics*, *33*, 159–174.

Lawless, R. M., Robbennolt, J. K., & Ulen, T. S. (2009). *Empirical Methods in Law*. New York: Aspen.

Lawthers, A. G., Localio, A. R., Laird, N. M., Lipsitz, S., Hebert, L., & Brennan, T. A. (1994). Physicians' perceptions of the risk of being sued. *Journal of Health Politics, Policy and Law*, *17*, 463–482.

Le, Q. V., & Mikolov, T. (2014). Distributed representations of sentences and documents. In *Proceedings of the 31st international conference on international conference on machine learning* (Vol. 32, p. 1188-1196).

Leeuw, F. L., & Schmeets, H. (2016). *Empirical Legal Research. A Guidance Book for Lawyers, Legislators and Regulators*. Cheltenham: Elgar Publishing.

Lewis, J., & Ritchie, J. (2003). Generalising from qualitative research. In *Qualitative Research Practice: A Guide for Social Science Students and Researchers* (pp. 263–286). London: Sage.

Lindegaard, M., Bernasco, W., & de Vries, T. (2016). *Overvallen in beeld [Robbery images]* (Tech. Rep.). Apeldoorn/Amsterdam: Politie & Wetenschap/NSCR.

Lindegaard, M., & Liebst, L. (2020). *Results of the NSCR COVID-19 behavior study (pre-print, version 2)* (Tech. Rep.). Amsterdam: NSCR. Retrieved from `nscr.nl/app/uploads/2020/08/Results-of-the-NSCR-COVID-19-behavior-study.pdf`

Malsch, M., Kranendonk, R., de Keijser, J., Elffers, H., Komter, M., & de Boer, M. (2015). *Kijken, luisteren, lezen. De invloed van beeld, geluid en schrift op het oordeel over verdachtenverhoren [Seeing, listening, reading. The impact of images, sound and writing on the evaluation of suspect interrogations]* (Tech. Rep.). Apendoorn/Amsterdam: Politie & Wetenschap/NSCR. Retrieved from `nscr.nl/wp-content/uploads/Kijken_luisteren_lezen_NSCR_Politie_Wetenschap.pdf`

Mascini, P., & Holvast, N. (2023). Does delegation of drafting duties to law clerks result in judgments that show lack of confidence in terms of writing style? A stylometric analysis. *Journal of Law and Courts*, *16*, 1–22.

Meernik, J. (2014). What kind of bargain is a plea? *International Criminal Law Review*, *17*, 200–217.

Meernik, J., & King, K. (2003). The sentencing determinants of the International Criminal Tribunal for the former Yugoslavia: An empirical and doctrinal analysis. *Leiden Journal of International Law*, *16*, 717–750.

Mello, M. M., Studdert, D. M., DesRoches, C. M., Peugh, J., Zapert, K., Brennan, T. A., & Sage, W. M. (2004). Caring for patients in a malpractice crisis: Physician satisfaction and quality of care. *Health Afflictions*, *23*, 42–53.

Miller, J. (2013). Epistemology and rigor in criminological research: An exploratory journey. In S. Ruiter, W. Bernasco, W. Huisman, & G. Bruinsma (Eds.), *Eenvoud en Verscheidenheid. Liber amicorum voor Henk Elffers [Unaffected and Diverse. Liber amicorum for Henk Elffers]* (pp. 491–502). Amsterdam: Nederlands Studiecentrum Criminaliteit en Rechtshandhaving (NSCR) & Afdeling Strafrecht en Criminologie, Vrije Universiteit Amsterdam.

Ostrom, B., Ostrom, C., Hanson, R., & Kleiman, M. (2008). *Assessing consistency and fairness in sentencing: A comparative study in three states* (Tech. Rep.). National Criminal Justice Reference Service. Retrieved from `ojp.gov/pdffiles1/nij/grants/223854.pdf`

Pearce, N. (2016). Analysis of matched case-control studies. *British Medical Journal*, *352*, 1-4.

Pennebaker, J. W., Francis, M. E., & Booth, R. J. (2001). *Linguistic Inquiry and Word Count: LIWC2001*. Mahwah, NJ: Lawrence Erlbaum.

Posner, R. A. (1985). *The Federal Courts: Crisis and Reform.* Cambridge, MA: Harvard University Press.

Ritchie, J., & Lewis, J. (2010). *Quantitative Research Practice. A Guide for Social Science Students and Researchers.* London: Sage.

Ritchie, J., Spencer, L., & O'Connor, W. (2010). Carrying out qualitative analysis. In J. Ritchie & J. Lewis (Eds.), *Quantitative Research Practice. A Guide for Social Science Students and Researchers* (pp. 219–262). London: Sage.

Robbennolt, J. (2003). Apologies and legal settlement: An empirical examination. *Michigan Law Review*, *102*, 460–516.

Robbennolt, J. (2006). Apologies and settlement levers. *Journal of Empirical Legal Studies*, *3*, 333–373.

Roberts, P., & Horney, J. (2010). The Life Event Calendar method in criminological research. In A. Piquero & D. Weisburd (Eds.), *Handbook of Quantitative Criminology* (pp. 289–312). New York: Springer.

Rooij de, S. R., Wouters, H., Yonker, J. E., Painter, R., & Roseboom, T. J. (2010). Prenatal undernutrition and cognitive function in late adulthood. *Proceedings of the National Academy of Sciences*, *107*, 16881–16886. doi: 10.1073/pnas.1009459107

Roseboom, T., De Rooij, S., & Painter, R. (2006). The Dutch famine and its long-term consequences for adult health. *Early Human Development*, *82*, 485–491.

Rubin, H. J., & Rubin, I. S. (1995). *Qualitative Interviewing: The Art of Hearing Data.* Thousand Oaks, CA: Sage.

Ryan, G. W., & Bernard, H. R. (2003). Techniques to identify themes. *Field Methods*, *15*, 85–109.

Saldana, J. (2013). *The Coding Manual for Qualitative Researchers* (2nd ed.). Los Angeles, CA: Sage.

Schmader, T., Whitehead, J., & Wysocki, V. H. (2007). A linguistic comparison of letters of recommendation for male and female chemistry and biochemistry job applicants. *Sex Roles*, *57*, 509–514.

Shadish, W. R., Cook, T. D., & Campbell, D. (2002). *Experimental and Quasi-Experimental Designs for Generalized Causal Inference.* Boston: Houghton-Mifflin.

Sherman, L. W., Gottfredson, D. C., MacKenzie, D. L., Eck, J., Reuter, P., & Bushway, S. (1998). *Preventing crime: What works, what doesn't, what's promising* (Tech. Rep.). National Institute of Justice. Retrieved from `ncjrs.gov/pdffiles/171676.PDF`

Spencer, L., Ritchie, J., & O'Connor, W. (2010). Analysis: Practices, principles and processes. In J. Ritchie & J. Lewis (Eds.), *Quantitative Research Practice. A Guide for Social Science Students and Researchers* (pp. 199–218). London: Sage.

Staring, R., & Kroese, G. (1991). Een kwestie van vertrouwen: Daderonderzoek in gevangenissen [A matter of trust: Studying offenders in prison]. *Justitiële Verkenningen*, *17*, 112–140.

Stern, P. N. (1995). Grounded theory methodology: Its uses and processes. In B. G. Glaser (Ed.), *Grounded Theory 1984-1994, vol. 1* (pp. 29–39). Mill Valley, CA: Sociology Press.

Strauss, A., & Corbin, J. (1990). *Basics of Qualitative Research: Grounded Theory Procedures and Techniques.* Newbury Park, CA: Sage.

Strauss, A. L., & Corbin, J. (Eds.). (1998). *Basics of Qualitative Research: Techniques and Procedures for Developing Grounded Theory* (2nd ed.). London: Sage.

Titiunik, R. (2021). Natural experiments. In J. N. Druckman & D. Green (Eds.), *Advances in experimental political science* (pp. 103–129). Cambridge: Cambridge University Press. Retrieved from `titiunik.mycpanel.princeton.edu/papers/Titiunik2021-NaturalExperiments.pdf`

Tollenaar, A. (2018). Repressive administrative law: Assessing culpability in Dutch social security regulation. *European Journal of Social Security*, 21–30.

Tracy, S. (2013). *Qualitative Research Methods*. Chichester: Wiley.

Tracy, S. (2020). *Qualitative Research Methods. Collecting Evidence, Crafting Analysis, Communicating Impact*. Hoboken, NJ: Wiley Blackwell.

Tudor, S. (2008). Why should remorse be a mitigating factor in sentencing? *Criminal Law and Philosophy*, 2, 241–257.

Tyler, T. (1990). *Why People Obey the Law*. New Haven, CT:: Yale University Press.

Tyler, T. (2008). Procedural justice. In A. Sarat (Ed.), *The Blackwell Companion to Law and Society* (pp. 435–452). Oxford: Blackwell.

Van Boom, W. H., Desmet, P., & Mascini, P. (2018). Empirical legal research. Charting the terrain. In W. H. Van Boom, P. Desmet, & P. Mascini (Eds.), *Empirical Legal Research in Action. Reflections on Methods and Their Applications* (pp. 1–22). Cheltenham: Edward Elgar.

Van den Berg, C., Blommaert, L., Bijleveld, C., & Ruiter, S. (2020). Employment opportunities for ex-offenders. A field experiment on how type of crime and applicants' ethnic background affect employment opportunities for low-educated men in the Netherlands. *Research in Social Stratification and Mobility*. doi: 10.1016/j.rssm.2020.100476

Vandenbussche, W. (2018). *Introducing apology legislation in civil law systems. A new way to encourage out-of-court dispute resolution* (Tech. Rep.). Ghent University. Retrieved from `papers.ssrn.com/sol3/papers.cfm?abstract_id=3237528`

Van der Geest, V. R., Bijleveld, C. C. J. H., & Verbruggen, J. (2013). *Vallen en opstaan. Mannen en vrouwen 17 jaar na vertrek uit een justitiële jeugdinrichting [Stumble and rise. Men and women 17 years after leaving judicial youth care]* (Tech. Rep.). Amsterdam: NSCR/VU.

Van de Weijer, S. G. A., & Bijleveld, C. C. J. H. (2016). *Military service as a turning point in the intergenerational transmission of criminal behaviour.* (Paper presented 2 April 2016 at the ESSHC conference, Valencia)

Van Dijck, G. (2016). Should physicians be afraid of tort claims? Reviewing the empirical evidence. *Journal of European Tort Law*, *2015*, 282–303.

Van Dijck, G. (2017). The ordered apology. *Oxford Journal of Legal Studies*, *37*, 562–587.

Van Dijck, G., & Hagenaars, J. (2017). *Empirical legal research: Principles and procedures*. Tilburg: Unpublished manuscript.

Van Kuppevelt, D., van Dijck, G., & Schaper, M. (2020). Purposes and challenges of legal network analysis on case law. In R. Whalen (Ed.), *Computational Legal Studies: The Promise and Challenge of Data-Driven Legal Research* (pp. 265–292). Cheltenham, UK: Edward Elgar.

Veerman, G. J. (2021). *Denken en Denkers over Wetgeving. Een Historisch en Systematisch Overzicht [Thinking and Thinkers on Lawmaking. A Historical and Systematic Overview]*. Nijmegen: Wolf Legal Publishers.

Venkatesh, S. (2008). *Gang Leader for a Day: A Rogue Sociologist Takes to the Streets*. London: Penguin.

Verbruggen, P. W. J. (2021). Methoden van systematische rechtspraakanalyse. Een inleiding tot het veld [methods for systematic case law analysis. An introduction to the field]. In P. W. J. Verbruggen (Ed.), *Methoden van Systematische Rechtspraakanalyse [methods for Systematic Case Law Analysis]* (pp. 7–25). The Hague: Boom juridisch.

Webley, L. (2010). Qualitative approaches to empirical legal research. In P. Cane & H. M. Kritzer (Eds.), *The Oxford Handbook of Empirical Legal Research* (pp. 927–950). Oxford: Oxford University Press.

Wermink, H., Johnson, B., Nieuwbeerta, P., & De Keijser, J. (2015). Expanding the scope of sentencing research: Determinants of juvenile and adult punishment in the Netherlands. *European Journal of Criminology*, *8*, 1–30.

Wesselius, E. P., Bijleveld, C., et al. (2023). *Workplace misbehaviour after MeToo: A vignette study* (Tech. Rep.). Amsterdam: Vrije Universiteit.

Wijntjens, L. (2020). *'Als ik nu sorry zeg, beken ik dan schuld?' Over het aanbieden van excuses in de civiele procedure en de medische tuchtprocedure ['If say sorry, do I then admit guilt?' On offering apologies in civil procedures and medico-disciplinary proceedings]*. The Hague: Boom Juridisch.

Wright, R., Decker, S. H., Redfern, A. K., & Smith, D. L. (2001). A snowball's chance in hell: Doing fieldwork with active residential burglars. In J. M. Miller & R. Tewksbury (Eds.), *Extreme Methods. Innovative Approaches to Social Science Research* (pp. 94–102). Boston: Allyn and Bacon.

Wulfgramm, M. (2011). Can activating labour market policy offset the detrimental life satisfaction of unemployment? *Socio-economic Review*, *9*, 477–501.

Zeng, J., & Eleveld, A. (2022). *To what extent do assumptions underlying the legal presumption correspond to the situation and needs of platform workers?* (Paper presented at the Reshaping Work Conference, 14 October 2022)

Subject index

A-select sample, see Random sample...
Absolute measurement level, 131
Accidental sample, see Convenience sample...
Acquiescence bias, 85
Agreement response bias, 85
ALLEA code, 36
α, 183–184, 194–196
Alternative hypothesis, see H_1...
Analytic memo, 74, 92, 161, 170
Analytical research, 159–160
ANOVA
  F-statistic, 231–232
  η, 235
  ω^2, 235
  'Between', 232
  'Within', 232
  contrast test, 235–237
  interaction effect, 233–237
  main effect, 234–237
  MS_A, 231
  MS_{error}, 231
  SS_A, 230
  SS_{error}, 230
Arithmetic mean, see Mean...
'As-if' randomization, 120–122
ATLAS.ti, 165, 178–179
Attrition, 65–67, 113
Availability sample, see Convenience sample...
Axial coding, 172–173, 244–248

Bar chart, 135–136
β, 185, 194–196
Bias, 61–63
Biographical interview, 73
Biotex effect, 119
Bivariate analysis, 138, 215
Bonferroni correction, 204
Building rapport, 80–81

CAPI, 80
CAQDAS, 164–165
Case-control design, 116–117
CASI, 80
Categorical variable, 131
CATI, 80
CAWI, 80
Censoring, 151–152
Central limit theorem, 199–200
Chance capitalization, 204
χ^2, 144–146
Classical experiment, 111
Closed-ended question, 77, 84
Cluster sample, 50–53
  design effect, 52–53
Clustered histogram, 149
Cohen's kappa, 25, 93, 255
Computer assisted interviewing, 78–80
Computer Assisted Personal Interviewing, 80
Computer Assisted Self Interviewing, 80
Computer Assisted Telephone Interviewing, 80
Computer Assisted Web Interviewing, 80
Conceptual definition, 23
Confidence interval, 202–203
  95% confidence interval, 202–203
Confounder, 28, 100, 156, 177
Construct validity, 26–27
Construct validity-in-the-narrow-sense, 27
Content analysis, 173–177
  themes, 173–175
Content validity, 26–27
Continuous variable, 132
Contrast test, 236–237
Control group, 107, 109
Convenience sample, 56–57, 235, 254

Correlation, 138–142
  Kendall's τ, 143
  Pearson product moment correlation coefficient, 138–142
  Spearman's ρ, 143
  spurious correlation, 104
Counterfactual, 108
Criterion validity, 27
Cross-sectional research, 117
Cross-tabulations, 144–147
  χ^2, 144–146
  odds ratio, 146–147

Data Privacy Impact Assessment, 35–36
Deductive codes, 166–167, 255–256
Deductive research, 159–160
Definition
  empirical legal research, 4–5
Dependent variable, 103, 209
Descriptive coding, 165–170
Descriptive statistics
  mean, 133
  median, 133
  mode, 133
  standard deviation, 134
  variance, 134
Design effect, 52–53
Deviant case analysis, 58, 161–162
Dichotomous variable, 132, 223
Distributions
  z-distribution, 190–191
  normal distribution, 188–190
  skewed, 136
  standard normal distribution, 190–191
Double-barrelled question, 84
DPIA, 35–36
Drop-out, 65–67
Dummy variable, 225, 263–264

Ecological validity, 119
Emic coding, 166–167, 255–256
Empirical cycle, 17–19
  deductive phase, 18–19
  evaluation phase, 19
  inductive phase, 17–18
  research idea, 17–18
  testing phase, 19
Empirical legal research
  definition, 4–5
Endogenous variable, 209

Error of central tendency, 85
Estimation
  95% confidence interval, 202–203
  99% confidence interval, 203
  confidence interval, 202–203
  point estimate, 201
Ethical rules, 36
Ethics committee, 37–38, 99
Ethnographic interview, 70
Ethnography, 91–92
Etic coding, 97, 166–167, 255–256
Event history analysis, 150–153
Ex-ante evaluation, 7, 102–103
Ex-post evaluation, 102
Exemplars, 170, 247
Experimental designs
  observational study, 116
  quasi-experimental design, 115
  time-series design, 116
  vignette study, 117–118
Experimental mortality, 113
Explanatory variable, see Independent variable...
External validity, 28–29, 118–119
  Biotex effect, 119
  Hawthorne effect, 119
  placebo effect, 119
Extreme response bias, 85

Face validity, 27
Face-to-face interviewing, 77
Fence sitting, 85
Field jottings, 74, 76, 91–92
Field notes, 74, 91–92, 161
First-cycle coding, see First-level coding...
First-level coding, 165–170, 243–244
  deductive codes, 166–167
  emic coding, 166–167
  etic coding, 166–167
  fractured coding, 169
  inductive codes, 166–167
  lumped coding, 169
  open coding, 166–167
  splitting, 169–170
Focus group, 76
Fractured coding, 169
Frequency tabulation, 135

GDPR, 35–36
green data, 35–36
orange data, 35–36
pseudonymized data, 35–36
red data, 35–36
General Data Protection Regulation, 35–36
Data Privacy Impact Assessment, 35–36
DPIA, 35–36
Generative questions, 80, 83
tour question, 80, 83
Goodness of fit, 212, 221–222
Graphics
bar chart, 135–136
clustered histogram, 149
histogram, 136–137
pie chart, 135
stacked bar chart, 149
Green data, 35–36
Grounded theory, 20–21, 160

H_0, 184
H_1, 184
Haphazard sample, see Convenience sample...
Hawthorne effect, 119
Heterogeneity, 233
Hidden population, 60
Hierarchical coding, see Axial coding...
Histogram, 136–137
History, 108–110

ICC, see Intraclass correlation coefficient...
Imputation, 264
In-depth interview, 72–75
In-depth interview, see also Unstructured interview...
Independent variable, 103, 209
Inductive codes, 166–167, 255–256
Inductive research, 159–160
Informant interview, 70
Informed consent, 34, 37, 72, 82, 91
Instrumentation, 111–112
Insufficient separation between groups, 113
Interaction effect, 209–211, 226, 236–237
Intercept, 216
Internal review board, 37–38
Internal validity, 28, 109, 110
attrition, 113
history, 108–110
instrumentation, 111–112
insufficient separation between groups, 113
maturation, 110–111
perceived differences between groups, 113
regression towards the mean, 114
selection, 112–113
testing, 111
threats to
attrition, 113
history, 108–110
instrumentation, 111–112
insufficient separation between groups, 113
maturation, 110–111
perceived differences between groups, 113
regression towards the mean, 114
selection, 112–113
testing, 111
Interpretative coding, 170–171
Interpretative research, 159–160
Interrater reliability, 25, 92, 93, 178–179, 255
Krippendorff's α, 178–179
Interval measurement level, 130–131
Interviews
building rapport, 80–81
in-depth interview, 72–75
open-ended interview, 72–75
semi-structured interview, 75–76
topical interview, 75–76
unstructured interview, 72–75
with questionnaire, 76–77
Intraclass correlation coefficient, 25, 93
In vivo coding, 169
IRB, 37–38
Iterative analysis, 161

Kaplan–Meier survival curve, 153
Kappa
see Cohen's kappa...
Kendall's τ, 143
Key informant, 57
Krippendorff's α, 25–26, 178–179

Life History Calendar, 71
Life-story interview, 73
Logical mistake, 86

Longitudinal research, 117, 122
Lumped coding, 169

Macro-level, 32
Maryland Scientific Methods Scale, 114
Matching, 116–117
Maturation, 110–111
MAXQDA, 165
Mean, 133
Measurement level, 129–132, 137
  absolute, 131
  dichotomous variable, 132, 223
  interval, 130–131
  nominal, 129
  ordinal, 129–130
  ratio, 131
Measurement strategy
  in-depth interview, 72–75
  interview with questionnaire, 76–77
  open-ended interview, 72–75
  semi-structured interview, 75–76
  topical interview, 75–76
  unstructured interview, 72–75
Median, 133
Mediating variable, 209–210
Memo, 74, 91–92
Meso-level, 32
Micro-level, 32
Missing values, 78
Mixed methods, 31
Mode, 133
Model fit, 212
Model misspecification, 213, 214
Models, 208
  dependent variable, 209
  fit, 212
  goodness of fit, 212
  independent variable, 209
  model misspecification, 213
  parsimony, 212–213
Moderator variable, 209–210, 234
Multicollinearity, 220–221
  Variance Inflation Factor, 221
Multiple correlation coefficient, 221, 260
Multiple regression
  see Regression analysis...
Multivariate analysis, 207

Narrative interview, 73
Natural experiment, 119–122
Negative case analysis, 58, 161–162
Network analysis, 179–180
Noise, 61–63
Nominal measurement level, 129
Non-probability sample, 45
  convenience sample, 56–57
  deviant case analysis, 58, 161–162
  negative case analysis, 58, 161–162
  purposive sample, 57–59
  quota sample, 57
  representativeness, 54–56
  snowball sample, 59–61
Nonresponse analysis, 66
Normal distribution, 188–190, 199–201
Null hypothesis, see H_0...
Numerical variable, 132
NVivo, 165

Observational study, 116
Odds ratio, 146–147, 258
Omitted variable bias, 225
One-sided hypothesis, 197–199
Open access, 21
Open coding, 166–167
Open-ended interview, 72–75
Open-ended question, 77
Operational definition, 23
Operationalization, 19
Orange data, 35–36
Ordinal measurement level, 129–130
Outlier, 133, 142
Overfitting, 222

Parameter, 212
Parsimony, 212–213, 221
Participant observation, 91
Pattern analysis, 171–172
Pearson product moment correlation coefficient, 138–142
Perceived differences between groups, 113
Percentage agreement, 255
Period effect, 122
Pie chart, 135
Pilot study, 24
Placebo effect, 119
Point estimate, 201
Population, 41–42, 254
  population member, 42
  sample, 42
Population member, 42

Positionality, 163
Power, 186–187, 195–197
  sample size, 197
Practical significance, 204
Predictor, see Independent variable...
Primary-cycle coding, see First-level coding...
Privacy
  green data, 35–36
  orange data, 35–36
  pseudonymized data, 35–36
  red data, 35–36
Probability density function, 188
Probability sample, 45
  cluster sample, 50–53
  random sample, 47
  stratified sample, 48–50
  systematic sample, 48
Prospective design, 117
Pseudonymized data, 35–36
Purposive sample, 57–59

qdap, 165
Qualitative data analysis
  in vivo coding, 169
  axial coding, 244–248
  deductive codes, 255–256
  descriptive coding, 165–170
  emic, 255–256
  etic, 255–256
  exemplars, 170, 247
  first-cycle coding, see First-level coding...
  first-level coding, 165–170, 243–244
  inductive codes, 255–256
  network analysis, 179–180
  primary-cycle coding, see First-level coding...
  second-level coding, 170–177, 244
  themes, 173–175
  vignettes, 170, 247
Qualitative methods, 13–15
Quantitative methods, 13–15
Quasi-experimental design, 115
Questionnaires
  CAPI, 80
  CASI, 80
  CATI, 80
  CAWI, 80
  computer assisted interviewing, 78–80
  Computer Assisted Personal Interviewing, 80
  Computer Assisted Self Interviewing, 80
  Computer Assisted Telephone Interviewing, 80
  Computer Assisted Web Interviewing, 80
  response styles, 85–87
  self-administered questionnaire, 77–78
Quota sample, 57

R^2_{adj}, 221–222
Random sample, 47
Randomized Controlled Trial, 111
Ratio measurement level, 131
RCT, see Randomized controlled trial...
Red data, 35–36
Reflexivity, 163
Regression analysis, 260
  bivariate ..., 215–219
  error term, 216
  goodness of fit, 221–222
  intercept, 216
  misspecified model, 214
  multicollinearity, 220–221
  multiple correlation coefficient, 221, 260
  multiple..., 219–223
  omitted variable bias, 225
  R^2, 221–222
  R^2_{adj}, 221–222
  regression weight, 216
  simple ..., 215–219
Regression towards the mean, 114
Regression weight, 216
Reliability, 24–25, 178–179, 255
  Cohen's kappa, 25, 93, 255
  in qualitative analysis, 178–179
  interrater reliability, 25, 92, 255
  intraclass correlation coefficient, 25, 93
  Krippendorff's α, 25–26
  percentage agreement, 25, 255
Replicability, 18–19, 170
Representative sample, 43, 149
  non-probability sample, 54–56

Reproducibility, 18–19, 22, 170
Research and Ethical Board, 37–38
Respondent interview, 70
Respondent-driven sampling, 61
Response styles, 85–87
 acquiescence bias, 85
 agreement response bias, 85
 error of central tendency, 85
 extreme response bias, 85
 fence sitting, 85
 logical mistake, 86
Retrospective design, 117
Robustness analysis, 264

Sample, 42
 bias, 61–63
 key-informant sampling, 59
 noise, 61–63
 non-probability sample, 54–61
  convenience sample, 56–57
  purposive sample, 57–59
  quota sample, 57
  respondent driven sampling, 61
  snowball sample, 59–61
 probability sample, 47–54
  cluster sample, 50–53
  random sample, 47
  stratified sample, 48–50
  systematic sample, 48
 representative, 43
 sampling error, 47, 51
Sample nonresponse, 65–67
Sampling
 attrition, 65–67
 drop-out, 65–67
 sample nonresponse, 65–67
Sampling error, 47, 51
Sampling frame, 43, 50
Saturation, 58, 161
Scatterplot, 138
Scoring protocol, 93
Screener question, 81
Second-level coding, 170–177, 244
 axial coding, 172–173
 interpretative coding, 170–171
 pattern analysis, 171–172
 typologies, 173
Selection, 112–113
Self-administered questionnaire, 77–78
Semi-structured interview, 75–77
Significance, 184
 α, 183–184
Significance level, 184, 194
Simple random sample, 47
Simple regression analysis, 215–219
Skewed distribution, 133, 136
Snowball sample, 59–61
Social desirability bias, 26, 79–80, 87–88
Spearman's ρ, 143
Splitting codes, 169–170
SPSS, 219
Spurious correlation, 104
Stacked bar chart, 149
Standard deviation, 134
Standard error of the mean, 200
Standard normal distribution, 190–191
Stata, 219
Statistical conclusion validity, 27–28
Statistical testing, 182–187
 α, 183–184, 194–196
 β, 185, 194–196
 alternative hypothesis, 183
 central limit theorem, 199–200
 critical value, 193
 H_0, 184
 H_1, 184
 normal distribution, 199–201
 null hypothesis, 183
 one-sided hypothesis, 197–199
 power, 186–187, 195–197
 significance level, 184, 194
 Student's t-distribution, 200
 two-sided hypothesis, 197–199
 Type I error, 183–184, 194–196
 Type II error, 185, 194–196
Statistical validity, 27–28
Stratified sample, 48–50
 disproportionate stratified sample, 50
Student's t-distribution, 200
Survival analysis, 150–153
 Kaplan–Meier survival curve, 153
Survival function, 152
Systematic case law analysis, 5, 172, 175–177
Systematic sample, 48

Testing, 111, 182–187
 α, 194–196
 β, 185, 194–196
 alternative hypothesis, 183

central limit theorem, 199–200
critical value, 193
H_0, 183–184
H_A, 183
H_1, 184
normal distribution, 199–201
null hypothesis, 183
one-sided hypothesis, 197–199
power, 186–187, 195–197
significance, 183–184
significance level, 184, 194
Student's t-distribution, 200
two-sided hypothesis, 197–199
Type I error, 183–184, 194–196
Type II error, 185, 194–196
Themes, 173–175
Theoretical sampling, 58
Theoretical saturation, 58
Time-series design, 116
Topic list, see Topical interview...
Topical interview, 75–76
Tour question, 80, 83
Transcription, 73–75
Triangulation, 30–31, 71
Two-sided hypothesis, 197–199
Type I error, 183–184, 194–196
Type II error, 185, 194–196
Typologies, 173

Univariate analysis, 133
Unobtrusive, 38, 90
Unstructured interview, 72–75
analytic memo, 74, 92
field jottings, 74, 76, 91–92
field notes, 74, 91–92
memo, 74, 91–92
Untreated control group design with pre-test and post-test, 111

Validity, 26–29, 178–179
confounder, 28
construct validity, 26–27
construct validity-in-the-narrow-sense, 27
content validity, 26–27
criterion validity, 27
external validity, 28–29
face validity, 27
in qualitative analysis, 178–179
internal validity, 28
social desirability bias, 26
statistical conclusion validity, 27–28
statistical validity, 27–28
theoretical validity, 58, 161
Variables, 128
Variance, 134
Variance Inflation Factor, 221
Vignette study, 117–118, 226, 235–237
Vignettes - qualitative, 170, 247

z-distribution, 190–191

www.ingramcontent.com/pod-product-compliance
Lightning Source LLC
Chambersburg PA
CBHW080938240926
51849CB00004BA/491
* 9 7 8 9 4 6 2 3 6 9 3 8 2 *